Lives of Courage

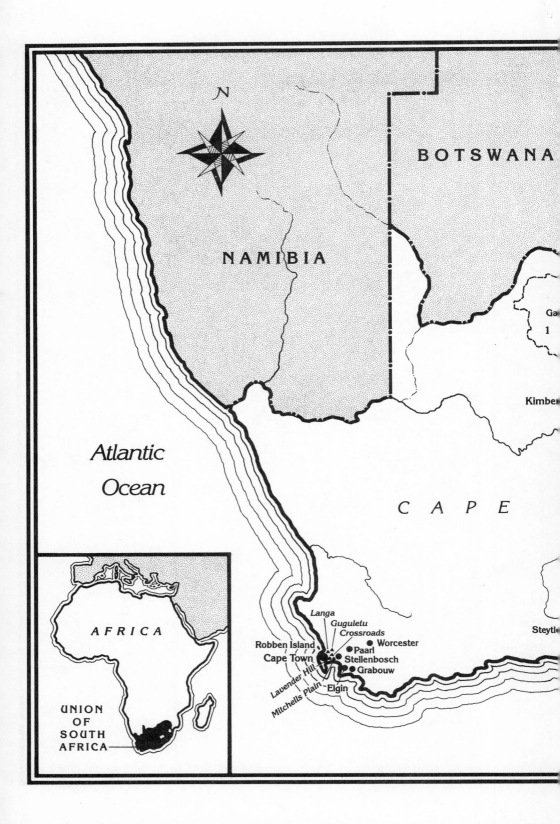

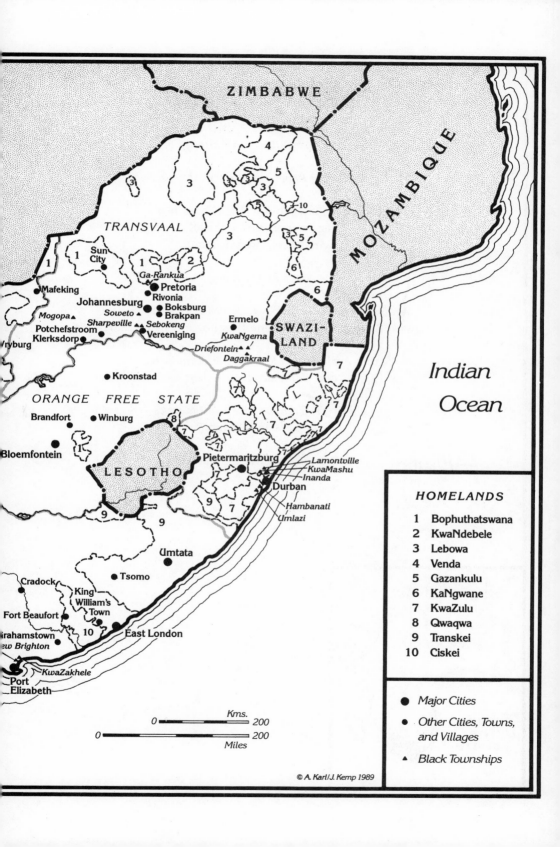

ZIMBABWE

MOZAMBIQUE

Indian Ocean

TRANSVAAL

Sun City
Ga-Rankua
Mafeking
Pretoria
Rivonia
Johannesburg
Mogopa ▲
Soweto ▲
Boksburg
Brakpan
Sharpeville ▲▲
Sebokeng
Potchefstroom
Klerksdorp
Vereeniging
ryburg

Ermelo
KwaNgema ▲
Driefontein ▲
Daggakraal

**SWAZI-
LAND**

Kroonstad

ORANGE   FREE   STATE

Brandfort
Winburg

Bloemfontein

LESOTHO

Pietermaritzburg

NATAL

Lamontville
KwaMashu
Inanda
Durban
Hambanati
Umlazi

Umtata

Cradock
King
William's
Town
Tsomo

Fort Beaufort

rahamstown
ew Brighton

East London

KwaZakhele
Port
Elizabeth

HOMELANDS

1 Bophuthatswana
2 KwaNdebele
3 Lebowa
4 Venda
5 Gazankulu
6 KaNgwane
7 KwaZulu
8 Qwaqwa
9 Transkei
10 Ciskei

● Major Cities
• Other Cities, Towns, and Villages
▲ Black Townships

Kms.
0 ━━━━━ 200
0 ━━━━━ 200
Miles

© A. Karl / J. Kemp 1989

Other Books by Diana E. H. Russell

Rebellion, Revolution, and Armed Force

The Politics of Rape: The Victim's Perspective

*Crimes Against Women: The Proceedings of
the International Tribunal*
(with Nicole Van de Ven)

Rape in Marriage

Against Sadomasochism: A Radical Feminist Analysis
(with Robin Linden, Darlene Pagano, and Leigh Star)

*Sexual Exploitation: Rape, Child Sexual Abuse,
and Workplace Harassment*

*The Secret Trauma: Incest in the Lives
of Girls and Women*

Exposing Nuclear Phallacies

LIVES
OF
COURAGE

WOMEN FOR A
NEW SOUTH AFRICA

Diana E. H. Russell

Basic Books, Inc., Publishers

NEW YORK

Photographs of Shahieda Issel, Florence de Villiers, Di Bishop, Gertrude Fester, and Rhoda Bertelsmann-Kadalie by Marie Hart. All other photographs by Diana Russell.

Distributed in southern Africa by David Philip, Publisher (PTY) Ltd., 208 Werdmueller Centre, Claremont 7700, South Africa

Library of Congress Cataloging-in-Publication Data

Russell, Diana E. H.
    Lives of courage : women for a new South Africa / Diana E. H.
    Russell.

    p. cm.
    Bibliography: p. 358.
    Includes index.
    ISBN 0-465-04139-6
    1. Women in politics—South Africa—Biography. 2. Women, Black—
South Africa—Biography. 3. Women in public life—South Africa—
Biography. 4. Feminists—South Africa—Biography. I. Title.
HQ1236.5.S6R87   1989
305.4'0968—dc20   89-42525
                                                   CIP

To the women of South Africa

who are risking their lives

to give birth to a

new South Africa

Contents

Contents

Acknowledgments

Of all the many people who made the publication of *Lives of Courage* possible, I am, of course, most indebted to the sixty women who agreed to be interviewed for this book. I am still unable to explain how it is that so many women in the embattled South African anti-apartheid movement were willing to open their doors and their hearts to talk to me. I know that part of the answer is that political activists there are so eager to have the real story of their struggle be known in the United States and other countries that they are willing to take the risks involved in speaking out. Answering my questions often meant saying things that are illegal in South Africa—for example, that they approve of sanctions and the withdrawal of foreign business as a strategy to try to bring down the government. While I hope with all my heart that the publication of *Lives of Courage* will not jeopardize any of them in any way, I know that, if it does, it was but one of the many courageous choices they have made in their lives in order to make a contribution to the liberation struggle.

I am also extremely grateful to Marie Hart for helping me through the many phases of work involved in this project, including agreeing to join me in South Africa and Zambia and assisting me with the work there in whatever way she could. Mostly, this turned out to be taping the interviews, enabling me to concentrate on the interviewing itself. But she also took photographs, participated in the interviews, helped me find obscure addresses, cared for me when I was sick, shared the driving, ran errands, and gave me feedback and moral support. She was my companion through it all—the fun parts and the all too frequent stressful parts.

In my introduction I have tried to convey what it was like to have to conduct this research in secrecy. It was a great luxury to be able to share and discuss the multitude of experiences as they happened with a good friend who traveled with me from Cape Town to Johannesburg, via Port

Elizabeth, Grahamstown, Umtata, and Durban, then on to Zimbabwe, Zambia, and England. And once we were back in the United States, we could talk about and relish our many experiences in Africa in a way possible only with someone who has shared them in person. Marie has also read and commented on drafts of many of these interviews. The fact that she was present during most of them has made her evaluations particularly important to me.

Anne Mayne and Hettie V. (pseudonym) are the two South African women who contributed most to this project. Both of them put me in touch with women political activists and recommended women to interview. Together, they also gave me a crash course on women political activists in South Africa, as well as on the anti-apartheid movement as a whole. Both also helped me in such practical ways as finding transcribers, providing equipment, advising on security issues, finding people with whom Marie and I could stay while traveling through South Africa, and so on. I don't know how we would have managed without them.

Hettie V. also read the entire manuscript to ensure, as far as possible, that the spelling of the names of people, towns, and cities is correct. In addition, she and Sheena Duncan inserted three small villages and twenty-one black townships on the map of South Africa appearing at the beginning of this book, since these proved impossible for the initial U.S. map maker, Vincent Torre, to locate.

My longtime friends Lindy and Francis Wilson and Sean Archer were also extremely helpful in advising me on many issues, suggesting who to interview, discussing with me what should be included in the interviews, listening to me talk about the problems I was encountering, and encouraging me during some low times by reminding me of the importance of this project.

I am grateful to my mother, Molly Russell, for providing home and board for Marie and me for the six-week Cape Town phase of our trip, and to my brother David Russell for the many ways in which he assisted me—most particularly, in my being able to use his name and reputation as an anti-apartheid activist to open many doors for me which might otherwise have remained closed. My sister Jill Hall, who was visiting South Africa during the early, most uncertain stage of my research, was also extremely encouraging at a time when I really needed it.

I am also indebted to the Cape Town attorney Essa Moosa for taking the time to read the entire manuscript, and for his welcome conclusion that it "substantially does not contravene any provisions of the Media Laws and Regulations," and that he therefore had "no hesitation in

Acknowledgments

recommending the publication of the manuscript without any changes."*

There were so many others who helped me to complete this work that it will be impossible to name them all. And I have deliberately chosen to omit acknowledging those for whom doing so would involve unnecessary risk—for example, those who came out of hiding to talk with me. They will know who they are, and that I appreciate their assistance. Those in South Africa, Zimbabwe, and Zambia who can be mentioned include Liz Abrahams, Leah Abramsohn, Margaret Auerbach, Jo Beall, Sally Brazier, Lynn Brown, Sandra Burman, Amina Cachalia, Judy Chalmers, Jacklyn Cock, Josette Cole, Eddie Daniels, Betty and Rodney Davenport, Amina Desai, Jessie Duarte, Andy Durbach, Gertrude Fester, Nyami Goniwe, Mildred Hallow, Karen Hurt, Kathy Jagoe, Leibe Kellen, Soraya Khan, Yashmeen Khan, Ilona Kleinschmidt, Susan König, Marian Lacey, Sheila Lapensky, Mildred Lesia, Lydia Levine, Hugh Lewin, Rozena Maart, Ann McCay, Tessa Marcus, Shamim Mare, Fatima Meer, Zora Mehlomakulu, June Mlangeni, Shirley Moulder, Thoko Mpumlwana, Phyllis Naidoo, Herscheler Narsee, Nomzi Notununu, Phumelele Ntombela, Regina Ntongana, Nozizwe Nyakaza, Rosalie Patterson, Jean Pease, Lillian Peters, Vicki Quinlin, Mamphela Ramphele, Carmel Rickard, Liz Rider, Rory Riorden, Denise Rudolph, Dorothea Russell, Kathleen Satchwell, Thabi Shange, Gertrude Shope, Mary Simons, Sandy Stewart, Sheelagh Stewart, Ginny Volbrecht, Cherryl Walker, and Mama Zihlangu.

People in England and the United States who helped me in significant ways include Sandy Boucher, Barry Fineberg, Louis Friedberg, Frene Ginwala, Pippa Green, Eleanor Khanyile, Mary King, Nona Kirk, Margaret Legum, David Mermelstein, Mary Orman, Stephanie Sachs, Adelaide Tambo, Stephanie Urdang, Randolph Vigne, Candy Wright, and Wendy Woods.

I also want to thank publicly my closest friends who gave me the encouragement and moral support, and sometimes editorial advice, which I sorely needed in order to get through the periods of doubt and frustration during the long months of isolated editing and writing involved in this task: Joan Balter, Sandra Butler, Kenneth Carstens, Marny Hall, Marie Hart, Nancy Howell, and Maryel Norris. Sandra Butler also offered excellent and extensive editorial advice on more than one draft of the entire manuscript, and patiently went over it all with me, despite my resistance. I am extremely grateful to her for the generous donation

* Personal communication, 18 August 1988.

of her skills to this project. And Kenneth Carstens assisted me greatly by correcting and adding to the chronology and glossary, commenting on selected chapters of the book, and advising me on certain political and publicity issues.

Others who assisted with the editing task include Barbara Austin, Jane Futcher, Grace Harwood, Annie Stenzel, Laura Tow, and the students in my class on "Contemporary Social Movements" at Mills College who were assigned to read a draft of the entire manuscript. The suggestions of Candida Ellis were particularly helpful. And Jan Dennie did her usual expert job of transcription and word processing of many drafts of this work.

Last but not least, I wish to thank my agent, Frances Goldin; Cheryl Friedman, coordinator of all work on *Lives of Courage* in the last several months of book production; and my two editors at Basic Books, Jo Ann Miller and Phoebe Hoss, both of whose editorial suggestions greatly improved this book, particularly its accessibility to an American and wider international audience.

Lives of Courage

Introduction:
Revisiting the Land
of My Birth

"The rest of the world doesn't know what it means to live with a people who are consumed by hate, a people who are so petrified of domination, who feel that if they share power, it means they will lose their identity. The Afrikaners' neurotic desire to keep their purity as a race is something like what Hitler must have had in mind when he flung the rest of the world into a state of chaos, with millions losing their lives because of their race."
—WINNIE MANDELA

I was born and raised in South Africa, a white child in an affluent English-speaking family, and left for the first time in 1959 when I was twenty years old. I am one of six children, just half an hour older than my twin brother, David, with whom I share position number four in our sibling hierarchy. Like many white South Africans, we were raised with and by servants who were black indigenous South Africans. This institutionalized form of racism was, I believe, my major instructor in racial prejudice.

When the power structure is as firmly in place as it was in my family, statements like "Don't let me ever catch you playing with a kaffir"* didn't need to be made. There were no black children around with whom to play, no black neighbors to disparage, and no black girls at my all-white, sex-segregated schools. A system of apartheid reigned in my world before the term was coined in 1948, and before the laws were passed to keep it that way.

My mother was born in Ireland to British parents. Her grandfather had been appointed Lord Chancellor of Ireland in 1885, after which time the title of Lord Ashbourne was inherited by the eldest male descendant, including her father and oldest brother. She and her other siblings were stuck with the more lowly title of "The Honorable." All

---

* A derogatory word equivalent to *nigger*.

this had so little meaning to me that I was seventeen before I absorbed the fact that Uncle Edward was the same person as Lord Ashbourne, and that my great grandfather was among those photographed in the picture of the House of Lords hanging near the stairs.

At the age of twenty-one, my mother had traveled to South Africa to take up a post as a school elocution teacher in the coastal city of Port Elizabeth. She met my father, a South African–born Rhodes Scholar to Oxford, on the boat trip out, married him, and made South Africa her permanent home.

Although English-speaking South Africans include a diverse group of immigrants and descendents of immigrants, most of them, like my mother, have British ancestry. Britons started to immigrate to South Africa when Britain took over its colonization from the Dutch in 1806.* Literally at war with each other from 1899 to 1902, Afrikaners and English-speaking South Africans today still practice a kind of voluntary apartheid, speaking different languages, attending different schools, living in different areas, and voting for different political parties. The one thing that unites them is their desire to keep all the power in the hands of white men.

I was seven years old in 1945, when my father, the son of lower-middle-class Irish immigrants, won a seat in the South African Parliament. Like most English-speaking South Africans, he was a committed United Party supporter. Although English-speaking South Africans constitute only about 43 percent of the white minority, and whites only 14 percent of the South African population, the Afrikaner-led United Party also enjoyed considerable support from moderate Afrikaners at that time, and was still in power when he entered politics.

Three years later, in 1948, the Afrikaners, descendants of the Dutch, German, and Huguenot settlers who started immigrating to South Africa in 1652, won political power on a platform that introduced an important new word to South Africans and the world—*apartheid*. Translating this euphemistically to mean "separate development of the races," the largely Afrikaner Nationalist Party† promised to implement an elaborate and unworkable plan to force millions of Africans, the original inhabitants of South Africa, to live in areas designated as "bantustans" or "homelands." Although the Africans constitute 75

---

* There is a chronology of the major events in South African history on pages 351–353.

† Although the Afrikaans phrase *die Nasionale Party* can accurately be translated as either "the Nationalist Party" or "the National Party," the latter usage has become increasingly popular as a way to underplay the nationalist values on which the party is based.

percent of the total population, the architects of apartheid expected this large majority of the South African population to live on, and have rights in, only 13 percent of the land. All Africans who lived and worked in the remaining 87 percent of "white" South Africa would be regarded as foreigners, without the right to own land in these areas, or to vote, or to continue living there if they lost their jobs, or to buy a house, or to live with their families. Proponents of apartheid were indifferent to the fact that many urban Africans had never even seen their alleged homeland, let alone lived there.

To implement this policy, the all-white government divided up the 13 percent of South African land into ten separate "homelands," one of which is made up of forty-four different pieces of territory. While four of these "homelands" are considered "independent," this term has no real meaning, since the white regime remains all-powerful on any issue that concerns it, and no country outside South Africa recognizes their independent status.

A divide-and-conquer strategy is at the heart of this apartheid policy. The designers' goal is to separate not only blacks from whites, but the different African groups—Xhosas, Zulus, Sothos, Tswanas, Vendas, and so on—from each other by forcing them to live apart. The government has made equally strenuous efforts to separate Africans from the other two major non-African black groups, the Coloureds and the Indians.

Nine percent of the estimated thirty-three million South Africans are referred to as Coloured. (Although politically progressive people have become uncomfortable with the term, no substitute has yet been invented.) Largely a product of miscegenation, most Coloureds speak Afrikaans as a first language and belong to the Dutch Reformed Church—the mother tongue and religion of their Afrikaner oppressors. Just under 3 percent* of South Africans are Indians, descendants of immigrants from India, most of whom settled in Natal Province between 1860 and 1911 as indentured laborers for the sugar plantations.

Both Indian and Coloured South Africans suffer less discrimination—legal, economic, social, and political—than do Africans. Nevertheless, their lives have more in common with Africans than with whites. They, too, are forced to live in segregated ghettos, separated from whites, Africans, and each other.

South African racial terminology is extremely confusing. Many politi-

---

* These percentages—75 for Africans, 14 for whites, 9 for Coloureds, and 3 for Indians—add to 101 because of rounding to the nearest whole number.

cally progressive South Africans reject the term *race* altogether, preferring the concept of *ethnic group*. And many reject as racist the classifications *Coloured*, *Indian*, and *African*, instead referring to all people of color as *black*. While there is no disputing the merits of this opinion, the fact remains that South Africa is an intensely racist pigmentocracy in which the lowest status is reserved for the darkest-skinned peoples, and in which very real differences exist in political rights and economic realities for different racial or ethnic groups. Hence the difficulty in dispensing with these terms altogether.

Other phrases are invented, such as *township people* to refer to Africans or *so-called Coloureds* for Coloureds.* But there is no consistency in usage, even among progressive people. For example, some use the term *black* to describe all people of color, while others use it synonymously with African.† Yet others are inconsistent, sometimes referring to Africans, and sometimes to all people of color, as black. Often one can gauge the meaning of the term only from the context. For instance, if someone mentions that all black people have to carry passes (or passbooks), South Africans know she or he must be referring only to Africans because this particular indignity has been limited to this group in recent years. Confusing as all this is to South Africans, it becomes trebly so for foreigners.

The Nationalist Party's ruthless commitment to the preservation of white privilege by subjugating the black majority, who together constitute 86 percent of the population, has been so popular with the all-white electorate that the party has remained securely at the helm ever since its 1948 victory. The Nationalist Party's continued success was a great disappointment to my father, who believed that he would have become a cabinet minister if his party had come to power again during his eighteen years as a member of Parliament.

Like the upper class in all societies, my family was intensely patriarchal. When I left South Africa in 1959, I was eager to escape its crippling effects, although I could not then have articulated my need in this way. As for many other English-speaking South Africans at that time, En-

---

* Because prefacing the word *Coloured* with *so-called* is cumbersome and awkward, I will not follow that usage here.

† Like the term *white*, *black* and *Coloured* are not typically capitalized by progressive South Africans; but *Coloured* uncapitalized looks odd when the terms *Indian*, *Asian*, *African*, *English-speaking South African*, and *Afrikaner* are all capitalized. In addition, some U.S. readers would interpret the uncapitalized usage as disrespectful, particularly since the term *colored* has negative connotations in this culture. Capitalizing the term also permits the preservation of the South African spelling.

gland was my automatic choice of destination. And as for so many other white South Africans, my three years away provided me with the opportunity to see through new eyes the political disparities in my homeland.

When I returned to South Africa in 1962, I joined the Liberal Party, which, despite its name, was considered radical in the spectrum of white politics at that time. (It disbanded just six years later, in 1968, rather than submit to new legislation that forbade multiracial political parties.) Within a few months, I became completely disillusioned with reformist politics. A pivotal experience in my transformation was my arrest for participation in a nonviolent protest against the banning (imposition of severe legal restrictions) of one of our Liberal Party leaders on the grounds that he was a communist. The South African government seeks to discredit its opponents by calling them communists, even those who are *anti*-communist. The law permits the government to ban whomever it chooses without having to prove the case in court or to justify it to anyone.

The futility of our disrupted protest demonstration was the last straw, convincing me that nonviolent resistance could not be effective in South Africa. Our rulers, I decided, were psychologically and morally un-reachable. From that point onward, I viewed the large majority of whites as unconvertible. They had too much to lose to surrender volun-tarily their monopoly on power, wealth, and privilege. Has a privileged élite class or ethnic group *ever* willingly handed over power to the less privileged in a country both inhabit? Why should white South Africans be different from others in this respect?

In 1963, hoping more radical action would bring change, I joined a small revolutionary underground group called the African Resistance Movement (ARM). The goal of this largely white group, most of whom were disillusioned former Liberal Party members, was to sabotage gov-ernment property in order to show the government and its white sup-porters that their racist policies would have to change. Although the ARM embraced violence as a means of trying to coerce whites into giving up their commitment to white supremacy, we did not intend to kill or maim human beings.

Despite my conviction that revolution was necessary in South Africa, I did not believe—unlike many other optimists—that it was imminent. And I was not willing to give up my future for my participation in a revolution whose time had not yet come. Consequently, I did not alter my earlier plans to attend graduate school in the United States later that same year (1963). If discovered, my participation in the ARM, brief and peripheral as it was, could have cost me several years in prison. Long prison sentences were the fate of several ARM participants who were unable to escape after the arrest of key members in 1964.

After four years of graduate school at Harvard University, a year at Princeton University, and three years of marriage to an American, I became a committed feminist. For the next fifteen years, I focused on understanding and writing about sexual assault and other forms of violence against women, and teaching sociology at a private women's liberal arts college in California. Although I eventually became very absorbed in my life in the United States and in feminist politics, the anti-apartheid struggle in South Africa continued to tug on my heart.

While the ARM is an important part of *my* history, it is of little significance in the history of the struggle for justice in South Africa. The African National Congress (ANC) is the giant among the many different anti-apartheid groups that exist today. Founded in 1912, it is also the oldest organization to fight for the rights of Africans and to struggle for a democratic, nonracist society. While the Pan-Africanist Congress (PAC), which broke off from the ANC in 1959, was a significant rival for a time, in the last decade the ANC has emerged as by far the most popular revolutionary political organization.

On 21 March 1960, progressive people in South Africa and throughout the world were shocked by news of the Sharpeville massacre. As part of an anti-pass campaign organized by the Pan-Africanist Congress, hundreds of residents of this African township located outside Vereeniging, presented themselves at the police station without their passes. Police fired more than 700 shots into the crowd, killing 69 and wounding 180 (Benson 1986, p. 84). Most of them were shot in the back, including children. This slaughter led to a political crisis of "unprecedented magnitude as riots swept the country" (Benson 1986, p. 84). The government responded by declaring a state of emergency and banning the ANC and the PAC under the Unlawful Organizations Act. From 1960 onward, the penalty for furthering the aims of either of these organizations was imprisonment for up to ten years.

Although the government banning of these two groups in 1960 forced them underground, increasingly repressive measures against these organizations (and any other group that tries to end apartheid) have not succeeded in obliterating them. The name of the ANC leader Nelson Mandela has become a household word throughout the world, despite his continuous imprisonment since 1962. The Freedom Charter, adopted as the ANC's fundamental principles in the late 1950s, and described by Mandela as "the most important document ever adopted by the ANC (Mermelstein 1987, p. 223), still serves as the bible for most of the anti-apartheid organizations in South Africa today. And Mandela's old friend and colleague, Oliver Tambo, still presides over a virtual government-in-exile in Lusaka, Zambia, where the ANC plans strategies on how to bring an end to white supremacy in the land that once belonged to the African people.

Since the anti-apartheid movement was effectively decimated following the 1964 life sentencing of Nelson Mandela, Walter Sisulu, and others, for sabotage and conspiracy to overthrow the government, I followed with great interest from the distant shores of the United States the emergence and growth of the Black Consciousness movement in the 1970s. Often associated with the name of a brilliant and charismatic leader, Steve Biko, this movement stresses the importance of black pride and the need for black people to liberate themselves from white domination as well as internalized racism. So threatening is this message to the white government that Biko was murdered by his interrogators while in detention in 1977.

The outrage that followed Biko's death led to the banning of eighteen black organizations, the detention of forty-two black leaders, and the banning of seven whites, most of whom were church leaders. My brother David, an Anglican priest who had provided his friend Biko with office space in his church for a while, was the only white person placed under house arrest on that fateful day of 19 October 1977.* House arrest—a uniquely South African method of trying to silence and immobilize the government's political opponents—is a more serious form of banning, which, along with numerous restrictions like being prohibited from meeting with more than one person at a time, also requires the arrestee to stay in his or her home for from twelve to twenty-four hours a day, seven days a week. Most house arrests last for five years, as did David's, after which time many are renewed for five additional years.

Arising partly out of the Black Consciousness movement, 20,000 schoolchildren in Soweto marched in 1976 in protest against the imposition of the hated Afrikaans language as the medium for their education. (Afrikaans, a simplified form of Dutch, is the mother tongue of Afrikaners.) Soweto—the largest township in South Africa, home of over a million black people, situated on the outskirts of Johannesburg —would never be the same again. The Soweto uprising is considered one of the major historic events in the annals of black resistance.

---

* Six other white men were banned—but not house-arrested—at that time.

Hundreds of unarmed children were gunned down, thousands wounded, and many crippled for life. These casualties provoked uprisings throughout the country. After 1976, many people talked about a new militancy on the part of young Africans, growing numbers of whom refused to be intimidated by the severe repercussions that seemed the inevitable consequence of political resistance, including the threat of death and the horror of witnessing the murder of loved ones. Many also fled the country to join the ANC's military forces, *Umkhonto we Sizwe* ("Spear of the Nation").

South Africa's response to the growing internal pressures and ensuing international attack on apartheid was to claim that the government was willing to make reforms, if only the world would stop interfering and be patient. One of these alleged reforms was to institute a tricameral parliamentary system with one chamber for whites, one for Coloureds, and one for Indians. Africans were completely excluded from this complicated and totally inadequate power-sharing scheme, and it was unequivocally rejected by the anti-apartheid movement. The "reform" was consistent with the government strategy I have already described —to try to maintain power by dividing black people and co-opting non-African blacks. The tricameral parliament was instituted despite the protests, because the white electorate wanted it. In response, the most significant legal anti-apartheid group of the past many years— the United Democratic Front—was formed in 1983. The emergence of the UDF, a coalition of over eight hundred anti-apartheid groups, was a dramatic renewal of the liberation movement within South Africa, and it became increasingly vocal.

After Bishop Desmond Tutu was awarded the Nobel Peace Prize in 1984, and Jesse Jackson made South Africa an issue in the United States' presidential campaign that same year, the anti-apartheid, pro-divestment movement became popular in the United States, where it had considerable clout. The combination of internal and international protest against apartheid in 1985 resulted in South Africa's President Pieter Botha's imposition of a state of emergency on 20 July.

A little over one month later, most international banks, including many in the United States, refused to reschedule South Africa's payment of its foreign debt, as they had always done in the past. The value of the rand, South Africa's currency, plummeted; and the South African government forbade its companies to repay their foreign debts for the rest of the year. Some people thought this might be the moment when the white regime would finally be brought to its knees. Although this thought proved overly optimistic, by 1985 the movement to overthrow apartheid was gaining tremendous momentum inside the country and significant international support outside it.

The government has effectively undermined this momentum by sheer brutal repression (killing hundreds, wounding thousands, and detaining tens of thousands), by trying to encourage or manipulate rivalries between blacks, and by deliberately arming the reactionary forces as vigilantes. For example, although the charismatic and interna- tionally known Chief Gatsha Buthelezi speaks out against apartheid and has refused to accept the farcical "independence" that the white regime has tried to impose on different African tribes, he and his sup- porters in the Zulu movement called Inkatha are used by the white government to do its dirty work by attacking the more radical members of the United Democratic Front. Many African critics who live near the territory over which Buthelezi has power are more afraid of being killed by his forces than by the dreaded security police of the white government.

In 1987, when I arrived in Durban, Natal—which is surrounded by some of the forty-four pieces of territory that constitute KwaZulu, the Zulu "homeland" over which Chief Buthelezi supposedly rules—I kept hearing about Inkatha's violent tactics. One of the victims of this vio- lence who is still alive to tell her story does so anonymously in chapter 20. This is a side of Buthelezi with which the international community is less familiar.

Although it is always difficult to say when a revolution has really started, I came in the mid-1980s to believe that South Africa was in the early phase of a radical transformation. This belief increased the ur- gency of my desire to reconnect with South Africa, and I decided in 1986 that the time had come for me to try to make some contribution to the progress and success of the revolution there. Facts and figures about the horrors of apartheid have little meaning for most people outside South Africa because they have no personal reference points: people's minds may be engaged, but their emotions are not. I decided to inter- view both black and white women involved in the liberation struggle about their lives and the risks they are taking to create a new South Africa. I wanted to convey the lived experiences behind the statistics because I am convinced that personalizing apartheid both makes it real and is the best way to reach a large international audience, many of whom know little or nothing about that country and its problems.

I decided to focus on women political activists because many other books on South Africa focus on the lives, activities, and experiences of men. Joseph Lelyveld's Pulitzer prizewinning _Move Your Shadow_ (1985) is a noteworthy example.* Many people are taken aback when feminists like myself express an interest in the question of how detention and torture or other kinds of oppression might differ for women and men in oppressive societies like South Africa, and see it as an irrelevant concern that only a narrow-minded feminist would wish to pursue. I have encountered the same response when I have tried to find out more about women's experiences in Nazi concentration camps. Only the belated efforts of some feminist scholars who have dared to investigate this question, despite public disdain, have enabled social historians to start to piece together some of the differences as well as the similarities in the ways women and men have responded to this extreme environment (Ringelheim 1985). The feminist historian Joan Ringelheim has pointed out that, prior to this work, "the experiences and perceptions of Jewish women have been obscured or absorbed into descriptions of men's lives" (Ringelheim 1985, p. 741). The same applies to many studies of South Africa.

As appalling as is the oppression of black men in South Africa, black women, particularly African women, are oppressed even more. They were referred to as "superfluous appendages" (along with children and old people) by G. Froneman, a prominent Nationalist member of Parliament who later became deputy minister of Justice, Mines and Planning. The so-called homelands have been turned into the only legal homes for millions of these so-called appendages (Bernstein 1975, p. 12). Grim as are the lives of the African men who are forced to look for work in the cities, it is even worse for many of the women, who must try to eke out a living for themselves, their children, and their elderly relatives, on the infertile land of the homelands, with only a portion of the meager pay check of their husbands if they're lucky.

In rural areas most African women still marry under customary (traditional) law.† Until 1988, the law considered married African women as minors under the tutelage of their husbands. The wife could not own

---

* Aside from a brief mention of Winnie Mandela and Mamphela Ramphele (a medical doctor and colleague of the late Steve Biko), women do not figure in this otherwise excellent book. Lelyveld devotes one chapter to a portrayal of five South Africans who exemplify moral courage to him, and not one of whom is a woman. In his thirty-six-item selected bibliography, not only is there no book about a woman or women, there is no book _written_ by a woman. This kind of male bias is so prevalent in our culture that few readers seem to notice it. Certainly, I have yet to hear anyone offer this critique of Lelyveld's book, and I would be willing to wager that Lelyveld himself is totally unaware of his bias.

† The main sources for this section on the legal status of women in South Africa are Bernstein 1985, and Burman 1984 and 1988, parts 1 and 2.

property in her own right, except for her clothing and a few personal possessions; and if she earned money or in any way acquired property, this became the property of her husband. She was also unable to make valid contracts without her husband's consent, or to sue or be sued. Her husband had to sue on her behalf (Bernstein 1985, p. 36).

Even worse, until 1986, commissioner's courts could confine any African woman to her kraal (home) if the court found that she was leading an "immoral" life, or if she was absent from her kraal and unable to "give a good account of herself" (Bernstein 1985, p. 36).

For all women married under *common* law (as opposed to *customary* law), as are most African women in the cities and towns, and all non-African women, the rights of wives were not much better than their country sisters until a new Matrimonial Property Act came into effect in 1985. Before then, the husband's marital power effectively turned the wife into a legal minor in terms of entering into contracts or opening credit accounts. And until the Matrimonial Affairs Act of 1953, the husband could even take his wife's earnings. Between 1953 and 1985, the husband could still take possession of anything the wife bought with those earnings unless she applied to the courts to change this rule.

The 1984 act abolished the power that made the husband the sole administrator of family property for white, Coloured, and Indian women, married after 1984. African women were only included in these legislative reforms in 1988. But even now that African women have the legal right to live in town, their right to housing still depends on their marital status. Housing restrictions are still used to keep African women away from the cities. For example:

> A woman must avoid the misfortune of being left without a husband, whether through desertion, divorce or death. She often loses her home as well as her husband. A divorced woman may be given permission to stay in her home only if she was not the guilty party in the divorce suit, and has been granted custody of the children; if she qualifies in her own right to remain in town; if she can pay the rent; and if her former husband has agreed to vacate the house. [Bernstein 1985, p. 40]

Until 1986, the infamous pass laws prevented African married couples from living together with their children. Africans were treated as expendable units of labor. When the "white" economy did not need their labor, they were forced to leave "white" areas, regardless of their family ties, or to live there illegally under constant threat of arrest and deportation. In spite of recent changes in the pass laws, many other controls remain to keep the unemployed reserve of African labor in the homelands, particularly women, children, the old, and the infirm. This situation, combined with the minimal legal status of women in South Africa, particularly African women, results in an extraordinarily low percentage of married African women. According to official census figures, only 23 percent of African women were married in 1980 compared with 46 percent of white women (Bernstein 1985, p. 45). Remaining single or divorcing does not, however, mean African women have the same rights as African men (Meer 1987, p. 238). For example, the right to stay in her township home of one divorced African woman I spoke to, was dependent on her son, since as a single woman, she was not entitled to housing.

Despite some improvements in the legal status of women in recent years, much oppression still exists through women's ignorance of these reforms as well as through the sexism that is so deeply embedded in all sectors of South African society.

While several books on women in South Africa have already been published, few of them are available in the United States. Most of them do not focus on women political activists, and most have not been written for the reader who knows little about that country but would like to know more.* I have written this book to tell both informed and uninformed Americans, women and men, what political South African women—particularly those who are black—are doing, feeling, and thinking. I have also written it for people in other countries, including South Africa, and for members of the liberation movement itself, both as a tribute and, as it turns out, a reminder. The reminder concerns the important contribution that women are making to the struggle and their feelings about sexism, both in the society and in the anti-apartheid movement.

The greater the unrest in South Africa, the more fervent the government's repressive measures have become. Audrey Coleman, an expert who has testified to the United Nations on detention in South Africa, and whose interview appears in chapter 5, estimates that only 5 percent of those detained are ever found guilty of any offense.

Although South Africa's Criminal Procedure Act requires that people who break the law be charged within forty-eight hours, Coleman stated in her interview that, of those detained, 75 percent are never taken to

* For example, see the selected bibliography on South African women at the end of this book.

court. Of the 25 percent who are charged, only an estimated 3 percent to 4 percent are found guilty. "There's no intention of trying to find a charge against most of them," explained Coleman, "because they haven't broken the law. And there is often no attempt to prove guilt, since South African law does not require it." "The government is using detention like internment camps," Coleman concluded. "People involved in democratic opposition are being removed from society because they are political opponents and dumped in prison for an unlimited time at the discretion of the minister of law and order without recourse to the courts."

South African law permits detention without trial on the whim of the police. After President Pieter Botha imposed a state of emergency on 20 July 1985, detention could be prolonged indefinitely by the minister of law and order. Less than four months after this state of emergency was lifted, another one was declared on 12 June 1986. It is still in effect today. Over thirty thousand people have been detained in prisons since then, without ever having been found guilty of any offense by a court of law (*Weekly Mail*,* 1988, p. 4). Women constituted approximately 12 percent of the twenty-five thousand detainees held in 1986–87, and 5 percent of the five thousand held in 1987–88.† Some of them were pregnant. Coleman mentioned that there have been several reports of miscarriages in detention, and that some pregnant women say they have been tortured with electric shock. She described one woman detainee she knew who had to be treated in hospital for an ectopic pregnancy. Although she suffered from cardiac arrest on the operating table, after convalescing she was taken straight back to detention, where she still remained eleven months later.

Girls constitute about 14 percent of the children detainees, some of whom are very young. "They are assaulted and tortured just like the boys," Coleman maintained, "and there have also been allegations of girls being raped by soldiers."

On their release, many detainees report that they were assaulted and tortured, according to Coleman. In addition, "some of them say that they were made to sign statements under duress. In some cases, they

---

* The *Weekly Mail*—an excellent publication, which still manages to publish astonishingly revealing information about what is going on in South Africa despite the heavy censorship laws—attributes the figure of these thirty thousand to "independent estimates," while pointing out that "the government's figure for those held for 30 days or longer under the emergency regulations since June 12, 1986 . . . is 17,723." The *Mail* goes on to say that Adriaan Vlok, the minister of law and order, refuses to provide information on the number of people detained for less than thirty days under the emergency regulations.

† Audrey Coleman, personal communication, 26 July 1988.

say they were not given the opportunity to read the statements; in some, they say that they agreed to sign a statement with which they did not agree because of the pressure that was applied to them."

The government is finding it impossible to deal with the growing discontent of the majority of the South African people. In an effort to regain control, President P. W. Botha decided in 1987 to extend, with additional restrictions, the 1986 state of emergency, and to restrict yet further the publication of information about the conditions of detention. "The reality," concluded Coleman, "is that there is greater repression today than there has ever been before in the history of South Africa." For example, people who oppose the government are killed more often now, according to Coleman, usually by agents of the government, both black and white. Some South African women I interviewed believe that unless there is much more international pressure against detention without trial than there has been so far, the state of emergency will never be lifted as long as the current government remains in power.

The issue of so-called black-on-black violence is one about which there are many serious misconceptions. The South African government spends millions of rand publicizing so-called black-on-black violence, although this violence is, according to Coleman, only a small percentage of the violence that occurs in the black townships. Most of the violence is perpetrated by agents of the state against the African residents.

The reason I preface the phrase black-on-black violence with the word *so-called* is that this phrase obscures what the violence is about. "In Germany or France during the [Second World] War, did people talk about white-on-white violence?" Coleman asked, rhetorically. "No," she answered emphatically. "They spoke about the resistance and the killing of collaborators." Similarly, "some of the township people are saying to those who have been co-opted into this Nazi-like situation: 'This is what will happen to you if you join forces with our oppressors.' It shows others that being co-opted is not worthwhile."

Winnie Mandela sheds further light on this issue by pointing out that the white government is actually behind a lot of the so-called black-on-black violence. "They kill the leaders of the United Democratic Front by using the so-called vigilantes—gangs comprised of the elements in black society who are the puppets of the state—and the black councilors who carry out the laws of the government against their own people," Mandela explained. "The government has always used blacks to elimi-nate blacks," she continued. "They want the rest of the world to see us as barbarians who don't know what we are doing, barbarians who are fighting each other, not Pretoria. They want to reduce the people's struggle to tribal frictions, to a civil war amongst ourselves. That is why they promote the frictions that exist between the puppet leaders of the homelands and the struggle."

In general, the South African government goes to extraordinary lengths—extraordinary, at least, to us in the United States—to keep down dissent, as I discovered on my four-month trip to South Africa in 1987 to do research for this book. It has become such a police state that I was not sure I would be granted a visa to enter the country, since Americans who are critical of the apartheid regime are frequently not permitted to visit. I became an American citizen in 1978, so for me to set foot on South African soil is now a privilege, not a right.

I worried about obtaining a visa because I feared that my relationship to David might make the security police more wary of me. In addition, my first book, *Rebellion, Revolution, and Armed Force* (1974), had been banned in South Africa, presumably because my support of a revolution there was quite apparent. While neither of these factors had caused problems for me when I had returned for brief vacations, I had never before applied to stay for more than three weeks, nor had I tried to enter the country during a state of emergency. So I was relieved when my passport arrived back from the South African consulate with the visa stamp in place. But my relief was short-lived: a small pamphlet inserted in my passport stated, "Your admission to the country is subject to examination by the Passport Control Officer at your port of entry." Apparently, my visa and a $1,800 plane ticket assured my entry only to the Johannesburg airport.

Despite the warning of friends that I should be prepared for a search on arrival in South Africa, my entry turned out to be a breeze. Instantly, I regretted my decision to leave behind the anti-apartheid books I had wanted to bring with me (hundreds of books are banned in South Africa, and people have been thrown in prison for being found in possession of one). I also regretted having mailed the names and addresses of anti-apartheid people instead of carrying them with me. Since mail tampering is also a common government-sanctioned practice in South Africa, I wondered if I'd made the wrong choice—a concern I was to have many times in the next four months.

I spent the first six weeks of my trip with my mother, in her Cape Town home. A week after my arrival, I received a phone call from a policeman in the so-called Special Branch requesting an appointment to see me. Members of this plainclothes wing of the police force deal exclusively with political crime. Also known as "security police," they have the power to arrest people "if considered desirable in the interests of public order" (Omond 1985, p. 161). In addition, they are the well-trained government agents who interrogate and torture political prisoners. At least fifty-seven people—almost all of them Africans—have died in detention since 1963 while under the "care" of the Special Branch. The officially stated causes of death include "fell out of tenth-floor window while being interrogated," "slipped in the showers," "slipped down the stairs," and—most common of all—"suicide" (Omond 1985, pp. 164–65).

As a white American professor with international connections, I was less afraid of being detained (although white Americans *have* been detained there) than of being deported. Not that deportation is such a horrible fate, but it would have put an end to my project, about which I had come to care a great deal. But I thought it more probable that I would be questioned, warned, and made to realize that the Special Branch knew exactly what I wanted to do; and I feared that this would make it impossible for me to interview women political activists. What Special Branch Officer Horne had in mind, I will never know. The intervention of my family lawyer, who told Horne that I would see him only in the lawyer's office with my lawyer present, ended with Officer Horne canceling our appointment the day before it was scheduled to take place.

My brief call from Officer Horne turned out to be my only brush with the security police during my fifteen weeks in South Africa. Yet the branch accompanied me and my traveling companion, Marie Hart, in our imaginations throughout our trip. It was only on departing from South Africa knowing that most of our tapes had arrived safely in the United States that we realized we need not have been so worried. My description of what it was like to conduct anti-apartheid research in contemporary South Africa will reveal many of the things we did not do, others that we did do, because of the security police. All these precautions, despite the fact that what we were doing was perfectly legal.

Hettie V. [pseudonym], a renegade Afrikaner and former journalist whose interview appears in chapter 21, was one of our major consultants, not only on whom to select for interviewing, but on how to protect our informants and the information they gave us. I was stunned to hear all the precautions she considered necessary.

"Before you leave Cape Town for your travels up country," Hettie V. said, "you must find a lawyer who knows what you're doing and where you're going, and who agrees to take on your case." Although the security police have a pretty free hand to do what they want, lawyers can still be helpful, acting as badgering advocates and sometimes a lot more. "You should call a friend every day at a particular time," continued Hettie V. "If your friend doesn't hear from you within a couple of hours of your prearranged time, she should call your lawyer, who will then try to find you." Could I be hearing correctly? The complexity of our calling at the same time every day while on the road and interviewing seemed awesome. Surely Hettie V. was being absurdly overcautious. Yet, as I was to learn from my interview with her, she erred, if anything, in the other direction.

Hettie V. was only warming up. "You'll also have to prepare for police roadblocks when you're traveling around the country. And they could happen here in Cape Town, too—particularly near the black townships.

"At certain points on the road, armed cops may order you to stop your car. They keep changing where they set up roadblocks, so it won't help for me to tell you where I've been stopped. If they have any reason to be suspicious of you, or if they're bored and want to amuse themselves, they will question and search you. If you suddenly see a roadblock ahead of you, don't try to U-turn your way to freedom. I was with someone who did that recently, and the cops shot at us. Fortunately none of us was hit, but it was pretty scary."

Hettie V. went on to warn us that suspicion would likely be aroused by our tape recorders, blank tapes, cameras, photos of black people and townships, names and addresses of people to visit, anti-apartheid literature, letters of introduction, notes about appointments or impressions of the people we met. Being caught with a collection of taped interviews with women in the anti-apartheid movement would be more than incriminating for us; it could be dangerous for the women interviewed.

The danger of losing our tapes was brought home to us by a U.S.-based journalist who must remain nameless. He kept many of his taped interviews with him in his car so that he could review them before writing articles for U.S. newspapers. The police found them when they stopped him for a search, and erased every one. They also told him he would never be allowed to return to South Africa. He guessed that they didn't throw him out of the country only because they feared the negative publicity it might create for the government.

Hettie V. was clear about another thing. "Don't imagine you will get away with hiding stuff on or in the car. These cops are trained to search people and vehicles, and if they find something that you are obviously trying to hide, they will know you are up to something." That put an end to my fantasies of squirreling away names and addresses in sanitary napkins and the like. "And you'll have to be ready with a good story about where you're going and what you're doing and about whatever they see in your car," continued Hettie V.

Another person advised us to rent a different car in every new city we came to so that the police wouldn't become familiar with our vehicle. Someone else suggested we purchase a tire pressure gauge and check our tires regularly because a favorite trick of the security police is to overinflate the tires of anti-apartheid activists to increase the chance of a serious blowout.

Because all post offices were closed in Grahamstown, where we stayed over the Easter weekend on our trip up South Africa's east coast, we were advised by a politically knowledgeable woman that the local university where she taught would be the safest place from which to mail our materials. Normally, we tried to mail our original and our duplicate tapes at different mailboxes to make less likely the interception of both. The consequence of departing from this practice was that both sets of tapes for three interviews were lost. Presumably they are in the hands of the security police.

If doing perfectly legal research is so fraught with frustrations and fears for white U.S. citizens visiting the country temporarily, imagine what life is like for black anti-apartheid activists who live with government repression day in and day out, year in and year out.

One of my goals was to represent the extraordinary diversity of South African women who are fighting apartheid—diversity in race and ethnicity, social class, age, occupation, political affiliation, as well as kinds of opposition work. Since a successful revolution requires that many people put their lives on the line, I also wanted to focus on women whose political work had required their taking significant risks.

The fact that phones are tapped in South Africa made it difficult to recruit women for interviews. I could not mention on the phone that I was writing a book, or convey the depth of my anti-apartheid sentiments, in an effort to engender trust. Here, the fact that my brother David is well known in South Africa, and highly regarded by many people in the anti-apartheid movement for his commitment to the cause, proved helpful. His political work has earned him several short prison sentences in addition to the five years of house arrest I mentioned earlier. (Helen Joseph, the first person ever to be house-arrested in South Africa, describes her experience of this particularly South

African form of punishment in chapter 15.) Mentioning my kinship with David opened many doors and evoked tremendous warmth and even excitement from some people, particularly Anglicans, since he has been an Anglican priest for many years, and is now a bishop. Being a staunch agnostic myself, I felt odd benefiting from this aspect of my connection with him. Nevertheless I was grateful for anything that helped provide me with the opportunity to learn about, and record, women's accounts of their lives as political activists.

Surprisingly, my necessarily cryptic self-introduction usually got me an appointment. My success is a tribute to the extraordinary openness and trust of women in the anti-apartheid movement.* I cannot account for these qualities, given the extremity of their suffering as a result of the relentless racism of white South Africans. The vast majority were also willing to allow me to use their real names and to include their photographs in this book. Some explained that the Security Branch already knew everything there was to know about them. Others believed that using their own name gave their words more authenticity and validity. They thought it important to inform the world about what is happening in South Africa, and were willing to take the risks involved, just as they frequently did with their other anti-apartheid work. Some believed that exposing themselves to an international audience could actually serve as a protection. I can only hope that their optimism will turn out to be well-founded.

The sixty interviews that I conducted were all with women who had been actively engaged in the anti-apartheid struggle. They were from all racial and ethnic groups—African, Indian, Coloured, Afrikaner, and English-speaking South Africans. They range in age from thirteen to eighty-two years. They live in Cape Town, Soweto, Cradock, Port Elizabeth, Grahamstown, Durban, Johannesburg, and the Transkei. Some of them are well known, like Winnie Mandela, Albertina Sisulu, and Helen Joseph. Others are well known only in South Africa. Still others are local activists who have maintained a low profile. All have been actively involved in trying to create a new, nonracist South Africa.

Fifty-four of the women I interviewed live in South Africa; five had fled the country to live in exile in Zambia, the location of the headquarters of the African National Congress, generally acknowledged as the most important organization in the South African liberation movement. One woman, Adelaide Tambo, wife of Oliver Tambo,

---

* It also testifies to their awareness of the prevalence of phone tapping and its constraints.

the president of the African National Congress in exile, lives in London, England.

Although the interviews had no rigid structure, each covered certain themes. I asked each woman: How and when had she become politically aware? What anti-apartheid activities had she engaged in? What were the consequences of her political involvement for herself and her family? Did she think the changes needed in South Africa could be achieved by reform or by revolution? If she believed a revolution was needed, when was it likely to occur?

Other themes included the role of the African National Congress in achieving revolution; the role of women in the struggle; the problems posed by sexism; the impact of economic sanctions on South Africa; and the importance of international pressure in bringing about change. In addition, I obtained basic demographic data, such as each woman's age, family background, level of education, occupation, marital and maternal status. All black women were also asked how they had been most affected by apartheid. Space limitations have necessitated the omission of portions of most of the interviews, most of which ran about ninety minutes.

Unfortunately, women in rural areas, including women in the so-called homelands, are severely underrepresented here. Although I sought to conduct interviews in a major rural area, the Transkei, where I spent eight days with my brother David, who was living there at the time, only two were forthcoming. One interview was with a radical white feminist, the other with a black woman attorney who turned out not to be an activist. I learned that the repression in many of the homelands—economically unviable land where the government dumps Africans based on their tribal affiliation—is even harsher than in the rest of South Africa. Many politically radical people gravitate to the cities, and African women activists who have stayed in the Transkei were presumably too afraid to talk to me.

But there was another even more serious problem. I do not speak Xhosa, Zulu, Venda, Sotho, or any of the other African languages. Nor do I speak Afrikaans, the mother tongue of most Coloured people as well as Afrikaners. (Twenty-eight years of living outside the country has made my Afrikaans unusable for interviewing purposes.) Since Afrikaans is seen by many black people as the language of the oppressor, even more than the English language, many blacks prefer not to use it, including politically-oriented Coloured people for whom it is a first language. Thus, my lack of fluency in Afrikaans was a relatively minor flaw compared with my inability to speak any African language.

Revisiting the Land of My Birth

There is a correlation in South Africa between the level of education of Africans and their fluency in English. English is sometimes the third language even of those who speak it quite well, their first and second being their native tongue and Afrikaans, or another African language. My decision to use the women's own voices in the form of edited interviews in English biases this study toward the more educated African women. This factor, combined with my inability to interview in any other language, partially explains why African women do not appear in this book in proportion to their numbers in the population.

Non-African women are also overrepresented in this book in order to correct the extremely simplified picture of South Africa that North Americans see in the media. The fact is that Coloured and Indian women play a significant role in the anti-apartheid movement, despite the government's many concerted attempts to co-opt them. A smaller but significant percentage of white women are also involved.

Undoubtedly, one measure of the success of apartheid is that white women were more accessible to me than were Coloured women, and Coloured and Indian women more than African women. Most Africans live in townships that are set apart from the so-called white areas. Many do not have phones. White visitors to these areas are conspicuous and likely to arouse police suspicion or the hostility of some of the township residents, particularly if unaccompanied by someone known to the community. Because of these problems, I frequently interviewed township women in areas reserved for whites—at my mother's, for example, or a friend's home. Meeting me in these settings was often not easy for these women.

No doubt my being white affected what black women were willing to say to me—particularly, perhaps, their feelings about white people. But most of the black women I interviewed were accustomed to working with white people in the anti-apartheid movement and to speaking their minds. Nor was my color the only fact about me that must have affected the interview situation; my gender, my age, my social class, my South African heritage, my living in the United States, my connection with David, all undoubtedly had an impact as well.

Despite these factors, I believe my knowledge of South Africa and the United States and my connections in South Africa place me in a unique position to convey to a North American audience what is going on in that country and to stress the urgency of the need for change. I strongly agree with a basic tenet of the African National Congress that people of all races and ethnicities can, and should, contribute to the making of a new nonracist South Africa.

Many of the women I interviewed stressed the important role women are playing in the liberation movement. For example, Albertina Sisulu, co-president of the United Democratic Front, maintained that "women are the people who are going to relieve us from all this oppression and depression." Ela Ramgobin, a leader in the Natal Indian Congress before she was banned, said, "From the time of the campaign against the pass laws, women have been quite militant. They have played a major role in the education campaign because they are concerned about their children's education. They are the ones who go on the marches about housing, and they have always been in the forefront of the rent boycotts." Women's strength was another common theme in these interviews. According to Florence de Villiers, a former domestic worker, "if given the chance, women are the most powerful force under the sun."

Several women maintained that, in their experience, women have shown more courage than men. According to the ANC representative, Mavivi Manzini, "Once women have committed themselves to the struggle, they do so wholeheartedly. That's why I think women don't break as easily as men. Even under torture, very few women break." Similarly, Feziwe Bookholane, who spent six years in prison, said, "My experience is that men break easily compared to women. I told a guy, 'I will never work with men again because you are afraid of being assaulted. A woman can still keep her mouth shut.'" When I asked Connie Mofokeng, whose torture was unusually harsh, what she thought of Bookholane's conclusion, she agreed, saying, "Because women are stronger."

When, however, I asked women why there are relatively few women leaders, many referred to women's internalized sense of inferiority, their poor education, their lack of assertiveness, and the strong beliefs in traditional gender roles that still prevail in African cultures. I find it difficult to reconcile these two perspectives. The fact that only 5 percent to 12 percent of the political detainees are women suggests that women are underrepresented not only in leadership positions but also in the rank-and-file of the movement. Although leaders are certainly primary targets for detention, the pervasiveness of detention (an estimated thirty thousand since June 1986) shows that this fate is extended to many others.

Perhaps a partial explanation for this paradox is that the women I interviewed recognize the crucial role that many women play in enabling men to be politically active. They often have to raise single-handedly and provide for their children on severely inadequate wages, as well as support their male activist relatives in whatever way necessary. Clearly, this way of contributing to the struggle takes enormous strength but does not necessarily receive much recognition. For example, the ex-detainee Elaine Mohamed said, "I think women's role in the struggle is a very strong one. Like my mother, they are the supportive base in holding families together. . . . If men had to cope with the responsibilities that women shoulder, their role would be much more difficult."

When mothers who are also the wives of political activists become politically active themselves, they often feel much more torn than men do about their other responsibilities. The interview with Winnie Mandela, for example, reveals the enormous additional stress in her life caused by having to combine motherhood with political activism. In talking about how it felt to be imprisoned, Mandela said, "At first I was bewildered like every woman who has had to leave her little children clinging to her skirt and pleading with her not to leave them. I cannot, to this day, describe that constricting pain in my throat as I turned my back on my little ghetto home, leaving the sounds of those screaming children as I was taken off to prison."

Several interviews show the crucial role played by relatives in helping politically active mothers take care of their children. For example, the ANC leader Ruth Mompati's mother took on the task of raising her two grandchildren when her daughter was unexpectedly forced to remain permanently exiled from South Africa. Mompati describes the agony this caused her. "I used to get ill thinking about my children," she told me. When she saw her sixteen-year-old son after a ten-year separation, she said, "I didn't know how to behave toward this boy. It broke my heart. . . . I can *never* explain the emotional suffering of this meeting. It is extremely painful for a mother to miss her children's childhood years. I died so many deaths. I felt, 'Good God, the South African regime *owes* me something, and that is the childhood of my children!' "

Although I told all sixty women that I wanted to interview them for a book on women in the anti-apartheid movement when I met with them in person, I also hoped to be able to give each of them the opportunity to see and, if necessary, correct the edited version of their interview before its publication. Yet another indication of the extraordinary trust of these women is that only two out of the sixty made their consent conditional on seeing what I did with their interview.

It would have totally interrupted the flow of the interview had I asked the women to spell each name of place or person at the time it was mentioned. I hoped later to obtain the assistance of the twenty-four women whose interviews I chose to include in this book, to check all such spellings. I also wanted to make sure that they felt comfortable with the material that had been included. Copies of the interviews were mailed or hand-delivered to each of them—many of them twice—with the exceptions of Winnie Mandela, whom I judged to be too busy to handle this request, and Gertrude Fester, whom I knew to be in prison.

Seventeen of the women responded to my inquiry, letting me know what corrections, if any, they found necessary. (They are, in order of presentation in this book, Elaine Mohamed, Connie Mofokeng, Feziwe Bookholane, Audrey Coleman, Ruth Mompati, Ela Ramgobin, Albertina Sisulu, Paula Hathorn, Florence de Villiers, Helen Joseph, Di Bishop, Anne Mayne, Rozena Maart, Sethembile N., Hettie V., Rhoda Bertelsmann-Kadalie, and Sheena Duncan.) While I would like to think the silence of the remaining four women and one child means that they could find no errors in their chapters, it would be naïve to believe that these manuscripts all arrived at their destination.

In a further effort to avoid spelling errors, I sent the entire manuscript to Hettie V., an extremely informed and helpful woman. This proved useful in catching several errors; but, clearly, she cannot be expected to know how to spell the names of every interviewee's friend or brother (for example), nor even of every informant. Hence, I can only apologize in advance for any errors in these chapters which may have occurred through clumsy editing or the vicissitudes of working with taped materials.

The map of South Africa at the beginning of this book includes only those cities, towns, villages, and townships mentioned in this volume, at least, those that could be located. Almost without exception, maps of South Africa do not include the townships in which most black people are forced to reside (with the exception of Soweto). Hence I asked Sheena Duncan and Hettie V., two very informed women on this subject, to try to place a list of twenty townships on the map I sent them. I also consulted the map published in Jane Barrett et al. (1985), and to a lesser extent, the map in David Mermelstein (1987). With this combination of sources, I was able to locate nineteen townships.

I cannot vouch for the accuracy or precision of their placement on the map, but I wanted to include them anyway, for both political and practical reasons. I think it is helpful for the reader to be able to see on the map where the places are that are mentioned in the text, including the townships. And I think maps of South Africa should not continue to exclude the places where most black people live, albeit not by their free choice.*

* Where there was a disagreement in placement of townships, I gave priority to the locations indicated in the published sources.

26

A glossary of words and abbreviations unfamiliar to non–South Africans, and a chronology of some of the key events in South African history, are included at the end of this volume.

Only eight out of the 112 people included in the 1985 edition of Shelagh Gastrow's *Who's Who in South African Politics* are women (7 percent). Of these eight women, four are included in this volume: Winnie Mandela, Albertina Sisulu, Sheena Duncan, and Helen Joseph. A fifth woman listed in *Who's Who*, the attorney Victoria Mxenge, subsequently shared the same fate as her attorney husband, Griffiths, who was murdered in 1981. Both murders are assumed to have been political assassinations. Dorothy Nyembe, the sixth woman, was one of the twenty-five thousand people detained after the 1986 state of emergency was declared. Prior to this detention, Nyembe had spent fifteen years in prison after being found guilty of harboring members of *Umkhonto we Sizwe*, the ANC's military wing.*

Although I never intended to focus my interviews on the recognized women leaders in the anti-apartheid movement, I did not intend to avoid them either. But the purpose of this brief analysis of the women included in *Who's Who in South African Politics* is to remind the reader how little credit women in the anti-apartheid movement have received for risking their lives in order to give birth to a new South Africa. It is to this end that I have dedicated *Lives of Courage*.

---

* I didn't even try to interview the last two women listed in Gastrow (1985)—Frances Baard and Helen Suzman. A short interview-based book had just been published about seventy-eight-year-old Frances Baard (Schreiner, 1986), and I decided not to try to duplicate this effort. Although Helen Suzman, a white member of the Progressive Federal Party and long-time member of Parliament, is a courageous and outstanding woman who has helped many blacks and political radicals and fought for many important issues, I do not think her participation in the white parliamentary structure in contemporary South Africa qualifies her for inclusion here.

The second edition of Shelagh Gastrow's *Who's Who in South African Politics* (1987) lists only six women, two fewer than the 1985 edition.

PART I

WOMEN IN SOUTH AFRICAN PRISONS

"I wasn't frightened because I used to tell myself that I wouldn't be the first one to die in prison. Also, it wasn't so different from the kind of life we lived outside where I never knew what was going to happen from one day to the next."
— CONNIE MOFOKENG

SINCE detention without trial outside of wartime first became legal in South Africa in 1963, it has become an oft-used feature of the legal system there (Foster 1987, p. 1). Since the beginning of the third state of emergency on 12 June 1986, for example, over thirty thousand people have been detained in South African prisons without having been found guilty of any offense. According to Audrey Coleman, who became an expert on detention in South Africa after her son was detained in 1981, many of the thirty thousand people detained after the 1986 state of emergency are still sitting in jail.*

One of the government's major goals in detaining so many people is to remove political opposition, not criminals. Another important goal is to frighten people into believing that it's too dangerous to oppose apartheid. But now, as Coleman says, "people who are detained who were not previously politically active often join the struggle."

While many of the women I interviewed had been detained at some

* Large numbers of detainees finally won their release after a very successful hunger strike in 1989 (Audrey Coleman, personal communication, 6 June 1989).

29

point in their lives, prison experiences predominate in the stories of four of the women included in this section—Elaine Mohamed, Shahieda Issel, Connie Mofokeng, and Feziwe Bookholane. Elaine Mohamed spent seven months in solitary confinement for participating in the production and distribution of illegal communist posters—a punishment that both reveals white South Africa's extremely harsh methods of repression, and reflects the intensity of the government's paranoia about communism. Connie Mofokeng, one of the participants in the Soweto uprising, did not expect to survive her second detention experience; she was the most severely tortured of all the women I interviewed. Feziwe Bookholane describes her trial on charges of terrorism—a charge she denies—and how she dealt with the ensuing six years in prison. Shahieda Issel's interview highlights some of the methods of psychological torture used by South African interrogators, as well as what it is like to live with constant police harassment outside of prison. Audrey Coleman, in concluding part I, provides an overview of detention in South Africa, including poignant descriptions of some of the young children who have been incarcerated for months or years on end.

1

Sexual Terrorism

"The way women experience detention is totally different from the way men do. I burst into tears when a security policeman said to me: 'I really enjoy interrogating women. I can get things out of them and do things to them that I can't do to a man.' "

ELAINE MOHAMED

*T*ENS OF THOUSANDS *of people have been held in solitary confinement—some for as long as two and a half years—without access to their families or lawyers (Coleman 1986). Many experts consider that this particularly traumatic form of detention should be regarded as a form of torture when used "for the purposes of interrogation, indoctrination or information extraction" (Foster 1987, p.68). Victims of it come to feel extremely vulnerable, especially women who are surrounded by male guards—an effect about which Elaine Mohamed is particularly eloquent.*

Mohamed, a single Coloured woman who teaches at Saint Barnabas School in Johannesburg, is an executive member of the Progressive Teachers' Union and, at the time I interviewed her, was attending training sessions of a feminist group called People Opposed to Woman Abuse (POWA), an organization that assists victims of battery and rape. "Wife battery is a big issue in all black communities," Mohamed explained, "and a lot of women get raped by soldiers." According to Mohamed, "Oppression, whether of women or men, of black or white, of gay or non-gay, Muslim, Jew or Christian, is all a political issue and must be challenged and defeated."

When I went to interview Mohamed on 18 May 1987, she described to me how it was to grow up in a political family. She was born in England in 1961, her parents having left South Africa about 1956 "when things got difficult for them here." They left England for Zambia and then went to Lesotho, where Mohamed got most of her education. Her family returned to South Africa in 1976, when she was fifteen years old. In her interview, discussing her arrests, detention, and solitary confinement for seven months, she dwelt especially on what such treatment means for a woman.

Mohamed is currently studying psychology through the University of South Africa, a correspondence school that has enabled many detainees (including Nelson Mandela) to obtain degrees, as well as black people outside of prison who frequently are not permitted to attend the largely white universities. She hopes to study for an honors degree in psychology in 1989.

Growing Up in a Political Family

I grew up in Lesotho [a small country encircled by South Africa] when it was a lot happier and more peaceful than it is now. I grew up without being racially aware, so I never learned to be racist. My parents had friends of all colors and religions. They have never pushed politics or religion or anything else down our throats. (My father is Roman Catholic, but he was an atheist for a long time, and my mother is Anglican.)

I think that my political consciousness only started in 1977 after I came to South Africa. But although I was very aware from reading the newspapers and talking to people of what was going on around me, I only became actively involved in politics two years later during my first year at the University of Witwatersrand. I joined the Black Student Society and worked with the Student Representative Council and in a local women's group. I was studying for a B.A. in fine art, and I produced and designed a lot of posters for political organizations. I preferred to work in the background because I hate being in the limelight, speaking on a public platform, and things like that. I was an extremely disciplined person at that time, and used to fast for long periods during my first year at university.

My father is an associate professor of math at the University of Witwatersrand in Johannesburg, and my mother is a chemistry technician there. They have been very politically involved, my mother more so in recent years. She is currently one of the vice presidents of the Federation of Transvaal Women. My father, Ismail Mohamed, has been politically active since the 1950s. He spent a lot of time in jail in 1976 although he was never charged with anything. By mistake, some of his clothing was sent home with blood on it. He'd been attacked by one of the guards who had set an Alsatian dog onto him. I was in boarding school at the time so my mother had to cope with this upsetting experience on her own. My father is on the executive committee of the United Democratic Front and was one of the seventeen or eighteen UDF leaders on trial for treason in 1984. The trial lasted over a year, but eventually they all got either suspended sentences or acquittals.

We're a very close family, perhaps because so many things have happened to us. My father has a history of heart disease and has been very ill. There are five of us: myself, Andrew, and Jenny, with two years between each of us, then there's a big gap between us and Ivor and Ingrid. Ivor is in early high school, and Ingrid is about to start high

33

school. My younger brother Andrew left South Africa to go into exile together with eight others in 1980, but six of them were arrested before they made it. Andrew was one of the two who got out, and he subsequently joined the ANC guerrilla forces. He left just before he matriculated when he was seventeen. He is now considered a terrorist by the government, so it's illegal for us to have any contact with him. We can't even correspond with him because then we'd be seen to be working with a terrorist.

At the end of last year [1986], our family was constantly harassed. We frequently got threatening telephone calls. Then my sister Jennifer was arrested in June or July, though we don't know why. Judging from the threats the police made, we don't understand why they let her go after two weeks. Security police were constantly around my parents' house, and my flat was broken into twice early in December while I was away in Durban. All that was missing was my diary. Security police had been around here a number of times to question the cook, the headmaster, his wife, and so forth, about my whereabouts. Recently mail from my sister had very obviously been opened.

We didn't know why the security police were coming after us, but each member of our family was aware of being followed. Our attorney, Priscilla Jana, told us that the police had made it clear that they are not prepared any more to try to get any of the Mohameds into court. They've had all of us in jail, with the exception of the two little ones. They've even opened a file on the youngest, Ingrid. She's only twelve now, but she's been brutalized by seeing my father and myself being arrested and the house being searched after my brother left. And she knows my mother has also been arrested and held for a few hours for participating in a demonstration.

My mother has held the family together and kept things going. I'm just beginning to understand the trauma that she must have gone through when my brother left home, not knowing where he was and if he was safe. Although we are all very proud of him, it must have been very hard on her to lose her child. Every time there's a report in the newspaper that another "terrorist" has been killed, we know it could be Andrew. I know it was also very hard on her when I was in detention. It's often harder for the people outside than for the detainees themselves because those outside have no idea what's going on or how the detainee is feeling. It was very traumatic when Jennifer was arrested last year because we heard that she had been seen in the hospital, but we had no idea if she was there because she had a toothache or because she needed psychological help. A lot of detainees land up in psychological wards.

Sexual Terrorism

I have lived so much of my life in fear, and there's pain wherever I look. There's always somebody who has been arrested or hurt. And when you become politically involved, there is always the fear of arrest. In December [1986], I started feeling terribly afraid that one of my family, or all of us, would be shot on the street, especially after our friend Dr. Fabian Ribeiro, who participated in the documentary "Witness to Apartheid" [shown in 1986 on Public Broadcasting stations in the United States], was gunned down outside his house together with his wife in the first week of December.

When my father was arrested in 1976, the University of the Western Cape fired him less than a month later. They said, "Look, we don't know how long you'll be in detention or what you've been arrested for." My mother wasn't working at the time, so we were left without any income. My mother started buying material at the factory and making track suits and T-shirts, and Jennifer used to go door to door selling them. We grew a lot of potatoes, and all we ate for a while were casseroles, potatoes, and carrots. It was crazy to be living in a big house with a swimming pool but have no money for food. My mother would buy a plastic packet of vegetables that were a little bit spoiled for a few rand [South African currency], and that's all we ate for the week. When some friends came that year to share Christmas with us, they brought a bottle of champagne. They were shocked to find that all we were having for Christmas dinner was potato chips!

Arrest and Conviction

I was arrested in the middle of my second year at university on 11 August 1981 under section 6 of the Terrorism Act for producing and distributing posters commemorating the sixtieth anniversary of the South African Communist Party, which is a banned organization in South Africa. I was interested in communism at the time, but those of us involved in the poster action didn't belong to a specific group. We were acting as individuals. I was the main person involved, although an Afrikaner called Ben took most of the rap for everything that happened. Ben and I had asked a few others to help us make and distribute a "Workers of the World Unite" poster. We wanted to put it up all over Johannesburg on 31 July 1981, because that was the sixtieth anniversary of the formation of the party. Ben and Gerhard were arrested as they were putting up the last poster. They were interrogated for ten days; then I was arrested after Gerhard gave them my name. The police assumed that we must be a Communist Party cell, but we weren't.

We were detained in solitary confinement for four months before we were charged in early December 1981 with attempting to commemorate the formation of the South African Communist Party and, in so doing, furthering its aims. I think the police detained us for so long before charging us because they were trying to build a case against us. They also wanted to break our spirits and find out if our action on 31 July had been instigated from somewhere else and whether we belonged to a Communist Party cell. We were brought to trial two months later on 8 February 1982.

After the trial had been going on for a while (it lasted a month in all), we decided to plead guilty. It was the first offense for all of us. Although we had already been in solitary confinement for seven months, we were sentenced to a year in jail. But only ten days were to be served, and the rest of the time was to be suspended for five years. We were finally released on 19 March 1982. I spent my twenty-first birthday in jail.

Although we all got the same sentences, I was given ten days' hard labor in prison, whereas Ben and the other two guys, all of them white, were allowed to read and sit around. The security guards made sure that I was aware that the guys had beds while I only had a grass mat to sleep on. They'd say, "These guys are white. They can get peanut butter on their bread but you're not going to get anything," or "These guys can have extra blankets but you will have to put felt on top of your grass mat to keep warm." It was a tactic to try to divide us and get us to hate each other, because they don't want whites and blacks to work together.

Seven Months in Solitary

After I was charged, I should have been placed with other women prisoners, but I was kept alone simply to try to break my spirit.

I was arrested on a Tuesday evening. On Sunday the police drove me around town trying to get me to point out the home of Shirley, the sister of my close friend Carmel. I refused to do this because I knew they were looking for Carmel. A policewoman said, "This dolly is going to have the time of her life. I can't wait to start!" That was her way of saying that they were going to force the information they wanted out of me. Because I felt an alliance with her as a woman, I felt more hurt by her saying this than if a man had said it. But I don't know what they did to me, because the whole next week is a total blank to me.

Sometimes I'd just wake up to find the security police in my cell. I became acutely attuned to the sound of keys, because that was how I listened for the police coming to my cell. They would take me for questioning at 3:00 A.M. Sometimes long periods went by without my being questioned, and I began to feel safe and forgot what I'd told them, and then suddenly they'd start questioning me again.

The security police tried very hard to break me. They'd tell me all the time, "You are going to be here for years." They'd ask me an innocent question like, "What did you do last Saturday afternoon?" I'd answer, "I was cycling." They'd say, "Do you know that you won't be able to cycle when you leave here because your legs won't have the strength?" I tried to be quite blasé with the security police, presenting myself as confident and assertive and not showing them when they were getting under my skin. I remember the humiliation of small things like trying to drink coffee but not being allowed to take my handcuffs off. I tried to get the sugar into the cup, stir it, then lift the cup with everybody waiting for me to spill it down my front so they could have a good laugh at me. I remember my total concentration as I told myself, "I'm not going to spill it," or "I'm not going to fall all over the place in the van." These experiences seem so unimportant in comparison with other things that happened to people, like having their heads ducked under water, but they were traumatic to me.

Why Detention Is Different for Women

The way women experience detention is totally different from the way men do. I burst into tears when a security policeman said to me, "I really enjoy interrogating women. I can get things out of them and do things to them that I can't do to a man." I was terrified by this statement. I felt far more horror and pain about it than when I was physically hit by the police, and I think the police realized this immediately. The first time a major smacked me, I had my hands cuffed at my back and I realized I was going to fall, but it didn't really touch me. Another time a policeman came into my cell and said, "You're not allowed tampons in here. You have to wear pads." And he shook the pad and hit it against the wall saying, "Put it on." I found this incredibly threatening. The first week I wasn't allowed to wash or have any change of clothing. After that when they brought in my fresh underwear, they flung it around and said how very small my panties were. I felt far more vulnerable with these kinds of experiences than when I was actually threatened.

I know a woman who was arrested in 1976 who was very brash and aggressive. Nine policemen interrogated her the first night, and they said, "If you don't talk, we're going to rape you, one after the other." She replied, "Oh great! The laws in this country never allowed me to have sex with a white guy. Who's going to be first?" And she started taking her clothes off, which totally shocked these guys, and they didn't do it. But this was something I just couldn't say or do.

At the Fort [a prison] they don't have a running-water system. I had three buckets in my cell: one for fresh water, one for waste products, and one for washing my hands in. They brought me a pad when I was menstruating and a clear plastic bag to put my used pad in. When I went to bathe in a big corrugated iron tub every morning, I'd put my pads into a big zinc bucket. These pads were then collected at the end of my menstruation. One day when I was taken to court I saw women prisoners in the courtyard working through a huge pile of soiled pads. I watched them feeling and shaking each pad while policewomen watched them to make sure that no one was trying to smuggle anything out. I couldn't see the point; it was only humiliating, degrading, and painful. Even if they'd found a note or whatever, surely they would not have been able to trace it to whoever had sent it in a huge prison like that.

The room in which I had my bath didn't have a light, but the sunlight used to come through cracks and holes in the wood. I used to see rats' eyes looking through these holes. I threw water at them and banged on the bath because I couldn't bear them to come into the small space I was in. They came because they smelled the blood on the pads in the zinc bucket. Coming into that room on the five days or so that I menstruated was terrifying for me. Bits of my pads would be scattered over the floor because the rats would eat them at night.

I know someone who had rats pushed into her vagina as a means of torturing her. Although I didn't have that experience, it was something I knew about and always expected. But I didn't cry about it because I didn't want to break down in front of the police. That's what they wanted. So I'd just pick up the bits of my pads, but that experience was terror for me. I always felt that the rats were gnawing at me. But how do I explain to someone that I found that more threatening than someone hitting me? It's those kinds of experiences that I couldn't talk about for a long time. Some of them I still can't talk about.

The police I dealt with at the Fort were women, whereas they were men at John Vorster Square [police headquarters in Johannesburg]. I felt very betrayed by what the women police did to me in prison, because I expected more of women. I always liked my breasts because they are very firm. The policewomen would flick them with their nails on my nipples, saying, "It's a shame nobody wants you. You've obviously never had a boyfriend. No one has touched these breasts, else why are they so firm?" I found this incredibly humiliating.

I was body-searched twice a day every day at the Fort, which was also very humiliating. They made me stand astride and do star jumps to check that I wasn't hiding anything in my vagina. I remember policewomen making me strip in front of men and people laughing at me. Stripping wasn't necessarily connected with being interrogated; it was just a normal prison occurrence. They were supposedly checking that I hadn't brought something into the prison. It was quite ridiculous because I'd go to see the lieutenant about something, and I'd get searched before I left as well as when I returned, although they *knew* that I'd never been left alone. I didn't even go to the *toilet* alone. Somebody was always watching me.

When they didn't strip me, they'd feel through my clothes, slipping a hand into my pants and bra. I found this much more traumatic than stripping. Sometimes this would happen regularly for a week and then it would stop; then suddenly it would start again. It was the same thing with being questioned. I used to almost blank out when they felt me like that. I learned to step outside of my body and ignore what was happening to it. I became aware of my doing this very clearly one day. One of the sergeants was reading the newspaper while another one was searching me. She made me take off my dress and my bra but not my panties. I looked over at the woman reading the newspaper and chatted to her while the other woman was checking inside my panties that I wasn't hiding anything. I was aware of the search happening to Elaine, and something else happening with me.

I remember lying on the bed with the prison doctor leaning over me and putting his forearm between my legs to examine my throat. When I stood on the scale to be weighed, he ran his hand over my behind and up between my legs and told me to walk across the room undressed. I found this traumatic because a doctor is someone I normally trust.

I'm vegetarian and for the first three months or so, all I had to eat was beetroot, carrots, and rice, and an occasional slice of bread, so I became *very* thin. They moved me to John Vorster Square, and my parents were then allowed to bring in food for one meal every day, because I became quite ill.

My mother brought food for me on a Thursday or a Friday. The guards would leave it in their car until they brought it to me on a Monday. I couldn't eat the food because by then it was spoiled. They'd say, "She only brought it this morning. Your mother obviously couldn't be bothered about you." I *knew* that that wasn't true, but it was very difficult sometimes to hold onto that knowledge. I got food poisoning once because I so wanted to eat the food my mother had made for me.

My family sent me other things—like once a week, I might get a parcel with a little chocolate in it. When I came out of prison they told me they'd sent me *more* than one piece of chocolate because they knew I was crazy about it, but the security police would take it. Someone I know, whose brother is doing five or ten years for treason, told me that they used a syringe to spike the fruit they sent him with alcohol. The police suddenly realized this, which must have been because they stole it. A lot of clothes that my mother brought for me were stolen. It snowed that year, and I only got the warm track suits she had brought for me after the snow was over. But I always knew that I had a family outside who cared about me. No matter how much the security police told me, "Your family has forgotten you," I knew that wasn't true. Having experienced my father's detention and knowing what we had done for him, I knew my family would be doing the same for me. That knowledge, and remembering that I was going to get out regardless of how long it took, enabled me to hold on to my sanity.

The police told me they were going to give me electric shocks. They took me to a room and told me to sit on a metal chair; then a guy went out and brought in boxes of equipment. They didn't do it to me as far as I can remember, certainly not on that occasion anyway. But I was so traumatized by thinking they were going to do it, I was almost ready to say, "Okay. These are the people that I know." But I told myself, "Just last one more minute," and focused on one minute at a time. I was very proud that, despite that scare, I didn't give the police people's names, so I knew that nobody would be picked up as a result of anything that I had said.

I started hallucinating in prison, presumably to try to combat loneliness. I remember someone asking me during the period of my trial, "Elaine, what are you doing?" I kept whipping my hand up behind me, and I said to him, "I'm stroking my tail." I had conceptualized myself as a squirrel. A lot of my hallucinations were about fear. The windows in my cell were too high to look through, but I would hallucinate something coming into my cell, like a wolf, for example. I hallucinated myself as different animals, as a squirrel, a camel, a giraffe.

And I started talking to myself. My second name is Rose, and I've always hated the name. Sometimes I was Rose speaking to Elaine, and sometimes I was Elaine speaking to Rose. I felt that the Elaine part of me was the stronger part, while Rose was the person I despised. She was the weak one who cried and got upset and couldn't handle detention and was going to break down. Elaine *could* deal with it. I spoke to my attorneys and Ben, my fellow-accused, about it when I came out. They had noticed it themselves, because sometimes I would say, "I'm not going to do that, but maybe Rose will." It was something that I almost couldn't stop. I had to learn to control it.

I would sit there for hours pulling the hairs out of my legs by the roots. The continual activity with my fingers and nails kept me occupied. The hairs on my legs don't grow any more because of this. When I got a Bible, I studied it to try to keep my mind alive and kill time, which sometimes seemed endless.

At one stage in my life I had wanted to do interior decorating, so I designed interiors in my head and worked out recipes. I got every civilian policeman who came into my cell to teach me one or two words of Sotho, and I gave a couple of English words to those who had poor English. I sat for hours worrying if my detention would ever end and wondering, "What are these people going to do to me? What have I said? How are the others?" because I didn't know what had happened to Carmel or another chap, Reavell.

I remember crying at night, although I was always afraid to cry, because I didn't want the police to see me like that. I'd constantly tell myself, "You've just had lunch, soon it will be supper time. Exercise for a while. Now you're going to sleep." And I told myself all the time, "Tomorrow you might be released." A big problem for a lot of detainees is that they lose hope, but I never did, and I think that kept me together.

My parents had an incredibly difficult time realizing that this person, Elaine Mohamed, was so different from how I'd been before I was arrested. And some of the changes were good ones. That's difficult to say, because it came out of such an awful experience. But it's like when some women come out of rape experiences stronger because they've managed to get their lives back together again. Before detention I rarely spoke to people. I was mainly interested in reading and painting. The comment I always used to get on my school report was that the headmaster didn't know if I was lonely or I just wanted to be alone. I was *very* shy when I went into detention, but I learned to make conversation with *anybody* who wasn't a security policeman. I remember one civilian policeman asked me, "Why do you always ask what the time is?" I did it just to talk to him. I'd ask him about his family, where he grew up—anything! I tried to interact with them as human beings because I became so desperate for conversation.

The first time I ever spontaneously hugged somebody in my life was in prison. I had been a very closed person before that. There was a change of duty, and the security police had accidentally taken me down to the ground floor where the civilian women were kept for engaging in prostitution, being drunk in public, shoplifting, and so on. That was the first time I had spoken to ordinary people for about six months. There was a young woman of about seventeen who was arrested for prostitution, though she denied being a prostitute. The next day she suddenly started crying, and I put my arms around her and she cried and cried. I felt so alone in solitary that I *had* to reach out to try to make contact with people to survive.

I often bite my cuticles when I feel hurt, but I didn't do that in prison. I remember being so proud of that. When I first saw my dad, I said, "Hey, look at my cuticles." It was a way for me to maintain control.

One time there was a breakdown in the pipes, so there was no hot water on the women's side of the police cells. I remember the police having this argument about whether I should be allowed out of my cell to shower, and one of them saying, "You can't expect a woman to shower in cold water. She'll get sick. Women need warm water and quiet time to shower." Despite the sexism, there was no way I was going to say, "My God, of course I can handle a cold shower as well as any man can!" So for a time I was taken to the men's side to shower every day and locked into a shower cell on my own.

The chaps there were pass offenders, not criminals. Some of these young sixteen-year-olds were very helpful. They would start whistling when the policemen were approaching. They'd steal *Scope*—a disgusting, very lightweight South African sex magazine—and lend it to me. That's all the policemen read. I used to absolutely *devour* that magazine when these guys brought me a copy. I read it twice through from cover to cover, including every advertisement. They brought it from the police barracks when they cleaned there, and pushed it up the drainpipe for me (there was a fairly big drainpipe going into my ground-level cell). When I was finished reading or when they began to whistle, I'd push it back up or tear it up. A young policeman also brought me a magazine to read for a few days. Then one day when I was being taken to shower, he ran his hand down my back and said, "Isn't it time to pay me back for getting you magazines?" I was very angry and told him, "Keep them, then! I don't want anything from you."

Sexual Terrorism

The pass offense guys used to sneak into the women's side sometimes. The nice ones used to bring me a magazine or tell me that they'd seen a political prisoner and they'd given my name to him. Sometimes somebody managed, while they were working outside somewhere, to buy a roll of sweets and throw it up the drainpipe to me. Whenever there was a tapping noise at the drainpipe, I'd rush out and listen eagerly. I remember one *horrible* guy telling me to take my clothes off and sit with my legs astride opposite the drainpipe. I remember another guy hiding in the cell I was going to shower in, and appearing after the policeman had locked me in. Fortunately, the policeman hadn't left yet, so I called him.

Not all the male prisoners are like that, as is also true of the police. When it snowed, a really nice guy, who was looking after the pass offense chaps, brought me tea in a milk bottle, although we weren't allowed to have any glass in our cells. He felt sorry for me because it was so cold. He never asked me for anything or made any disgusting, indecent suggestions, but there were other policemen who did.

The Aftermath of Detention

When I was released, my parents took me straight to my doctor. He said my arches were severely damaged and asked me what had happened to them in prison. He said that this kind of damage happened to people who were force-marched for days or had weights dropped onto their feet. But I can't remember anything happening to my feet. As I mentioned, I can't remember an entire week at the beginning of my detention. I blank out very traumatic experiences. For example, I had a very bad car accident the same year that I came out of detention, which is also a total blank for me. I do have a memory of waking up in a room where I was lying on the floor with a noose around my neck and a security policeman holding it, but I don't know whether it really happened or was a dream or a hallucination.

I had a lot of problems when I came out of detention. My father insisted that I see a psychologist, which I did for two years after my release. My father noticed that whenever somebody spoke to me, I would look away. I also couldn't look at people when I found it difficult to talk about something. My concentration was terrible because I had no reading matter most of the time. Although I was released from prison over four years ago [1983], I am still feeling some of the effects; for example, my concentration is still terrible. I had previously intended to do an honors degree, but after I came out of detention I didn't do it because of this problem. Although I did get my B.A. degree, I decided I couldn't complete my work in fine art.

I continue to step outside of myself without realizing it. One of the women who teaches with me said to me a year ago, "Sometimes I get the feeling that you've gone off somewhere. I don't know if it's you I'm talking to." I remember a concrete example of this. I used to undress in my cell quite often when I got very hot because there was no other way to cool down. The concrete cells get either very hot or very cold. Because there were four gates into my cell, I had time to dress when I heard the first gate being unlocked. The day I came out of prison, a lot of people came to my parents' house to see how I was. I suddenly became aware that these people were looking at me. My mother told me afterwards— which is the only reason it's part of my memory now—that I'd taken my skirt off and folded it very neatly and hung it over the back of a chair and then sat down again. People were dumbstruck by my sitting in the lounge in front of them all in only my T-shirt and panties.

I needed a very strong acknowledgment of my body when I came out. Because of my disciplined attitude before I was arrested, boyfriends had not been part of my life, so I was very young in terms of relationships when I was released. I remember being in a car with a chap I got involved with and taking off my shirt and wanting him to tell me that my breasts were beautiful. I needed reassurance that my body was fine because it had been hurt so much, or my conception of it had been. Whenever I'd been touched during my seven months in solitary, it had been to degrade or to physically hurt me.

2
From Soweto to Exile

"I didn't think I'd come out alive; in fact, I was seeing death. But I was prepared to die as long as I died for the truth, and I knew that people would know that this was the case."

CONNIE MOFOKENG

*T*WENTY-EIGHT YEARS OLD *in 1987, Connie Mofokeng is a single, African woman who used to be a social worker before she went to live in Lusaka, the capital city of Zambia. She fled there from South Africa in 1986 because Lusaka is also the headquarters of the African National Congress. Although not—contrary to the police's contention—a member of the ANC when she was in South Africa, she is a hard-working member now. She reported that a lot of women are now actively involved in* Umkhonto we Sizwe, *the military wing of the ANC.*

It is a near miracle that Mofokeng is still alive. As well as being poisoned while in prison, she was subjected to electric shocks more times than she can remember. (Mofokeng reported knowing other women who had been similarly tortured.) Looking at Mofokeng with her warm smile and gentle demeanor, I found it difficult to take in the horrendous and almost fatal brutality she had suffered over an extended time, until she showed me the scars on her breasts and back from the electric shocks. Despite the torture, Mofokeng never gave her torturers the information they sought. As is clear from the epigraph, she was willing to accept death for the cause of liberation.

Growing Up African

I was born in Johannesburg, the youngest in a family of four girls. My father died when I was very young, so I was brought up by my mother. I was lucky to be the youngest because all my sisters had to help my mother in the house whereas I did not. She was a domestic worker who struggled a lot to earn enough to educate and take care of us. She had to work at night as well as during the day. When I was about twelve years old, she explained to me that very few black people live better lives than we did. She told me that because whites dominate, they do less work but earn more money than black people. She also told me about the ANC and the struggle of black people to change the situation.

I joined a youth organization during high school when I was fifteen or sixteen years old. That was when I learned that education in South Africa indoctrinates whites and domesticates blacks.

The Soweto Uprising

I was eighteen years old and living in Soweto in 1976. I was a member of the Soweto Student Representative Council [SSRC] at that time, then later a member of the Soweto Student Organization [SOSO] but not very active in it. Later, after the arrest of the leaders, I became the secretary of SOSO. The government passed a law to force us [Africans] to get all our education in Afrikaans because they wanted Afrikaans to be known to all black children. But we didn't want to have all our classes in Afrikaans, so SSRC worked hard to stop this from happening. They decided that on 16 June 1976, the first day all subjects were to be taught in Afrikaans, all the students should stay away from school. Instead, we planned a peaceful march to make our demands known to the authorities.

When we were marching peacefully on that day, the police started to shoot at us with tear gas at first, and then with bullets. Thirty-five people died on that day. More died later, and many people were injured.

I had to go into hiding for some time after that. When they knocked on my door, I didn't realize it was the police at first. Then I looked through the window and saw many cars and torches [flashlights], so I knew it was them. Someone must have tipped them off that I was there. They detained everybody in the house, but they let all the others return in the morning.

First Two Detentions

They never charged me with anything, but about eight policemen beat me and kicked me, even before I said anything. They didn't give me a chance to talk until they thought they had exhausted me. I had discussed this sort of behavior with my comrades,* so it didn't come as a surprise to me, but it was tough. I had been told not to talk, and I thought that meant that I must keep completely quiet rather than that I mustn't reveal anything important. As young and inexperienced as I was, I kept quiet, and maybe that's why they kicked me so much.

They interrogated me to try to find out who said we must stay away from school. After I realized that they were hitting me more because I

---

* The term *comrade* is used by many people in the anti-apartheid movement and does not necessarily indicate that they subscribe to a communist ideology.

wasn't saying anything, I said, "All the students who were marching decided to stay away." But they wanted to know the person who *started* it, which I refused to say. The interrogations lasted over a period of about six weeks. After that, I sat in my cell day and night for three months in solitary confinement without reading material. It was very hard for me. A day seemed like a month, and a month seemed like a year. I never knew if it was morning or evening. Others had written poems and slogans or drawn pictures on the wall, so I read what people had written and wrote my own poems and stories on it with little stones.

Outside prison the police don't admit that they have killed detainees. They say that the people who have died in detention have committed suicide. Inside they told me they were going to kill me, and they told me about some of the people who had died in detention. I believed them, but I wasn't frightened because I used to tell myself that I wouldn't be the first one to die in prison. Also, it wasn't so different from the kind of life we lived outside where I never knew what was going to happen from one day to the next. And conditions are even worse now. Kicking small kids or a woman and her child is nothing unusual to the police outside prison any more.

They finally let me out after three months. I had been in standard eight [tenth grade] when the Soweto uprising occurred, and I was expelled from school for being detained. Fortunately, my father was a priest who was well known, so one principal who knew my family allowed me to attend his school.

What happened to me happened to about one hundred fifty of the other young people who had participated in the Soweto march in 1976. About thirty-eight of the one hundred fifty were girls. The number who were detained was much higher if people who only stayed for a short time are included. If boys were carelessly dressed, that was enough for the police to detain them. With the girls, they'd pick up those who their informers said were involved.

The SSRC and SOSO had dissolved by then, because all the leaders had been arrested and faced trials and the other members were too afraid to continue.

My second detention was in 1979. I was one of the people who organized the funeral of Comrade Matsobane who died in prison on Robben Island [a maximum-security prison for black political prisoners]. We were all arrested, but I wasn't held for very long.

The Vaal Triangle Uprising

I moved from Soweto to Sebokeng, a new township in Vereeniging, which is in an area known as the Vaal Triangle.* I helped to form a women's organization in the Vaal Triangle in 1984 called the Vaal Organization of Women, and became its secretary. I also participated in an action committee that worked toward the formation of the Vaal Civic Association. I was elected as its chief representative and an area committee chairperson in Zone 7 of Sebokeng. People in the Vaal couldn't pay the high rents. The lowest rent there was fifty rand [$25], but people only earn about sixty rand [$30] per month. So we helped to organize the very first rent boycott as well as a boycott of the community council which had just started. The community council is made up of puppets who are working for the government. But the people have to pay them, despite not having the money for this.

The Vaal Civic Association organized house meetings in all areas of the Vaal Triangle and called mass meetings on 24 and 25 March 1984. Many resolutions were passed, one in favor of a rent boycott. We also demanded that the community council resign because nobody had voted for them; that all the shops, taxis, and garages of the community council must be boycotted; that on the day of the rent increase, nobody should go to work or school in protest, and the buses and taxis must not operate; and that the people at the meeting must tell those who weren't there about all the resolutions that were passed.

Two days after that meeting, the police came to my place. They said I must tell people that they must go to work on the day of the stayaway. I told them that the people were going to march peacefully to the administration board on that day to present their demands, and I emphasized that there would be no violence on that day. I said that the people had decided to do this because when they keep quiet, the administration board thinks they are happy. I also told the police that the people themselves had decided not to work. It wasn't me who had told them not to. They responded, "You must go and tell those people to go to work. Otherwise, we're going to lock you up." But there was nothing that I could do. I met with other members of the Executive Committee and asked them their feelings about the police's demands, but nobody was willing to try to stop the stayaway.

* The Vereeniging/Van der Byl Park/Sasolberg/Sebokeng/Sharpeville triangle-shaped region, south of Johannesburg on the Vaal river.

On 3 September, everything stopped. People were to meet at a certain Roman Catholic church and march to the administration board quite a distance away. When the marchers passed the home of one of the councilors, they shouted, "As a person who's also a resident of the Vaal Triangle and who is also going to pay a higher rent, come and join us." But instead of joining us, the councilor took out a gun and started shooting at people, injuring some of them. People were very angered by this and started to stone his house. The police then arrived in a helicopter and also started shooting at people. (Other helicopters were flown to other areas like Sharpeville, Bophelong, and Boipatong, and the police shot people there also.) The people became more and more angry at what was happening, so instead of taking their demands to the administration board, they started stoning, burning, and looting. Some of us tried to control people, but things were totally out of hand by then. After the councilor had killed about five people, people stoned his house until they got him out of it. Then they stoned and burned him. He was the first councilor to be killed. The whole Vaal Triangle was on fire.

We tried to take injured people to the hospital because no taxis were running. Ambulance drivers were also afraid of being stoned and shot by police in the townships, so they refused to help. People who were injured but not unconscious didn't want to go to the hospital for fear they would be arrested. But some nurses were willing to help the injured people, and UDF sent out mobile units to assist them. The upheaval continued for a whole week.

When I went home, my mother told me that the police were looking for me, so I went into hiding. But I continued to work while in hiding, making pamphlets to tell people to stay at home because it was dangerous to move around. On 18 October, I was arrested due to my own carelessness. Because I had managed to visit my lawyer in town without being caught, I went to town again to make some pamphlets and to collect some documents from my workplace. That's when they got me. They were also looking for my friends who were in hiding, but fortunately, when they heard I was arrested, they were able to skip the country.

Torture

I was taken to John Vorster Square in Johannesburg. A policeman had told me in 1979, "If I see you here again, I'm going to be very tough on you." And they did treat me much more harshly than before. They told me that they were going to kill me. They kicked me before even asking me anything. They gave me electric shocks on my bosom and on my back. It was like a burn. They beat me with a baton and threw me against the walls. They kept asking me who my contact was in the ANC and what work I'd done for them. I told them I had no contact. They asked me why I told people to revolt, saying that everybody in the Vaal Triangle blamed me for what had happened. They accused me of having brought all the activities of Soweto to that region.

For about six days they gave me no food. But I didn't feel hungry. I only started to feel hungry when I was alone for some time in my cell. The cells were very filthy. The food was terrible. The porridge was half cooked. I wasn't allowed to change my clothes, and I wasn't allowed visitors. They were hiding me from other detainees, and only one comrade saw me by accident. At some point near the end, they allowed me to wear clean clothes and get food parcels, but they would keep the fruit until it spoiled before they brought it to me.

They continued torturing me for about six months. They put me in a cold bath before assaulting me. When I started to become dry, one of them would say, "Take her to the bath and make her wet." I think maybe this stopped me from bleeding because I noticed I didn't bleed at all that year. They undressed me for the electrical torture, but they put me in the bath with my clothes on. I can't count all the times I was shocked. It was as often as they took me to the office to interrogate me over a period of many months. After a while I wasn't even sure that I was still alive. And they kept me in solitary confinement for the whole time, which was over a year.

There was only one woman among the men who tortured me. One woman was also there during the interrogation, but she just sat there doing nothing. It's hard to know which kind of torture was the more painful. I had become a thing. I even thought that I was dead. On the eve of the July 1985 state of emergency, I was taken to the hospital unconscious from the torture. That is where I learned that some doctors are collaborators. I was there until August.

I never told them anything. I was so angry because of the way they treated me. What's the use of talking when people are hitting you? I became a very stubborn person, though I wasn't that way by birth. But in truth, I wasn't working with the ANC then. If I'd had a way to work for them, I would have, because I wanted to work for an organization that would destroy apartheid. But all my activities were actually quite legal, and they simply blamed the ANC for everything that happened.

Attempted Rape

I always knew that if I had a chance to escape, I'd do it. One day the watch policeman wanted to sleep with me. I fought with him, and fortunately he didn't manage to overpower me. I pulled his hair, and he fell down. The door was open so I left my cell. I wanted to run away, but I realized that if they caught me, he'd say I was fighting with him to escape. Then the case against me would be very serious. So I stayed in my cell where police found me after they came running in thinking that I had escaped. So the watch policeman's story that I tried to escape wasn't very convincing. But when I told them what had happened, their reaction was to assault me. Two weeks later, a prison inspector asked me and the other prisoners if we were having problems. I made a statement to him about what had happened on that day in my cell, but the only thing they did as a result of my report was to transfer me to another prison.

This wasn't the first time something like that happened. They would usually try to sleep with me when they came to look into my cell in the evenings. When I heard the door opening, especially in the evenings, I had to be ready for anything. I often couldn't sleep because I felt so unsafe. But they never succeeded because I used to fight them.

Escape

Because I was sick from the torture, they had to take me to the hospital. I finally managed to escape from there. I was very fortunate that a car was coming by as I came out of the building. I stopped the driver and told him I was going to town on business and asked him for a lift. He was attracted to me, and I made it seem that I was also attracted to him. He asked where he could pick me up later, and I said, "You can pick me up this evening at the same place you dropped me today." That's how I escaped.

But I was nervous, especially when I saw someone looking at me for a long time. I decided not to go to the comrades because I no longer knew who would be safe. I went straight to my family, who took me to another place. From there, I met up with some comrades who found a place for me to stay that even my family wouldn't know about. They were afraid my family might not be strong enough to remain silent if the police asked them where I was. The police locked my family up for some days, including my seventy-eight-year-old grandmother, to try to get them to say where I was. They looked everywhere for me but couldn't find me.

I didn't leave South Africa for some time because I was so sick. But finally I escaped to Botswana. I stayed there for some time, too; then I came to Lusaka. I've been here for over a year now, working for the ANC.

I don't think they would ever have released me. Either they were going to charge me with terrorism or kill me. They were even talking about a murder charge against me because of that councilor who was killed. They might have blamed me for that murder.

Physical Aftereffects

My period stopped until July 1986. The doctor said there was a blockage in my fallopian tubes because I had been kicked there. But it came back after I had received a lot of medical treatment, and they told me that I can still have a baby. Also, I couldn't hear with my right ear because of being kicked and hit there. It's better now although sometimes I still can't hear properly. The electrical torture made it very painful for me to wear a blouse, even after I arrived in exile. And I couldn't wear a bra.

I have also had a severe stomach problem. For a very long time, nothing used to stay in my stomach when I ate. Although I was vomiting all the time, my stomach kept getting bigger and bigger. I also developed a lot of pimples on my face. I still have the scars from them. All these problems made me look quite horrible. The treatment I got in Botswana didn't help, but the treatment I got in Zambia for about six months did. When I was taken to Moscow for further treatment, I thought my stomach was healthy again. I thought I'd only be there a month. But I had to stay about three months because they found so many complications. The doctor told me the poison had been eating away my intestines, and that they would rupture without an operation. I believe a slow poison had been put in my food deliberately.

But I am happy to be alive, and I know what I'm fighting for. Every time I go to the bathroom and see my scars, I feel angry. The doctors tell me I will have them for the rest of my life. But the revolution has already started and will be completed very soon. The only victory remaining is a military one. Politically, we've already won.

3

Six Years Inside

"My youngest child was three years old when I was first detained. Early on in my detention, I was very concerned about
her, but it got to a stage where I even forgot about *her*. Maybe
that was how God protected me, because if I had thought about
my child all the time I don't think I would have come out sane."

FEZIWE BOOKHOLANE

F

EZIWE BOOKHOLANE, an African, spent six years in prison, longer than any of the other women I interviewed. She was forty-four years old and separated from her husband when I interviewed her in her apartment in the so-called white section of Johannesburg; she was living there with her twelve-year-old daughter, her youngest child. The Group Areas Act, which makes it illegal for people of different races to live as neighbors, has not been rigorously enforced in a few city locations in the past few years—in part, because of the extreme housing shortage for black people. I could see, when riding the eleva-tor in the high-rise apartment building in which Bookholane was living, that many other black people were making their homes there.

Although living in Johannesburg now, Bookholane comes from Port Elizabeth, the port city where she engaged in most of her political activities. It is situated in the heart of the militant eastern Cape area, where government repression is now so intense that it was difficult to find people, particularly blacks, to interview there. The large majority of political activists in Port Elizabeth appeared, when I was there, to be in detention or in hiding. As Bookholane said, "If there is a con-sumer boycott in Port Elizabeth, then virtually no black man is going to buy from town. People in the eastern Cape are the most militant in the country."

A nurse by profession, Bookholane began her political work by treating people who had been injured by government forces. Greatly affected by the murder of her stepson by the South African army, she decided to take on the risky task of helping young political people to escape from the country. This led to her conviction on a trumped-up charge of terrorism.

Bookholane described all but one member of her family as "political fireworks." One of her sisters, currently a member of the African National Congress in Lusaka, left South Africa in 1977 for political reasons. Two of her other sisters are active in women's organizations.

She speaks here eloquently of how it felt to be incarcerated for so many years, particularly the torture of long spells of solitary confine-ment. More surprising for many people, however, is her description of the trauma of being free again: "It got to a stage where I almost wished that I was still in prison." Three years after her release in 1984, she was still suffering from the experience.

Growing Up African

I was born in Port Elizabeth in October 1942, the first-born of seven children. I went to various boarding schools; then, after passing my matric [final examinations at the end of high school], I joined a Catholic convent. During my seven years in the nunnery, I was the only black nun. The mother superior told me, "You'll feel out of place here because you haven't lived with whites before," and, "You can't have recreation with the other nuns because this is a community of whites." I was expected to read books on my own during recreation. I was even given different food from them. My meals were leftovers from the wards like sliced polony [cheap sausage], bread and jam. I told the mother superior that I wouldn't stand for this. "I may be from a poor family," I told her. "I may be black. But my parents didn't feed me such food at home." In my seventh year, I wrote to the bishop to get a dispensation, and I left the convent. It was such a bad experience that I didn't go near a church for a very long time after leaving there.

I decided to become a nurse and worked at the Livingstone Hospital in Port Elizabeth for a while, then was transferred to a day hospital in a township called KwaZakhele. After completing my midwifery training, I married an actor, Fats Bookholane, who already had two children. In 1973, I gave birth to a daughter who is fourteen years old now and staying with me here. Thabang, one of Fats's children, also lived with us, and I looked after and educated him.

Political Activity

I started to get politically involved for the first time when I was working in the day hospital during the 1976 and 1977 uprisings in Port Elizabeth. These started in August, just two months after the Soweto uprising. I was looking after bullet victims, and I found out firsthand that some of them simply happened to be in the streets, coming home from work, when they were shot. Despite their lack of political involvement, those who had been shot were automatically held prisoner and charged with whatever the police deemed fit. After I saw a number of children getting killed, I decided I had to do something about it.

Six Years Inside

I started working together with some doctors to remove the bullets and treat the wounds of injured people off the record. We had to keep what we did secret because we would have been in trouble if the police had found out about it. People knew who to contact when they needed this kind of help, and we treated injured people wherever they happened to be. We also carried them to the doctors' rooms when necessary, but some doctors volunteered to go to where the people were.

I was very close to my stepson Thabang. We would go together to meetings and funerals, and I became very aware through these experiences with him of what was happening politically. He was very active in the student movement and in the 1976 uprising in Port Elizabeth. It was very painful for me when he decided to leave the country in 1977, but he said he couldn't stand it here any more. I missed him a lot. He joined the ANC when he was in exile, and he was killed together with seven other ANC members in the Maputo raid into Mozambique by South African forces in 1981. The police were disguised as blacks. They say he was the last one to die because apparently he saw through their masks and realized from the way they were talking that this must be a raid. Then a confrontation took place, and he was killed. I am told that his one leg was literally tattered.

I was in prison at the time, and my husband couldn't go to Maputo for the funeral because the South African authorities wouldn't give him a passport. My mother and my sister tried to attend it, but they were held up at the border, so they only arrived the day after the funeral.

I was in close touch with other students besides Thabang. They would come to me for help in drawing up their protest pamphlets. I started working with five other people, two in Johannesburg and three in Port Elizabeth, to assist students who were being sought by the police in getting out of South Africa. I was responsible for helping them to get from Port Elizabeth to Johannesburg. Two out of the six of us were women.

We heard that the first group of students who left the country in 1977 had gone to Swaziland. Some of them went to further their education, and some went for military training. People were so afraid of being detained, they often didn't care what happened as long as they got out of the country. We began to be bombarded with children and parents asking us to please help their children to leave. We realized what we were doing was risky, so when we were finally detained it didn't come as a surprise. The other three Port Elizabeth people in my group were caught about three weeks before me.

Detention and Trial

On 23 March 1978, I got a phone call at the hospital where I was working, requesting me to go to the matron's office immediately. I was on my way there when I met a nursing sister who told me, "There are four white guys standing next to the matron's office who look like security police." Some people knew that I was involved in something because of all the groups of children that would come into the hospital. So I rushed to the loo [toilet] and hid there. But finally I went to the matron's office.

These guys were standing there, and it was as if they already knew me. I said, "Hi," and they said, "You had better take your bag. We are picking you up." Shivering and scared as I was, I decided to put up a front. I said, "May I ask who you are?" They said, "Yes, we are from security." They took out their identity badges and said, "We are detaining you under section 6." I asked if they had a warrant, and they said yes, and one of them brought it from their car. I was too nervous about what would happen to me to read what was written on that piece of paper.

Six white men were waiting for us at the police station. They were very excited that "the nurse" had been found. They fired so many questions at me it was impossible to answer them, so I told them, "Guys, I cannot respond to all these questions. I am confused." So one fellow said, "You are not going to address us as if you are here with doctors and matrons. We are the *police*." Then they removed my glasses and boxed my ears. One of the others said, "No, no, no! Let us not assault her now. The time is still coming for that." I was then taken to an identification parade. Some people who had been arrested said that they knew a nurse who helped people to leave the country, but these children didn't know me.

The colonel came in to tell me that they had a search warrant to search my house, so we went in nine cars to my home. I had a number of cards from a friend of mine, Olive Theodora, who had signed her initials O.T. at the end of each card. They were bubbling over with excitement thinking this was Oliver Tambo [the president of the ANC]. And there were a number of letters from Frances Baard [a well-known political activist] who is my husband's aunt, which they also confiscated. They said that they thought they had found a stronghold of the ANC.

My husband had been very close to the late Steve Biko, so pictures of him were on the walls. The one fellow said, "Remember when we used to come here to look for Fats." The other guy responded, "*Ja*, we should have detained that guy a long time ago." And the first fellow said, "No, you've got it all wrong. The one who has been doing underground work is his wife, so we have the right person now."

A policeman called Wilken was there. He had featured prominently in the Biko case, so I knew of him from newspaper stories. Wilken asked me if I knew of him. I said, "No, I don't." He said, "That means you don't read your papers. I'm the one who featured prominently in the Biko affair, and I know how to handle cases like yours." From there they took me to a police station outside Port Elizabeth and locked me into a cell.

My cell had a cement floor, one small window, and the toilet system was a pit privy which was full, with no way to flush it. They said it was flushed from outside and the flusher was out of order. There was no mattress or bed. And the blankets were so dirty and full of ticks that I told myself I wasn't going to sleep in them. But it was so cold that in the middle of the night I stuck myself in between the blankets and slept.

The police didn't believe that I and my colleagues were only involved in sending children out of the country. There had been a bombing in Port Elizabeth in early 1978, and they were trying to force us, by assaulting us, to admit that we knew the people who were responsible for it. They said they knew that the ANC uses educated people for this kind of thing. The truth is that no one in my group knew people who were bringing arms into South Africa and engaging in bombings. But they told me that the riot squad would deal with me if I didn't cooperate. After this threat was made, the warrant officer said on the phone in my presence that he was withdrawing from my case because he knew no one could guarantee that I'd survive after the riot squad had handled me, and he didn't want to have to testify to the fact that he was present when it happened.

The warrant officer's stand spared me from the riot squad but not from being assaulted. I was beaten on my face and became semiconscious, so I don't know exactly what happened after that. My eyes were so swollen up I couldn't see. I remember getting antibiotics in capsular form after a while. By this time I had been detained for over two months. When the swelling subsided, I was taken back to Port Elizabeth.

The police were now satisfied that they had arrested our whole group. They said that all I needed to do now was to give evidence against the other five people, then they would let me out and find me a job in some hospital. I said, "To hell with it!" So they said, "If you don't, you'll just stay here." They thought they could break me and force me to be a state witness. They sent lawyers to tell me that I wouldn't get less than fifteen years if I didn't testify against my colleagues, whereas I'd be free if I did. I said, "Fine. They can go up to twenty years, but I will never turn against my own people." They left orders that no one should be allowed to see me, no food parcels should get to me, and so forth.

Time passed and another lawyer was sent to tell me that the police had told him that I would be inside for ten to twelve years, and he thought that the best thing for me to do was to give evidence. I said, "My dear friend, go back to the other lawyers and ask them to give you some kind of education." He said, "I know if you do this, you will lose your associates." I said, "Besides losing my associates, I don't want to lose my dignity."

By this time I had been charged, and on the way to court they said, "Feziwe, we are giving you one last chance. You are now going to court, and Shun Chetty [a lawyer] refuses to get you representation because he says your case is hopeless. You are going to get convicted, but you still stand a chance if you give testimony against the others." I said, "My dear people, let me go to court and get convicted. I don't mind getting convicted for doing what I have done." In court I found out that they had been lying about Shun Chetty because he *had* obtained legal representation for me.

The six of us were charged with acting in concert to incite people to undergo military training. They had found two state witnesses to tell that story. They are the people who destroyed us. They just made it up. One girl from Port Elizabeth gave evidence in another case here as well. They were going around testifying against people. The state witnesses reported that when we bade them farewell, we said, "Train well. Then come back to overthrow the state." We now believe that they were both plants. The one student who had frequented my place had taped everything we said. They were being paid to spy and to lie. I wish I knew why they did this. The woman had appeared to be a great person and was very dynamic. It was hard to believe that she could stand in that witness box and say the incredible things she said.

Six Years Inside

We were convicted of terrorism and sentenced on 4 April 1979, over a year after I had first been detained. The first accused was sentenced to nine years in prison; the second, a woman, to three years, two of them suspended; the third was acquitted; I got eight years; my fifth co-accused got ten years; and the sixth one was acquitted. We appealed against the severity of the sentences, and after a year my sentence was reduced to five years; the sentence of the person who got ten years was reduced to eight; and the sentence of the one who got nine years was reduced to seven.

Convicted Prisoner

My first reaction to being searched when I was an awaiting-trial prisoner was one of absolute horror. They had to call the major of the prison because I said, "I refuse to undress in front of this crowd." The prisoners had to stand in front of everyone stark naked while the police opened up their buttocks. I saw it being done to other people, and when it was my turn I said, "I'm very sorry, but I cannot undress in front of this crowd. To me this is not decent." The major said, "O.K., go into this room. They will search you there." Because I put up that kind of protest, they didn't treat me like the other prisoners. I also said, "I refuse to speak Afrikaans, and I refuse to stand up for you." And they left me in peace. But all this changed after I was convicted. They insisted I stand up for them when they entered the cell.

I was in Potchefstroom Prison for almost a year. I became ill with typhoid while I was there. When they changed my treatment in the hospital, I developed strange scales on my skin. When my mother came to visit me, they said, "You have come on the wrong date. It is supposed to be her husband visiting her today." And when my husband came, they said, "It's the wrong date. It's supposed to be her mother today." They did this because they didn't want my family to see the condition I was in.

There were cockroaches and worms in the food, so we went on a hunger strike several times to protest this. After our third hunger strike had lasted eleven days, they decided to transfer us to Klerksdorp Prison. I gave a wardress there a hard clap on the face when she threw my toilet bag into the yard. I was charged for assaulting her and given thirty days on a spare diet and three months in solitary confinement with all privileges withdrawn.

Solitary confinement was the most terrible time for me. Even the Bible was confiscated. It got so that I didn't know what day it was. My cell was directly facing the section where they execute people. When I stood at the window, I could see the visitors of the people to be executed. I saw the people crying on the day of execution and heard the prisoners on the other side praying. It was a kind of torture that I thought I couldn't stand. They kept me in segregation for eight months that year, not just the three months they had told me I'd get. There is a prison regulation that says, "For a prisoner to be segregated for longer than three months, the approval of the state president must be obtained." But apparently the state president didn't know about it. When Helen Suzman [the most liberal member of Parliament] came to see me and the others who were segregated, she reassured us that we would be removed from it. The following month we were put with others.

But trouble started again with the food. We were given bread for supper one night which tasted of tobacco, so I didn't finish eating it. In the middle of the night, two of the people who had eaten the bread started vomiting. They had to be given injections and other medicines for their condition. When the doctor came the following morning, he wanted to know exactly what had happened, so I told him that the food had been poisoned. Immediately after that episode, I was moved to Pollsmoor Prison [in Cape Town] for a year on my own. I was again in solitary confinement because I was the only prisoner being held there under the security act.

Being segregated was the hardest part of prison for me. It got very boring because I didn't have anything to read. The only person I saw was the one who locked and unlocked me. I couldn't even see the prisoners who cleaned the passages. I wasn't allowed to receive letters from home or to write letters to anybody. I didn't know what was happening around me. I was very worried that I would become mentally deranged. I wondered how a person feels when they go mad. I still don't know how I survived. It took me time to try to recall what date it could possibly be. I decided to keep a calendar and play Scrabble with little pieces of toilet paper to keep myself going because I realized that it is very easy to lose your mind.

Children were not allowed to visit until 1982 when I was in Kroonstad Prison. When I saw my [youngest] child for the first time since I had been imprisoned in 1978, I was so excited. But at the end of the visit when I went back to my cell, I was so upset that I hoped and prayed that they would never bring her to visit me again. The pain afterwards was too much to bear.

Six Years Inside

My imprisonment upset my husband very much. At one point he had run away because the police were looking for him, thinking that he must be in the know about what I had been doing. He didn't take care of our child properly, which was another trauma for me. Being an actor and traveling all over the country, he didn't have the time. He would leave the child at various places with friends, until I put my foot down and insisted that she must go to my mother, which she did.

The Aftermath of Detention

I was finally released in January 1984. I am grateful to the people in the office of the Eastern Cape Council of Churches because they organized for me to see a psychologist on the very day of my release. She prepared me for what would happen. She told me, "I know it is very exciting to be released, but you must remember that you have been out of this society for virtually six years. Your child was not at a stage to understand that you had to go to prison because of politics. She has been wondering what has happened to you, and for a time she will be withdrawn, and then she'll become very dependent on you. You have to go through these phases with her until she understands and pulls herself out of them." My child is twelve now, and she wants to be with me all the time. She has been severely psychologically affected by all this. I am still trying to nurse her as much as I can because I was not there for her when she needed me most.

I have been scratched off the nursing roll. This means I can't get a job nursing because I am not registered. I would like to be registered because nurses have a lot of privileges now. But I got a job immediately after my release working for the regional office of the South African Council of Churches as a fieldworker for interchurch aid in the Port Elizabeth region. I am now working for an organization which funds small self-help projects. Most of the funding comes from overseas. We have set up various projects like soup kitchens, crèches [day-care facilities], sewing groups, and garden projects.

My mother felt I wasn't ready to be in my house on my own after my release, so she said, "We'll take care of you." My brother and child were staying with her and I agreed to join them. When I was still in prison I told myself that the first thing I would eat when I got out was bacon and eggs with toast and ice cream. This food was now available to me, and my mother and brother would leave the house and say, "Eat whatever you like." But when they returned, they found that I hadn't eaten a thing. I don't know why. I was scared that they would disapprove, and I was afraid to cook. I was afraid to be in groups of people, and I always got anxious when a group of people came to see me.

People didn't understand that I had been totally out of touch with what had been happening outside prison. I never saw any newspapers. UDF wanted me to address a rally, and AZAPO [the Azanian People's Organization, a black nationalist group] people were calling me to take part in their annual general meeting. I told people that I couldn't address rallies and organize people after six years inside. I wanted people to understand that I was very confused psychologically, and I didn't want to get more confused. I said, "If you'll just leave me in peace, I will go to these rallies and these meetings until I can see for myself what it is that I need to do." It got to a stage where I almost wished that I was still in prison. I felt I wasn't ready to be out making decisions. My brother understood this because he had talked to a psychologist who had prepared him for my reactions. Even now over three years after my release, I can carry around fifty rand for two weeks and not spend it. I go into shops, but I find it hard to choose things.

A fellow who was released recently after eight years on Robben Island asked me, "How do I handle this situation?" I said, "You just have to tell people that you aren't well yet." I have seen people destroyed by coming out of prison and not knowing how to handle it. I am fortunate because I have a job, but many former prisoners have been unable to find work. Their grants are cut off and some can't even afford a pack of cigarettes.

Despite all these problems, I have never regretted my political work or my experience in prison.

4
Balancing Motherhood and Politics

"I started to cry. But then I said to myself, 'The only thing they can do is kill my body. They are not going to get my mind, and my soul will live on in my children and in other people.' "

SHAHIEDA ISSEL

*S*HAHIEDA ISSEL *has faced with extraordinary strength the double task of trying to be both responsible parent and dedicated political activist: "I have to be strong because I have three kids and people have a lot of faith in me. . . . There are so many of our comrades in hiding, and they expect those of us who are not in hiding to take the struggle forward. It's my duty to do that."*

A thirty-year-old, divorced mother of three in 1987, she lives on her own with her children, then aged thirteen, eleven, and nine. Issel's ex-husband, Johnny, is a well-known political leader with a long history of persecution by the police. After their marriage ended, Shahieda became a political leader in her own right, although she has clearly been subjected to more police harassment because of her connection with him. Her loyalty to Johnny—even after their divorce—in the face of police attempts to divide them, is quite touching.

Unlike many mothers who feel constrained by their responsibility to their children to stay out of politics, for Issel, motherhood increases her motivation to participate in the liberation movement. She has also chosen to involve her children in her political activities. Leila, her thirteen-year-old daughter, started to make political speeches at the age of seven (see chapter 23). And Issel's two younger sons were also politicized at young ages.

Today Issel continues her political activities despite constant and sometimes devastating harassment, the inner turmoil and despair she sometimes feels, and the painful dilemmas risk-taking places her in as a mother.

Issel attended college for two years. She took a one-year course at the University of Cape Town on marriage counseling and community work, and also holds an accountancy certificate from the Technicon in Cape Town. She is currently working at an advice office, an agency that advises and assists members of the community in myriad ways, from helping them to deal with evictions to seeking help for an aged parent. When I asked Issel about her political affiliation, she said she had been the secretary for the past two years of the Mitchells Plain branch of the United Democratic Front—the largest grouping of legal anti-apartheid organizations in South Africa today.

Always referring to herself as black, Issel did not identify herself as a member of any specific ethnic group (although she may have, had I asked her to). She is a practicing Muslim who lives in a Coloured area called Mitchells Plain, a place of luxury compared with the African townships, with its own quite modern-looking shopping centers. But it is modest compared with the white areas. Issel's parents live nearby, which makes a crucial difference to her life, since her mother takes care of her children when she is arrested, detained, or in hiding.

Growing Up Muslim

I am the second eldest of four children. I come from a very strict Muslim family which is a bit old-fashioned. Although I am a Muslim myself, I don't practice it much mostly because I don't have the time, but my heart is there, and I encourage my children to practice it every day.

My parents aren't rich people, but they wanted the best in life for us. They really struggled to rear us in the proper way and to give us an education. I was the type of child who would question my father at length on everything. I liked reading, and he had cabinets full of books, and he used to like us to read good stuff. But my father used to get very upset with my questioning. Firstly, because I'm a female. Secondly, I'm his daughter and I am the soft spot of his heart, and he was scared that if I became involved politically, I would be taken away. He explained what people like Ray Alexander, Albert Luthuli, and Nelson Mandela [all famous anti-apartheid leaders] had gone through, and told me that they had never achieved very much. We had heavy debates about these issues. My father didn't like white people at all, but he has changed over the years due to my involvement. He came to trust me and have a lot of respect for my political work.

My mother was not political herself, though she was forced to become politically aware later. When I came out of detention, I said to her, "Mommy, I don't have the courage for this situation much longer. I've got three kids I have to see to." And she said to me, "My daughter, you are on the right path. There is no turning back." I looked at her in amazement, wondering, "Is this really my mother saying this?"

Our family comes from a place called Worcester, which is a very small country place [near Cape Town]. There were Boers [farmers] in Worcester who would buy kids from their parents: they would give the family one rand fifty [$0.75] to keep the child and have him work on the farm for a couple of months. And when it came to Friday, the farmer didn't pay the child in cash but, instead, gave him liquor. The child became drunk because his body wasn't used to liquor, so children were in a constant state of drunkenness. This practice is known as the "tot system," and it happened to a lot of children in Worcester. It starts when they are very young. My cousin Ann was about seven years of age when it happened to her.

We went to Worcester every holiday because my father was born there, and his mother, father, and brothers, all live there. One holiday when I was about thirteen years old, I and my two sisters were a bit naughty and we wanted to make a bit of money by working on the farm. When we got there, we saw young kids lying around drunk and a guy standing there with a whip. We got so frightened by this sight that we left right away. We didn't dare tell our father. The tot system is still used for women on the farms in Philippi [a white farm area] near here, but I'm not sure if children are still involved. We have received a lot of complaints from the women there at the Advice Office, but we don't have the power to do anything about it.

Marriage and Early Political Activity

I was still in high school when I persuaded one of my sisters to go with me one night to a weekend seminar. We could only go for a couple of hours because we had to be back before my father came home so he wouldn't have any idea that we were out.

Because I feel women are doubly oppressed in South Africa, the first organization I joined was a women's organization. Most men still think that women should play a subordinate role. I have been at a number of workshops where men object heavily to women being there. They think our role is in the kitchen. But I'm not going to stand down because I'm female. I support the need to have a separate women's organization at this time, and I have participated in the United Women's Congress.* I feel that women have problems which can't be addressed in a broader organization. It really helped me to be in the Black Women's Federation.† It's not that we want to be on our own. It's merely that women need to get the confidence to speak up.

* The work and significance of this Cape-based women's organization is described by Gertrude Fester in chapter 18.
† Founded in 1975, this federation was an exclusively black women's organization that was banned in 1977.

Balancing Motherhood and Politics

In my own family, my mother used to take my father's underwear to him. She'd iron his shirts and do all those typical sort of things. But I've grown up in a different society, and I feel that for her to do these things is oppressive. Fathers must also participate in the household.

When I met my husband, Johnny, he belonged to SASO, the black South African Students Organization. He was the regional secretary at that point and very actively involved. In October 1977, he was banned along with many other individuals and twenty black organizations. He only respected his banning order for one day. On that day nobody could come into his office or talk to him, but on the second day he said, "This is nonsense! Who's going to respect this piece of paper?" Not him! He was arrested for breaking his banning order quite a number of times. One time he got a one-year suspended sentence as a result, and another time he was in prison for seven days. After a much longer detention, he came out with a lot of new ideas. I was quite glad because I didn't really like the Black Consciousness idea [stressing the need for black people to separate themselves from whites] he had subscribed to. It was very important for all of us to go through, but as the times changed, we needed to change our ideas and develop a new strategy. And people like Braam Fischer [a well-known Afrikaner leader in the anti-apartheid movement who died in prison] and Neil Aggett [a white medical doctor and trade-unionist], who was killed in detention a couple of years ago, and a number of other white people, have shown us that being a good person doesn't depend on your color; it depends on what is inside your heart.

When I got married, we didn't have a house of our own. Because Johnny was banned at the time, there was no place he could get work. I was just out of college and pregnant and couldn't get a job immediately, which made life very difficult. We had to live on fifteen rand [$7.50] a month, which was extremely hard. Often we would not have food in the house. Milk for us was a luxury. I couldn't buy new clothes, and we lived for five years without a mirror. I married just after I turned eighteen. But when I was about twenty-one, I moved back to my mother's house because I couldn't take the poverty. Also, it had been really hard for me having a child and being only eighteen. Because my husband was banned, he couldn't move to my mother's house with me. But one evening Johnny pitched up [arrived] at my mother's, and the police knocked on the door just at that moment. It was a very frightful situation. We thought they had come because of another contravention of his banning order, like that he was not supposed to be in that area. But they were actually bringing papers to show that his banning order had been lifted. So then he got a job with the Food and Canning Workers' Union, and we could buy a house here in Mitchells Plain. Altogether, we were married about ten years, but my husband's banning order was lifted for only one of those years.

When I was pregnant with my first child, the police came to arrest my husband. They had already given him his banning order and had harassed him a great deal. I wanted to know why they were taking him because he hadn't done anything to contravene his banning order. They said it wasn't necessary for me to know, and they started insulting me, and I got furious. When I saw the way they were handling Johnny—they had him on the ground—I became very disturbed. So I walked over to the senior officer and gave him a karate chop in the neck, and I kicked him on his leg. He lost control and couldn't handle Johnny at that point, so Johnny got away. They were furious. I had gone mad, but they were a bit frightened to touch me because I was already eight months pregnant.

The police threatened to lay charges against me as a result of my attack on one of them. They also told my father what I had done, but he just said it wasn't his business. He brought us up to believe that if somebody threatened us and we were in the right, we have to defend ourselves. We used to train a lot. My father does weightlifting, and every night at our place my brother and my sister's husband would train and they would teach us how to do street fighting.

The police were quite scared of me also because of what I said. For instance, when they came to detain Johnny, I would say, "My husband does not leave this house unless a doctor comes here and states that he is in a very healthy condition and not in any state to commit suicide." If he then killed himself in detention, it would be known it was because of his treatment by the security police. So I would get a doctor to come and sign a statement. The police used to freak out about things like that.

When I took food parcels to Johnny in prison, I would stand there waiting day and night with my baby tied behind my back. The police would remove me, and I would fight them, then stand there again. Finally, they'd take in my food parcel. Johnny had to sign that he'd received it, and I'd insist on seeing his signature because I wanted to see whether or not he'd been killed in detention. That was the type of person I was then, but I've calmed down a lot now, partly because the police have become so vicious and violent. People just disappear. Now, if I see them in the street and they say, "Hi," I say, "Hi." If they swear at me, I'll swear at them. For instance, a policeman came to read Johnny his third banning order. This guy could not read English, but police are now forced by law to do this and to tape-record it as well. It was so embarrassing for this guy. I really pitied him, and we asked him if we could read it for him to lessen his embarrassment. He said that he had to read it in his own voice, which took him three hours. But he really appreciated our offer, and up till today, he would never treat us badly.

When we moved here to Mitchells Plain, we went to a rate [tax] payers' meeting, and we both spoke quite a lot. A couple of meetings after that, Johnny was made chairperson of the rate payers, and I became the secretary. We participated very actively in a health campaign, and I got all the women together, and we had art classes on a Saturday morning and got the children together in our yard. So that is how people got to know us in Mitchells Plain. Our involvement started by getting people's confidence in us.

Police Harassment and Detention

I was not detained at all while we were married, but I was harassed a lot by the cops because of Johnny's involvement as well as my own. Immediately after we divorced, I started playing quite a leadership role in Mitchells Plain. From that time on, police harassment intensified, and I would spend weekends in prison or be taken there for a day of questioning. Then about two years ago [1985], I was taken in for a month, then released for about two weeks, and then taken in for another three months.

During my first detention, the sexual harassment was mostly psychological. There would be about ten men there, and they would force me to say who I was going out with. They'd ask me personal questions about my love life for four hours on end. It was very embarrassing. They'd swear at me and call me a dirty person. They'd take out a list of names of people that I'd supposedly slept with. In fact, I had been married to Johnny for ten years, he had been my first boyfriend, and I've never known any other man in my life. Because they know I'm that kind of person, they knew how to embarrass me. They would tell terrible, dirty stories, and I've never been sworn at like that in my life before. They'd call me a slut and say that my children will become sluts, and —— I don't even want to repeat their dirty words. It's very embarrassing. For me, all this is sexual harassment.

They never explain why they detain you. At that time a lot of the houses of the Labour Party MPs [members of Parliament] were attacked by hand grenades, and since I was one of the leaders in Mitchells Plain, they figured that I was the commander. Johnny is still considered the commander of the whole western Cape, so they thought surely he would be in contact with me locally. The idea that I would have a hand in any grenade attack in Mitchells Plain I found extremely absurd.

After my divorce, I worked at the Advice Office. People's rentals were so high they couldn't pay, so they were being evicted. I was working at the Advice Office and felt that we had to respond immediately to the situation. We had a protest march from the Advice Office to the city council's office, and we rallied people on the way. Most of the participants were women, many pregnant or with babies. There were about fifteen men and sixty women. People made their own placards, and we made it very clear that it was a peaceful demonstration. When we arrived at the city council, it was surrounded by police in lorries [trucks], casspirs [military vehicles], and helicopters. The colonel in charge came into the rent office, where I was on the phone with the head councilor trying to get her to promise that people wouldn't be evicted. The colonel, who was four times bigger than me, got so upset that he pulled me by the hair, threw me against the fire extinguisher, and then hit me. He took a gun and shoved it down my mouth and said that he would shoot me immediately. Next he lifted me up with my clothes all torn and threw me down the stairs. After that he started kicking me. The people outside got very upset. All this had happened right in front of them, so they became violent and charged him. The police then ordered them to disperse within three minutes.

The colonel had assaulted me so terribly that my leg was broken. But the police had the audacity to say that my participation in the hand-grenade attack on a man called Fischer was the reason for my leg injury. I had laid a charge against them for assaulting me before the Fischer attack had even happened. A doctor had examined me, stating the condition I was in after the assault.

In court, police officer Van der Merwe said of me: "Your Honor, this lady claims to be a lady, but she is no lady at all. The policemen were all lying on their backs." He was suggesting that *I* had beaten all of them up! Meanwhile I was in such pain from the way he kicked me that I had to lie in bed for a month. I couldn't even walk. And he expected the women who saw it all to say and do nothing. They had attacked the policemen, but they didn't hurt them to such an extent that they had to get medical attention. They merely gave them a fright because those people really adored me. They were not going to tolerate my being attacked—especially by a man. But it was I who was blamed for what happened. I appeared more than seven times for charges against me, though the case was finally kicked out of court. But I am still under three suspended sentences.

Balancing Motherhood and Politics

I spent one month in hiding. I couldn't sleep at home and had to leave my children with my mother. I would wake my mother up at 3 A.M. or 6 A.M. to bring her money for the kids. She wouldn't mind if I didn't, but I felt I had to support them and I also wanted to see them. I missed them. I get very upset if I can't be with them for a couple of days. One Sunday morning, I walked to my mother's house, and as I arrived, the police pulled up. So I walked out the back door, climbed over the fence into somebody else's yard, and escaped. Things like that happened all the time, 'til one night I couldn't take it any longer. I had worked until two o'clock in the morning. We still had to distribute pamphlets that night, and I went home because I had messed up my suit with ink and I wanted to change my clothes. Also, I wanted to go to my home. I was hardly in the house half an hour when the phone rang. I didn't want to answer it, but I thought maybe something serious had happened. It could be my parents. So I picked up the phone and said, "Hello," but there was no answer. Then before I could get out of the house, the whole place was surrounded. That's how they got me.

I refused to open the door to the police because I was very scared. The whole riot squad was outside my door. There were two big trucks, four police vans—what we call "chicken vans"—and about ten cars to arrest me. It was amazing. When they kicked the door open, Colonel Du Preez said, "Don't shoot! She is not armed." They had all these machine guns with them. Then they took about four hours to turn my whole house upside down looking for grenades. I don't know where in God's name I would have obtained such things. I showed the police that I had the support of the people on my street by greeting each and every woman and man. They came out of their doors and stood outside their homes. The colonel looked quite impressed with it. He said, "No, no, no! Give her a chance. Let her greet the neighbors."

Living in hiding was terrible because although my mother and my whole family were very supportive, I felt guilty putting so much responsibility onto them. Also, I could not be seen anywhere, I had to meet with people in a secretive manner, and I couldn't sleep at home. Yet I still had to work, and I was under a great deal of pressure. And the police harassed my family, even my granny. They went to her place twice to look for me there. They arrived with all their machine guns to intimidate my family and the neighbors. They searched all the houses in her street on the morning that they arrested me. The people were sitting with their Bibles praying for me.

Second Detention

I was detained again after the 1985 state of emergency was announced. They didn't give me a chance to take any clothes when they came to take me away. They just took me in my nightie to the Mitchells Plain police station and refused to allow my father to bring anything to me. The following morning they took me out onto the grass and told me that I was being released. I thought, "Thank God! I'm going back home." Then they said to me, "No, no, no! Not so quick! You are being redetained under section 50." I felt sick to my stomach, but I had to go back to my cell and sign the papers for section 50. I was then taken to Pollsmoor Prison [in Cape Town] where I stayed for a number of weeks.

There were quite a number of women detained with me. Though we all had single cells, we saw each other at exercise time. The detention there was O.K., except the food was very bad. We decided to go on a hunger strike, so we were then separated and couldn't exercise together any longer. The hunger strike made me quite weak, and since I was also menstruating, I would faint. After two weeks, people started being released. After the second month, only about ten of us were left. Julie Esau, who also came from Worcester, was one of them. One morning they took Julie and me to Caledon Square Police Station [also in Cape Town]. Our lawyer used to tell us, "When you are at Pollsmoor Prison and they question you, you shouldn't worry. But when you get taken away to Caledon Square Police Station, then you should start to worry." Julie and I were taken in different cars to Caledon Square.

I had a curly perm at that point, and this guy in the lift said to me, "Oh, you've got nice curls," and started playing with my hair, then gave it a pull. "This is just the beginning," I thought. "The rest is coming. I'm not going to get upset about it." In the foyer of the Caledon Square Station, I saw the most hated man in the security police—Colonel Mostert. He asked me, "What have you got on?" I said, "I've got a dress on." He said, "I want to know what you have on underneath." I replied, "I've got underwear on." Then he wanted to know the color of my underwear. I said, "I've got black panties on." Then he said, "That is not all I want to know. I want to know what is inside your panties." I thought, "This man is totally crazy." I said, "Look, this is my personal affair. It has got nothing to do with you." Then he walked over to me, pulled at my dress, and started unbuttoning it while he said, "Well, if you won't tell me, I'll find out for myself." I was very intimidated, but I said, "I am menstruating. I've got a tampon in." I was completely devastated. I didn't know what to do, and I prayed to God to help me. I was afraid that he would rape me. I thought, "Oh my God, is this what is going to happen?" I've always heard people speak about it but I had never been subjected to it myself. But I couldn't even scream. I just stood there saying nothing. By the time he had unbuttoned my dress, another guy walked in, but Colonel Mostert wasn't even embarrassed. He said, "I am Frans Mostert. That is normally how I introduce myself," and he shook my hand.

I was taken to a large room where about ten policemen started questioning me. After I sat down, one of them pulled me up and said, "You've got no right to disrespect us like this. You have to stand when you speak to us." "O.K.," I said, "Fine, I'll stand. Whatever you say." Then he said, "Now, show us how you are going to faint. We know that you have this problem of fainting." They had received a detailed report from Pollsmoor Prison about what I and every other detainee had gone through, so they could use this information against us. They used their knowledge of my divorce in this way. They would say how Johnny had left me for another woman; how I am stupid and the other woman is more intelligent; that Johnny thinks nothing of me; that they—the police—respect the other woman more than me. These were all ploys to make me feel bad. And they also wanted me to rebel against Johnny, which I refused to do. Whatever problems Johnny and I have, that is our personal business, not to be used politically. Johnny was a Christian, and they could not understand how he could be with a Muslim woman. To them I was a dirty person.

When Mostert questioned me, I said, "I don't know anything about what you people are asking me." Here and there I would give a bit of information to satisfy them, but nothing that they could use against anyone. They got very mad, and Mostert walked behind me. I didn't expect him to hit me, but he gave me one shot from behind, and I went sprawling over the floor. I got up, and he hit me again. I started to cry. But then I said to myself, "The only thing they can do is kill my body. They are not going to get my mind, and my soul will live on in my children and in other people." So they were actually wasting their time, which I told them.

They also assaulted Julie in the room next door, and I had to hear her screams. It was awful and made me feel completely helpless. Then they brought a tape in with what appeared to be my sister speaking. She said that the family was disgusted with me and that they didn't want anything more to do with me. But I had a strong belief that my family would never say something like that. They next brought in another tape in which my daughter was screaming that she was being raped. This finished me completely. I just looked straight ahead, but I couldn't function. They left me on my own for a couple of minutes, and at that point I felt that I was going to jump through the window. They had left it open, and there were no bars on it, and I felt I couldn't take it much longer. I felt that I'd never, ever want to have anything to do with politics again. I asked myself, "How did I get myself into this situation?"

Then a policeman pulled a gun on me which he said didn't have a safety catch. He held it at my head and said, "I know you were thinking that you were going to jump through that window." I felt devastated. "They can even read my mind," I thought. I felt so at their mercy. They kept me there the whole day until the following morning, questioning me all the time. I had to stand all that time, too, and my feet were quite swollen when I was taken back to Pollsmoor Prison the following morning. Then they measured my neck and Julie's neck to make us think we would be taken to Guguletu [an African township near Cape Town] to be necklaced [murdered by having a gas-soaked tire put around the neck, then set on fire]. They did it to scare us, and it put me in a hell of a state.

Julie and I traveled back to Pollsmoor together in the car, but we were not allowed to speak to one another. They had a gun between us at all times, and if we had dared to speak one word, we would have been shot. The minute we got to our cells, we flaked out completely. We went into such a state that they had to give us sedatives for quite some time. It was the first time I went through an experience like that. Other people have been harassed much worse. Johnny has been assaulted much more than I was—but for me, it was quite an experience.

Later I found out how they made the tapes of my daughter and my sister. They get to know how you speak. Then they find somebody with a similar voice. They have equipment that enables them to listen in to what you say inside your house. They listen to your telephone conversations. They get to know what problems exist in your family, and they use this knowledge so they can make the tapes seem real. When I came out of prison, my father told me that they had gone to my home many times. They wanted pictures of my children to see how they looked. They went to the school to get my daughter. When you are already in a terrible state, not thinking very clearly, it is easy to believe it is your family speaking.

My children could not play outside because the police harassed them so. They would also phone up the neighbors and say real weird things about me. Because I am a divorced woman, they'd say I am jolling [fooling] around with their husbands. When I got out of prison my father took me to the neighbors and told them that his daughter would never behave in that way, so the neighbors didn't believe it. The police even wrote to the neighbor next door saying that I am a weird person, and the neighbor came to show me the letter. So we laid a charge against them. We had taped all their anonymous telephone calls to us, which would often be very rude, full of all sorts of swear words, and these calls were traced to the police. Although we got lawyers to lay a charge against them, they refused to accept the case.

After coming out of detention in 1985, I went away for two weeks. I was completely disoriented and could not even take being with my children for half an hour. I was quite devastated. I couldn't even walk straight! And almost immediately after I came out, I was charged with possession of banned literature. They then changed the charge to "furthering the aims of the ANC." I just got off that charge a couple of months ago.

Motherhood

Having children makes me more determined to fight for liberation. My reasoning goes like this: I have three children whom I love very much, but I also think of the thousands of other children who have to go through much worse experiences than my children have to go through. And when I'm detained, I know my mother will always take care of the kids, so that is one problem off my shoulders. In fact, we have an arrangement to that effect. I would never allow the cops to take me away and leave my children behind. Once when they came, I was alone with my kids, and I insisted my children go with me. And my thirteen-year-old daughter also intervenes and says that I am not going anywhere unless she goes with me, and the police feel a bit pressured by something like that. Sometimes they wait until my mother comes to fetch the children. My children are very aware of the political situation.

Their father would also take responsibility if he could, but he is not in a position to. Being politically involved sometimes means I am out of the house most of the time. I may be home for just half an hour in the day, maybe at breakfast or sometimes not even then. But I have a very good relationship with my children. I always try to make it up to them; on a Saturday we may go for lunch somewhere, or we may take a drive and spend some time together. But it is difficult, and they do complain: "You don't have time for us." I explain to them why I have been so busy, and then they understand. The main thing is that I explain my involvement to them.

I normally take my kids with me when I hand out pamphlets because I want them to see and understand what I am doing. One time my youngest son was pulled into a police van to be taken to the police station and I got so upset, but he said, "Mommy, I want to go. I want to ask the police 'What is wrong with giving out these pamphlets?' He must tell me why this pamphlet is banned and why it is wrong." My daughter Leila also challenged the police on this occasion. I didn't have to say anything.

Many black children in South Africa today are very political. For example, just before I was detained about two years ago, I went to the town center with my youngest son Fidel who was dressed in a UDF T-shirt. In the middle of the road, a five-year-old stopped him and said, "I like your T-shirt. *Amandla*! [the power salute of the liberation movement]" I looked at my son who was only seven or eight years old at the time, and I said, "Fidel, aren't you going to respond?" He said, "I'm not sure, because nowadays you can go sit for two weeks in prison for just saying *Amandla*!" So I said to him, "But you have to respond to this young son here, otherwise I will have to take off your T-shirt and give it to him because you aren't worthy of wearing it." So he turned around and he said, "*Amandla*!" Judging from an incident like that, I would say that the children are quite aware. They know who the enemy is. They speak politics. They know when things go on. They have to survive.

When Leila, my thirteen-year-old, was seven, she read a message from her father at a meeting. She does "speech and drama" at school, and she read it very beautifully. The people in the hall went berserk. They shouted so loud "Attack the terrorists," that I was afraid that they were going to go out of there and do something. The police were outside, and they saw people's response, so they wanted to know who gave Leila the message. We sent her to stay in a safe place, but the police then harassed her school, and every day they sat parked outside the house waiting to see when Leila would come home. My husband was in detention at that point, and I was in a state of nerves. I got all these advocates [lawyers], and we studied section 6 of the Terrorism Act to see whether it was legal for the police to harass a seven-year-old child. We discovered that it was. I was so upset. But they couldn't find her.

I've traveled a lot and one time I saw a mother working on a farm in the rain with her seven-day-old baby wrapped in a newspaper lying there screaming. I got so furious about this that I screamed at the white boss of the farm, and I asked him what right he had to let the child lie there like that. He just swore at me, saying it was none of my business. I witnessed lots of cases like that. For me, the more poverty I see, the more determined I am to fight for our liberation. There is no turning back for me now.

5

South Africa's
Internment Camps

"Anyone involved in opposing the system is in danger of breaking some law or other because the definitions of what is illegal
under the Internal Security Act are so wide. By giving this interview, it is possible that I could be accused of making subversive
statements."

AUDREY COLEMAN

*A*UDREY COLEMAN *was fifty-four years old in 1987 and had graduated from high school but not attended a university. Born of South African parents, she married her husband, Max, when she was twenty years old. He is a successful businessman, and the Colemans live in an affluence characteristic of upper-middle-class whites in South Africa.*

Both Audrey and Max Coleman, white South Africans, were radicalized by the detention of one of their four sons, and became active members of an organization called the Detainees Parents' Support Committee (DPSC). Although Audrey has no official position in DPSC, she has become an informal kind of ambassador for them, traveling all over the world to publicize detention issues, particularly the detention of children. Last year, for example, she spoke to the media and other audiences in Britain, Sweden, and France, including an interview with President François Mitterrand of France. When in South Africa, it is she who often finds herself speaking to the press, embassies, and foreign visitors.

The South African government threatened to impose a restriction order (the new term for banning) on Coleman when she was away publicizing the Free the Children Campaign in Europe in 1986. She refused to be intimidated by this, merely informing everyone she spoke to of the government's efforts to stop her work. The government, whose actions are frequently arbitrary and unpredictable, decided not to carry out their threat after all. Today Coleman continues to be undaunted by the risks she takes. "Personally," she said, "I feel the need to speak out today more than ever before, because people are becoming so frightened and intimidated that I feel that the people who are able to, must do so."

Coleman had testified to the United Nations earlier in 1987 about the detention of children in South Africa, and here cites a few telling cases, while also providing a valuable analysis of why black children are so politically active and sophisticated in South Africa today.

Coleman pointed out to me that by the government's own admission, between June 1986 and June 1987, children constituted thirty-four percent of the approximately 25,000 detainees held under the emergency regulations, including children as young as twelve years old. Thirty-four percent of 25,000 comes to about 8,500 detained *children. High as these figures are, Coleman maintains that forty percent is a more accurate figure.* And this policy of detaining children is not new. During the 1985 state of emergency, 2,106 children under the age of sixteen were held, the youngest being but seven years old.*

These and other facts (such as, that "people who oppose the government are being killed more often now") lead Coleman to conclude that "there is greater repression today than there has ever been before in the history of South Africa." She believes that the reason for this is that the government is finding it impossible to deal with the growing discontent of the majority of the people. This is why they declared the third state of emergency and severely restricted the publication of information about the conditions of detention. "If they were running decent prisons and everything was above board, why would they worry if people wrote about them or went to see them?" she asked. She went on to argue that "if the townships were being properly run and it was just a matter of wild animals running around necklacing people, they'd want the press to be in there to show the world what sort of people these are." Not surprisingly, the DPSC has been included in these repressive efforts. Their offices all over the country have been raided by the police, and in early 1988, DPSC was one of many anti-apartheid groups to be banned in a mammoth repressive action. The Human Rights Commission is now carrying on the work previously undertaken by DPSC.

Since this interview, due to the success of the Free the Children Campaign, there are now approximately one hundred children detained (Coleman, personal communication, September 1988). The government has expressed its disapproval of Coleman's role in this campaign by refusing to renew her passport since 1987. She believes her testimony to the United Nations in March 1987 also contributed to their anger. It took the efforts of Senator Edward Kennedy, and the United States Ambassador to South Africa, Mr. Perkins, as well as

---

* Wendy Landau, a representative of the Human Rights Commission, said that this forty percent figure includes 18-year-olds with those who are under 18 (the official definition of a child in South Africa). She added that between June 1987 and June 1988, children constituted twenty percent of the 5,000 people detained under that state of emergency, and that between June 1988 and June 1989, they represented ten percent of the 3,000 emergency detainees held (personal communication, 7 June 1989). According to Coleman, the Human Rights Commission, like the DPSC before it, is the best source of national detention statistics in South Africa.

many other well-known people, for Coleman to be permitted to attend her son's wedding in the U.S., "on compassionate grounds." For this to be granted, Coleman had to sign a paper promising that she wouldn't make any public speeches (Coleman, personal communication, 6 June 1989).

Coleman's analysis of detention as South Africa's version of internment camps provides a valuable context for the accounts of Elaine Mohamed, Connie Mofokeng, Feziwe Bookholane, and Shahieda Issel, as well as those of the other women in this book who have lived through this traumatic but commonplace experience.

Growing Up White

My parents' attitudes were typical of conservative whites, but I had been aware of racism and the iniquities of this society as long ago as I can remember. I have a brother, who is ten years older than I, who educated me politically. He was chairman of the now-banned Congress of Democrats in Cape Town [a radical white anti-apartheid organization], and was held in prison for three months during the 1960 emergency. After that he was harassed, and eventually left the country in about 1964 on an exit permit* with his family. He moved to London, where he's lived ever since.

Amongst his friends were leading political figures, like Dennis Goldberg and Ivan Schermbrucker. Ivan had a big influence on me and taught me at a very early age about the rights and wrongs of our society. I was very young when I began speaking out. I remember challenging a policeman when he loaded a group of black people into a police van because their reference books were not in order. My parents didn't agree with the political stand my brother and I took, and our two sisters weren't politically aware or interested.

I didn't participate in politics when I was a young mother because I was involved in bringing up my four sons. When the boys were grown, I decided it was time to get involved in community work. I began working in the Black Sash Advice Office [a largely white women's political organization; see chapters 16 and 24] about twelve years ago, and eventually became national secretary. Working in the Black Sash was a very important step in my life, and I definitely grew as a result. I couldn't have gone on living in South Africa if I hadn't started speaking out.

---

* An exit permit requires permanent exile from South Africa.

Son's Detention

My son, Keith, was detained in 1981. He was twenty-one at the time and an honor student at university. He was—and is—very opposed to this government and was outspoken in his criticism of the apartheid system. He was an editor of a student newspaper which deals with grassroots issues, and was detained together with his co-editor. I was shattered by Keith's detention. I had previously dealt with families of detainees, but to experience the removal of a loved one oneself is different. He was taken away and put into a prison. He had no rights other than to a Bible and one hour a day of exercise, and we were powerless to help him.

It is very important to understand that ninety-five percent of the people who are detained in South Africa are not detained for breaking the law. We went to see Louis Le Grange [the minister of law and order at that time] about Keith's detention, and were told that he had done something terrible and that he was going to be charged in a treason trial.

Keith was held for five months in solitary confinement. After the fifth month, we got a call from him saying, "If you're doing nothing, would you like to come and fetch me?" It is in this arbitrary fashion that people are released. Keith had been interrogated for something like seven weeks, but they never assaulted him. It could have been because my husband had told them at the very beginning of his detention that Keith had a bad back, and that if anything happened to him, he would hold that captain responsible. Keith said that they looked as if they wanted to hit him, but they never did. When he was released, he was banned for two years in order to silence him.

The Detainees Parents' Support Committee

When Keith was detained, Max and I joined DPSC, which had just been formed in August of that year. DPSC was a spontaneous coming together of the families of detainees to share our problems. At the beginning, I was only thinking of my son, but very soon I and others realized that detention will occur as long as apartheid exists, so we have to fight the whole system. The committee included people from all groups—black, Coloured, Indian, and white, though the majority of the detainees come from the [African] townships, where most of the harassment and repression is taking place.

Many of the people on the committee didn't have a political background like my husband and I. They were parents who didn't necessarily agree with their children's politics. They included people like Professor Koornhof whose daughter was in detention and whose brother is Piet Koornhof, now South African ambassador in New York. Professor Koornhof demonstrated with the rest of us on street corners with placards saying, "RELEASE MY CHILD, HELD [SO MANY] DAYS" and "RELEASE ALL DETAINEES."

We only opened our office in 1985. Until then we worked as an ad-hoc committee and met at the university. DPSC grew very fast, and township people began to seek us out for help. Then in 1983 with the formation of UDF, with which we are affiliated, we were able to set up structures throughout the country. At the last national conference, forty-four areas were represented. Our office is now staffed by five workers chosen by the township people. I and a couple of others work here purely on a voluntary basis. We also have committees in small outlying areas. These are the structures that the police try to break at a time of repression. In many areas, the structures have been totally broken in the last couple of years by detaining all the activists.

We publicized detentions for the first time. We demonstrated outside police stations and the supreme court with our placards. I came to learn that a criminal has more rights in South Africa than a political detainee. We had to fight to get even small things like food parcels and clean clothing in to our loved ones and to make people aware of what was going on. There was a tremendous response to DPSC from the townships where most of the detentions had occurred, but where people had never had such support before.

Our work informed people about the type of person being detained. We wrote profiles of the detainees and a monthly report. These were disseminated both locally and internationally. Ex-detainees began attending our meetings and speaking about their experiences of torture. There had been rumors of torture, but allegations had not been openly made before. We compiled seventy-nine affidavits of torture into a document called "The Memorandum of Torture." Of course, the government tried to discredit DPSC but did not succeed.

In 1983, DPSC started monitoring public violence cases because we observed that young activists involved in democratic opposition were being charged with public violence and other criminal charges. We realized that the government was trying to criminalize political opposition. By 1985, we could no longer monitor public violence cases because the numbers had escalated to something like twenty-five thousand cases in one year.

During the state of emergency, we're not allowed to give food parcels to detainees, so instead we give their families twenty rand [$10] a month to take to the prison so the detainee can buy food. We used to give track suits to all detainees, but because of the enormous number of detainees —at least twenty-five thousand in the last eleven months—we couldn't keep doing this for everyone.

We take a statement from all detainees when they are released, and we arrange for them to see a doctor and a psychiatrist. We feel that *all* people who have been in solitary confinement need help. We have a panel of lawyers who we instruct on behalf of the families to represent the detainee while in detention. They obtain confirmation of the detention and apply for visits. When the detainees are released, the lawyers get statements from them about their detention experiences and, where necessary, enter into litigation on their behalf. The lawyers also represent the detainees who are charged.

We also monitor allegations of assault and torture of detainees, as well as allegations from township victims who have been shot or assaulted. Also, all the information from the different centers comes into this office, so we get a national picture of what is happening rather than a fragmented one. For example, people will ask, "Don't you think that torture is just occurring in one area? That it's just one mad policeman who is doing it?" And we're able to say, "Absolutely and emphatically not. Torture is nationwide. Even the type of torture and the way it's done is occurring systematically throughout the country." We put the responsibility firmly at the door of the government because we know they are aware of what is happening. We believe that torture is part of the strategy to break people as well as to gain information. The number of detainees we are now seeing suffering from severe trauma is horrendous. People are being held for such long periods in detention that they feel forgotten and lose hope of being released.

Most of the people seeking our help are women. They are the ones who are most involved with the detainees. In the majority of cases where it's the child who is detained, the mother plays the main role. It could be because they're not working and have more free time than their husbands. But I see a lot of very concerned and worried fathers here as well. When wives are detained, their husbands are just amazing. They take off from work and try to fill the gap in the home as well as tend to the needs of the detainee. In some cases, the husbands have spent many hours trying to locate where their wives are held. And in the rural areas, men are more politically involved in this work than women because the women play such a subservient role there.

Police Harassment

The plainclothes police stole our posters when we were demonstrating. An instance of this was when my husband was dressed in his suit ready to go to work. He was demonstrating with his poster outside John Vorster Square when a plainclothes policeman snatched his poster and ran down the street with it. My husband ran after him. The next day on the front page of the *Star* newspaper was a picture of Max Coleman running down the street after the man. This was a fine advert for the DPSC—one we could never have afforded. These recurring incidents put us on the map.

Many parents are harassed during the detention of their children. Homes of detainees' parents are petrol-bombed. I've also noticed that the security police are bullies. The parents in our group who were the weakest were the ones who were harassed the most. They were called in to John Foster Square, the husband taken to one room and the wife to another, and lectured to. One such case involved a mother. She was screamed at and asked, "Aren't you ashamed of your daughter?" She was told that her daughter had never loved her. They reduced her to tears. She was very relieved when we explained to her that this was part of their strategy to alienate her from her daughter. This type of sharing and knowledge that the committee has enables us to inform people about the divide-and-rule strategy of the system and enables people to withstand this type of bullying more easily.

The Brutalization and Politicization of Children

Black children who grow up in the townships are growing up in a very violent and insecure society. They are watching, daily, their parents being beaten up, their homes being broken into, their brothers and sometimes their mothers or their fathers being taken away. Out on the streets, they see the army, the police, guns, tanks, shooting. They see all the violence of a war. So even from the age of two, some will pick up a stone when they see a soldier or a policeman because they're frightened. They don't have to be told to pick up that stone; it's a natural response to feeling insecure. The youth are having to fight with stones against very sophisticated arms. They try to protect their homes by putting furrows along the roads so that the casspir [a large army vehicle] will fall into it. And sometimes they put stone barricades up across the roads when they know that there are going to be rent evictions and their families will be thrown out of their homes.

The majority of the people in the townships totally identify with the ANC, and Nelson Mandela is their leader. You ask a little child, and they'll tell you that. Many parents don't know where they get this information from. It's the children who are in the forefront of the struggle. There's no question about that. At the age of eleven, if they're intelligent kids, they will be harassed because they are already articulating certain demands. They're not necessarily stoning or burning, but they *are* a threat to the state even from that tender age. I can hardly believe what comes out of the mouths of some thirteen- or fifteen-year-olds. I feel I am talking to politicians. They understand that they're living in an abnormal society, that their education is unequal, that their parents are struggling and cannot pay the rent. Some children see their parents get up in the early hours of the morning to catch the bus and come home late at night because of the distances they are forced to live from their places of work. The children are no longer going to accept what their parents have endured all their lives.

The outbreak of unrest in the schools in 1976 politicized the children irreversibly. Their leaders were put into prison for many years at that time, but they *saw* what happened. They were part of it. They don't need television or newspapers to tell them what is happening. They are there living it. So that's why we're seeing the children being targeted. But the police efforts to intimidate and harass them are not going to work. Because if you brutalize children by taking them into prison and trying to subjugate them into submission, it won't work.

Children in Detention

Very young children have reported to this office after their release from detention. For example, eleven-year-old William Modibedi was one of four children detained in one family. The reason given to the lawyer by the minister of law and order for detaining this child was that he was one of the ringleaders of the boycotts. So that little boy was held for three months until our lawyer took up his case. The authorities gave all sorts of reasons why William had to be detained, like that he was a very, very dangerous person. Shortly thereafter he was released, but his three brothers are still in detention and have been for a long time. When William came out of prison he had lost four teeth. He told me he had been electric-shocked and very badly assaulted. I said to him, "William, what did they do to you?" And he showed me. He said a big white man had smashed his fist into his mouth.

The reasons the government gives for the detention of children are that they have been involved in necklacing and other criminal acts. But I believe that those involved in criminal acts are charged under the Criminal Procedures Act, and that the detained children are mobilizing the townships to oppose apartheid in a democratic manner, and so cannot be charged with an offense. Being a student leader is enough to get them detained. I know the case of a kid who was seventeen in 1985. He was detained on the first day of the state of emergency, then released seven and a half months later on the last day of it. We heard that he had been tortured, so we sent him to our doctors who proved that this information was correct. In fact, they believed he had suffered brain damage as a result of it, and arrangements were made for him to see a neurosurgeon. But he was redetained under the second state of emergency before this could happen, and he has been held in prison ever since. So from 1985 until now [May 1987], he has been out of detention only about four months of the two years.

I asked his mother to ask the police why he was taken in again, and the reason they gave her was that he was a student leader. Similarly, as soon as they know someone is a street committee member, boy, they're in there! People are not allowed to have meetings or to boycott. Street committees have been set up to mobilize people very quickly by word of mouth. When someone in the community blows a whistle, everyone immediately comes out to either witness what is happening or to defend their homes. In addition, street committees are targeted by the state because they are a very effective way of mobilizing people.

The security police also detain unpoliticized kids to frighten them. There was one case which shook me, as hardened as I am. He was thirteen years old. He came into this office a couple of weeks ago with a friend who had been detained. His friend was sitting talking to me, and because I love kids, I said to the other little boy, "So you missed being detained?" And he looked at me and said, "No, I've been detained." And I said, "For how long?" And he said, "Nine months." I didn't have his name on my list because his mother had never heard of us. He told me he had left home barefoot to go to the shops for his mother. A car was parked in the street with a friend of his in it. As he walked past the car, his friend pointed at him. He was immediately picked up by the police. He said, "Please, can I go home and get my shoes?" They said, "No," and took him off to be questioned about stoning and burning a house. He denied having done either, so they said, "Fine. If you're not going to *admit* to doing it, we're going to hold you here." He said he couldn't admit to doing it because he hadn't done it. They said, "O.K., you're going to stay in prison for ten years, and there is nothing anybody can do about it."

That little boy was held in prison for nine months believing that he was being held for ten years. He wasn't assaulted or physically tortured, but what they did to him was certainly mental torture. They didn't even speak to him again after that first day, and his parents were never notified about what had happened to him. For two weeks they went from one police station to the other, to the hospitals, and to the mortuary, looking for their little boy, but they couldn't find him. Eventually when a neighbor whose child was in detention went on her biweekly visit, her little boy said, "You know, Mommy, who is here? Eugene."

There are thousands of children being held as awaiting-trial prisoners on criminal offenses, and some are held with hardened grown-up criminals. The terror for them that results from that is absolutely mindblowing. Children are often brought into court without the knowledge of their parents and without a lawyer. Some kids have been sentenced to six years for throwing stones. I happened to go into a court in the eastern Cape just after the Langa Massacre [the murder of twenty African mourners by the South African police in 1985], and I saw a little twelve-year-old sitting there. His feet didn't even reach the floor. He was there without a lawyer and without his mother's knowledge. It's the children who are not represented who are getting the longest sentences.

The children who are being brutalized cannot grow up into soft, caring people like the present anti-apartheid leaders are. The UDF leaders who are standing trial for treason are the moderates in this country. They are still saying, "We want to negotiate." One told me, "When we come out [of prison], we're going to be told we're redundant. Where did our talk of negotiations get us?" These kids are definitely not going to want that. They cannot experience what they're experiencing now, and choose a peaceful solution. I don't know what will happen when these children become the future leaders.

PART II

THE ANTI-APARTHEID MOVEMENT: IN SOUTH AFRICA AND IN EXILE

"In South Africa you don't decide to join politics; politics decides to join you."

—RUTH MOMPATI

I T WOULD BE impossible to include in this section all the major anti-apartheid organizations or movements in South Africa. Before the United Democratic Front was banned in February 1988, it was an umbrella organization for over eight hundred different anti-apartheid groups with a combined membership of over two million people. Of the many other anti-apartheid organizations that did not choose to unite under the UDF rubric, one of the most important is the Azanian People's Organization. In addition, there are banned organizations that have to operate underground. Although part II is thus necessarily incomplete,* the accounts of the six women included here, as well as those

* The lack of representation of the Pan-Africanist Congress and the Black Consciousness movement constitute the most serious omissions here. It appears that no PAC women were ever recommended by those I consulted, for reasons I do not know. It could be that this organization and its descendants have very little following inside South

of other women in this volume, demonstrate some of the diversity in the anti-apartheid organizations, past and present, that make up the South African liberation struggle.

The African National Congress is by far the most powerful and the most popular of the many anti-apartheid organizations. Founded in 1912, the ANC was banned in 1960 along with the Pan-Africanist Congress, which had split off from it in 1959 because of the ANC's willingness to work with whites and communists. The ban is still in effect today. Consequently, no one in South Africa can openly admit to membership in these organizations.

Although I interviewed some women in South Africa who talked about their participation in the ANC before it was banned, I spoke to no one who admitted current involvement in the ANC underground. Indeed, I did not ask women whether they were thus engaged, or seek out such women, lest I endanger them. In order to get an up-to-date view of the ANC, I interviewed women at the ANC headquarters in Lusaka, Zambia.

I was ushered into the ANC Women's Section* office, where I sat in a circle with eight of the women who worked there. They asked me to explain my project, its goals, who I am, and who I had seen in South Africa. Although I was aware that I had to win their approval, they were friendly and intensely interested in news from their homeland. I was struck by the modesty of their office facilities and the ANC headquarters in general. Clearly, the funds donated to them are not spent on fancy desks and wall-to-wall carpets.

After about an hour of questions, the women made it clear that they wanted to assist my project; now the problem became how to keep the number of interviews manageable. I was pleased with their choices, but space permits the inclusion here of only three of the five women I interviewed: Ruth Mompati, the most senior woman in the ANC power structure; Mavivi Manzini, secretary for publicity, information, and research for the Women's Section; and Connie Mofokeng, who in chapter 2 describes her escape from a South African prison after being severely

---

Africa, and/or that women play a very insignificant role in them, and/or that their members would be less willing to be interviewed by a white woman.

The interview with Thoko Mpumlwana, a representative of the Black Consciousness movement in its heyday when her friend and colleague, Steve Biko, was still alive, could not be included here because the changes she wanted made in my editing of her interview failed to reach me in time.

* Before the ANC was banned by the government in 1960, the separate women's arm of the organization was referred to as the Women's League. After the ANC went into exile, its name was changed to the Women's Section.

tortured. All five women came to my hotel room to be interviewed at prearranged times over a two-day period. While this arrangement was convenient, it deprived me of the opportunity to see the women in their usual work or home settings.

Chapters 9, 10, and 11 are presented in order of historical occurrence. First, Ela Ramgobin describes the famous Defiance Campaign, launched by the ANC and the South African Indian Congress in 1952, in which thousands of people participated in civil disobedience. She also gives an account of the revival of the Natal Indian Congress in the early 1970s, and the important role it played in bringing to life again the long-dormant anti-apartheid movement.

Although Albertina Sisulu's political work predates by many years the formation of the United Democratic Front in 1983, I have included her here in her role as co-president of UDF. As already mentioned, this organization has undoubtedly been the most significant legal anti-apartheid organization in South Africa in recent years. Although most UDF members and leaders have been black, a few whites have also been active participants. Because the UDF chose for its patrons all the long-term ANC prisoners, many people have seen it as a child of the ANC. What will happen now that it, too, has been banned, I cannot say.

In chapter 11, Paula Hathorn, chairperson of the End Conscription Campaign in Cape Town, describes the philosophy and actions of this important white anti-apartheid organization since it was launched in 1983. Despite ECC's commitment to work within the limitations of the increasingly repressive South African laws, this organization was also banned in August 1988.

This part begins with Winnie Mandela, one of the most famous people in South Africa, and without a doubt, the best-known woman there.

6
A Leader in Her Own Right

"The years of imprisonment hardened me. . . . Perhaps if you have been given a moment to hold back and wait for the next blow, your emotions wouldn't be blunted as they have been in my case. When it happens every day of your life, when that pain becomes a way of life, I no longer have the emotion of fear."

WINNIE MANDELA

A Leader in Her Own Right

*A*LTHOUGH *her fame used to be due in large part to her marriage to Nelson Mandela, the most revered and popular leader of the South African liberation movement, Winnie Mandela is a powerful personality and leader in her own right, with an extraordinarily strong and regal presence. It was all the more painful, then, to read the news, which made world headlines in late December 1988 and the first months of 1989, alleging that she had participated in the beating of four young anti-apartheid activists. (One of these victims, fourteen-year-old Stompie Moeketsi, was later found dead, allegedly killed by members of the Mandela United Football Club, who served as her bodyguards.) If there is any truth in these ugly accusations against Winnie Mandela, made by Stompie's three companions and some of the leaders of the United Democratic Front, it is important to remember what we have learned from the literature on torture and concentration camps—including the torture of battered women: that every human being has a breaking point. It is clear from Winnie's interview here that she has been subjected to decades of intense persecution by the government and its agents—the security police—and has suffered long years of separation from her husband and children. Her present situation may well be a tragic consequence of this persecution and of the great isolation that, as a black woman and famous anti-apartheid leader in an extremely racist and sexist society, she has had to endure. The possible role of infiltrators and provocateurs among her football players-cum-bodyguards (a common weapon of the South African government against the anti-apartheid movement) may also turn out to have played a pivotal role.*

While we may never know the full story, nothing can take away from the tremendous courage and spirit that Winnie Mandela has shown in the face of painful and often devastating experiences that would have broken ordinary people years ago.

Born Nomzamo Winifred Madikizela in 1934, Winnie Mandela (as she is usually called) is an African and mother of two daughters, Zeni and Zindzi. Mandela, passionately committed to the struggle, has been in and out of prison so many times that she cannot keep track of the dates.

In the following interview, Mandela gives a poignant description of her childhood years in a rural area of Pondoland, now part of the Transkei. One of the poorest parts of the country today, the Transkei became the first of the so-called homelands for Africans—specifically for Xhosas—in 1976. Despite the opposition of many Xhosa people, Chief Kaiser Matanzima, the traditional leader of the Transkei, accepted the white government's offer of a kind of nominal independence. But this manifestation of apartheid occurred after the sixteen-year-old Mandela had left the area for Johannesburg, where she still lives in the large black township of Soweto.

We learn about the infamous treason trial in which 156 leaders of the congress movement, the major coalition of anti-apartheid organizations during the period when it occurred (1956–61), were charged with high treason. Among them was her future husband, Nelson Mandela, whom she first met when he called her up to ask her to raise funds for this trial. Sixteen years her senior, Nelson was—in 1956— already one of the most outstanding of an impressive group of African National Congress leaders. After a grueling five years, all 156 of those charged with treason were acquitted, much to the chagrin of the South African government.

Three months after Winnie Mandela married Nelson in 1958, she was arrested for participating in the historic anti-pass campaign organized by women in an effort to prevent the hated passes—an identity document men had been forced to carry for decades—from being extended to women. (The African women's militant and effective campaign against passes, as early as 1913, was one reason they did not have to carry passes sooner.) This arrest was just the first of many for Mandela, who remained under banning orders continuously from 1962 to 1975.*

In 1969, Mandela was detained under section 6 of the Terrorism Act, without having been found guilty in a court of law. She was held in solitary confinement for seventeen months, an experience she describes in the following pages. She was finally released in 1970 after having been acquitted twice. Her relief was short-lived, since she was immediately banned and house-arrested on leaving prison. She was subsequently charged many times for breaking her banning orders.

---

* I am indebted to Shelagh Gastrow (1987) for many of the facts mentioned here.

A Leader in Her Own Right

One of these contraventions resulted in another six-month jail sentence in 1974.

Since nothing seemed to stop Mandela from continuing with her political work (for example, helping to found the Black Women's Federation in 1975 and the Black Parents' Association in Soweto in 1976), the government finally banished her in 1977 to Brandfort, a small, conservative, Afrikaner dorp [town] in the Orange Free State. Mandela explains in her interview why she found living in Brandfort for eight years one of the most painful times in her life. After her home there was fire-bombed in 1985, she defied her banishment order and returned to her Soweto home amidst a great national and international furor. Her determination and courage paid off, and she was finally allowed to stay in Soweto.

In earlier years, Mandela had been active with the Women's League of the African National Congress and with the Federation of South African Women (described by Helen Joseph in some detail in chapter 15). Despite her leadership role in the anti-apartheid movement, Mandela explained to me: "I have really been more engaged in the struggle at the grassroots level. Partly because of my training as a social worker, I have always considered myself as belonging there. I prefer to work with ordinary people and to be part of them. If I had had a choice, I would never have wanted to be in the limelight."

Despite the extremity of the persecution to which Mandela has been subjected, she does not hesitate to say that she is willing to suffer more. The depth of the religious feeling and commitment evident in her interview is in sharp contrast to the South African government's portrayal of the African National Congress (with which she is identified) as a godless, communist organization.

Of the sixty interviews I conducted, the one with Mandela was by far the most difficult to arrange. It involved a visit to Mandela's lawyer, Ismail Ayob; a visit to Soweto to hand-deliver a lengthy handwritten plea to Mandela to consent to an interview; more than fifteen phone calls; one inexplicable failure to connect with each other at a prearranged meeting place; a postponement of my flight out of the country; and a mysterious tape-recorder failure when I finally started the long-awaited interview at Mandela's home in Soweto. Her response to the last of these calamities was one of total equanimity. "I'm used to sabotage," she commented, as she went out of the room, leaving me in a state of suppressed hysteria and shock. Fortunately my frantic random fiddling somehow got the treacherous machine to work again, and I was able to proceed with the interview.

Growing Up African

I come from a remote country village in the Transkei, one of nine children. I grew up in the countryside looking after cattle and sheep. It was a wonderful childhood in a way, although I felt the pains of apartheid from an early time. But the environment was very healthy. We were not in an urban situation where you are confronted with apartheid every day of your life. As a child I used to wake up at three in the morning to go to the fields to hoe and look after the crops. I would come home with the other girls who lived in the area, wash up, and then go to school. At times we used to alternate between going to school and working in the fields. We knew that if there was no harvest from the mealie [maize] fields we were going to have worse times. Our livelihood depended on it.

We learned from the white local traders and their families that there were people of another color and standard of living. We knew from a very early age that our parents were peasants and that, in order to maintain us, they were dependent on a white man who looked down on us. We found ourselves in a derogatory kind of environment with supercilious white children, our counterparts, who wore better-quality clothes than we did.

I wore shoes for the first time when I passed my standard six [eighth grade] and went to boarding school. I was just beginning puberty, which was a difficult age for a deprived child. I wanted to look like other little girls. I was beginning to be conscious of who I was, and wanted to have so much, but there wasn't any money. I came from a very large family. There were eleven of us, and I came right in the middle, so my birth was of no particular consequence. I was a very difficult child—extremely naughty—and, because there were fewer boys in the family, I tended to regard myself as a boy. I was a terrible tomboy, the truth of which is borne out by the fact that my body is full of horrible scars. I used to fall from trees and that sort of thing, but I wouldn't report these mishaps to my mother. According to the adults, I gave my mother a lot of trouble.

My parents were on the fanatical side. My mother was an extremely devoted Christian who taught me to respect adults, and part and parcel of that was to respect the missionaries who were invariably white. We literally had to revere the white missionary because he commanded so much authority, and in a rural setup, he was one whose advice everybody sought. These were Methodist missionaries, and we attended Methodist missionary schools. So we grew up becoming subservient to men of another color, whether they were missionaries or local traders. But then one day, when I was in standard three or four, I suddenly asked "But why? This is *my* country."

My father was our teacher, and he taught us the history of our country. "This is what you are going to find in the text," he would say. "This is how the white man wrote your history. But I am telling you that, contrary to what this white man says, it is so and so. These books were written to condition you into believing that the whites are your masters." I learned this for the first time from my own father.

And my grandmother, his mother, was an extraordinary woman who exercised a great deal of influence on all of us. She was a tough, robust woman with the physique of a fighter. She was the woman who taught me the power and strength of a woman, and that the real head of the family is a woman. My grandfather was a chief (my father refused to take up chiefdomship) and my grandmother was one of twenty-nine wives and was widowed very early in her life. She was the first woman in that part of our country to have owned a small trading post, by virtue of being a senior wife to the chief. My grandfather is reported to have worked hand in hand with the local traders. Because he had given them a large piece of land, they thanked him by giving him a little trading post, which was run by my grandmother. She must have resented whites very deeply because when the particular whites she had dealt with left, the subsequent local traders took this small trading post from her. She was extremely bitter about this. She taught us that these people of the other color are thieves. All they are here for is to steal our land and our cattle. With what my grandmother instilled in us at home and my father taught us in school, I realized I was growing up in a blistering inferno of racial hatred which was, of course, emphasized by the Afrikaner when he took over the government in 1948.

Some of my uncles worked in the gold mines, so I learned about migratory labor in my childhood. I was very fond of these uncles who would disappear for months. I saw their young wives toiling. They would come to my mother who was a senior wife, and I would listen to them crying and telling her tales about their hardships: how difficult it was for them to bring up children; how they were no longer hearing from their husbands. I began questioning why the children would be deprived of their parents for so many months when the local traders and the local priest never left their children. We witnessed this agony and learned of the horrors of migratory labor in a physical sort of way, so when I talk about these things on the platform, my heart bleeds from many generations of pain.

Political Activity

I first heard of the names of Mandela and Tambo in 1953 when I was doing my matric. There was a Defiance Campaign in Johannesburg at that time, and I heard that these leaders had told the country to defy unjust laws. The level of consciousness at our country high school was already far advanced at that time, and our interpretation of that instruction was that we must defy school authority. We didn't even write exams that year because we went on strike because of insufficient food and complaints about the general administration of the school. As long ago as that, the name of the African National Congress was instilled in our minds. Immediately after I graduated, I lived in a girls' hostel in Johannesburg. There were political discussions at the hostel almost daily, and it was there that I came across the names of Mandela and Tambo.

I was the first black medical social worker in the country. I worked at the Baragwanath Hospital, specializing in pediatric social work. It was one of the most painful fields to work in because I came into physical contact with the infant mortality rate and the gross malnutrition my people were suffering. I witnessed the pains of bringing up children without any means. I was aware of the desperation of my people trying to make ends meet in a society which was entirely capable of looking after all of its inhabitants. I began to question the role of social workers and felt that we were not being effective at all. I saw us as nothing more than civil servants. All I did was to refer cases to white institutions because there were no facilities for black people. We had no orphanages, we had no homes for disabled children, we had no homes for cerebral palsy cases. It was then that I really became conscious of the fact that if one was to be counted as a human being of fiber, one has to play a role in changing society. So I only worked as a medical social worker for three years.

I was doing social work at Baragwanath when I was telephoned by Nelson Mandela who wanted me to assist him with raising funds for the 1957 treason trial. Although Mandela* was a patron of the Ann Hof-

* Almost invariably, Winnie referred to her husband by his surname only.

meyr School of Social Work where I had trained, I had never met him before. But I used to read about him like all the other girls. When he called me up and asked me to help raise funds, I agreed because I wanted to be more involved in the liberation of my people. From that moment on, I attended the treason trial regularly and came into direct contact with the leaders of the people for the first time. Then in 1958 we married.

Attending the treason trial was for me the greatest thing to happen in my life. I was able to meet for the first time great Christians and great leaders like Chief Albert Luthuli [a former president of the ANC and Nobel Peace Prize winner]. I met Oliver Tambo, Duma Nokwe, Moses Kotane, and Walter Sisulu [well-known ANC leaders]. And my greatest experience was meeting a woman who was my hero at that time, Lillian Ngoyi [a former president of the Federation of South African Women]. We all worshiped her. Her name was a legend in every household, and we all aspired to be a Lillian Ngoyi when we grew up. When I actually met her, I found out how down to earth this great woman was. I subsequently attended meetings because I wanted to hear her and experience the power she had to grip the country. She was one of the greatest orators I have ever heard, one of the greatest women I have lived to know. And you could feel she was self-taught. I felt some kind of physical identity with her because she belonged to the working class. She spoke the language of the worker, and she was herself an ordinary factory worker. When she said what she stood for, she evoked emotions no other person could evoke. She was a tremendous source of inspiration. She spoke on behalf of the Women's League of the African National Congress and the Federation of South African Women, of which she was the president at that time. She worked closely with Mama* Helen Joseph [a leader in the now-defunct Federation of South African Women; see chapter 15] and various other great women like the late Florence Matomela and Frances Baard [former leaders of the ANC Women's League and the Federation of South African Women], whom we also worshiped very dearly.

And then there were my immediate seniors like Albertina Sisulu [see chapter 10], a woman who was a tremendous source of inspiration and who gave me a lot of courage when Mandela went underground. I went to her when times were very hard and it was very difficult to pull through. I had been jailed with her in 1958, which was my very first experience in prison.

* Black South African women frequently refer to an older woman as "Mama" so-and-so.

[Before the Soweto uprising,] I was very involved in organizing the people and conscientizing [a South African word for "consciousness raising"] them about the extremely dangerous situation that was developing. Walking in the streets of Soweto in 1976, you could feel that we were heading toward a climax between the security forces and the oppressed people of this country. I met with a few leaders here and suggested that we form the Black Parents' Association to encompass the entire country, because it was obvious then that the outbreak of anger against the state wasn't necessarily going to be confined to Soweto. The government regarded me as having played a major role in the formation of these organizations and in generally encouraging the students' militancy toward the state. Although it would be wonderful to imagine that I have such organizational powers, it was madness to think I was responsible for these things. This was a spontaneous reaction to the racial situation in the country—an explosion against apartheid.

I don't think I will ever erase the memory of those days from my subconscious mind. It was the most painful thing to witness—the killing of our children, the flow of blood, the anger of the people against the government, and the force that was used by the government on defenseless and unarmed children. I was present when it started. The children were congregated at the school just two blocks away from here. I saw it all. There wasn't a single policeman in sight at that time, but they were called to the scene. When they fired live ammunition on the schoolchildren, when Hector Petersen, a twelve-year-old child, was ripped to pieces, his bowels dangling in the air, with his little thirteen-year-old sister screaming and trying to gather the remains of her brother's body, not a single child had picked up even a piece of soil to fling at the police. The police shot indiscriminately, killing well over a thousand children.

Prison, Banning, Banishment

I was one of over six hundred women arrested in the anti-pass campaign of 1958. We were trying to stop the extension of the pass laws to women. These laws had already caused tremendous damage to black people by causing the disintegration of black family life. Black men had been carrying the hated pass for years—a document that was calculated not only to prevent the influx of blacks into the urban areas, but also to dehumanize those of a darker skin and to make them feel nonpersons and sojourners in urban, white, racist South Africa. We had completely lost the concept of the family as the nucleus of our community. Men were imprisoned endlessly. The laws declared them automatic criminals by virtue of their color.

Because of the physical brutality of prison life, I nearly lost my eldest child, who I was three months pregnant with at the time. I was fortunate to be there with Albertina [Sisulu], who is a nurse. Most of us were in prison for six weeks on this occasion, but the movement decided that Albertina and all the nursing sisters were needed during the crisis, so they had to leave prison. Although she only stayed there for a few days, she helped me a great deal.

I have spent most of my life in and out of prison. I can't remember how many times I have been inside, and it isn't possible to give dates. At first I was bewildered like every woman who has had to leave her little children clinging to her skirt and pleading with her not to leave them. I cannot, to this day, describe that constricting pain in my throat as I turned my back on my little ghetto home, leaving the sounds of those screaming children as I was taken off to prison. As the years went on, that pain was transformed into a kind of bitterness that I cannot put into words.

Solitary confinement was frightening at first because my thoughts were with my children all the time. Their father, whom they had never known, was in prison. They had never known the pleasure of having a family, of having a father figure, and there I was in prison without having had the opportunity to make arrangements for them. I didn't even know where they were, nor what had happened to them that night. That was the only thing that frightened me. What was going to happen to my children? What would become of them? What if I was held for ten years? What if whatever they would cook up as evidence against me, stuck, and I was sentenced to many years of imprisonment? How was I going to bring up my young children from prison? Those were my only fears. The police made me believe that I would be in prison forever—that I had reached the road to the end of eternity. Even experienced politicians come to believe this kind of threat because of the psychological warfare that is conducted.

It was my nine years in exile in Brandfort that was the worst experience of my life. They banished me there because they believed I was in the forefront of the 1976 Soweto uprising. The government imagines it can solve the country's problems by uprooting human beings and exiling them to deserts. Those years have brutalized me more than all the times I was in prison. My experience there was calculated to leave my soul in shreds: to so dehumanize me that nothing would be left in me to fight with; to tear apart my spirit so that life wouldn't be worth living.

I was flung into a crude, dirty, three-roomed building in Brandfort, which was without water or electricity and which was full of soil. They brought prisoners to scoop up the soil, and they threw water on the floor and walls to settle the dust. Zindzi [her youngest daughter] and I spent the first night sitting on bundles of our clothes because there was nowhere to sleep. They had taken everything I had possessed with pride, Mandela's last possessions, little things that make one what one is. They threw them onto bedspreads and sheets—whether it was cutlery or breakable plates or my house ornaments—and tied them into bundles. That is how everything was conveyed to Brandfort, and most of the things were broken in the process.

Zeni was sixteen and a half and living in Swaziland when I was banished. Zindzi was fifteen and on vacation from school. Banishing me meant banishing her as well. To do that to a little girl that age in her developing years is unforgivable. That kind of scar never heals. One of the most painful things for me was seeing that child in exile with me.

I refused to stay in Brandfort. I wanted to set a precedent that unjust laws are meant to be defied, and that I could no longer continue obeying an immoral government. Half of my life I have spent complying with their regulations to satisfy their sadism. It has become a personal vendetta by the state against me. I came back to Johannesburg not only because I was imprisoned in that ghetto home in Brandfort for nine years, but because they finally destroyed the very ghetto home they had exiled me to by firebombing everything I possessed. Everything I had went up in flames forcing me to start from scratch again.

The government has kept harassing me and treating me like a common criminal. I asked myself what it meant for them to be so scared—despite the fact that I hadn't any power to do anything in retaliation for what they were doing to me. Does it mean that what I stand for is so true that it is like the story of Jesus Christ? Is that story of the Bible the real story of life? That for one to attain one's aspirations, one has to pass through this road of crucifixion?

The years of imprisonment hardened me. I no longer felt their powers of harassment. Later I was transformed from that bitterness into the realization that those who are fighting like me, and the cause we are fighting for, must be worth a great deal; and that if this is the path through which I have to tread in order to reach that goal, then God has designed it that way. It is God's wish that those He handpicks to tread on this path must reach that Golgotha, because that is then the end of that journey to liberation. Perhaps I am one of the chosen ones, and therefore God gives me the strength and the energy to carry on, no matter how bitter the struggle. And if He wishes that my blood, as in the case of Jesus Christ, be spilt for this purpose—then, God, let it be. Because He made us, He alone determines our path, He knows whom He has chosen for which task.

Marriage and Children

I've never had the opportunity to live with Mandela. When we got married in 1958, he was being tried for treason, and he lived in Pretoria where the trial took place. And when the treason trial came to an end, he went to address a convention in Pietermaritzburg. We were together when he had time to come home for weekends, but those times wouldn't add up to even six months. So I have never really known what married life is. I have always known him as a prisoner. I feel deeply wounded about this and very angry that human beings can be kept apart for a lifetime, not because they committed any capital offense, but because they simply disagree with another man's ideas. But I'm convinced that Mandela will be released because of the pressure of the international community, the internal pressure from the oppressed people themselves, and the deterioration in the political situation in this country.

The historical period in which our children, Zindzi and Zeni, live has made their experiences no different from the ordinary black child in the street. It is a life of deprivation, a life in a sick society that deprives families of what belongs to them; that even deprives families of the duty of parenting their own children. My daughter Zindzi was detained for three weeks about three years ago. Zeni hasn't been detained only because she is a Swazi national and carries a Swazi diplomatic passport because she is married to a young prince in Swaziland.

I have had to live with a permanent threat to my life, a permanent threat to my family, and a permanent threat to almost my entire extended family. This includes my brothers and sisters who are not political at all. One of my sisters died in exile in Botswana, not because she was political herself, but because I was closest to her. She had to leave this country and live as an expatriate in Botswana.

I can no longer say what many of my colleagues find themselves having to say at one stage or another: "Off the record, I can tell you this is so and so, but I can't say it publicly because I have a family to feed. If I am known to expound such views, I'll be jailed." In my case there is no longer anything I can fear. There is nothing the government has not done to me. There isn't any pain I haven't known.

7

The Most Powerful Woman in the African National Congress

"As a woman, not only do you have to be good, but you've got to be better than the men. This is the load that women have to carry. You can't afford to make the slightest mistake."

RUTH MOMPATI

The Most Powerful Woman in the African National Congress

*R*UTH MOMPATI has the powerful presence and style of someone accustomed to leadership. Such was this sixty-three-year-old
African woman's intelligence, experience, and charisma that, after
spending only two hours with her, I thought she might well one day
become president of South Africa. No doubt my assessment was
also influenced by the fact that she is currently the most highly
placed woman in the exiled African National Congress, being one of
only three women on its thirty-five-member National Executive
Committee.

A teacher by training and many years of experience, Mompati gave
up her profession in 1953, just one year after she had married and
moved to Johannesburg to be with her husband. She felt she could no
longer teach after legislation was passed in 1953 requiring that edu-
cators train their black pupils to fit into the subservient roles they
were expected to play in South Africa. Mompati soon became a
member of the ANC, and spent the next ten years working as Nelson
Mandela's secretary in his and Oliver Tambo's Johannesburg law
firm.

In addition, Mompati was active in the Women's League of the
ANC before it was banned in 1960, and was among those who
founded the Federation of South African Women in 1954. Six years
later, when the ANC was banned, she was asked by this organization
to work underground, which she did for five months. When the ANC
asked her to leave South Africa in order to learn certain skills they
needed, she also agreed to do so since she believed it would only be for
a year. She reluctantly left her two-and-a-half-year-old baby and her
six-year-old son with her mother, her sister, and her sister's husband,
and went abroad in September 1962. "With my children so young, I
had no intention of staying away for more than a year," she said
emphatically. On the eve of Mompati's return twelve months later,
because of events in South Africa which she describes in the interview, she was forced to realize that returning meant certain imprisonment. Her description of how she felt as a mother to be forced to
live apart from her children for the next ten years are among the most
moving passages in this book.

Mompati first became a member of the ANC's National Executive

Committee in the 1960s, and then again in 1985. She is currently the administrative secretary of the National Executive, which means, she said, "that I have the very great responsibility of more or less administering the whole organization." Mompati's work for the ANC has made her into a widely traveled and very cosmopolitan figure. She lived in Lusaka, Zambia, working at the ANC-in-exile's international headquarters until 1976, after which she was sent to the Women's International Democratic Federation in the German Democratic Republic to represent the Federation of South African Women. She spent three years in the GDR at this time, and another three years (from 1981 to 1984) as the chief representative of the ANC in Britain and Ireland. Since then, Lusaka has been her main base.

Because of Mompati's role in the ANC, which many regard as the South African government-in-exile, what she has to say about her organization's position on violence and communism, two of the major preoccupations of international opinion, is of particular interest. Mompati also provides a vivid picture of the acute dilemma felt by many women in the anti-apartheid movement. On the one hand, she (and many others) recognize the seriousness of the problem of sexism women are faced with; while on the other, she believes that the national struggle, as she refers to it, is the priority. However, she also maintains that the women's struggle cannot be divorced from the national struggle and that national liberation is a prerequisite for women's liberation. Nevertheless, Mompati is an extremely articulate spokeswoman for one of the most common perspectives on black and women's liberation in South Africa.

Growing Up African

I come from a family of peasants and was born in a small village, Ganyesa, in the northwestern Cape between Mafeking and Kimberley. My father worked on the land in this village as well as in the diamond diggings. His work in the mines was periodical, so most of the time he was in the village. There were six of us in the family, three girls and three boys. One of the boys died as a child from a common children's ailment which doesn't necessarily kill children in other countries.

My mother only went as far as standard three [fifth grade]. My father, who comes from a family of thirteen, taught himself to read and write when he was working in the diamond diggings. I don't know what put the idea into his head that we should get an education, because no one in his village or in his family was educated, but he said that he wanted his children to live a better life than he had led, and he felt that education would make this possible. So he moved to a small town in Vryburg to be closer to the school we attended. Interestingly, we never considered this little town our home. The village was always home to us because our grandparents lived there. They lived to quite a great age—my grandmother until she was over a hundred. She was such a wonderful, strong person, and she had a wonderful memory. She would relate a lot of things to us like how they suffered during the Anglo-Boer War [1899–1902]; how they were treated by the soldiers; and how she had to carry her many children from one place to another with my grandfather.

My father died when I was fourteen, and it became impossible for me to continue at school. I had to work for a white family looking after their young daughter. The child was very close to me—you are really the mother of the white child in South Africa; and I think that she loved me because I was the closest person to her. I was with her all the time. I took her everywhere, played with her, and put her to bed. She had a sister who was about two years older than her, and these children were around me all the time. I hadn't had anything to do with white families before, but I became aware that the parents of these children treated me as something completely different from themselves. When I told them that I would like to go back to school, it didn't interest them. They sent me on errands, so I also had to deal with whites in shops. This placed me in the presence of older African people—whom I looked upon as parents because we Africans are taught that anyone older than you is a parent—who were sometimes humiliated in front of me. They stood there mutely not saying anything, and as a child I couldn't say anything if *they* didn't say anything. I couldn't stand another year of this, so I told my mother, "I don't mind what you do, but do something! Find money! I *must* go back to school!" I don't know how she got the money, but the following year she sent me to school.

Teaching was the cheapest profession for Africans to train for, so that's what I and my two sisters did. I started teaching when I was eighteen in a village fifteen miles away from my home. The children had to walk to school, some of them six miles each way every day. It was extremely cold in winter and extremely hot in summer, so these children had to walk these twelve miles in extreme circumstances. When you teach in that type of situation, you have to be a doctor, a nurse, a social worker, and an advisor. The nearest real doctor was fifteen miles away. You are the center of wisdom. Everybody comes to you for help, so you get to know the difficulties of these people.

On a cold winter's morning, I'd see the children come to school with only one garment covering their little bodies. It may have been the elder sister's dress or a shirt three sizes too big, and they'd sit there shivering. I was expected to teach them in these circumstances, and they were expected to learn. It used to break my heart. I was born into apartheid, and I grew up with it, and I knew these children were in this situation because of the racial discrimination in our country. Their parents worked very hard from dawn to dusk, but they couldn't buy more than what these children had. They couldn't feed them more than they fed them. And some children in my class died at an early age, six years, seven years, eight years. By the time I'd taught for a year, I'd seen many little lives ending. And I knew from my reading that children in other countries don't die from diseases like measles. They don't die from malnutrition. There was no need for these children to die.

As I mentioned, another distressing experience was going into a shop. The first thing the white woman or man would say to me was, "Annie, what do you want?" They didn't say, "What can I do for you?" They didn't ask what my name was. Because I'm black, any name would do for me. All this generated such anger in me, I wanted to shake them. My response was, "Yes, John, can you give me a loaf of bread?" That used to incense them! I started fighting back at a very early age. I think I was a rebel by nature. I didn't necessarily plan to say something like that, but the anger would well up in me, particularly when there was an old man in front of me who'd be asked by a young person, "Yes, John, what can I do for you?" "This is my *grandfather*," I'd think, and this young person is calling him "John"! I wasn't only fighting my own battle but the battles of everybody else.

It's very difficult to say in what ways apartheid hurt me most. There were so many arrows striking into me all the time. If ten people are all shooting at you at the same time, one shot is not less painful than the other. To me, that's how apartheid attacks you as a child. The constant brutality of seeing whites push my people around when I *knew* this shouldn't happen, hardened me, made me grow up before my time, learn to defend myself so I wouldn't get destroyed inside, and forced me to live for the future when I could change these things.

Political Activity: The African National Congress

When I was a student, I became a member of the students' union, which fought for the rights of students. And later I became a member of the teachers' union. I started thinking that things could be changed when I became a teacher, but I wasn't yet thinking of *political* change. At that time I still believed there was a place for my people somewhere in the South African setup. I thought that we could fight for better working conditions for teachers. But the longer I taught (I taught for eight years in all), the more I realized that under apartheid there is no place for me or my people.

In 1950, a teacher who was a member of the African National Congress came from Mafeking to teach with us. He introduced us to this organization. It hadn't occurred to us that we could work for the ANC. Teachers weren't allowed to be members of political organizations because we were supposed to be civil servants. But it was possible to work as an associate without taking the official membership. There were a number of us in our early twenties, and we did just that. We started by raising money for the ANC.

But as for how I became politically conscious, I think that politics just caught up with me. The racial discrimination, the brutalization of the African people around me, the contempt and the arrogance of white South Africans, made me defiant and eager to fight back.

My marriage in 1952 meant moving from a fairly small, quiet town to a big city where people like Nelson Mandela and Walter Sisulu and many others had been arrested for their participation in the Defiance Campaign. I joined the ANC properly in 1953, and I also became a member of the Women's League of the ANC. I couldn't go back to teaching because the Bantu Education Act [which imposed a highly inferior education on Africans in 1953] had been passed, and I refused to teach according to this law. Since there were no secretarial schools for Africans, I had to attend a private school to learn to be a shorthand typist.

I got a job [in 1953] in the law firm of Mandela and Tambo—the first African attorneys' partnership in South Africa. I was a typist in their office and a secretary to Nelson Mandela. It was a very wonderful experience to work with them because they were *the* attorneys who dealt with political cases, so everybody went there: people who had money to pay for their cases and people who didn't. They were very popular and very good lawyers. We always said that if they had been interested in money, they would have been among the rich in South Africa. But they chose their mission in life as leaders in the struggle because they felt that a rich slave was no better off than a poor slave. Working with those two leaders was one of the best times of my life. It meant a lot to me to come into contact with ordinary African people and their political problems, and to come into contact with people from all walks of life. These two men were not just leaders of the black people and of low-income people. They were leaders of everybody. People of Asian origin and white people came there, too. That's where I met most of my friends from other racial groups.

I worked in that law firm for ten years until our president, comrade Oliver Tambo, left the country to open an ANC mission outside. Then, under the instructions of comrade Nelson Mandela, I and the account-ant closed the firm. We took the files to other attorneys and asked them to deal with them. I then went to work for the Defence and Aid Fund [which contributed funds for the legal defense of political activists] before it was banned.

Motherhood and Exile

I was expecting my first child during our campaign against Bantu education in 1954. I was so busy running around, I always remember my colleague, Tambo, saying to me, "One day you will drop that baby and jump over it whilst you are still running." But I was very healthy, so it didn't worry me. And after the baby was born, I was just as involved with my work. We women always used to carry our babies to whatever work we were doing.

In September 1963, after I had been abroad for a year at the request of the ANC to work in their mission, I was all set to return to South Africa, hoping that I would be able to slip into the country without the police knowing that I had come back, but knowing that maybe I would spend a few months in prison because I had left without a passport. Then I learned of the Rivonia arrests.* Every week they were picking up more people, until most of the leaders were arrested. Then the man with whom I had worked underground for those five months became a state witness, so the ANC told me not to come back. I said I *had* to return to my children, but they said there was no point because I would just go to

---

* Rivonia, a suburb on the outskirts of Johannesburg, was the underground head-quarters of *Umkhonto we Sizwe*. Nine of the leaders were arrested there on 12 July 1963.

prison. So the next time I saw my children was ten years later. The baby was twelve and the older boy was sixteen.

I used to get ill thinking about my children. After ten years of separation, I wrote them a letter and gave it to somebody to hand-deliver to them. In it I said to them, "If you want to join me, I'm in Botswana. You know what to do. Just cross the border and come over." So the children packed and came to join me. It would have been very difficult for them to join me sooner because before then, Botswana and Zambia were not independent. Only Tanzania was. When I had left South Africa to go to Tanzania, it was *very* difficult to get there. Many of our people were arrested in Northern Rhodesia [now Zambia] or Southern Rhodesia [now Zimbabwe] and sent back home. If you arrived in Dar-es-Salaam [in Tanzania, East Africa] you always considered yourself lucky. I had been one of those lucky ones.

I had left a baby of two-and-a-half years and a child of six years. I discovered that there's no way that you can see the growth of your children in absentia. You always think of them as being the age when you left. It doesn't matter how many years pass. When I met the twelve-year-old after ten years it wasn't too bad; I could still cuddle him. He hadn't shot up as one would have expected. But my other boy was a tall sixteen-year-old. I didn't know him. I didn't know how to behave toward this boy. It broke my heart. And neither of them knew how to behave toward me. I was watching their reaction, and they were watching mine. I can *never* explain the emotional suffering of this meeting. It is extremely painful for a mother to miss her children's childhood years. I died so many deaths. I felt, "Good God, the South African regime *owes* me something, and that is the childhood of my children!" But I'm not unique. Indeed, I'm lucky. I met my children after ten years. There are those mothers who never meet their children again, who just hear that their children are dead. In contrast, we were able to sit down and discuss what happened, and they were able to begin to understand why I had stayed away from them for ten years. We could build a relationship again. They came to live with me here in Zambia in 1972. There are many parents who never get that chance.

The Federation of South African Women

We founded the Federation [of South African Women] because we felt we needed an organization for *all* women of South Africa. But because the African people are the majority in South Africa, the ANC

Women's League was its biggest affiliate. However, we also had very strong membership from the Indian women's organization, the Coloured women's organization, white women from the Congress of Democrats [an organization for white radicals], and women from the trade union movement. And we had a working relationship with women from the Liberal Party of South Africa who used to come as observers when we had conferences, and women from the Black Sash.

Working with all women in the federation enabled us to realize that there were no differences between us as mothers. We were all women. We all had the same anxieties, the same worries. We all wanted to bring up our children to be happy and to protect them from the brutalities of life. This gave us more commitment to fight for unity in our country. It showed us that people of different races could work together well.

When it comes to the work of liberation or *any* work in *any* society, men are always in the leadership positions. There are very obvious reasons for this—not only amongst Africans but amongst whites, too. Usually it is men who get a better education than women, so they know more and become more articulate and are more easily able to get jobs. And there's the historical tradition of women's place being in the kitchen whilst men's place is in leadership. So we felt that, even in an organization like the African National Congress where there is no discrimination based on sex, we needed to have an organization which would tackle problems that are specific to women. We women have always been on the bottom rung. We felt that we needed to educate our women that this is not our place. Women have occupied that place by accident of history, but we *can* participate and we *can* lead. But the oppression of African people has always been the key problem in South Africa. We are not on the same level as the white, Indian, and Coloured women who were also members of the federation.

Fighting the Pass Laws for Women

Because the pass laws formed the cornerstone of our oppression as Africans in South Africa, the Federation of South African Women took up this issue. Apartheid has to have a reservoir of cheap black labor, and the pass laws helped to provide this by controlling the movement of African people. Africans were completely controlled by the pass laws, including where they could stay and where they could work. So when we realized in the early 1950s that the pass laws were going to be extended to women, we knew we had to fight this.

The Most Powerful Woman in the African National Congress

In taking up this struggle, we were taking up a powerful tradition. Already in 1913—one year after the founding of the African National Congress—[African] women had been put into jails in Bloemfontein in the winter of that year. Their men wanted to bail them out, but the women refused, saying, "We will serve the sentence. We have burned the passes because we don't want to be controlled the way our men are controlled." That's why women didn't have to carry passes like the men for all those years. And in 1929 and 1953, the women fought against passes again. They were successful until, I think, 1962. It was only after the government had amended the laws in such a way that anything one did could be seen as sabotage, that they were finally able to extend passes to women. So the pass was a very important issue to the Federation of South African Women as well.

Fighting Bantu Education

Bantu education was another issue the federation addressed. [Hendrik] Verwoerd, who was the minister of so-called Bantu affairs at that time, said, "There is no place for the African in the European community, save as certain forms of labor." His idea was that when black people are educated, they see the green pastures on which the whites are grazing and become envious, then rebellious. So Bantu education was instituted to make it very clear that black children had to be educated to know their place in South Africa. They must only be given enough education to be useful to whites, which meant being manual laborers and being able to carry messages intelligently for the white population. The African National Congress itself had taken up the question of Bantu education even before the Federation of South African Women was founded. Indeed, the program of action of the federation could not be different from the program of action of the African National Congress and of its Women's League, because removing racial discrimination was the first priority.

The Role of Women in the Struggle

Even in an organization that supports the liberation of women, we have had to work hard to build the confidence of our women, because we are victims of history, victims of our traditions, victims of our role in society. Despite this, African women have always been part of the lives of their communities. Actually, they have been the *strength* of the communities, but they've always been a *silent* strength. But in the past years, our women have come forward and taken the lead more. They are not just supporting the men and pushing the men in front.

The National Executive is outside the country. One of the reasons there are only three women [out of thirty-five] on it is that very few senior women have left the country. But also there are a lot of women leaders *inside* the country who, if we had a free South Africa, would be on the National Executive. So we can't really judge the representation of women in leadership positions by looking at the National Executive of the ANC. Secondly, we have to continue to fight to put our women into leadership positions and to make them more able so that they can lead and articulate their problems. We still suffer from the old traditions.

Inside South Africa, we have Albertina Sisulu, [see chapter 10], Frances Baard [a trade-union leader who was jailed and banished in the 1960s], and Helen Joseph [see chapter 15]. But also, the very reason for forming women's organizations is to try to change the tendency for men to always be the leaders. Even in the most developed countries of the world, men are in the leadership positions. How many women are in the British government today? That's why Margaret Thatcher makes world history. It's a pity that she's not a very good example of women's leadership. And how many women leaders are there in the United States? So this is a historical phenomenon which we have to attend to.

About two years ago, we were discussing with the leadership of the movement what liberation for the people of South Africa really means. Will women find themselves in the same position as they have always been? Or do we see liberation as solving the conditions of women in our society? We have brought these questions up with our own leadership because we want them discussed now. If we continue to shy away from this problem, we will not be able to solve it after independence. But if we say that our first priority is the emancipation of women, we will become free as members of an oppressed community. We feel that in order to get our independence as women, the prerequisite is for us to be part of the war for national liberation. When we are free as a nation, we will have created the foundation for the emancipation of women. As we fight side by side with our men in the struggle, men become dependent on us working with them. They begin to lose sight of the fact that we are women. And there's no way that after independence these men can turn around and say, "But now you are a woman."

If you look at the role of women in South Africa, you find that they are the breadwinners because the men are not there. They also bring up their families because the men are either in prison or they are working away from home. And they are in the fight for national liberation. They are the supporters of those who are fighting in South Africa, and they themselves are fighters. They are in *Umkhonto we Sizwe,* the military wing of the African National Congress. They are in the community organizations, the health-improvement organizations, the organizations that look after prisoners, and those that look after the parents of prisoners, encouraging the parents to come together and attend to prisoners. They are in the churches, they are in every organization in the country that you can think of. For us, this is one of the first victories as a people. We've got our women feeling that the liberation struggle is their responsibility, and also that they've got a responsibility to their nation to bring up children into a happy world; and since there is no happy world for us, to bring about that happy world. We have seen that, because of this increase in women's participation, our movement has become stronger. The community organizations inside the country have organized alternative structures. For example, in places where the usual services are no longer being rendered because the people have refused to pay rents, the people themselves have made it possible for those services to continue. An infrastructure has been created by the people, and our women are the strength in these structures.

In Angola, for example, the majority of women were illiterate. Although the women who participated in the struggle were not educated, they had confidence. It wasn't a confidence brought about by being able to read or write, but a confidence from being part of a movement that did away with the oppression by the Portuguese fascist regime. They drew up their own programs of what they wanted to do, and they actually won a medal from UNESCO for the way they tackled illiteracy. They could only do these things because they were free as women to move forward with their own programs. And they were respected. A number of the women who had participated in the struggle were given positions in the ministries and the central committees, even those who didn't have a high-level education. So, what happens to women after liberation depends on how much women are part of the liberation struggle itself. But the national question is our central task.

The African National Congress and Communism

The South African regime has always been paranoid about communism. My first understanding of communism was that communists are the people who fight for their rights and who support the struggle of people who want freedom. For example, in the past if there was a strike for better pay, there would be a witchhunt, and people would be arrested and fired because they were communist. It didn't matter *what* you did, you would always be called a communist.

The Communist Party of South Africa has been banned for many years now. Some of their members are also members of the African National Congress. As far as we're concerned, this has never been a problem. Some of them have been among the finest people I know. For example, a person like Moses Kotane was a communist and also a leader of the African National Congress, but he never used his position in the ANC to organize people into the Communist Party. What was primary for him was the liberation of the people of South Africa.

The African National Congress is a movement which brings together people from all walks of life, people of different races and religious beliefs who are against apartheid. When we have liberated our country, when we are free, maybe we will begin to look at what we think of communism. The issue of communism has never interfered with our work. But we know that every time anyone is active, they are considered a communist. When we do anything intelligent, it is seen as influenced by Moscow. If we organize a campaign that is successful, then so-called troublemakers and communists are held responsible, not the movement.

I have been described as a moderate with strong nationalist leanings, and I have also been described as a communist. Other members of the ANC have been called communist because they were trained in the Soviet Union—as if that made them communist. Meanwhile, for us, the question of who is a communist is irrelevant. The relevant question is who is actively involved in the struggle for a new South Africa.

The Issue of Violence

It is important to know why the African National Congress is involved in an armed struggle. For a very long time, we thought we could fight for our liberty peacefully. We thought we could discuss, plead, petition, and demonstrate for it. The last thing that Nelson Mandela did before he was imprisoned [in 1962] was to call for a convention where all South Africans could come together to discuss what should be done. The South African regime rejected his proposal. All the time that the African National Congress was using peaceful means to try to bring change in South Africa, the reaction from the regime was violent. People were shot at peaceful meetings. I can't count the number of meetings of the Women's League of the ANC which were surrounded by armed police peering through the windows with their guns pointed at us. Since I wasn't used to guns, I didn't see the danger of this at the time. Nor can I count the number of meetings of the Federation of South African Women when we were given five minutes warning at gunpoint to close our meetings. We knew that if we didn't do so, we would be shot. This violence also occurred when our people were arrested. Thousands upon thousands of South Africans have died violently at the hands of the police. We've got *hundreds* of children in prison today. What crime can be committed by an eleven-year-old that he should be in prison? Teenagers have been imprisoned in Robben Island's maximum security prison. What crime can be committed by a teenager to justify this? When our people carry to the graveyard the coffins of their loved ones killed by the police, they are shot on the way or at the grave site itself. As they are burying one, others are falling dead.

But it's not only direct violence that we are concerned about. There's also the violence of the conditions of *living* in South Africa. The deaths of our children from malnutrition, the short life span of our women and our people, the violence of the education where our children are condemned to a life of ignorance. The violence of the working conditions of our mine workers who bring gold from the bowels of the earth, but whose *safety* is not even thought about. How many of them have died from miners' phthisis or because the mines have fallen in on them because the necessary precautions were not taken? The whole life of an African person is a life of violence! The African National Congress looked at all this, including the fact that we have done everything to try to speak to the white people of South Africa. But they have even closed our mouths. Our people are banned and banished. Our organizations are outlawed. Even the nonviolent methods which we had were made illegal. We had to look at our children suffering and being shot by the police, but what could we do as a people to change the situation? We decided that, if the gun is what the South African regime has used to rule us, it will have to be the gun that breaks that rule.

On the issue of necklacing [murder by placing a burning tire around someone's neck], sometimes people take actions which they would not have taken under normal conditions. A few people are using methods that they would *not* have used had they not been faced with so much violence. For example, a young man put a limpet mine in a supermarket, and five whites died. And the *whole world* went *berserk*. We pointed out that forty-one black people had been killed in Lesotho in cold blood by the South African regime. And this boy who put a mine in the supermarket had played with many of those people who were killed in Lesotho when they were children. They had all grown up together. If they had been shot fighting the police with arms, that would have been different, but they were sleeping! And this young man said in court that he couldn't take what had happened to his friends, so his mind became closed to any reason. It's very easy for the world to look at what the African National Congress or what the black people in South Africa are doing, but not at the scale of the violence against us. The South African townships are occupied by the police and the army. There's violence every day. The South African regime pays young black people to *kill* those who are struggling for better conditions. It's a hungry society, so it's not surprising that some accept this money so that they can eat.

And some of the violence which is often blamed on the African National Congress is really perpetrated by the police. They necklace people, and then they say it's the ANC. They kill people, and then say it's the comrades [young radical opponents of apartheid]. This has been proved a number of times where they have been caught redhanded. But the press is not even allowed to report this, and this censorship is even worse now under the state of emergency. The ANC has a very clear policy that we only attack apartheid's instruments of repression and its supporting structures—the police, the military, and the economy of the country. We believe that if we destroy the economy of the country, we are destroying apartheid. If innocent people are hit, it will not be because our policy has changed, but because there is a war going on in South Africa. And the world must recognize that where there is a war, a lot of civilians suffer, as they did in Europe in World War II.

8

Women and the African National Congress

"We women students actually accused the men of being cowards because time and again it was us who had to be in the front of the demonstration facing the guns and the bullets."

MAVIVI MANZINI

*M*AVIVI MANZINI *has been working full-time for the Women's Section of the African National Congress since 1979. She is a thirty-one-year-old African who escaped from South Africa in 1976 (as she describes here) when she was twenty. She obtained a B.A. degree in political science and sociology from a Zambian university in 1979. A year later in 1980, Manzini married a man who is now working for the ANC Youth Section. Their only child was born in 1984. Although Manzini's three siblings were, like her, involved in the student movement in South Africa, she is the only one who now lives outside the country.*

Manzini speaks of her work in the ANC underground and is particularly informative about how the ANC's Women's Section (to be distinguished from the earlier Women's League) is organized, and what its current thinking is about the status of women and women's issues. I was impressed by her willingness to talk about the fact that sexism is a serious problem within the ANC-in-exile (for example, ANC women often feel they cannot attend meetings because of their domestic responsibilities), but even more serious inside South Africa. Manzini's thinking on this question suggests the heartening possibility that the ANC-in-exile may be significantly more progressive in understanding the importance of women's liberation than its sister organizations inside the country.*

In this connection, Manzini reports that the Women's Section is currently engaged in drawing up a bill of rights for women. They have been both gathering information about family codes and laws on women in different countries in order to try to arrive at the best possible bill of rights for women, and also seeking input into this document from women in South Africa. Manzini said that it would include policy statements about lobola *(paying to obtain a bride) and polygamy, both controversial issues in South Africa. White South Africans have typically responded to African traditions in such a heavy-handed and racist manner, that many African people are defensive about them. Africans have the task of deciding which traditional practices are positive and to be preserved, and which are*

---

* This is heartening because of the anticipated role of the exiled ANC in the creation of a new South Africa.

negative (even if they were once positive) and in need of change. Manzini was definite that the traditional practices of lobola *and polygamy are oppressive to women. "If we want equality," she declared, "*lobola *has to be scrapped."*

With regard to the ANC-in-exile in general, Manzini reported that it has been growing "because lots of people are leaving the country." The ANC community is even larger in Mazimbi, Tanzania, than in Lusaka, because this is the location of their school. It is, however, too dangerous for ANC people to live in countries close to South Africa, and thus relatively few are living in Zimbabwe. My own experience in Zimbabwe helped me to understand this in a personal way. The ANC member Phyllis Naidoo invited me to stay with her, but warned me that it was at my own risk, because the ANC offices had just been bombed the previous day. When I went to visit her at her home, two soldiers were on guard. Even in faraway Zambia, ANC members are not safe. "According to the Boers," Manzini explained, "they have the capability to strike up to the equator. So at times we have to live in hiding, and we live scattered throughout Lusaka."

Even those in exile, then, have to fear the power and military might of the South African police state.

Growing Up African

I was born in 1956 in Alexandra township in Johannesburg, then moved to Soweto when it was established. I am one of eight children, of whom only four are still alive. I suffered from polio when I was about two years old, and spent most of the next four years in hospital. But from the age of six, I was well and started at school.

Apartheid affects people from childhood. We lived in a terrible part of Soweto, and although my father and mother were both teachers, they had a very hard time making ends meet. Sometimes there'd be no food. Later I became aware that our situation was connected with the political system, but I understood it only as poverty when I was young.

My school was quite a distance from my home so I had to wake up very early in the morning to get there. There were only about four school buses to collect people all over Soweto and drop us off at different places. By the time the bus got to my place, it was often full. On the way to school, I'd see white school buses that were empty, so I started to question this difference. As I grew up, I began to notice that it was our people who were working so hard but who continued to suffer, and I realized that my parents were getting a raw deal. The ANC was banned when I grew up, but I learnt about it from my parents who were very active members in the 1950s. They would tell us about detention, the Mandelas, and how difficult it was to do anything against the regime.

Political Activity

In 1973, when I was seventeen and at high school, I got involved in the South African Student Movement. I continued with this involvement when I went to Turfloop University in the northern Transvaal. The South African Students Organization, SASO, had been banned on campus by the university administration in 1974 following a rally. The students had demonstrated in solidarity with the people of Mozambique when they won their independence from Portugal. Most of the students who participated in this demonstration were expelled. After that the Student Representative Council, which had been the mouthpiece for student grievances, no longer existed because most of its members were among those expelled. Many of them went into exile, but some were tried and sentenced to five years in prison.

It was a very difficult time to be politically active on campus, but some of us decided that we wouldn't be silenced. We organized SASO meetings in a church off the campus to discuss the state of student rights, and this kept at least some political life going at the university. I was in my second year at university when the Soweto uprising started in 1976 and spread throughout the country. When the high school students started demonstrating against the Afrikaans language being made the medium for their education, we at the university wanted to show our solidarity with them, so we organized a demonstration on 18 June —two days after the shootings in Soweto. The police came on campus and arrested and detained many students. Although I was involved in the planning of this demonstration and participated in it, I wasn't detained on this occasion.

I became involved in the ANC underground earlier in 1975. I was in a unit with four other campus activists. We carried out tasks to assist the ANC, especially *Umkhonto we Sizwe*, by reconnoitering and giving them information about the whereabouts of the police, especially in the northern Transvaal area where there are military bases. I lived around that area at that time and knew it very well.

Women and the African National Congress

We got most of our political education from the ANC, who supplied us with literature that was otherwise unavailable in the country. After reading it, we'd pass it on to others in the student movement. We also used to listen to Radio Freedom* which helped us with our political development.

We'd talk to other students about the ANC because we were convinced that the time had come for our methods of protest to go beyond demonstrations. Most demonstrators end up being detained or shot without having really contributed to the struggle. Of course we had to be very careful who we approached. Because the ANC was a banned organization, it meant five years in prison if we were found to be involved in it.

Then one of our unit members was detained in May 1976 before the Soweto uprising. The police had trailed him when he went to meet with the ANC outside the country. They detained him at the border on his way from Swaziland. We informed the ANC of his detention, but decided to remain in the country because it is so difficult to leave. We hoped that they wouldn't come after us, but if they did, we thought there wouldn't be a very heavy charge because we didn't actually *carry out* any operations, we had only reconnoitered.

I think they tortured our comrade. He resisted talking to them for a long time, but he broke down after two months, resulting in detention for the rest of us and a ten-year sentence for him. I was detained on the third of July. It was the day I was supposed to have left for a SASO conference. The police had been watching my movements and knew when I would leave, so they picked me up from my home that morning. After the university was closed down, it became difficult to maintain contact with the other comrades in my unit so I didn't know that they had been detained before me. So by the time they took me in, the police already had a whole file on me filled with information that had been sucked from my comrades.

I was transferred to another police station out of my home town where I was held in solitary confinement. After leaving me in my cell for about three days without questioning me, the police repeated the same questions about the other people in my unit that they had asked me the first day. When I denied something, they'd open my file and read out the information they had been given. I felt very helpless, even though they didn't actually have a lot of the most significant information.

* Radio Freedom is administered by the ANC in Lusaka, Zambia. It beams ANC news into South Africa from broadcasting facilities in Zambia, Tanzania, Ethiopia, Angola, and Madagascar (Davis 1987, p. 54).

But they knew that I was in touch with the ANC and had propounded its aims and objectives amongst the students. I was afraid that if I continued to deny everything, they'd torture me. To be held in solitary confinement, to be given food only once a day, to be taken out of the cell time and again for questioning, is itself torture. But I think they didn't hit or torture me further because they thought there was no more information to extract from me.

They kept me in detention for two months. One day in September 1976, I was told, "We are releasing you, but you must report to the police station every day to tell us where you are going and what you are doing. And we might call you in later." They wanted to monitor my movements, and I think they planned to charge me later. I was released with the three other people from my unit including Joyce Masamba, the only other woman member. One month later, they detained Joyce and the other two comrades again. Immediately after I learned this, I left the country.

Two of my comrades were charged with terrorism for aiding the ANC and were sentenced to five years in prison. The other two, both of them men, were used as state witnesses. Joyce is presently in detention again under the 1986 emergency regulations, together with her sixteen-year-old son.

Other people connected with the ANC were supposed to help me escape, but they were all in detention. So I didn't know how to leave or whom to contact. I was left in the lurch. But I finally managed to contact people who assisted me in working out an escape route to Botswana. Botswana is quite a distance away from where I was in the northern Transvaal, but I had a few pennies, and these people gave me a few more pennies, and I took a train which stopped at a place about an hour's drive away from the border.

I took a bus to a village near the border, but I couldn't simply go to the border post and show them my passport because I was afraid that a message may already have reached them that I had not reported to the police station back home. And if they were looking for me, I'm easily identifiable [because of being partially disabled by polio]. There had been lots of peasant revolts in this border area, so most of the people there were quite politicized and gave assistance to those who needed it. But still, I had to be very careful. My story was that I was very sick, that I had to see some traditional healers who stayed next to a river, and that only the water from that river could cure me.

The borders were heavily patrolled, especially after the uprising in 1976, because the government knew large numbers of people were leaving the country. The woman villager whose help I sought told me, "We hear these days there are a lot of people who are leaving. Where do you come from?" I mentioned an area where there wasn't any political activity, and said, "Yes, I hear this too, but I'm not involved in all those things. I am sick and on my way to see a traditional healer." Because it was quite a wild area with wild animals roaming about, I needed an escort to show me the exact route over the border. This woman asked a young man to help me. I think he was quite aware that my story might not be true because he kept telling me that the Boers [police] usually patrol in that area and I must be careful. He took me some of the way, but then I had to continue alone. I was scared because people had told me how wild the area was. I had about ten kilometers further to walk. I saw the claw marks of wild animals on the way. Although I became more and more scared, I had no choice but to continue. I'm able to walk without any problem [despite a partially disabled leg], except that I can't walk very fast and it's tiring if it's a very long distance. But on that day I was more concerned not to be detained and have to serve five or ten years in jail. It was with great relief that I finally made it into Botswana.

In Botswana, I had to report to the police station and ask for political asylum. After explaining why I had to escape from South Africa, the police granted it. When I told them that I wanted to get in touch with the ANC, they contacted them for me, and the ANC came and picked me up at the police station.

I stayed in Botswana for about three months while the ANC looked for a scholarship for me. Then I went to Zambia to continue my studies at the university there. Because there was a lot of sympathy for students from South Africa, the university authorities accepted me and other comrades despite our lack of certificates.

The Women's Section of the ANC

On completing my degree in 1979, I joined the ANC Women's Section secretariat full-time and worked as an assistant editor for *Voice of Women* [an ANC publication]. I've been working here full-time now for eight years. The Women's Section was set up when the ANC went into exile, and it operates differently from the way the Women's League used to operate in South Africa. The Women's League was an independent body with its own constitution and laws, and it could make its own decisions. But the ANC felt that there should only be one organization in exile, and that we should carry out our work collectively. Our decisions are also made in consultation with the people in South Africa. So the constitution of the ANC has been suspended in exile, and new structures like the Women's Section have been developed.

The ANC Women's Section is charged with the task of mobilizing women inside and outside the country to enter and continue the struggle. Outside of Lusaka, the Women's Section is organized on the basis of regions. If there are five or more women anywhere who want to join the ANC, they can form a unit of the ANC Women's Section and elect a secretary and a chairman and follow the Women's Section's program. Within the Women's Section, the highest body is the conference which meets every five years. The first conference was held in 1981. This is the body which elects the National Women's secretariat and discusses all matters relating to women. And the highest body within the conference is the council, which consists of members of the National Women's secretariat and women from different regions. These council members are appointed by the National Women's secretariat according to how active and how big their units are.

The secretariat of the Women's Section consists of nine people each in charge of a "desk": for example, there are desks for logistics, international relations, politics, education, projects and finance, and internal mobilization—meaning mobilization within South Africa. There are also subcommittees, which people in charge of the different desks work with. Women here in Zambia who may not be working full-time in the Women's Section can serve on these subcommittees.

All women who belong to the ANC-in-exile automatically belong to the Women's Section. Once a woman is accepted as a member in the ANC, her name is sent by the mother body to the Women's Section. If a member is under thirty-five years of age, he or she automatically becomes a member of the Youth Section. But not all women actually *work* in the Women's Section; they work as well in other departments of the ANC.

Our view is that women's emancipation in our country cannot be separated from the struggle for national liberation. That's why we have sought to participate actively in the struggle. But we have realized from observing the experiences of other struggles, even those of our neighbors in Zimbabwe and Angola, that the question of women's liberation has to be addressed now, and not left to later when national liberation has been won. And we think the best way of addressing it is to repeatedly raise the problems of women sharply, because they are usually dealt with only in passing. If *we* don't raise women's issues, nobody will. That's our experience in all the forums, be it youth, trade unions, or wherever we are.

We think that this is a struggle which has to be fought by both men and women. It should be the whole movement, not only women who take an interest in it, because by liberating women the whole nation will be liberated. By educating a man you are only educating one individual because he doesn't usually pass it on. But by educating women the whole nation is being educated because it's usually women who teach the future generation. Our president, Comrade Oliver Tambo, expressed the same view at the Luanda Conference. We consider his speech there a major ANC policy statement on the question of the emancipation of women.

Major Issues for Women

We have recommended to the ANC that there has to be a concerted effort by the movement to uplift women politically because it's very clear that, with only three women on the [thirty-five member] executive committee, there's still a problem. In our recommendations, which have been approved by our National Executive, we proposed discrimination *in favor* of women. Of course, a person must be appointed on the basis of merit, but when a man and a woman have equal merit, the woman should be chosen. For a long time there was only *one* woman on the ANC Executive, Florence Mophosho, who was on the National Executive from 1975 onwards. After the last consultative conference in Luanda in 1986 when Gertrude Shope [head of ANC Women's Section] became a member of the executive, there were three women [Ruth Mompati being the third] until Florence passed away recently.* Lillian Ngoi was on the national executive at home [in South Africa] before the banning of the ANC, and Charlotte Mqxeke was on the executive right from the founding of the ANC. So even three women is quite an improvement over the past.

We must raise our political awareness through education. Most women cannot participate in the struggle, cannot actively articulate their needs, their grievances, their wishes, because of a lack in confi-

---

* Jaqueline Mlefe has become the third woman member of the executive since then (Ruth Mompati, personal communication, 6 April 1989).

dence, which in turn comes from a lack of education. So the Women's Section has a political program to train women in formal and informal education. Many women cannot go to school because they are too old, so we are addressing the importance of adult education.

Other important women's issues are rent, the high cost of living, children in detention, education of women and children, participating as equals, and not being discriminated against because we are women. The women at home [in South Africa] are also pushing for a fairer reflection of the role they play within the UDF because they think that they do most of the work at the grassroots level, but when it comes to leadership there is Mama Sisulu [see chapter 10] and Cheryl Carolus [formerly on the National Executive of UDF] and that's all.

Even in the Women's Section, we find that women cannot come to our meetings because they say, "I have to cook first," or "There's nobody to remain with the child," and yet their husband is there in the house. Our men must take part in looking after the children. If I'm going to a meeting and there's no cooked food in the house and he's there, then he has to cook, not wait until I come back or expect that I shouldn't go to the meeting. We have recently received reports from one ANC unit that the women are too busy to meet because after work they still have to attend to their family's needs. But we don't accept this. It's a question of attitude. Our men think that our place is in the kitchen. Even when our president, Oliver Tambo, says women's place is in the battlefield, the men don't readily accept this in practice. But I think it will happen, and it's better outside here than at home in South Africa— maybe because of the various tasks we do here. Sometimes we travel, and our husbands have to remain at home, and in some places we live communally and we all have to cook, wash, and clean the house. We women also go to the office in the morning and come back tired, so most of the men here are accepting more equality.

Violence against women is an important issue, but I believe that the major violence we have to address is state violence. Violence starts with the state, then goes down to others. Women, being on the bottom, receive the most. South Africa is a very violent society, not only because of the use of armed force against us, but in the working and living conditions of black people. When men go home, they let the violence out on women. After their bosses have called them "boys" at work and kicked them around, they have to find some way to let off steam. So when you analyze the problem of violence against women politically, you find that it emanates from the system itself.

But the Women's Section *is* addressing the issues of wife beating and child bashing. We are trying to educate our people about them and trying to put them in a political context. The attitudes toward women and children are wrong and must be corrected. We have taken these issues very seriously within the movement. The External Coordinating Committee has issued circulars about wife beating and child bashing because of pressure from the Women's Section.

In Lusaka and at home [in South Africa], we are also taking up the issue of rape and other violence against women very seriously, especially on campuses. The young women in the student movement are addressing the problem of sexual harassment in the schools by the teachers and the male students. When I was in SASO, most of the women in it didn't seem to know their rights. They just followed their boyfriends. And the treatment they got was quite awful. But some of us insisted that we had rights and were not at the mercy of the men.

Lobola is one of the issues that the Women's Section will be addressing in the upcoming conference in September [1987] along with the question of polygamy, because these practices serve men and oppress women. We feel that we cannot be liberated and still accept *lobola* to be paid for us when we get married, because it creates a lot of marriage problems. A man who has given *lobola* to his wife's parents regards her as his property with whom he can do anything because he has bought her.

Of course, there are other views of *lobola*. Some people think there is nothing wrong with it or that there used to be nothing wrong with it. According to this view, it was only with the coming of capitalism with its money economy that it [*lobola*] became a problem. But we live in a different era now, and if we have to fight a system we have to fight it in its entirety. And I don't think it is possible to go back to the traditional way of life where *lobola* used to be respected, and where the men used to respect their wives. If we want equality, *lobola* has to be scrapped.

We are telling our movement here that we have to send more women cadres into the country. Most of us women end up being in the offices. We feel that our revolution would advance faster if more of the women were sent to work in South Africa because that's where the struggle is. *Umkhonto we Sizwe* cadres also do political work, and it's advantageous for women to be trained militarily. If there is a struggle around rent and people see the rent office being demolished, it boosts their morale and they continue to fight. But if there is a demonstration and people are shot and there is no retaliation, then people get demoralized.

I think the movement realizes that the women are the best cadres because they do lots of work. That was also the case when I was a student. We women students actually accused the men of being cowards because time and again it was us who had to be in the front of the demonstration facing the guns and the bullets. The men stayed behind saying, "It's better for the women to be in front because the Boers [police] still have some respect for women." But when the police start shooting, they don't look to see if you're a man or a woman. The bullet will hit the first one on the line.

9

An Indian Woman
Confronts Apartheid

"Once you are involved in politics, the most difficult thing is to go for hang [be sentenced to death]. That is how we look at it. . . . So until you are killed, you can't say that you have really suffered."

ELA RAMGOBIN

*A*FTER AGREEING *on the telephone to be interviewed, Ela Ramgobin told me to meet her in my car at a particular intersection in downtown Durban, the major coastal city of Natal Province. "I know my telephone is tapped," she explained later, "and we just don't say exactly where we'll meet a person on the phone." This precaution in no way indicated that Ramgobin was unwilling to take risks. She was one of only two black women willing to criticize Chief Gatsha Buthelezi, the much-feared chief of the Zulu people, without requesting a pseudonym for protection. (The reason he is so feared will become clearer in chapter 20.) "When you are quoted anonymously," Ramgobin said, "people don't pay as much attention to what you say. As long as it helps the movement, I don't mind if I'm quoted."*

Ramgobin's grandfather was Mahatma Gandhi, who started the passive resistance movement in South Africa and then continued it in India. Indeed, three generations of her family—her grandfather, father, and eldest uncle's son—were involved, in the early 1940s, in the Salt March in India to protest British rule. Ramgobin's father was beaten up by the police there and spent a year or so in prison.

Ramgobin speaks here of the Defiance Campaign of 1952 and of the revival of the Natal Indian Congress, the major Indian anti-apartheid organization in Natal. She was also a founder of the Natal Organization of Women and the Women's Congress of the United Democratic Front, and has been active in organizing women at all levels, including in the community and as workers.

Ramgobin, forty-six years old in 1987, is married to the politically active Mawalal Ramgobin, to whom four pages are devoted in Who's Who in South Africa *(1985). They have known each other since their childhood years in Inanda, Natal, where they grew up, and were married in India in 1961. They have five children, ranging in age from twenty-three to sixteen-year-old twins. Two of the children were injured in 1973 when a parcel bomb exploded in their father's office.*

Ramgobin got her B.A. degree at Natal University; then at the University of South Africa (UNISA), a correspondence school, she obtained another social science degree and an honors degree in social work. She has been a social worker since 1973. After her 8 A.M. to 4 P.M. stint at work, Ramgobin is studying for a law degree, also through UNISA, "because I have no time to attend classes." When she has completed this degree, she will decide what to specialize in—whether constitutional law, as she thinks right now, or something else.

Growing Up Indian

My family has always been very politically involved. My father was in prison on and off here and in India for a number of years. My mother and my brother and sister and I remember attending meetings in Red Square in Durban, South Africa, from the very early days. My mother was very active in India, but after she came out to South Africa she didn't engage in any of the passive resistance struggles. She is well educated but not in English, so she's had a bit of a problem communicating with people here.

My grandfather started *Indian Opinion* [a newspaper] and a community known as the Phoenix settlement in Inanda, where I was born. The settlement was governed by a board of trustees, and when my grandfather left South Africa he left my father with the responsibility of managing the whole settlement together with the newspaper. My father would visit India for six months or so and then come back here.

I have one sister and one brother, both of whom were politically involved in their early years. But now my sister is involved in her own family life and hasn't been politically active for a long time. And my brother got married in India and settled there, so he hasn't been politically active either.

Ever since I can remember, I was aware of living in the apartheid system. I traveled to school by train, and I always had to use the nonwhite compartments. Often I would see that the white compartments were empty while ours were full, sometimes necessitating my standing all the way from Phoenix to Durban, which is about a forty-five-minute journey. The amusement parks were only open to whites, the beaches were separate, and so on. These things made me bitter and aware that the whole system is inhuman. And the Africans suffered more than the Indians. The system is about ten or fifteen times worse for them. We have a better system of education, more facilities, and better welfare services. I was aware of all this from an early age because I was born and brought up in the Inanda area where members of all races lived together—Indians, Africans, whites; and we always had members of all races coming to our house.

The Defiance Campaign of 1952

My father and my sister participated in the passive resistance campaign in South Africa in the 1950s. Since I was only twelve years old, I couldn't actively participate in it. A law was passed declaring the African areas as places into which other racial groups could not go. Thousands of people participated in civil disobedience against this law in 1952 in what has come to be known as the Defiance Campaign. Together with others, my father defied this law by entering African townships. The organizers addressed a meeting there, after which they were immediately arrested. They could have paid a fine and come out of prison, but my father chose to remain there. This, his last imprisonment, lasted three months.

My father's imprisonment was a bitter experience for us because the prison conditions were absolutely inhuman at that time. I have a very vivid memory of the day we went to fetch him from prison. His whole body was covered with little black spots caused by body lice that he'd been exposed to there. It was very painful to see him like that. My father was always very strong, so his state of mind was all right. But I think that the prison diet and the conditions had a physical effect on him from which he never recovered. He died from a stroke four years later. We think that it all started in prison because it was soon after his release that he started getting pains in his fingertips and other signs like that. He must have been about fifty-four at that time. He wrote a series of articles about prison conditions after he came out.

After the Defiance Campaign, the government passed a new law equating defiance of a law with committing treason. Now you could be sentenced to death or to life in prison for defiance, so the whole question of defiance as a political strategy had to be rethought.

Marriage and Political Activity

My husband has been banned for a total of fifteen years. In the early days he was involved in student activities. At that time there was a black section of the University of Natal, and my husband was the president of the Student Representative Council there. He was called by the judge and told that he must resign or action would be taken against him. He said, "I am not going to resign. Only the students can force me to resign, not you." He was banned for five years after that. It was 1963, and we had only been married for three years. Of course, this affected my children and myself because we generally stuck together as a family. If he couldn't go out, none of us went out. As near as possible, we stayed together.

The banning order prevented him from going out of Durban, but it didn't prevent him from working as such. He is an insurance broker, but he was working as an agent for a company at that time, not as a broker. For the first five-year banning order, it wasn't so bad; but after the second banning and house arrest order, he was demoted in his firm. We think it was as a result of pressure from the state. So he gave up his job in protest, after which he had to start out on his own. He had to be at home from 7 P.M. to 7 A.M. every day so he couldn't go out and see any clients at night. And people couldn't visit us during those hours either.

Next my husband had to close his office in Durban because he was banished to the Inanda district, which meant that he couldn't move out of Inanda. He had to find offices and clients in that area. So his work was affected quite a bit, including his income. But the community has been very supportive. Generally business people have to go looking for business, but in our case people came to him. So in that respect, it wasn't so bad. He had to stop his overtly political work at that time, but he did a lot of work on community issues during that period.

I didn't get involved in student politics because I was living some way away from Durban and so, being female and having to travel at night, it was impossible for me to attend meetings.

I worked as a social worker for a child and family welfare agency, and I also did a lot of community work. The community's suffering is related to political issues, because the community doesn't have a vote, it doesn't have a say. I work in areas where communities don't even have a basic necessity like water. So I tried to get them to get together to demand these kinds of facilities, and in the process I also tried to educate them to understand why they were in the position they were in.

In the early 1970s, my husband was unbanned for a short while, and the first thing we did was to form a national committee and call for the release of all political prisoners—Braam Fischer [an Afrikaner, communist, lawyer, and well-known leader who died in prison], Nelson Mandela, and all the others. We started this campaign during an Anti-

Republic Campaign at the time of the tenth anniversary of South Africa becoming a republic [1961]. This was the first call for the release of political detainees, and it was the beginning of the community becoming politically involved again. We got a lot of activists involved in this campaign, and lots of prisoners were given clemency.

The Revival of the Natal Indian Congress

NIC had never been banned as an organization, but its leadership had been imprisoned and then banned in the 1960s. As a result, it became dormant for a number of years. After the success of our campaign to release political prisoners, we felt we needed to get all the energy that was generated into some kind of an organization. So we decided to revive NIC. We had a big public meeting in the early 1970s, at which a mandate was given for its revival. I wasn't on the steering committee that actually revived NIC because my children were quite small at that time and I didn't have time to go to the meetings.

Soon after we revived NIC, my husband was banned and house-arrested for the second time. His banning occurred on the eve of the conference which we had organized, so he couldn't participate in it. We had organized branches in various areas, and I went to the conference as the delegate from one of them. There I was elected onto the executive of NIC, the only woman on it.

The revival of NIC has played a significant role in the history of the Indian people. We have never wanted to work only within our ethnic group, but because we live in ethnically segregated areas, we have been forced to do this. We go to ethnic schools, and there are differences in the kind of oppression we are subjected to and the way we perceive our oppression. So if we want to organize the Indian people, then we have to work within the Indian community. But our actions have always been nonracial, and we have always worked toward nonracial ends. For example, the first thing we did after NIC's revival was to rededicate ourselves to the Freedom Charter.

NIC was the first political organization to start remobilizing after the heavy repression of the 1960s. There were student organizations which were fairly active, and they were very supportive of our revival. The trade unions were started after NIC was revived, and there were massive strikes in the 1972 period. A lot of community action around issues of rent followed. All the different groups worked together, and that laid the foundation for the United Democratic Front. NIC has not been banned, but once again, they have banned many of the leaders.

Banning and House Arrest

I continued to be involved in the organization until I was banned and house-arrested about six months after my husband's banning. I was amongst the first NIC executive members to be banned. The NIC president was also banned, as were quite a few other people. I was banned again for another three years after this five-year period. But I am still active in NIC today.

I expected something to happen to me, but at the same time I was quite surprised when I was actually served with a twelve-page document about my house-arrest restrictions. Everybody expects to be detained nowadays, but when it actually happens to them they are surprised. It was my son's birthday on the day the security branch came to house-arrest me. We wanted to give him a little party, and I was busy cooking for it. Of course, we had to put off the party. As long as my husband was under house arrest and I was free, I could have visitors at home. But when both of us were house-arrested, we couldn't have visitors any more.

For five years I was confined to Inanda. I had to report to the police station every Saturday. I had to be in my home from 7 A.M. to 7 P.M. every day, and I had to be inside the house the whole weekend. I wasn't allowed to attend any social gatherings, to enter educational institutions, to enter factories, to be quoted, to speak in public, to communicate with any other banned person, and so on. My husband and I had to have special permission to communicate with each other.

Living under house arrest was really difficult. It was very difficult for my children because throughout their childhoods we couldn't go out, so they didn't know what it was like to go for holidays and to participate in social activities. They had to be with us all the time. My second son became such a racialist for a time. He began to hate whites so much. We didn't realize this was happening until it hit us one day when we wanted to get a little pet for him and he said, "Mummy, whatever happens, don't get me a white dog. You must buy a black dog." He was quite small then, and his seeing anything white as bad turned out to be just a phase.

I was working in Durban at the time. I couldn't keep my job because I couldn't go to Durban any more. So I applied for a job where I was living, but for a long time I couldn't get one because I was restricted from visiting most places and from entering a court. This made it difficult to do my job as a social worker. I had to get special permission to be present at a children's court inquiry. This meant that each time I went there either the commissioner had to subpoena me or refuse to allow me to be present. My clients suffered because they had to be there without a social worker's support.

My son was detained for the first time for just under three months about six months ago. It was totally unexpected and a really trying experience because my son is very claustrophobic. But he was fairly strong and came through it. But it is very hard to be a parent when your children are in detention and there is nothing you can do about it.

The Natal Organization of Women

Some women felt the need to come together and observe South African National Women's Day on the eighth of August [1983]. Although they continued to meet after that, they didn't consolidate into a group at that time. When I was unbanned, I joined the group and we developed it into an organization called NOW.* This was before UDF formed. It was tremendous because when UDF started, we could participate in it as women. We made a resolution about not forgetting the women's struggle and to remind people that our struggle is very much part of the rest of the struggle.

The Women's Congress of the United Democratic Front

I was one of the 250 to 300 women to launch the United Democratic Front Women's Congress in Cape Town in 1987. Women came from all over the country, and the spirit there was tremendous. This new organization is comprised only of the women within UDF, but the foundation was laid when it was launched for the formation of a new [all-inclusive] national women's organization. We started making connections with the different women's political organizations all over the country. Student organizations and trade unions that are within UDF were there, too. Our idea is that by consolidating ourselves into this national organization, we will strengthen our presence within the UDF as well as our

* This organization has no affiliation with NOW in the United States.

activities outside UDF within other women's organizations. Because until we women are powerful and confident enough, we can't expect to participate fully in the struggle.

We didn't want to have a formal constitution, just an informal organization. There will be a twenty-person committee and council with four convenors, one from each province. We adopted the Freedom Charter [a document drawn up in 1955 by a coalition of anti-apartheid groups, known as the Congress of the People, outlining principles for a nonracial democracy for South Africa] and the Women's Charter, and we resolved to play a role in all the campaigns like the Free Our Children Campaign and the Living Wage Campaign. The demand for living wages affects us most of all because women workers are the lowest paid. Now we can develop national policies and have uniform methods of participating in the struggle.

The launching of our congress would have been prevented had the authorities known about it. It was really something for all those women to manage to get together for a day in secrecy during a state of emergency.

Inkatha

Once you are involved in politics, the most difficult thing is to go for hang [be sentenced to death]. That is how we look at it. We can't cry over what has happened to us because other people suffer lots more than we suffer: for instance, people in the townships are being much more persecuted. If it's not the police persecuting them, then it's Inkatha [a Zulu movement headed by Chief Gatsha Buthelezi]. So until you are killed, you can't say that you have really suffered.

Inkatha is being portrayed as a liberation movement, but the basic question is, What has it done for the liberation of the black people? As I see it, it spends most of its time criticizing other people and destroying organizations that are involved in the struggle and, in so doing, it is supporting the state. The least they could do is to leave us alone and do whatever they want to do. Lots of countries have had different liberation movements. We've got PAC and ANC in this country, but they have never killed each other.

What Inkatha has done to a lot of our people is gruesome: the murders and the burning of houses, for instance. And they get away with it. They are not even charged. Buthelezi can say that UDF also perpetuates the violence or that these people are defending themselves, but he can't prove a single case in court. The fact is that all the people who have been convicted of murder have been Inkatha people.

The UDF does not go out and mass-kill or destroy grassroots community organizations that are fighting for their rights. I know of Inkatha's responsibility in such incidents, like in Hambanati [an African township in the Durban area], for example, where people who formed themselves into a residents' organization to fight for decent housing, education, and transport in a peaceful manner were destroyed by Inkatha. They drove the people out of Hambanati.

In all these years that Inkatha has been in existence, when has it ever fought for any rights for the people? When has it made wage agreements for its workers? When has it fought for better transport or better housing for the community? The answer is never. I see Buthelezi as a dictator.

10
Co-President of the United Democratic Front

"Women are the people who are going to relieve us from all this oppression and depression. The rent boycott that is happening in Soweto now is alive because of the women. It is the women who are on the street committees educating the people to stand up and protect each other."

NONTSIKELELO
ALBERTINA SISULU

*O*N ARRIVING *in Johannesburg with only ten days at hand, my first priority was to try to make appointments with Nontsikelelo Albertina Sisulu (known by her middle and last name; also often referred to as Mama Sisulu) and Winnie Mandela. Although I had no wish in this book to focus solely on the leaders in the anti-apartheid movement, I wanted to include these two women, if at all possible. While Mandela is more widely known outside South Africa, many people regard Sisulu as the most important woman leader in the country because of her role in the organized anti-apartheid movement. Her most significant leadership role at present is as co-president of the United Democratic Front, the largest and most important anti-apartheid organization within the country. In addition, Sisulu's entire life over the last forty years has been enmeshed in the liberation struggle, as she recounts in her interview.*

Like Winnie Mandela, Sisulu's fame, persecution by the state, and opportunities for leadership have all been greatly affected by the status of her husband, Walter Sisulu, who, after Nelson Mandela, is the best-known ANC leader in South Africa. Walter Sisulu became the secretary-general of the ANC in 1949 and was imprisoned eight times between 1953 and 1964. In 1964, he was sentenced to life imprisonment for treason with his friend and colleague Nelson Mandela. Now, still serving his time in prison, he has become a heroic legend second only to Nelson Mandela himself.

I interviewed Albertina Sisulu, an African mother and grand-mother, in the office of her lawyer, Priscilla Jana, a well-known defender of anti-apartheid activists. Despite having a cold, the sixty-nine-year-old Sisulu had come all the way from her Soweto home for the interview. Unfortunately my time with her was limited to just over an hour, far too brief to interview this woman whose political life spans over four decades. One of Sisulu's many experiences that we did not cover was her indictment in 1985 for high treason, along with fifteen others, all members of five organizations: UDF, the Release Mandela Committee, the Transvaal Indian Congress, the Natal Indian Congress, and the South African Allied Workers' Union. The state attempted to prove that they "were part of a revolutionary plot and that treason had taken place without violence" (Gastrow 1987).

Co-President of the United Democratic Front

Later that year, the charges against twelve of the sixteen accused were dropped.

Frequently, when I asked people who didn't want to admit that sexism is a problem in the anti-apartheid movement why it has so few recognized women leaders, they cited the names of Winnie Mandela and Albertina Sisulu. When I asked Sisulu whether she thought that sexism holds women back, she replied emphatically, "No! In fact, that is what has made women stand up and play their role." When I mentioned that there aren't many women leaders in UDF, she countered that there are many women leaders in UDF-affiliated groups like the new Women's Congress that had just been launched (about which Ramgobin spoke in the last chapter). "And," she added, "we have classes that are preparing women leaders, so a lot of them will emerge in the future."

In 1988, a year after my interview, I learned from the newspapers that the government had banned the UDF and restricted Sisulu once again. I found her a surprisingly low-key, modest, warm, and gracious woman, and was very touched when she thanked me at the end of the interview for the work I was doing.

Growing Up African

I was born in the district of Tsomo in the Transkei. I was the second eldest in a large family, but never had a normal family life. I think that is why I've been able to stand the strain I've had to live with all these years. My mother died when I was fifteen, so I grew up as an orphan. I had to leave school to nurse my young six-month-old sister because my grandparents were too old to do this, so for this reason I missed at least two years of school. My hope when I got married was that this time I'd have a normal family life with my children and my husband around me, but unfortunately history has repeated itself.

I was lucky that my grandparents on my mother's side were able to see me through with my education. When I was in standard six [eighth grade], the top students who did the examination that year in the district of Tsomo were given an aptitude test, and I came second. But I was older than many of the other students at school because of missing those two years after my mother died, so I was already sixteen when I passed my standard six. Some jealous people said that I only came second because of my age, so my bursary was taken away and given to the person who came third.

A Roman Catholic priest read about what happened in the local paper and went to my grandparents to ask them if they would pay to educate me. He told them that when I was through with my education I could refund them. Although they were old and helpless, they agreed to do this. That is how I managed to go to a boarding school. After that, they decided that I should take up nursing to help support my brothers and sisters. I managed to pay my grandparents back the money for my school fees within a year, and after that I helped take care of my four younger brothers and sisters. I had to do this because my grandparents were very old. Although they had sheep and earned money from the wool, it wasn't much for their whole family as well as our family.

I had wanted to be a teacher, but unfortunately it would have meant more years at school than was needed for nursing. I wanted to build a home for my brothers and sisters because we never had a home of our own. I wanted them to be comfortable and to get an education. I had also wanted to be a Roman Catholic nun. At that time I thought I wouldn't get married and have children. Once I was through with taking care of my brothers and sisters, I'd look after other people who needed help. But I wasn't accepted by the church. They said, "Look, if you are a nun you must be entirely for the church. You can't have anything to do with your family." So I had to take up nursing, but still I vowed that I would never get married until I had seen my brothers and sisters through.

Because I grew up in a rural area where I rarely saw a white face and I had nothing whatever to do with the government, I thought we were independent. Our grandfathers had cattle and sheep and fields to plow, so I wasn't disturbed about the political situation when I was growing up. I only started seeing the unfairness when I trained for nursing at the Johannesburg General Hospital. There was a white hospital and a black hospital. Ours was called the Non-European Hospital and the white hospital was called the Johannesburg Hospital. Even when I was the most senior in my ward, when the sister in charge left, she would fetch a junior nurse from the European section to be in charge although she didn't know how it was run.

Because of apartheid I have never had a normal family life. My husband has always been in and out of jail. Also, I have been in jail, and my children have been in jail and in exile. For a mother, this is very painful. Sometimes I couldn't even nurse my children when they were ill. At other times I didn't know where they were. Bringing up my children alone because of my husband's life imprisonment has been very difficult. There are six in my family who couldn't even bury me if I should die today. Aside from my husband's life imprisonment, two of my children are in exile—the first-born, Max, and the fourth-born, Lindiwe. The youngest, Zwelakhe, is in jail. My seventeen-year-old grandson who was born of my first son, Max, was arrested in November 1986, and he is also still in jail. And my adopted son, Jogomsi, is serving five years on Robben Island.

Political Activity

I accompanied my fiancé, Walter [Sisulu], to meetings and listened to the young men discussing the conditions under which we were living. I was the only lady there, but I was very impressed because what they said reminded me exactly of what was happening in the hospital where I worked. The meetings were only open to men at the beginning. At that time the ANC was an organization of old people who discussed the situation but didn't do anything, so the youth decided to put new blood into it by starting the Youth League. They eventually allowed women to join.

So when I married Walter in 1944, I was already in politics. After my marriage I joined the ANC's Women's League. Lillian Ngoyi was instrumental in forming this league to discuss women's problems. Men really don't know much about the home and things like that. We tried to understand the conditions that directly affect women, such as children and salaries, because in most cases women are the hardest hit. For example, they don't get maternity grants. It doesn't matter how many years they have been working in a factory, when they become pregnant they have to resign their jobs in most cases, and when they return to work they have to start at the bottom again. We were worried about the education of our children, and the cost of living was skyrocketing. This affected women in particular because we're the ones who have to feed the family.

Unfortunately, although I wanted to participate in the Defiance Campaign in 1952, I couldn't because my husband was involved. We had small children at the time, and the ruling of the ANC was that only one parent could participate. Walter led the first batch [of passive resisters], and they were arrested in Boksburg for breaking the permit laws. By law, they were not supposed to enter the township without a permit and without being accompanied by a policeman. Lillian Ngoyi defied the law at post offices where we had our own entrance and whites had theirs. She went into the white section where black women were not allowed. Because I wasn't able to participate directly in the campaign, I helped feed the families of the people in jail.

I missed my husband as part of the family and a father for the children. Time and again they would ask me, "Where is Daddy? When is he coming back?" Although I was allowed to go and see him in jail, they were not. That really affected them. But for myself, I understood why he was in jail and wasn't worried because, as I said, I also wanted to protest.

But the years that followed the Defiance Campaign were hard, I must say. Financially, my salary was very low—seventy-two rand [$36] a month to support a family of seven children. I had five children of my own, and I had two of my deceased sister-in-law's children. I had to borrow money to manage, which I found very difficult.

Then in 1954 we formed the Federation of South African Women. Not every woman was interested in joining the ANC—in fact, some women were afraid of it—so we wanted an organization that would involve all women—churchwomen, trade-union women, and so on. I was one of the founders of this organization. Ida Mdwana was our first president, followed by Lillian Ngoyi in the Transvaal; then I became president when Lillian Ngoyi died.

My first arrest was in 1958 when the Federation of Women protested against the introduction of passes for women. We went to the pass office with duplicate passes, which we'd tear up; then we'd drive the women out of the pass office. I led the second batch of women there. We were arrested and awaited trial in jail for three weeks. Fortunately my mother-in-law was still alive, so I left my little ten-month-old girl with her. But I had been breast-feeding her, and I became sick in jail because my breasts were so engorged. Winnie [Mandela] nearly lost her first baby in jail. She would have lost her had we nurses not been there to demand that she be treated in the hospital. Nelson Mandela was our lawyer, and we were fortunately discharged in the fourth week.

Jail conditions were terrible for the nonpolitical prisoners who were already there. They were made to kneel and scrub a very long passage in the prison while an old white lady with a cane whipped them. I don't know whether she thought they were loafing or what. Also, immediately when they were through with the food on their plates, each and every one of them would be sjamboked. I remember the noise of the whip. It made us angry and nervous, so we protested saying, "Look, these people are punished enough. They shouldn't be assaulted as well." So the sjamboking was stopped after that.

The next time I was in jail was in 1963, when I was detained for three months in solitary confinement under the Suppression of Communism Act. That was one of the worst experiences I ever had. I would sit there on a thin mat on the cement floor. It was cold, the blankets were dirty with lice, and the food was only half cooked. Oh, it was terrible! A Special Branch policeman came to question me. In those days we were told by the movement not to answer any questions. They asked a lot of questions about my husband and the activities of others who had been members of the ANC and about the organization itself. I didn't answer them, so this policeman said to me, "We know you are told not to answer questions, but if you don't, you will die in this cell or you'll sit here for the rest of your life." To torture me to try to get me to talk they told me, "Your children have been removed from your house by the government." After ninety days [the legal limit for detention without trial at that time], they released me.

I was banned in 1964. The first five years of my banning order restricted me from meeting with more than five people at a time in my house. I couldn't leave the district of Johannesburg without informing the chief magistrate of Johannesburg, and so on. When that banning order expired, I was put under ten years of continuous house arrest. This was the worst experience. I had to be in my home from 6 P.M. to 6 A.M. the following day without leaving the house. I had to report to the police station once a week. I could not receive any visitors, and I could not be seen near any courts or in any educational centers. That hit me hard because my children were in school. I couldn't consult with the teachers when something was wrong with one of them. If a child was late with school fees, I had to ask friends to go and explain and ask for an extension from the teachers for me.

Another very frustrating thing about house arrest was the isolation. I think the government thought they would succeed in forcing me out of work by house-arresting me. I was told by the city department that because my case was still in question, I must stay away from work until they called me back. When they tried that, I applied to my nursing association for help. They sent a hot letter saying, "Look, no court of law has convicted her of anything. Detention is not her fault, and according to our records we have no case against her. If the city health department of Johannesburg and the government feels that she must stay away from work, then you must continue to pay her salary monthly until she is finished with house arrest." So the following week I was called back to work. I had been away for two weeks in all, but I never had to leave my job after that. The nursing association and lawyers did not permit it.

In 1981, Rose Mbele died and I was one of the speakers at her funeral. I was asked by the women to give her life story because she had been my patient. A green, black, and yellow flag [the colors of the ANC flag] was flying at the funeral. The authorities said that I was responsible for it being there. So I was arrested for furthering the aims of a banned organization, the ANC. In my speech I didn't say anything against the government, and I didn't have anything to do with an ANC flag. What the judge said when he summed up his case against me was so amazing. He said, "You allowed yourself to be used by the ANC by allowing yourself to be introduced to the public as Mrs. Walter Sisulu, the people's secretary." You see, my husband had been the general secretary of the ANC before it was banned in 1960. "That was another way of introducing the ANC to the people," he [the judge] said, "and showing that the ANC is still alive." He also said that "we want to scare others and stop them from doing these things." Can you imagine a magistrate saying this when he sums up his case? I got four years in prison for this, and spent seven months in solitary confinement before any charges had even been made. I came out in February 1984.

I was detained again in 1985, and held in solitary, this time for nine months. I was one of several UDF people to be put on trial. In the end, we were all acquitted [in 1986].

To visit my husband, I had to first get permission from Robben Island. Then I had to take this permission to the chief magistrate of Johannesburg for approval. This took time. Sometimes I would receive my permit just two days before the date given me by Robben Island for my visit. But my train journey alone took two and a half days, so I'd have to cancel my visit. When I managed to get permission in time, I had to report to the local police station with a permit telling them when I was leaving Johannesburg and arriving in Cape Town. Then at every stop on the way to Cape Town, a policeman came looking for me, and there was also a policeman in the next-door compartment.

When I got to Cape Town, I had to report to Caledon Square Police Station that I had arrived and where I would stay and the time I would be visiting Robben Island. The strain of being watched and constantly having to report to the police stations was terrible. Sometimes I missed my train coming back home because the police at Caledon Square would take their time to attend to me. This is how it was for ten years whenever I visited my husband. Because I was also working full-time, I would only be able to see him twice or three times a year.

The United Democratic Front

In 1983, I became the Transvaal president of the UDF. I was elected in absentia while I was in jail. Although I was in solitary confinement, I was allowed newspapers, and I read about it in the paper. Before UDF, everybody was standing on their own. It was formed to unite the people and give them a direction, and it worked wonderfully. Now when we have boycotts, we speak with one voice. Even more than unity, people needed to understand who the enemy is. For example, the government says the ANC is a terrorist organization. We explain to people that the real terrorist is the government. Take the case of Sharpeville in 1960, when the government bulldozed the people down with bullets. Women were lying dead in that open square with their babies on their backs. And when the government decided in 1985 to send soldiers into our townships, they killed the children mercilessly. Children would be playing in the playgrounds, and the soldiers would tell them to disperse. When the children were running in all directions, they were shot in their backs like wild animals.

Women in the Struggle

A woman is a mother, and women are the people who are suffering most. Look at the forced removals. People are put in the open veld [countryside] where there is no water, where there is no transport to get to the nearest town. Who is suffering? The mother. Because she looks at her children who are thirsty and crying, "Mama, we want water." If the government continues killing children, the women will become even more angry, and these are the people who will take up the struggle. The government has killed our children mercilessly since 1976 [in Soweto], which has left an unhealing sore in our hearts.

I have been talking to people in the white suburbs. Some of them don't know what is happening in our townships. Some white women shake their heads and whisper to each other, "Is she telling the truth?" My approach to the white sisters is, "Our children are dying in the townships, killed by your children. You are mothers. Why do you allow your children to go to train for the army? There is no country that has declared war on South Africa. Do you want your children to come and kill our children?" Because that is what is happening. We want to know from our white sisters why there is not a word from them about this. Our children are being killed mercilessly, but what do they say? How can they, as mothers, tolerate this? Why don't they support us?

11
The End Conscription Campaign

"Conscription is one area where whites actually *do* pay a price for apartheid and where they are prepared to organize around it. We, as well as a lot of other white anti-apartheid organizations, often get saluted by black organizations for the work we are doing."

PAULA HATHORN

*P*AULA HATHORN, a white woman, graduated from the University of Cape Town with an honors degree in linguistics in 1986.
Twenty-five years old when I interviewed her, she is single and works
full-time in the Lodgings Bureau at UCT, a bureaucratic job in the
administration. Hathorn worked in a conscientious objectors' support
group in 1983, and was also elected to the Student Representative
Council at the university, where she became the representative for the
End Conscription Campaign. Then in November 1986 she became the
chairperson of ECC in Cape Town. Hathorn had been moved to work
on the conscription issue when her brother, Peter, became a conscientious objector.

Peter was the first man to refuse army service on political grounds
alone, without any religious reason. He spent a year in prison as a
result. He now works for ECC in Port Elizabeth. I met him and his
woman friend, Barbara, quite by chance at a small dinner party when
I visited that city. They told me that one night when Peter was out of
town, Barbara was attacked and beaten with sjamboks by four men
wearing balaclavas [hoods that conceal all but the eyes] in an attempt
to intimidate Peter.

Every white South African male has to register at the age of sixteen
for the South African Defense Force and, soon afterward, do two years
of army service. In her interview, Hathorn describes conscription and
army life, and told me that the membership of ECC is all white
because only white men are conscripted. But the fact that only men
are conscripted does not mean that ECC is an all-male movement;
indeed, Hathorn mentioned that there are probably more women than
men involved in it.

Although ECC was launched in 1983, and is therefore only a few
years old, it has had a significant impact on the white community;
consequently, its members are severely persecuted. In 1988, approximately a year after my interview with Hathorn, ECC was banned by
the government.

Here Hathorn describes her involvement in student politics at UCT
and her experiences of arrest and detention for demonstrating with
other students and for her ECC work. I interviewed her at my
mother's house in Cape Town. Hathorn is a very soft-spoken, modest

young woman whose style belies her strength, determination, and commitment to the anti-apartheid movement.

Growing Up White

I was brought up in a middle-class Natal family, the youngest of five children and the most spoiled, they say. When I look back, I'm really quite shocked at the isolation of my childhood. I was terribly protected. I went to private boarding school, and I remember learning about the Nazis and Hitler and thinking it must be a very good feeling if you are able to be involved in opposing something as bad as that. I felt that I wouldn't have my chance to do something as worthwhile as that because Nazi Germany was over. I had no idea then that the situation here was very bad. It was coming to university when I was seventeen that first started to open my eyes. It gave me access to alternative literature, hearing black speakers and meeting black students.

I confronted a lot of feminist issues before I got actively involved politically. I was living in residence at UCT where sexist stereotypes are very prevalent. I spent a lot of time talking about this with a small group of friends. I think South Africa is a *very* sexist society, and it was quite a revolutionary personal experience to work through some of the effects this has had on me, on the level of shaving legs and things like that. It was really important for me. I needed some understanding of who I was and where I came from. It gave me a lot more confidence and made me feel a lot better about myself. It gave me the courage to get involved. I haven't been involved in any feminist groups since I left the campus, which is a lack, but I have a full-time job and I'm chair of ECC in the Cape so I don't have time to belong to any other groups.

Brother's Trial and Imprisonment

Perhaps for me the most pivotal event—not in my becoming politically conscious, but in making me politically *active*—was when my brother spent a year in jail because he refused to go into the army for political reasons. The rest of our family in Natal didn't understand what he was doing. I was the only family member with him here in Cape Town, and I completely supported his stand. When he went to jail, I did a lot of support work for him. This made me realize that I had to really *do* something about the situation here.

Peter's statement at his trial focused on the fact that we are fighting a civil war in this country. At that time troops hadn't yet gone to the townships, so the sense of it being a civil conflict was quite difficult for people to realize. But Peter pointed out that the purpose of the South African Defense Force was to defend a minority government, and that some of the people they were fighting on our borders—like in Namibia —were young black South Africans who had left the country in 1976 after the Soweto uprising. He spoke about destabilization and how the South Africa Defense Force has gone into neighboring states quite regularly, without provocation, and killed civilians supposedly to root out ANC people in those countries. This has happened in Zambia, Lesotho, Zimbabwe, and Mozambique.

Peter faced a maximum of two years in prison for his stand, but only served one year beginning in early 1983.

The Formation of the End Conscription Campaign

Nineteen eighty-three was the year in which the sentence for conscientious objectors changed. Alternative service was introduced for religious pacifists, while the sentence for people who objected to serving in the army on moral or political grounds was increased to six years. This, in conjunction with the fact that in March 1983 the Black Sash called for an end to conscription at their annual conference, led to the formation of ECC. Previously, anti-militarization work had focused on individual conscientious objectors, but with such a severe sentence, we didn't know whether people would continue to object. In July of that year, the conscientious objectors' support groups in Johannesburg, Durban, and other parts of Natal got together for an annual conference. They decided to try to set up End Conscription Committees in each of those centers; and by the end of 1983 or early 1984, these committees were set up.

ECC focuses its efforts on the white community because white men are the ones who are conscripted into the South African Defense Force. Our issue defines our constituency. In Cape Town there are fourteen organizations that come together to form ECC and to call for an end to conscription. While those organizations all have their own programs, they also take up our issues. But ECC also has its own subcommittees made up of ECC people.

Although there are probably more women than men involved in ECC, it's not a huge imbalance. It's a bit more dangerous for men to get involved because they need to lie low if they're wanting to get out of their call-ups. I've spoken to a lot of men who've said, "I really appreciate the work you're doing in ECC, but it's too risky for me." White women are a bit more secure. The majority of our members are English-speaking South Africans, though we now have branches in the Afrikaner communities of Stellenbosch and Pretoria. Our Stellenbosch University branch has really struggled. The university administration banned them before they were even launched, so they've had a really difficult time. We're hoping to be able to make more inroads into the Afrikaner communities.

Conscription and Army Life in South Africa

Young white men spend the first few months of their two years of army service at basic training. Training involves a lot of political lectures about who the enemy is, the left, the ECC, the ANC. It's a lot of propaganda. Then these young men are sent to Namibia or into the [black] townships or used in whatever way the army wants. After those two years, they are due to do another two years, but this time it is split up into 90-, 60-, or 30-day stretches. They have to leave their jobs or whatever they are doing and go off to army camps. Some of them get called up to do these camps every single year.

After completing these camps, men can be called up for ten to twelve days of active duty every year until the age of fifty-five. After that, a man can no longer be called up. Camps for men in their middle-age years are referred to as Dad's Army. In the eastern Cape, the Dad's Army has been used to man roadblocks and to look after the searchlights that scan the townships. It involves playing a support role for regular army work.

Being in the army for two years has an incredible effect on men. It destroys a lot of them. It destroys their relationships, and it destroys their families. I've seen this happen and know people who have known men it's happened to. A lot of men go into the army feeling that they have no choice, and they spend two years in conflict about having to be prepared to kill and die for a system that they don't believe in.

But much more often I see men who have decided they're *not* going to go into the army and who realize they're either going to have to leave their country or they're going to have to live underground. These men often become very insecure. Most of the men I know don't know what their future holds. They're living from year to year. For example, if they've reached the fourth year of doing a master's degree—because academic work can get deferment from the army up to a point—they wonder if they will get a deferment. There are weeks of crisis while men wait to find out if they've been lucky or not. If they don't get deferment, they'll have crucial decisions and arrangements to make in a very short period of time. I see how freaked out they get and how unstable their lives are.

The effect of conscription on me is knowing that I'm not going to have most of my close male friends around very much longer. They'll have to disappear. Quite a lot of these men leave the country, but this, too, isn't easy. People often wind up going to places that they don't want to go to.

In 1986, [Minister of Defence General Magnus] Malan said in Parliament that eight thousand five hundred people had failed to report that year for the basic two-year military training. That is eight thousand five hundred out of the thirty thousand who are generally called up in one year. That's a hell of a lot of people. There is some confusion as to whether that figure includes people who were at university and who were deferred on that basis. The government wouldn't release comparable figures in Parliament at the beginning of this year, because they said they had been misused by certain organizations. Statistics are getting very difficult to obtain because the government refuses to release any that might be damaging to it. The conclusion we draw from this is that a lot of men aren't reporting for service.

The resistance to conscription has become much bigger than the numbers involved in ECC itself. I think there are vast numbers of young men drifting around the country keeping their addresses quiet. These include men who aren't politically involved in any organizations but who don't want to go into the townships where the South African Defense Forces have been since 1984. The wool can't be pulled over people's eyes any more. If they go into the townships, they know who their guns will be aimed at. No one can pretend that there's no civil conflict in this country any more, contrary to the propaganda we used to get fed that the South African Defense Force was fighting the war on our borders against the Russian onslaught.

Student Political Activity

I was at UCT at a time when the campus was very militant. There were a lot of marches and demonstrations. In February 1985, I woke up at 2 A.M. to my housemate turning on the light of my room and saying,

"Paula, the police are here. They've come to detain us." The next minute a burly policeman shoved him out of the way and said, "We are here to detain you under blah blah blah," and read out some law. I was terrified out of my wits. He said I was to put my clothes on and come into the passage. I did so only to find, to my delight, that the rest of my housemates were also being arrested. The police had identified us from the photographs that they had taken from the bushes opposite our demonstration.

We were dragged off to the police station where the police spent a couple of hours recording information about us, then shoved us into a cell. There were only six of us at that stage, until the police drove around and picked up eight more. We were charged with participating in an illegal gathering. It's illegal under the Internal Security Act for more than three people to gather out of doors with a common purpose, unless it's a bona-fide sports or religious gathering. We were kept in the cell overnight, then appeared in court the next morning and were released on bail. The charges against us were dropped after quite a long time.

Although political demonstrations are illegal, people defy this law all the time, but they pay the price. After the Pollsmoor march at the end of 1985, the goal of which was to call for the release of Nelson Mandela, half of Cape Town was on trial for participating in an illegal gathering. There was a whole spate of marches and demonstrations at that time. Nuns and priests and academics and everybody else who had participated in the march was picked up and charged.

A week or so before the Pollsmoor march, we at UCT decided to march to the state president's home in Cape Town. About two thousand to three thousand students came to the bottom of a small road in a residential area and found a casspir parked across the road. We took another route but soon found ourselves facing a line of policemen in riot gear, which was terrifying to me. One person told us to disperse on a walkie-talkie, but nobody heard. The next minute, our march leaders told us to sit down.

The policemen then came and belted people with sjamboks, which was also absolutely terrifying. Unlike black South Africans living in townships, I'd never been exposed to such aggression before. I was part of a group of mostly women who were trapped, which is why we were eventually arrested. There were people running in all directions and screaming in fear. A friend of mine was lying next to me on the pavement, and she looked up at a policeman and said, "Please don't hit me. Please don't hit me." I could see the look of hate and aggression in this guy's eyes as he sjamboked her on the head.

The whole experience was very scary. I told black students on campus afterwards that I had been so absolutely terrified that I almost felt ashamed. They said that the police had been gentle with us compared to what they're like in the townships where they normally trample all over people. Nevertheless one person who had been sjamboked had to have an operation on his eye. Somebody else who was arrested with us was bruised all over. These two people sued the police, and I think it was settled out of court. They were paid quite a lot of money. The rest of us had to spend hours in court, and we won the case on a technicality.

This experience was a turning point for me in many ways. It didn't change my thinking; it was more an experiential change. It gave me a very important, day-to-day sense of what being a South African anti-apartheid activist entails. It was the start of all sorts of demonstrations and confrontations on campus. A couple of weeks later, there were casspirs on campus for the first time. By the end of 1985, the whole western Cape was alive with these kinds of confrontations happening daily. It made the struggle real. It made the fear real. And it made the hate real. It made me understand why people are violent.

What the police did was disgusting and unforgivable. We were so vulnerable, and they just tramped over us. It almost seems arrogant to say that I understood so much after one experience, which is so little compared to what somebody in the townships goes through, but it gave me that additional inch of insight, which was very important to me. Our lawyers found it interesting that most of the arrested students were women. At one stage they even wondered if the police intentionally picked out innocent-looking white women to drag off, but I think it was probably just chance. Our lawyers warned us to be cautious about getting arrested again. At that time I was on trial for the first time and I had been arrested for the second time, so I avoided other demonstrations after that. This experience has made me very scared, but the fear won't stop me from being part of demonstrations in the future. I'll just be far more nervous about it.

The ECC's Response to Repressive Legislation

The emergency regulations of 12 June 1986 made it subversive to incite anybody to undermine or discredit the system of compulsory military conscription. This obviously curtails ECC's work. We immediately stopped all public work for a month or so to consult with all the other ECC branches in the country and to get proper legal advice on the implications of this regulation for us, because ECC considers it important to work within the law. Our lawyers said that there was a lot of related work that ECC could still do. For example, we could oppose militarization in general or cadets in the schools, so we cautiously started doing some public work again.

We had a Give-ECC-the-Right-to-Speak Campaign in about August of 1986, which went fine. Next we decided we needed an offensive campaign, so we organized a War-Is-No-Solution Campaign. It was a campaign that focused on apartheid but which was directed at the white community. Noting the kind of war the South African Defense Force is involved in, we argued that war is no solution. We had a lovely picnic, and we planned to walk from Rondebosch [a white suburb] to Guguletu [an African township]. We distributed a lot of pamphlets and had a meeting in the city hall.

We've done quite a few actions that involve the public. For example, we organized a fast in connection with our call for the troops to come out of the townships and for a just peace in our land. One of our members, a man called Ivan Toms, fasted in a crypt at a cathedral for three weeks. A lot of people went to see him, and we called on everybody to fast for one day, which gave them an opportunity to get involved.

Last year we ran a national campaign called Working-for-a-Just-Peace: Construction-Not-Conscription. We distributed pamphlets inviting people to be a part of a whole range of projects that we felt would provide examples of a type of national service that would benefit the nation, rather than being conscripted into the South African Defense Force. For example, we built a concrete cycle track at a school on the Cape Flats [a black area near Cape Town], and we cleared the ground at a home for underprivileged children. Also on the Cape Flats, we cleared the garden and painted a mural at Cowley House, where people stay when they visit family members on Robben Island or at Pollsmoor Prison. About five hundred Capetonians participated in different projects, and it was great to give people an opportunity to feel they were able to do something constructive, because a lot of people get frustrated not knowing what they can do. In Port Elizabeth, the ECC and the public helped to build a crèche in one township.

We do other kinds of activities that are symbolic and fun and that hit the press. On ECC's birthday last year, we decided to make a big castle on the beach out of sand. We built it in the shape of a castle that represented the defense force headquarters in Cape Town. The police ordered us to destroy it, and there was a public outcry at their actions.

And we've done fun runs where we all put on our ECC shirts and jog along the beach front. These creative actions are very good for us as an organization. They're very bonding, and they also interest people on the beach, and they have a publicity value as well. We've also brought out a record called "Force's Favorites," which is the name of a radio program played by the South African Broadcasting Corporation to South African soldiers on the border. We've often used concerts and drama and all sorts of other means to get our message across.

Detention

On 3 December 1986, they detained nine of us for two weeks, then charged and released us. Again, our charges have been dropped. But thinking for two weeks that we might be there for a few months is very different from being in jail for a night. We had to try to prepare ourselves for whatever happened.

We're not sure how they picked us. We had all been actively involved in ECC at some time, though some weren't actually involved in the War-Is-No-Solution Campaign. The security police get to know you when you put up posters. Even if you have permission to do this, they take down your name and address which, by law, you have to give them. We know that the security police also keep tabs on us by listening to our telephone conversations and coming to ECC meetings. All of those detained were white, and three of us were women.

From the time that we were in Pollsmoor Prison, we were aware that we were treated very differently from black detainees. We never felt under any threat of torture or physical violence against us. We all had beds with blankets and sheets. We were able to spend twenty rand [$10] each week for food the prison wardens bought for us from a local supermarket. We got a lot of the things we asked for. It was a comfortable detention in many ways. At times we felt guilty about this. Although we didn't deserve to be in prison in the first place, it was terrible that black people are treated so much worse than us—even in prison— because of their skin color.

The biggest thing about detention is the isolation and boredom. There were three of us in a very small space without much to do. The hours passed very slowly. We were exhausted because we had been working on the campaign at absolute fever pitch, so we slept a lot. We gave ourselves seminars. We did quite a bit of exercise. But it was boring to be isolated from the rest of the world for two weeks. Unlike us, the men who were detained when we were had some contact with other prisoners. The radio was played into our cells so we heard the news, but there's never very much news on the radio. Very important things could be happening in the world, and we wouldn't know about it. We got hungry for real news and frustrated to be totally cut off from it.

Because I assume I will be detained for much longer than two weeks at some time in the future, I felt my detention was a useful learning experience. I didn't have to make decisions in detention. I could use all my resources to cope with being there because I didn't have to cope with much else. The day after I came out, I found myself baffled by the number of things I was expected to do in a day. For example, I had to buy food at the supermarket for thirty people, and I thought, "I don't know how to do this! I don't know how *anybody* does it!" I imagine those who've been in for a long time come out feeling very ill-equipped to cope with such a demanding world, and relating to people again must be difficult.

The thought of being detained for a longer time in the future scares me at times. We prepare ourselves for this by attending security workshops, where we hear about other people's experiences of detention. We study the laws and find out what you must ask for in detention. I think all anti-apartheid organizations in South Africa go through a similar process. Confining ourselves to activity that is legal doesn't mean that we won't have to pay for it. All of us who are involved politically take it for granted that we're going to have to go through a much harder and longer detention than my two-week experience.

The ECC as a White Organization

Civil disobedience is something we're discussing at the moment, but although ECC might engage in it, we try to do work that is legal. Our work is aimed at a white constituency, and the white community finds it difficult to accept illegal, underground-type work. With underground work we'd risk cutting ourselves off from the people that we are targeting for our political work. We also think it is very important that people see who we are and what we are doing, and that people who are interested in our work can join us. I'm not saying that illegal organizations don't have a role, but I think it's very important that ECC remains a legal organization at this stage.

There is a danger, particularly if you're a white activist, of committing suicide politically by cutting yourself off from your own community. Even though our campaign is directed at the white community, if there were only about fifty individuals in ECC it would be easy to go off on a tangent. But since a whole range of organizations are involved, our campaigns are appropriate and directed to reach our community.

We can't hope to convince every white South African to agree with our point of view, but we try to draw a substantial number of them behind us and to pull them into working for change in some way. For whites it's such a big jump to support organizations like UDF. They have to give up and change so much, and many of them aren't going to be able to make that big a leap. But ECC is an issue that affects all white South Africans, and we work in a style that is suitable for them. We try to use symbols that potentially liberal white South Africans can relate to.

Black men aren't conscripted so there's not much point in blacks being part of ECC, but we receive a lot of support from the black community. At one stage we had a strong call for "Troops Out of the Townships," a call which was also taken up by the black community. It served as a very good bridge between the work that our two communities do and showed how our struggles fit together. We are not a member organization of the UDF, but we have regular discussions with them about what we are doing, and we try and keep in contact with some of the black organizations.

Women in the Struggle

White women in South Africa have pretty much been relegated to the role of looking after men and providing a home for them. The situation of black women is much worse. They live with extreme sexism, and on top of that, suffer other forms of oppression. But I have a fair amount of faith that women won't sit back and allow South Africa to become a totally male-dominated new society. The women in South Africa have shown that they are strong, and I think they will make their voices heard.

PART III

SOUTH AFRICA'S BLACK GOLD: TRADE-UNION WOMEN FIGHT FOR WORKERS' RIGHTS

"I don't think the workers' struggle can be divorced from the community's struggle because the workers become community at the end of the day."

—LYDIA KOMPE

T HE TRADE UNIONS have grown dramatically over the past decade in number of members, rights won, and political power—a success story revealed in all three of the following interviews with Florence de Villiers, Emma Mashinini, and Lydia Kompe. Mashinini was one of several women to articulate the view that "the trade-union movement is the most important part of the struggle in South Africa." After all, she explained, "our political organizations are banned or in exile, so who else is there?" Even my hometown newspaper carried an article in 1987 written by Michael Parks, foreign correspondent for the *Los Angeles Times*, declaring, "Black workers have moved into the forefront of the fight against apartheid" (p. 1). Parks cites as evidence of both the growing politicization and strength of the black unions the two-day general strike that occurred during the whites-only parliamentary elections in May 1987. I was conducting interviews with women in the coastal city of Durban at the time, and one of them canceled because of it (she was unable to get public transport to meet with me). An estimated 1.5 million workers participated in this strike.

Frank Meintjies, a top official of the Congress of South African Trade Unions (COSATU), argues that workers are the vanguard of the anti-apartheid struggle because they "have the most muscle. Students can boycott classes for a long time, but that does not hurt the regime. Workers, when united and motivated, can take strike action that could be decisive" (Parks 1987, p. 4).* And even the South African minister of finance, Barend du Plessis, admitted in his budget address to Parliament in March 1988 that the number of strikes in 1987 had increased by 69 percent since the year before.

COSATU's increasing militancy made it the target of a damaging bomb attack on its headquarters in Johannesburg in May 1987, just a couple of days before the election. (This event is discussed by both Emma Mashinini in chapter 13 and Sheena Duncan in chapter 24.) Parks mentions that five of its regional offices have been bombed, set on fire, or burglarized since then.

Mashinini explained why it doesn't make sense for trade-unionists in South Africa "to limit our concern to the worker's rights in the workplace. That's all right in comfortable countries," she observed. "But in South Africa we've got to follow the worker out of his place of employment to see how he travels home, where he goes to, where his children go to, that there is no adequate housing or education. Everything around him is distorted."

Of the five women union organizers whom I interviewed, it is Lydia Kompe (chapter 14) who expresses the most concern about sexism in the union movement.† This is not to say that de Villiers and Mashinini did not see sexism as a problem in the trade-union movement. For example, de Villiers said, "It still is a man's world in COSATU." And Mashinini stated, "I have attended several world conventions and have seen large international trade union organizations being led by men. This concerns me. Are we South African women still going to be led by men when we get our liberation although we were oppressed together with them and fought against this oppression together?"

* Meintjies was explicit, however, in excepting those in the underground and the armed struggle from his comparison of the relative strengths of workers, students, and other anti-apartheid groups.
† Two other impressive union organizers whose interviews are not included here for lack of space are Liz Abrahams of the Food and Canning Workers' Union and Zora Mehlomakulu of the General Workers' Union.

Trade-Union Women Fight for Workers' Rights

In an interview with Kompe published elsewhere (Barrett et al., 1985), she pointed out:

> No union has yet elected a branch chairlady. Offhand, I don't know even a chairlady of the shop-stewards committee. . . . The women officials should have their own grouping to discuss the day-to-day problems that we encounter in the union. Having meetings of women is the first step. . . . We pay subs equally, we work the same shifts, we work the same jobs, we participate in the same way in the unions. I don't see why we can't have an equal say and equal rights! . . .
>
> I think it's the time for women to come together and see this thing as a major problem for us. . . . In Fosatu [the Federation of South African Trade Unions] we tried to have a women's group. But our male members felt very threatened. . . . [T]he men are still taking the lead. It will take a few years for women to move towards proper leadership in the unions. . . . These men feel threatened when we push to be equal.

No feminist will be surprised by Kompe's criticisms. But why should South Africans be expected to solve a problem before people in other countries?

12

From Domestic Worker
to Head of the
Domestic Workers' Union

"If other people have to go through it [detention], why should I be spared? I know that we won't get our freedom on a silver plate."

FLORENCE DE VILLIERS

Head of the Domestic Workers' Union

I WAS in the audience on 8 March 1987, International Women's Day, when forty-six-year-old Florence de Villiers delivered a brief but fiery speech about the need for solidarity among women. Although I had interviewed this so-called Coloured woman nine years previously, I didn't recognize her. Since people referred to her affectionately as "Auntie Florrie," her name also rang no bell for me. But mostly, I didn't recognize de Villiers because she had been transformed by her determined and successful efforts to build the Domestic Workers' Union to serve and organize the second biggest workforce in South Africa. In 1977, it was only a dream, conceived by de Villiers and Maggie Owies. Today it is a national organization with a membership of fifty thousand. "Auntie Florrie" is its general secretary, who now believes that "if it wasn't for the unions, I don't think we'd be where we are today in the anti-apartheid struggle."

This is a phenomenal and moving story of the personal and social transformation of a woman who considers herself to be the "child of slaves"; a child who was so hungry for learning that she broke the law and endured her mother's beatings to pay for her schoolbooks. Later, de Villiers became a domestic worker who rebelled against the oppressive maternalism of her employers. Finally, there was de Villiers the wife, who realized she was in prison and broke out. De Villiers is also profoundly committed to trying to improve the lot of others, particularly domestic workers, farm workers, squatters, and women. Because of the Government's attempt to force Africans out of the cities or to prevent them from migrating there, in order to make cities a little whiter in complexion, many Africans are not allowed to live there. Illegal squatter communities emerged in many of South Africa's urban areas in the 1970s and 1980s because it was impossible for many Africans to survive in the impoverished rural areas where apartheid had consigned them. When the government moved against these communities, "it found itself challenged by organised resistance in the Western Cape for the first time since the 1960s" (Cole 1987, p. 9). De Villiers participated in this struggle as a dedicated outsider, and her vivid account of her work among the squatters in Cape Town depicts both the everyday horrors of apartheid as well as her own tenacity and courage in the face of it.

Although de Villiers was forced to leave school after completing standard six (eighth grade) at the age of fourteen, she has pursued several adult education courses in her later years. Her husband, who completed standard eight (tenth grade), works in a furniture factory. Their four children are now adults. De Villiers said that she encouraged them "to go the whole way with their studies." The eldest is a teacher; the second, a radiographer; the third, a plumber; and the fourth, at eighteen, had just completed high school. She had promised herself that "my kids were not going to be slaves like my parents and I had been. I did everything possible to encourage them to stay out of trouble. And as much as I have worked and not been home, they've done well and never stayed out of school once," de Villiers said proudly.

Growing Up Coloured

I am the product of two very proud slaves who didn't want to become beggars and who worked very hard. Seventy years ago my father was taken from his home when he was about seven years old and given to a white family so he could work for them as a farm laborer until he was eighteen. He earned next to nothing for all those years. After that he was allowed to find his own way in life.

After my mother's father died in the First World War, her mother got herself another man. When my mother became a problem to him, he gave her to some white people to work for them for a pittance. Like my father, she was only about seven years old. She did domestic work on a farm until she married my father and had us. She also became a midwife, and, as illiterate as she was, she was accepted by [the midwifery authorities in] Pretoria. Before he died, my father said to me with tears in his eyes, "You know, this was not the life that I wanted for you. But the white man knew better what was good for us." I realized then that he had wanted a better life for us.

I come from a big family of nine kids, and I was squeezed into the middle as the fourth eldest. Both my parents were totally illiterate. They were wonderful parents and they taught me a lot, but to them religion was the answer to all problems. We had to get up at four o'clock in the morning to pray, and then we prayed again at night before we went to bed. We weren't allowed to go to bioscope [movies], to dance, or to play on a Sunday afternoon. It made me feel different from other kids.

I was born on the apple farm my father worked on in Elgin in the

Grabouw area. There was no school on the farms there, so my father decided to move to a fishing village where there was an Anglican school. There my father made a living by selling the vegetables he grew, the wood he cut, and the fish he caught. He was a good farmer, and I was very proud when I saw what he grew.

Often my parents didn't have the money for my schoolbooks, but I didn't want to tell the schoolteacher that I didn't have a half a crown to pay for them. My mother's only brother would go to sell wild flowers along the road on a Sunday, which was against my mother's religious principles. But I would run away to sell flowers with him because it was important to me to be able to proudly say to my teacher, "Here is the half a crown I owe you for my book." I knew I would get a hiding when I got home because I had sinned in my mother's eyes. Sundays were for church and Sunday school and that's all. It was also against the law for me to sell flowers at fourteen years of age. The people driving by felt sorry for me and preferred to buy my bunch of flowers than my uncle's. He would get mad at me and say, "If the police catch us, you'll get me into trouble." When I got home, my mother would give me the expected hiding, but it was worth it as long as I could pay for my books. But eventually I decided to respect my mother's wishes, and I'd earn the money instead by washing nappies [diapers] and looking after children. I was obsessed with the idea that I had to have money like some of the other kids.

When I was only about ten years old, I very much wanted to have a professional job when I grew up. I loved history and would sit for hours with my history books. I found my school work easy and was always amongst the first in my class. In fact, I did better than my older sister and brother at school. My principal spoke to my mother about sending me to high school, but she told him she didn't have the money. So I had to go to work after finishing standard six [eighth grade] when I was about fourteen years old. I was very sad to have to leave school.

I never wanted to be a domestic worker. I did it after I left school until I married at nineteen. Then I continued doing it on a part-time basis. I always hated it. My human dignity was removed from me completely. I was told, "Do this. Do that." I wasn't allowed to think for myself. I had to say, "Yes, yes, yes." I could never say, "No." Because I am black and my employer was white, I couldn't convince her that I had a mind of my own and that I wanted to use it. She kept telling me things that I knew. It was degrading. It made me want to do something to make these people realize that I have a mind that can develop in the same way as theirs if I am given a chance. I think that is why I got involved in organizing other domestic workers. I thought there must be many women like myself who hate the treatment I got from people. But for many years this was a painful thing I just had to live with.

I married at nineteen hoping to get out of the trap I found myself in as a domestic worker. I soon realized it wasn't all roses. My mother taught me that the husband is the head of the house, and at first I went along with this idea. When I married my mother used to say, "Now, you must always have a tray to serve your husband when he comes home." I said, "No, he can make his own coffee." She would get a fit and say, "It's not Christian. I didn't raise you like that." Because that's how she used to behave. She was a slave to my father.

There is also a tradition that if your mother or your mother-in-law had eight or ten kids, you should have the same number. I said, "No! This is my body and I have the right to say how many kids I want." My sister-in-law said to me, "But my mother had eight and your mother had nine." I said, "Having one baby after the other without having any say? Not on your life!" Then I started asking myself, "Should I allow people to use me body and soul?" And I answered no. I told my sister-in-law, "Religion or no religion, I'll leave my husband before I do that!" But my husband also didn't want more than four kids. Even that was too much for my liking. Although we loved kids, it was tough wanting to give them everything in life but having very little money.

I found I couldn't do what I wanted to do when I married. It dawned on me that I was in prison. For example, I loved doing things, and my next-door neighbor told me, "The women are getting together this afternoon at the church." I joined them, but my husband didn't like it. I realized I was actually a slave in my own home. After going to work, I'd come home and have to cook and clean all over again while my husband sat with his newspaper. And I thought, "To the devil with you! You've got to share this with me. You should wash the babies and assist me in washing and drying and cleaning the house." He didn't accept this at first. He said that I might leave him later on if I carried on in this way. Finally I told my husband that he had to either divorce me or accept me as I am. I was not turning back. But it took time before I made this stand. I knew I had to get out of this situation so on top of raising my four kids and working, I also started taking night classes in math, English, and history, which I still loved. Later I did accountancy and typing. Sometimes I wouldn't finish cleaning the house until two in the morning. But my husband did come around to sharing the housework.

Then there was an uprising and people were killed at the night school I attended, so it closed.

The Black Women's Federation

I got involved in the Black Women's Federation when it started in 1975. To protest the increase in bus fares that year, we walked with placards from the townships to our workplaces many miles away. We kept this up for more than a month, and our efforts were quite effective. The following year we had rummage sales and cake sales and collected money to give to people to visit their families in detention. Then in 1977 our organization was banned along with all the other black organizations.

Working in the Squatter Camps

I worked in a very liberal organization called the Christian Institute from 1969 until October 1977, when it was banned. I worked in their restaurant for a while. When the people there learned about my involvement in the bus boycott, they asked me what sort of work I would like to do. I told them I preferred to work in a squatter camp than in a restaurant feeding people. Theo Kotze, the head of the institute, told me I could do that, so I worked in a squatter camp called Kraaifontein for a year, beginning in 1976.

Most of the people there came from the Transkei. Just like all human beings all over the world, they wanted their families to be able to stay together. I tried to teach the women there to be proud of themselves as women, that we cannot do things unless we become aware of ourselves and our woman-power. They were very responsive, and over the next weeks I'd find a women's committee, a health committee, and a food committee when I went back, and I'd see real growth. Women are a great encouragement to men, especially in our situation in South Africa. For example, I found a man sitting behind a bush at the squatter camp, crying. I asked him, "What are you crying about?" He said, "I've just lost my job. I've been a bricklayer and look where I've landed." I said, "Hold it! Just get up. You are not going to cry. You've got a family to see to. Before the sun sets tonight, they must have shelter." I brought that man's courage back. If given the chance, women are the most powerful force under the sun.

I encouraged men as well as women not to accept their squatter situation, but to fight for justice. I would look at whatever problems they were having and try to find ways and means to bring in other people to assist me in helping them. For example, when their shanties were demolished by the government, we would get more building materials and assist them in rebuilding their homes.

I didn't shed a tear in that camp, but I learned to fight there. I came across an old man of sixty-eight who was chopping through the jawbone of a cow. It was absolutely bare, so I asked him, "What are you doing?" He said, "I might get something out of it." I thought, "Here is a man who has helped to build up this country over the years. He has been pushed into a squatter camp to wait for his dying day, and on one of his last days he has to try to get marrow out of bone on which there is no meat." Then and there I promised myself that I will always fight for what is just. I got my degree in that camp to do the work I am doing today.

A huge complex called Brackenfell Hypermarket was built near another squatter camp where people weren't even given water. The people in Brackenfell were told, "If you give water to people in the squatter camps, you will have to vacate your council dwellings." The women in the camp came to me crying, "Florrie, come and help us." I would carry in water in plastic cans from where I lived and I would go to the ministers nearby and say, "Come and assist me."

By then, the people were living in tents. All their building materials had been taken away from them in an effort to force them to go back to the Transkei. A woman with seven kids was living in a tent which we had provided. She was very ill and I was giving her pills when the police came to remove me from the camp. The police called me a terrorist and turned the car of the person who brought me into the camp upside down. The woman I had been giving the pills to died afterwards.

The police would normally demolish the squatters' homes during the heavy rains in winter. People would be crying around me so there was no time for me to cry. They needed help, and I had to get it for them. Some of them were actually living in the ground by then. Working in the squatter camps made me very determined to do everything in my power to help my people, even to give my life if necessary. I prepared my family for what might happen to me by showing them how people had to live in the camp. I said to them, "Don't shed a tear if I have to go to jail for this, because you will know what I am in there for." Eventually the entire squatter camp was demolished, and we moved the people into Crossroads [another squatter camp with an awesome record of resistance].*

* See Cole 1987 for an analysis of the making and breaking of this community.

The Domestic Workers' Union

I met a woman called Maggie Owies at the Christian Institute when I was still working at the squatter camps. She was involved in organizing recreation for domestic workers, which I found interesting. When the institute was banned in 1977, I immediately said to her, "Look I'm free now"—because the banning meant I'd automatically lost my job. "Let's start something for domestic workers," I said. But I was interested in more than their recreational needs. "I'm prepared to work with you," I said, "but I'm not prepared to assist in making better slaves of women like myself." Maggie was trying to find accommodation for herself at that time, and I said, "Look, you can come and stay with me." I had about one thousand rand [$500] saved at that time, and I suggested we try to get this thing off the ground by selling apples from my husband's brother's farm and baking bread to raise some more money. So this is how we started the Domestic Workers' Union.

Most people saw organizing a domestic workers' union as impossible. But with the help of a friend, we opened a small office in central Cape Town. All we had was a telephone in the corner on the floor. We started to talk to domestic workers on the streets and in the parks and at the shops. "Are you happy with your working and living conditions?" we asked. Some of them would invite us to their rooms. We'd ask them, "What do you want for your family? Do you have kids? Where are they? What do you want out of life? Are you happy with your life style?" Women would pour out stories about their experiences and how they so much wanted to do things that they couldn't do. And it would click with us because both Maggie and I went through the same kind of experiences.

One of the first things that I did was to teach people to read and write. We had meetings at our office on a nightly basis and at weekends. We had meetings in people's rooms, in church halls, wherever we could talk to people. We encouraged women to get involved, to become organized, to see themselves as women not as slaves. The women were very receptive because of the exploitation they had experienced.

When we got a little bit of money from overseas, I initiated our union becoming a national one. I said to the others, "Let's make do with what we can and assist the other regions." By then, we had taken courses on trade unionism. So I went to Port Elizabeth to help them start a union there, and I did the same in East London and Durban. About seventeen hundred people attended the launching of the National Domestic

Workers' Union in Cape Town on 29–30 November 1986. There were supposed to be two thousand but road blocks prevented many people from getting there. We now have a membership of fifty thousand. The head office is in Cape Town, and I've been elected general secretary. I really love this work and can't see myself anywhere else now.

We've drawn up demands for a living wage and better working conditions, nationally. If a woman wants to be a domestic worker, fine—but she mustn't be trapped in that choice. We don't want women doing domestic work when they don't want to do it. We also resolved that we would get involved politically as well as socially and economically, so we're affiliated to COSATU.

Sexual Harassment of Domestic Workers

Domestic workers are sexually harassed because some white employers think they can do whatever they want with these women because they are black. We know of endless numbers of cases where women are beaten up if they don't give in to their employers, and others are sacked [fired] and made to leave the premises immediately without pay. Sometimes it really disturbs the family life of the domestic worker as well. Some employers of husband-and-wife teams expect the husband to accept the harassment of the domestic worker as if to say, "This is my property. The job includes her working for me body and soul."

In one incident a domestic worker came to the union office crying. She said her employer came home at lunchtime and made sexual demands on her. She refused him so he told her to get off his premises immediately. Fortunately there was a white student at the house that day (he was using the servant's quarters and the worker was sleeping underneath the stairs); otherwise, the employer might have forced her. I phoned the employer and got his wife. I said to her, "This person is here and she is making a serious statement about your husband, and your husband told her to get off the premises without giving her any notice money. She said she doesn't want to make a case against you as long as you pay her." The woman was very shocked. She said absolutely nothing, but two days later the money arrived at the office by mail.

There is another case of a young twenty-year-old woman who did domestic work for a man and his son. They both had intercourse with her, and when she became pregnant she didn't know who the father was. Her whole life was messed up because of their demands and her fear of losing her job. We take such cases to a lawyer if the worker requests it. We feel strongly that this issue needs attention because it happens so often and has been going on for so long.

Harassment by the Security Police

I was detained overnight once in 1975 when I was on my way to the Black People's Convention to discuss the situation of black people in South Africa. The security police heard about it, put up a road block, and took us in. They called us terrorists and kept us overnight. Theo Kotze came to release us at about four o'clock the next morning. Some of our people had to appear in court the next day. We waited until they were released, and then we left for the convention in Pretoria, so we managed to attend it anyway.

The security police raided our union office this year [1987] for the third time. They just take what they want to, and there's nothing we can do about it. People in detention have told me that they've been questioned about me by the security police and told to give me the message that the police will get me. But I'm not afraid of detention. I've heard so much about it from other people that I will know what to expect if my turn comes.

13
Life As a
Trade-Union Leader

"That was the most horrible day of my detention. The whole day
I could see my baby's face and wanted to call her name, 'Dudu,'
'Dudu,' but my mind was blank. I couldn't recollect it. 'Can a
mother forget her baby's name?' I wondered."

EMMA MASHININI

Life As a Trade-Union Leader

*L*IKE *Florence de Villiers, the fifty-seven-year-old African Emma Mashinini also told a remarkable success story about how she started a black shop-workers' union in 1975, now called the Commercial Catering and Allied Workers' Union, and worked as its general secretary from its inception through to its emergence as the second largest union in South Africa, with a membership of seventy thousand.*

Mashinini is married and has two daughters, one of whom is married with two daughters, and the other of whom is pursuing her education in the United States. Mashinini is currently writing an autobiography called "Dudu"—the name of one of her daughters—about her life and work in the trade-union movement. She lives in Soweto and, since her retirement from the union, now works for a church group called the Department of Justice and Reconciliation.

Mashinini is an Anglican; and since my twin brother David was about to be enthroned as a newly elected Anglican bishop, my relationship to him was a definite asset in gaining access to her. She holds strong views about what the church should be doing about apartheid. Just as she believes that the trade-union movement has to embrace political issues as well as economic ones, so she argues that "the church must also face that it has to be involved in the political situation. We are extremely lucky that the highest person in our church, Desmond Tutu, speaks out about injustices. When he was elected as a bishop, and then as archbishop, some people chose to pull out of the church because they thought that he was too involved in politics. But his being political is very important to us [black people]. Priests must not just stand in their pulpits and preach about the suffering of the people. They have to do something about it. The church must follow people out of church. It will suffer if it doesn't get involved."

On 27 November 1981, Mashinini, then fifty-two years old, was detained in solitary confinement for six months along with other trade-unionists. In the interview to follow, she describes how traumatized she was by this experience. Although her spirit is not broken, she finally decided to resign from her union responsibilities a year ago in 1986—"because I was so exhausted," she said. Mashinini also describes how affected she was by learning of the death of Neil Aggett,

179

a dedicated trade-unionist and medical doctor, and the first white person to die in detention. Although it could not be proven whether he was murdered by the Security Branch or committed suicide, people in the anti-apartheid movement do not regard this as a salient distinction. His death caused an international outcry, as Mashinini describes in this interview.

Mashinini said that she was surprised that her husband, not an outspoken person, became "very conscientized by my detention," and turned into "a very active anti-apartheid fighter. The security people don't realize," she observed, "that these continual detentions educate people. They harm the people detained, but they conscientize others." Her husband was among the first people to become involved with the Detainees Parents' Support Committee (described by Coleman in chapter 5). "He stood as a lone demonstrator demanding my release in front of the Supreme Court and many other places," she said. He traveled from Johannesburg to Cape Town to see the minister of justice and police to demand her release. Mashinini also describes the other ways he supported her during this difficult period of her life.

I interviewed Mashinini in her Khotso House office in downtown Johannesburg, the recently bombed anti-apartheid building where I also interviewed Lydia Kompe and Audrey Coleman.

Growing Up African

I was born in 1929 in the city center of Johannesburg, and have lived all my life in the urban areas. I am the one with the least education in a family of six. My eldest sister went to a boarding school and she managed to pass her matric exams there. I was the next eldest, and because my mother wasn't well, I had to assist her at home with my younger sisters, so I couldn't pursue my education any further than standard eight [tenth grade].

I am a product of many forced removals. My father was a dairy man, and he and my mother lived in the backyard of a white family when I was born. Then they moved to a place called Prospect Township—one of the first areas subjected to forced removals in the 1930s. People were forcibly removed from there to Orlando—the place which is called Soweto today. My parents, not wishing to go to Orlando, because it was like a very wild forest at that time, chose to go to Sophiatown. That's where I had my schooling. I went to Bantu High secondary school—the same school that our Archbishop Desmond Tutu went to. Little did my parents know then that they and others would again be forcibly removed from Sophiatown in the 1950s.

There was no separation in Sophiatown of people who were Zulu or Sotho or Coloured or Indian. The only people who didn't live in Sophiatown were the whites. My home was next to the veld, as was a white area called Westdene. Like the white children, we only had to cross the road to play in the open, green veld. We didn't realize then that one day we would all be separated and see each other as enemies.

I can vividly remember the bulldozers coming to destroy our home in Sophiatown. A big truck would come, and people threw our things and the belongings of other families onto it. When we got to the new place, we had to try to find the bits and pieces that belonged to us. After Sophiatown was demolished, there was no alternative for my parents but to move to Soweto. It's inhuman not to be able to choose where you want to live. I got married in Soweto, and my father, who is now eighty-six years old, still lives there.

I married quite young at the age of eighteen and had my first baby on my birthday when I turned twenty. I am still married, so I've had a very long marriage. I had six daughters, but three died of yellow jaundice at a very early age due to the poor conditions of health care in our area at that time. Nobody recognized what they were suffering from, otherwise they maybe could have been saved. My third daughter died in an accident when she was seventeen years old. I stayed at home with my children until I was twenty-seven, when I started working outside the home.

Becoming a Union Activist

Because I had little education, I had no training for a profession, so when I started working in 1956 I became a garment worker in the clothing industry. At first all I had to do was to clean cotton from the edges of the cloth. Then I was promoted to the job of machinist, and later I became a team leader and a factory supervisor. This factory was producing men's clothing, mainly uniforms for policemen, men at sea, and in the air force. I joined the union immediately. I started working there in 1956 and stayed there for nineteen and a half years.

I saw the white employers pushing [black] people around at the factory. I never used to keep quiet on these occasions. I always wanted to help in settling whatever problem arose. I spoke out from an early age, so the workers chose me to be their shop steward. After that I was elected to serve on the national executive of the union, which I did for twelve of the nineteen years that I worked there. I remember a time when we were earning only one penny short of the amount needed to qualify to be a contributor to the unemployment insurance fund. We actually went out on strike to get an increase of a penny because we felt that it was so important to belong to this fund.

There were not many unions at that time. I was invited on several occasions to start a union, but I wasn't ready at that point because of the promotions that I kept getting. Each time I thought, "Oh, now I've made it. I've got what I wanted." But eventually I was approached by several people about the need for a union for black shop workers, and I myself also felt this need. Because this job had been reserved for whites in the past, only white shop workers had a union. Then Coloureds and Indians were hired as shop workers, so they also got a union. When a sprinkling of black [African] workers' faces started showing in stores like the OK Bazaars and Checkers, it became apparent that they needed a union, too.

The Industrial Conciliation Act had an exclusionary policy for unions. Black people were not regarded as workers, so the unions didn't accept us. If not workers, I don't know what we were supposed to be. Just objects, I suppose. Although joining a union with people of other races was forbidden, the law didn't stop us from forming our own union, so that's what we did. I resigned from my job in August 1975 to start a shop-workers' union for black people.

There were many strikes in Natal Province in 1973. After that there was a mushrooming of black trade unions, though not all of them were legally recognized. That is also when we started our union. I wondered, "Where do I get my first people from?" Shop workers are very difficult people to organize because they have canteens within the workplaces for their tea and lunch breaks. So I visited them at their homes and told them about the new union that they must join. The best time to approach them was in the morning before they went to work or at their homes after work. If you stand around a supermarket you see them stream by, so I found them mostly very near their work.

I had a colleague who belonged to the whites-only union, Morris Hagan, who helped me a lot in the formation of this union. We made leaflets which I distributed to the workers. These leaflets informed the employers immediately that a union was being organized, and I am sure that it was they who set the police on me. One time the police confiscated the leaflets I was distributing, and arrested me. They kept me at the police station for a while, but eventually they had to let me go because there was nothing they could charge me for. But their harassment made things very difficult. They had destroyed the few leaflets that I had, and it was an effort to get access to equipment to remake them. That was my first encounter with the police.

Another time I was distributing leaflets with my husband. He used to assist me in this way or by giving me a lift to the shopping centers on his way to work since we didn't have such centers in our black townships. We were arrested and told that we would be charged for trespassing because the supermarkets are built on private property. I wish I had asked in court, "Is it only private property when you are organizing a union?" because I have never been stopped there as a shopper and told I'm on private property. This kind of harassment continued.

When the employers realized that I wasn't intimidated, they came up with something they called the "Liaison Committee." They said that the workers should belong to this committee instead of the union, and that there was no need for a union because the Liaison Committee would deal with the work conditions. Because some of the workers were taken in by this, the first thing I had to do was to track down who the Liaison Committee members were. Then I went to their homes and organized *them* into the union. Since the Liaison Committee people were already recognized by the workers on the shop floor as their representatives, it made my life very easy. The Liaison Committee members started organizing the union within the workplace which I had no access to. So the union started growing bit by bit, and then postal workers were included with the shop workers. I was so excited when I got the first rand [$0.50] in the post for somebody's subscription.

When I first started working for the union, the employers would refuse to talk to me. But I knew the day would come when they would want to talk to me. The workers finally forced the management to recognize the union, and today they sit down and negotiate with us for everything. There are agreements which regulate even how people must be dismissed from work. This union—now called the Commercial Catering and Allied Workers' Union—has become very powerful and now has more than seventy thousand members.

Detention and Solitary Confinement

The police came to fetch me in about ten cars. There were more than forty of them armed with rifles. As soon as the police entered our house, they ordered my husband out. I have lots of trade-union books, and when they had finished searching the house up and down, they collected piles of these books while my family was outside. Then they wanted my husband to attach his signature to confirm that they had removed the books. My husband refused, saying that he ought to have been present when the books were collected [to ensure none were planted]. They said, "You are making things worse for your wife," but he still refused to sign.

I was kept in solitary confinement for six months. When they took me to John Vorster Square the first day, a policeman was standing next to a Bible and he said in Afrikaans, "Is jy 'n kommie? [Are you a commie?]" I'm not very good at Afrikaans and I thought he was asking, "Are you a communicant?" So I said, "Ja, ek is 'n kommie." So he said, "Since you have admitted that you are a communist, you won't get a Bible."

The police told me they detained me because of my political activities, but I believe it was because of my trade-union work. I can never know for sure why, because I was never brought to court. They interrogated me about my travels, about the people I had met when outside the country, about my behavior toward employers when I negotiated with them, about the strikes that had occurred in the industry. Little did they know that many more strikes were going to occur, proving that they didn't occur because of my telling people to strike. The workers chose to strike because of the frustrations that they experienced at work.

Being in solitary confinement was very bad. For the first three months, I just had my hands and fingers to help me pass the time. I had nothing to do, just nothing, nothing, nothing! It was only when I was moved to another prison that I managed to get a Bible and so had something to read for the first time. There was some elastoplast [elastic adhesive bandage] on the outside of the little window of my cell, and whenever the prison guards wanted to see me, they would peel it back. It could be quite frightening because I would see two eyes looking at me through the glass when I was least expecting it.

I slept on the concrete floor, and although it was summer, it was freezing cold. The cells themselves are designed by the South African authorities to torture you. In my first prison there was a laundry machine on one side and a lift [elevator] on the other. The laundry machine operated from about 4 A.M. right through the day, except for Sundays. I knew it was a Sunday the day that machine didn't run. The lift on the other side went up and down all the time, so I was entertained by this continuous noise. It drove me mad. In the other prison where I was lucky to find a Bible, the trains constantly ran overhead.

There was no chair. There was nothing to sit on but a small bundle of blankets. There was a day when I sat and thought about my family. I saw my husband, I saw my father, I saw everybody, and then I saw my baby's face. I wanted to call her by name, but I had forgotten what it was! That was the most horrible day of my detention. The whole day I could see my baby's face and wanted to call her name, "Dudu," "Dudu," but my mind was blank. I couldn't recollect it. "Can a mother forget her baby's name?" I wondered. That experience hurt me terribly. Mostly I worried about my dad when I was in detention. I wondered if he understood that I hadn't committed any crime, that I had not shamed my family by being detained. I knew my children understood this, but I wished I could talk to my father and make him understand it, too. I was so pleased when I came out to find out that he knew that I was detained because of apartheid.

They kept the fact that others were detained secret so that I would think I was the only one. One time when I was being driven to another place for interrogation, I saw newspaper posters saying, "Detainee Dies in Detention." I knew that Neil Aggett, a friend and colleague and a trade-union organizer, had been detained because when I was escorted to the loo on the day I was detained, he walked out of the lift and said, "Hello, Emma." For some reason I never said hello back to him, but it was an immense relief to know that, "Oh, my God. I am not the only one who is detained." I regret to this day that I never responded to Neil's hello because I never saw him alive again. But he was so fit, so strong, I didn't think it could be he who had died in detention.

When I was returned to my cell, I became very furious and demanded to know who this dead detainee was, but the senior police officer wouldn't tell me. It was about two months later that I heard one morning on a transistor radio that Australian trade unions refused to offload goods from South Africa because of Neil Aggett's death in detention. That was the way I had to receive the news about Neil—a person whom I had worked with very closely. I was all by myself in my cell without anybody to share it with or ask about it. There are many deaths in detention in South Africa, but Neil was the first white to die in detention. He was a medical doctor who had sacrificed a great deal to assist the workers.

It was because of social pressure about prison conditions after Neil's death that we were eventually allowed to have these transistor radios in our cells, and to get love novels as well. The security branch maintained that Neil committed suicide, but many people came forward to testify that he was murdered. I can't imagine him committing suicide.

From the day I was detained in November, my husband sent me fruit and other food, toothbrushes, toothpaste, and so forth, but I never received these things. My husband only found this out after he visited me for the first time late in December.

I don't know if it was my husband's efforts that helped me to be released. It could have been pressures from others as well. Fortunately I am quite well known. When I came out, I saw copies of letters from all over the world that had been sent to the state president demanding my release.

I hadn't realized that another woman I knew—Rita Ndzanga [a very active trade-unionist]—had been in detention at the same time as me, also for about six months. When we saw each other on the first day of our release, we were both very surprised. Like me, Rita didn't have the money to get home. The police had fetched us from our homes, but they weren't going to take us back there. Fortunately I managed to send word to my husband, and I told Rita, who also lived in Soweto, that he could take her home. But Rita couldn't *find* her home. My husband, Tom, had to drive toward the station to see if this would remind her how she came home from work, but she still couldn't remember where her home was. Eventually Tom went to the superintendent's office, where we pay our rent, to ask him for the number of her house. Because she was known in the community, some people became excited when they saw her, so we asked them, "Can you tell us where Rita lives?" Then we took her home. This is how horrible detention can be.

I wasn't physically assaulted in prison, but I was psychologically assaulted. I was very ill when I came out. I had a terrible backache from sleeping on the concrete floor, and I suffered from a loss of memory. I had to go for treatment to a hospital in Copenhagen, Denmark.* At that time it was one of the only hospitals in the world that treated victims of detention and torture. I stayed there for about six weeks, but I think I didn't go there at the right time for me. They gave me the best treatment they could, but it was very hard having been separated from my family and home when in detention, then leaving them again so soon after my release. I didn't respond well because I was thinking of them so much and missing being home. Also, all the tortured people from different countries couldn't understand each other. So I wasn't cured. When I came back, I thought I was O.K. but I had lost my memory again. I have been admitted to the hospital several times since then. In December of

* Presumably, Mashinini's trip to Denmark was funded by some organization, such as the International Defence and Aid Fund for Southern Africa, that assists political prisoners in South Africa.

1982, I found myself in a hospital in Johannesburg without knowing how I got there.

These attacks of forgetting came on the anniversary of my detention each year. I had blackouts and amnesia every November/December. In 1985, I decided that I should go on leave and not be in South Africa during those months. I visited one of my daughters last year [1986] and it didn't happen, so I think I am outgrowing it. But the doctors say this sort of problem can persist for about ten years. There are others, however, who have suffered worse problems than I have as a result of detention.

I went back to work at the union because I wasn't going to be intimidated by the police to leave my work, but my concentration had become very bad. And you've got to be all there when you work for the union. The doctors advised me to work for two or three days in a week, but you can't work like that as a trade-unionist. Others said I should work for half a day, but then I would have to take the work home. During the time that I continued working, I paid dearly for it. I had to pay for treatment every fortnight to keep me going. I finally decided to stop working for the union because it was taxing me so much. I had to go back to the hospital about twice, but after that I had therapy with a private doctor.

The Commercial Catering and Allied Workers' Union

Our greatest achievement during my time with the union was that we made management talk with us as workers. Another great achievement is that we improved the workers' salaries. An annual salary increase has to be negotiated now by the union. The workers are still not earning enough because the basic wage was so low at the beginning, but there has been an improvement. My greatest joy of all is what we have achieved for women workers. We were the first union in South Africa —black, white, or Coloured—to have an agreement that protects women's maternity rights. It does not extend to women being paid during their maternity leave, except for what is required by law, but women cannot now lose their jobs or be demoted because of pregnancy. They can stay at home for up to twelve months and return when they are ready to work again.

Before this, pregnant women were moved from their jobs because they were considered an ugly sight. They would be dismissed or, if they

were lucky, they would only be moved from view. If they were fortunate enough to work until their time of confinement, they couldn't
return to their jobs afterwards. They lost their jobs for having a baby. If
they were workers who were approved of, they'd have to start again
with a beginner's salary when they returned. So having a family resulted in many hardships for women. The agreement we reached with
one of the largest retail stores, OK Bazaars, covered all women workers,
not just black women. So the very deprived black workers had achieved
something which also benefited the comfortable white workers of
South Africa. That was very fulfilling for me.

The Congress of South African Trade Unions

Another fulfilling experience has been my involvement with the formation of the Congress of South African Trade Unions in 1985. I was
involved in the unity talks that led to the inauguration of COSATU. So
the union that I and the workers organized was in the safe home of
COSATU before I retired a few months later. COSATU is very important because it is one of the largest federations of national unions in
South Africa. It is a nonracial federation of unions that are worker
controlled. There are other federations as well, and I look forward to the
day when there will be only one federation in our country. I think the
results of the recent election [in May 1987] show us that we must stand
together and be united against our enemy because the situation seems to
be getting worse and worse.*

The COSATU office in Johannesburg was destroyed by bombs last
week [May 1987]. Before this happened, there was a siege on COSATU
by police. They searched the building in which COSATU was housed
during the two-day election stayaway, then claimed that people had
been killed there. The next morning we learned that COSATU has been
wrecked by bombing. According to the media, there has never before
been that type of a bombing in South Africa.

The security nightwatchmen who were in the building saw a few
policemen immediately after the first explosion, but the policemen said
they didn't see anybody who could have planted that bomb running out
of the building. So who put the bomb in COSATU? One can clearly see
that the enemy of COSATU is the government. Now workers have no
place to meet and discuss the problems they are faced with, and their

* There was a significant swing to the right in this election.

printing press in the basement was destroyed. But I don't think the government's efforts to destroy COSATU will be effective. The more the police do strange things, the more the people are mobilized to get together.

If anybody in my age group is angered by what is going on, you can imagine what it means to the younger generation who are not afraid to die like we are.

14

Sexism in the Union
and at Home

"It was very difficult for a woman to organize men. . . . Some of them would say, 'If you don't make love with us, we're not going to join your union.' "

LYDIA KOMPE

Sexism in the Union and at Home

"**Y**OU must try to meet Lydia Kompe," advised the political activist and researcher Stephanie Urdang, one of the women I consulted about whom to interview in South Africa before I left the United States. Urdang proceeded to tell me about the important union-organizing done by Kompe, an African woman, adding that, "Lydia was the strongest black feminist I met on my trip to South Africa in 1986." But when I asked Kompe, "Do you consider yourself a feminist?" she replied, "What's that?" Nonetheless, as her interview makes clear, Kompe is very concerned about women's issues: sexual harassment of working women; the sexism she has endured from her husband, workers, and her fellow union organizers; and lobola, the African custom that has become akin to buying wives. Had Kompe been familiar with the term feminist, however, she would probably still not have identified herself as one because of its negative connotations in South Africa. (For further discussion of this issue, see pages 197–199.)

Born in 1935, Kompe is a mother of three children—two girls and a boy—the youngest of whom will soon be twenty-one.

Since I was aware that Kompe had talked about the taboo topic of female "circumcision"—a practice feminists refer to as genital mutilation—in a previously published interview (Barrett et. al. 1985), I had hoped that time would permit me to ask her about this subject. Unfortunately, it did not. But Kompe mentioned in the earlier interview that she herself had not been circumcised, and thus it was hard even for her to find out about it. "My friends didn't tell me that they cut off their clitoris," she said, but "I discovered that [this was done] when I worked in a hospital." "Today, people don't see circumcision school as a first priority, but they still believe that it must happen," Kompe continued. She said the practice is "very common" where she grew up in a rural area of northern Transvaal, so she and other women who are opposed to it "are very careful to prevent our children going [to circumcision school]. My daughters went to live in that area when they were quite big. So they could decide if they wanted circumcision" (Barrett et. al. 1985, p. 98).

Kompe's willingness to talk about the topics of genital mutilation and lobola publicly and in print—surrounded as they are by silence if

191

not denial, at least as far as outsiders are concerned—reveals her considerable courage, as does her work as a trade-union organizer, which she describes in the following interview.

Kompe lives in Yeoville, a legally white section of Johannesburg where I was also staying. Of her current circumstances, Kompe said, "I'm getting old now, and I don't even have a house, though I've been working all my life since I was nineteen years old." Needless to say, Kompe's situation is a common one for Africans.

I interviewed Kompe in the frenetically busy DPSC offices in Khotso House in downtown Johannesburg. Khotso House is a large several-storied building housing the offices of an assortment of anti-apartheid groups. It was an extraordinary place to visit, vibrant and collegial, and distinctly multiracial. It was hardly peaceful, however, and interviews there had to be conducted with many interruptions and background noises. Since my interview with Kompe, this building was severely damaged in a bomb attack and condemned as unsafe for use.

Growing Up African

I was one of seven children born in a village called Matlala in the northern Transvaal. My father was a peasant farmer. We coped quite well until 1949 when the government came to take away my parents' cattle and donkeys. I was fourteen years old at the time. This hit us very hard and forced my father off the land. Before this my father had enough livestock so he didn't have to work for the capitalist system. Because my parents were now very poor, I didn't manage to go further in school than standard eight. I was eighteen when I left school.

I started working as a nursing assistant in Potgietersrus Hospital in 1954 when I was nineteen years old. I wanted to go on to train as a registered nurse, but after one year my husband pulled me out of the hospital because he didn't want me to be a nurse. He blocked me from getting trained in my profession because *he* didn't finish his teacher's course, which I thought was very unfair. He also thought a nurse wouldn't have enough time for her family. I chose not to continue because I really loved him and wanted to marry him.

We came to Johannesburg in 1955, and in 1956, I had my first baby. We married in 1958 after I had my second child. I was about twenty-three years old then. My husband was very cruel. He didn't want me to communicate with other women. He just wanted me to be a housewife sitting at my sewing machine. All he wanted was to work for his own personal gain. After we divorced in 1974, I immediately got involved in the struggle. In 1975, I got married again to a man called Smile.

The Metal and Allied Workers' Union

I went to work in a factory after I split with my first husband and got involved with the Metal and Allied Workers' Union. We participated in a big strike in 1976 to try to get our union recognized. But the management still had all the power at that time, and we were all dismissed. But we won a civil case against the police because they had beaten us when we tried to disperse and their dogs had bitten us. I only got a bruise on my head, but other people were very badly injured. It took more than two years to win our case, but finally the government had to pay the court expenses and damages.

Because I was a shop steward and I was seen as one of the instigators of the strike, they wouldn't take me back. I was unemployed for about five months and really had to struggle to pay my children's boarding-school fees. But I didn't regret losing my job because I was very committed to the union. Eventually I found a job as a packer at a Checkers store where I worked for nine months.

In 1977, the Metal and Allied Workers' Union asked me to be an organizer for them because two of their organizers had been banned. I became the only female organizer amongst six men. At first this was really difficult because I felt quite intimidated. Because women are seen as inferior to men in African tradition, it took me a while to get over my inferiority complex. Every lunchtime we put money together to buy lunch to eat together. These men would collect their fifty cents and dump them on my desk saying, "You are the woman. You can choose better food at better value than we can." So I would leave my job to buy the food, then put on a kettle, and prepare the lunch while they continued doing their jobs. I realized that I had to fight this because otherwise it meant that I was partly an organizer and partly their maid. So I said, "If you don't know how to buy food, I'll show you how to do it. We must have a roster of who will buy food and who will wash and clean up." Their resistance to my suggestion was quite strong, but I refused to continue doing these jobs, and in the end we started to share them.

It was very difficult for a woman to organize men. At forty-two years old, I was a bit young, and men didn't respect my age as they do now. We went to talk to the workers at lunchtime because we weren't allowed to go into the factories. We had to organize very secretly because the management was very against the unions at that time. It is mainly men who work in the metal foundries, so I would be the only woman surrounded by men. Some of them would say, "If you don't make love with us, we're not going to join your union." I couldn't tell them to go to hell because I wanted their membership, but I couldn't say yes, just because I wanted them to join my union. I told the other organizers about the problems I was having. Sometimes they went with me to tell the men that they had to respect me because I was also an organizer and had been a shop steward before. The men started to recognize that I had once been a worker like themselves. And when the shop stewards saw me negotiate with their bosses, they also started to respect me.

The Transport and General Workers' Union

After working for the Metal and Allied Workers' Union for about two years, I became an organizer for the Transport and General Workers' Union. I started the union from scratch in Johannesburg and became the head of the Transvaal region. By this time I was quite used to men's tricks and could overcome them easily. I wasn't even scared to go and organize them on my own, and I got a lot of memberships. We negotiated for higher wages, holiday allowances, and the right to participate in stayaways. We managed to break down a lot of concrete walls which the management had built around the workers, and we grew tremendously. When I left the Transport and General Workers' Union, there were about twenty-four thousand members and six organizers. It had become a national union with its headquarters in Durban.

Security guards approached us to join our union, so we started organizing them. Then the women cleaners wanted to know why we weren't including them, so I said to my executive committee, "We must extend the constitution to cover the cleaning sectors so we can include these women." So in 1982, I started organizing women cleaners, a very neglected group.

The management employed men as supervisors over the cleaning women who worked at night, and these men were sexually harassing the women. The men did whatever they wanted to because the women would lose their jobs if they resisted. The men would report that the women had refused to work if the women wouldn't sleep with them. Every day women would come to my office weeping about being threatened the previous night by this man or that one. I called meetings with the managers about this and woke up the foremen and confronted them. As a result, some of the supervisors were dismissed and the male foremen are being replaced by women in most cases.

We now have about three thousand cleaners involved in this union. When we first organized the night cleaners, these women didn't have any facilities whatsoever. They had to sleep on concrete; there was no carpet, no cooking facilities. They had to eat cold food at 2 A.M. that they had cooked at two in the afternoon before they left for work. They had no resting time. We got them tea and coffee to drink, a little stove to warm their food. They now have an hour or two to sleep and rest. They get two overalls and soap to wash them in. They now work for eight hours, and then they can sleep at their place of work until it is light. We won all these rights for them. The only thing we are still fighting to get is transport to take them home.

Lobola and Women in the Struggle

The men are starting to realize that they cannot win the struggle on their own. But when we return home, men still think we have to do all the shit work because they paid *lobola* for us. It is as if they have bought us to work for them and we have become their slaves. The men in South Africa are still very backward about this.

I went to a Federation of Transvaal Women workshop on *lobola* in 1984. It was a really big issue. Some women in FEDTRAW—particularly the older women—still believe that we shouldn't throw away our tradition. They think we must educate men not to misinterpret *lobola*. But given the way *lobola* is being interpreted, I think it should be stopped. I don't believe that the objective of *lobola* in the past was to exploit women. It used to bring two families together. For example, if your family is much better off than mine, that means you have more cattle. If I give you my daughter, you give me a share of your cattle so that I can improve my standard of living. So in the past *lobola* wasn't the same as buying a woman but an exchange of resources and trying to live more equally. But now the paying of *lobola* exploits a woman because once a man has paid it, he believes he has bought his wife. That's how my husband interpreted it. I had no voice because I was the woman he had paid for. I had to do everything for him and he could tell me what to do.

I wouldn't accept *lobola* for my children if it wasn't our African tradition, but I can't change this tradition on my own. I can't give away my children for free. I have one married daughter, and *lobola* was paid for her. It would have been seen as an insult for me to refuse it. People would say, "Ah, your mother gave you away for nothing. You're just a parcel. You've got no dignity. You've got no right to be here because nothing was contributed for you."

Men have understood that to be sexist at work is to oppress themselves because management then replaces men with women for lower wages. The men are also fighting for maternity benefit agreements together with women against the management. But men need very strong education about being equal at home and sharing the caring of the children with women.

We women have been having workshops on women's double work load. Women are ready to sit down and discuss it, but we don't know which group to discuss it with. We don't have anywhere to negotiate and bargain and resolve these issues unless the political organizations come together to discuss and confront them.

PART IV

WOMEN
ORGANIZING
WITH WOMEN

"Although men may say it is sexism in reverse, I think women's organizations are very important. Women have to encourage one another as women so that they can go out and face the world, including men. They need to talk to each other about the intimate issues that affect them and that they can't talk about in front of men."

—SETHEMBILE N.

ALTHOUGH FEMINISM in South Africa is still at an embryonic stage of development, women's organizations are a very significant force in the anti-apartheid movement. Even the large majority of women's organizations, which are not feminist, have been formed in recognition of the fact that women do not play anything like an equal role in gender-integrated groups, and that women's organizations are therefore likely to be more successful in mobilizing women.

The chapters in part IV are presented in order of historical occurrence. Helen Joseph, in describing the formation of the Federation of South African Women in 1954, sets the stage for their two most dramatic actions involving marches of two thousand women in 1955 and twenty thousand women in 1956. Joseph, an active participant and organizer of these historic marches, brings them movingly to life.

One year after the federation was formed in 1954, six women started an organization that has come to be known as the Black Sash because the women in it wore black sashes when they demonstrated as a symbol of mourning for the laws they were protesting. The women believed that if there was a substantial public outcry about the unjust laws being passed, the government would have to desist from whatever they intended to do. Although Di Bishop does not describe the early history of the Black Sash (Sheena Duncan, whose mother was one of its founders, does so in chapter 24), she gives a lively and humorous picture of the kinds of activity she has undertaken as a member of that organization from 1978 or 1979 when she joined it, until today. Despite a conservative beginning, this still largely white women's organization has radicalized over the years, with several of its members now in detention. It remains, however, adamantly nonfeminist, an issue addressed by Bishop in her interview.

Anne Mayne, the woman who initiated the movement against rape in South Africa in 1976, describes the trials and tribulations entailed in the development of Rape Crisis into a national organization that also now assists women battered by their partners. Rape Crisis has almost become synonymous with feminism in South Africa, with budding feminists gravitating toward that organization even if they have no particular interest in rape or battery.

Feminism in South Africa is frequently dismissed as a white, Western, bourgeois movement, thus making it very difficult to take root in a country where progressive people are understandably preoccupied with the anti-apartheid struggle. But once the issue of rape has been forced out of the closet, it may be less easy than with some other issues to include women's work on it in the general disparagement accorded to feminism. For example, Mayne has informed me, since my interview with her, that the women in Rape Crisis have recently been invited to train both men and women who work in anti-apartheid advice offices all over the country, as well as in Namibia, in how to counsel rape victims.

The Black Women's Federation was founded in 1975, one of the many organizational manifestations of the Black Consciousness movement [started by the charismatic Steve Biko and others]. In 1977 it was banned along with all the other Black Consciousness organizations. However, shortly afterwards, the United Women's Organization was formed in the Cape in 1979, the Federation of Transvaal Women was started in the Transvaal, and the Natal Organization of Women was founded in Natal.

In May 1987, the UDF Women's Congress was formed in an attempt to bring together groups affiliated with the UDF on a national level. A year after my departure from South Africa in May 1987, a new National

Federation of Women—much talked about during my visit—was also successfully launched. These are but a few of the many women's organizations in South Africa.

Gertrude Fester describes in her interview the evolution of the Cape-based United Women's Organization, from its beginnings in 1979, into the United Women's Congress (UWCO) in 1986. Of great historical interest is the fact that UWO "was largely instrumental in the formation of the United Democratic Front in the western Cape," according to Fester (as well as Hettie V. [see chapter 21]).

Although UWCO, like UWO before it, is a women's organization that deliberately excludes men from its membership, it would not consider itself feminist, in part because of the negative connotations of feminism for many black women. For that reason, I rarely asked a black woman whether she defined herself as a feminist. In South Africa, I met several black women who, though fitting my definition of feminist, didn't identify themselves that way. For example, I did not ask Fester whether she would describe herself as a feminist, but she certainly appeared to be both conscious of sexism and committed to doing something to change it in a way that fits my notion of that term.

Rozena Maart is one of those rare women—a self-defined black feminist. She is one of five black women who founded an organization called Women Against Repression (WAR) in April 1986, just a year before I interviewed her. WAR gives priority to street actions against child sexual abuse in schools. Maart focuses on this issue in the context of gender oppression because she considers sexism to be, not a more serious problem than racism or classism in South Africa, but the most *neglected* form of oppression. Thus, she and her group have made it their priority.

15
The National Federation of Women

"I think it's very important for [progressive] white people to stay in this country. They are needed here. What those who leave are losing sight of is the tremendous rewards and riches that you get from feeling that you are part of the same cause."

HELEN JOSEPH

*A*S *the first person in South Africa to be subjected to the unusual punishment of house arrest in 1962, Helen Joseph—a warm, intense, and vivacious white woman of eighty-two with a wonderful sense of humor—has been called the "mother of the struggle" by some members of the anti-apartheid movement. Her interview provides, among other things, a thumbnail sketch of the history of some of the early anti-apartheid women's organizations in South Africa, including some of the women who have dedicated their lives to the liberation movement. Annie Silinga, for example, was one of the three women to be accused in the 1956 treason trial. Silinga refused to carry a pass all her life (she died in 1984 at the age of seventy-four), despite the severe consequences her refusal entailed, such as constant police harassment and not being able to claim a pension (Bernstein 1985, p. 110). Lillian Ngoyi, a former president of the Women's League of the ANC and the second president of the Federation of South African Women, was a charismatic leader who "spent the last eighteen years of her life (she died in 1982) banned and silenced, struggling to earn money by sewing in her tiny house" (Bernstein 1985, p. 113). Silenced, but not broken, according to reports (Bernstein 1985). Ruth First, author, teacher, and ANC organizer, was blown to pieces by a letter bomb in 1982 while living in exile in Maputo, Mozambique (Bernstein 1985, p. 110). Her assassination is assumed to be the responsibility of the South African government, which has made it a practice to kidnap and murder anti-apartheid activists, successfully extending this policy as far away as France. Joseph describes Ray Alexander, born in Latvia, as a legend in trade-union circles for her tireless efforts as an organizer in the early days of union organizing. Alexander was elected to Parliament as a Communist Party member by Africans when they (Africans) were still permitted to have three representatives, but was "barred from taking her seat through the provisions of the Suppression of Communism Act" (Joseph 1986, p. 3). She now lives in exile in Lusaka, Zambia, working full-time for the ANC. Hilda Bernstein, who was born in London in 1915 and emigrated to South Africa in 1934, became in 1943 the only communist ever to be elected by whites to the Johannesburg City Council. Arrested three years later for assisting striking African miners and detained in 1960 during the state of* *emergency, Bernstein now lives in exile in Britain as an active ANC member (Bernstein 1985). Dora Tamana was a founder of the Federation of South African Women and its national secretary after Ray Alexander had been banned, and until she also was banned (Joseph 1987). Mary Moodley, an organizer in the Food and Canning Workers Union, had—"from the time she was banned in 1963—only three days in which she was not restricted and silenced until she died in 1979" (Bernstein 1985, p. 79).*

Joseph vividly describes the historic demonstration of the Federation of South African Women in Pretoria, in 1956, in which twenty thousand women protested the issuing of passes to African women. Unfortunately, time, as well as Joseph's diminished energy (owing to a recent heart attack), did not permit her to tell me about her experience as one of 18 women out of the 157 people accused of treason, also in 1956. In her recent autobiography, Side by Side (1987) (though banned in South Africa, it is now available in the United States), she describes at length the four-year treason trial, along with numerous other remarkable experiences that could not be included in our one-and-a-half-hour interview.

Growing Up British

I was born in England in 1905. My parents were very ordinary, run of the mill, middle-class people. My father was in the civil service, and I grew up in a suburb in the London area. There were two of us: my brother, who is fifteen months older than I am; and myself. Only one of us was destined to go to university because my father couldn't afford to pay for both of us. It was never intended to be me. I was going to be a music teacher because I was good at the piano. Then my brother failed his matric. Being a very stubborn young man, he said he wasn't going to write it again. He went into the insurance world and stayed there for the rest of his life. This opened the door for me, and I went to King's College in London and took an honors degree in English.

On graduating, I was told by a big scholastic agency, "Although you don't have the training, you'll be able to get a job abroad." So I got a job in India, and out I went on a three-year contract. When I was near the end of it, I had a riding accident and fractured my skull. I was advised to get a light job for the next two years. I was engaged to be married to somebody there who was tied up by his contract with Imperial Tobacco Company. I was going to marry into this big capitalist firm which sent their men out into the bundu [boondocks] in India to teach the Indian villagers how to smoke so that they could sell them their cigarettes. To tell you the truth, I couldn't see anything wrong in it then. I was totally apolitical. I was drunk with the lovely life I was living. We few white teachers were terribly spoilt and absolutely unaware politically.

While my fiancé was away on an extended leave during the Depression in 1931, I cast around for something to do for another year. I wrote to a friend in South Africa who had been at university with me in London, and she said, "Come over here. My father's got a little school. I've just married, but you can come and stay with my parents and do a bit of teaching until you want to go back to India." So I went there, but I didn't go back to India. I met somebody in Durban and married him instead.

Then I moved into Durban society. My husband was a very popular dentist, and we lived a very gay and totally apolitical life. I played bridge. I played with my garden. I was very interested in languages, so I studied Afrikaans. And so it went on until the war came. My husband joined up in the dental corps, and the following year when I was in my late thirties, I thought it might be fun to do the welfare information officers' course, and to my amazement I was accepted. This meant I was in the air force, which was a wonderful experience for me. I had to give information lectures on current affairs to the women in the air force. Amazingly, our mandate was to inculcate a liberal, tolerant attitude of mind, and we were fed with masses of left-oriented material from England. So I learnt about conditions in South Africa, and that's when I began to realize that I was living in the middle of a totally unjust society.

I was about thirty-nine when the war ended, and I didn't go back to my husband. Our marriage had packed up, and I took a job as director of a community center here in Johannesburg. Then I went to Cape Town for two years and worked amongst the Coloured people. Gradually I realized that all I was doing was giving aspirin for a toothache. It was wonderful to build these community centers, but it didn't do much for people's lives. I began to feel it was the whole system that had to be dealt with, and that means engaging in political action.

In 1953, I accepted a job with the Transvaal Clothing Industry's Medical Aid Society in Johannesburg. There I met a man called Solly Sachs who had an enormous influence on my life. He put my foot onto the political path. I was dealing with an enormous clothing industry in which seventy-five percent of the workers were black. So I got very close to black workers and began to get the feel of black society.

The Congress of Democrats

Within a couple of years, I was visited in my office by Ruth First who invited me to be on the founding committee of an organization called the Congress of Democrats. She, Trevor Huddleston [an Anglican priest of Sophiatown who left South Africa in the 1950s and currently heads the Anti-Apartheid Movement in England], Padre du Manoir—a very well known Roman Catholic priest—Cecil Williams, and Hilda and Rusty Bernstein, were also on the founding committee. This was a very small, very radical organization. It was not communist, but inevitably it provided a political home for some of the people who had been members of the South African Communist Party before it was banned. We were called into action by the African National Congress when it became evident that there was quite considerable white sympathy for the defiers in the Defiance Campaign. The ANC didn't accept white members; the Transvaal Indian Congress was confined to Indian members; and the South African Coloured People's Organization worked amongst the Coloured people, so there was no place for white radicals. Look, none of these organizations had a color-bar clause in their constitutions, but they did state that their organization was for a specific group.

A meeting for whites was held in which the ANC took the chair. Oliver Tambo, Walter Sisulu, and people like that spoke. They called upon whites who had been moved by the Defiance Campaign, who had understood its goal to highlight the grievances of the people, to form themselves into an organization. There was a good deal of argument at the time about what form the organization should take, but finally, at the request of the ANC, it was decided that it would be an all-white organization whose job would be to work in the white areas. The ANC made it quite clear that they didn't want us nosing around in the townships recruiting black people into our organization. We would try to work on changing white opinion. The ANC has always said, "We want a South Africa for all people who live in it, black and white together." They never worked for an Africa for the Africans only, but as Z. K. Matthews [professor and former ANC leader] put it at the treason trial, for "Africa for the Africans, *too*."

The Congress Alliance was formed to link all these groups together on an equal footing, including COD. Incredibly so, because we were very small. We never had more than a few hundred members. Here in Johannesburg there were perhaps a hundred or a hundred and fifty. I think the ANC was very gracious to us, although I must admit when I say equal footing, some were more equal than others! The ANC was accepted as the mother body.

We organized into branches and had weekly branch meetings. We were great propagandists. There wasn't an issue on which we didn't bring out a pamphlet or a little booklet or something to circulate. We had to try to sell our literature like *Counter Attack* and *Fighting Talk* and all the Congress journals. I used to go on these selling expeditions, but I was hopeless. I couldn't put my foot in the door unless I was invited. So I made more use of my long legs and just shoved pamphlets under doors and scuttled down the corridors.

Nobody had any money in the 1950s. We had to earn every damn penny, which meant book sales, food sales, and jumble [rummage] sales. We also did an enormous campaign of writing letters to the papers on every possible subject. And we had our national conferences. Our total support of the Congress Alliance meant that our members also actively worked on the campaign against Bantu Education, helped to organize cultural clubs, and opposed the forced removals of black people. We spoke up publicly, organized meetings, educated the public, got people to sign postcards and send telegrams. I was so frightened that we might get arrested at my first political activity that I literally prayed, "Please, dear God, let it rain tonight so I won't have to sit there!"

The Federation of South African Women

Then in 1954 the Federation of South African Women was started by Ray Alexander and Hilda Bernstein—two very brilliant women. Ray was one of the most famous women trade-union organizers that we have ever had, and a very outstanding woman. Hilda was the only member of the Communist Party who ever got into the city council. She was also a commercial artist who was very busy bringing up a family. I was called in to help Ray and Hilda organize for the launching of the federation. About 90 percent of the women at the launching conference were black. We elected a national executive committee and then those of us on that committee went to our own provinces and started drawing women's groups together to form the federations regionally. And that's how it grew. I was on the executive committee and became a regional secretary as well.

Hilda Bernstein and Ray Alexander wanted to bring women's rights into the forefront, and we had a fantastic women's rights charter. But we didn't actually work to implement it. It didn't get as much attention as it should have, because the organizations that were affiliated to the federation were basically national liberation organizations, and we were so involved in the general struggle that women's rights got pushed aside to a great extent. But we firmly believed that when we got our freedom it would be universal freedom. I think we were very naïve about this, but don't forget feminism wasn't all that established in the 1950s. It certainly wasn't in South Africa. And the fight for women's rights in South Africa really had been conducted *by* white women *for* white women. For example, Olive Schreiner [well-known novelist and feminist] turned her back on the League of Women Voters because they were only fighting for the rights of white women. The Business and Professional Women's League was really confined to white women from its inception. I withdrew from it for that reason. So women's rights hadn't infiltrated into our political thinking very deeply. Although the Freedom Charter doesn't say there shall be *votes* for men and women—it says there shall be votes for all—it means the same thing, and we were satisfied with that. We'll fight for women's rights after we get our freedom, if we still have to.

I had been more or less ordered by Johanna Cornelius [an Afrikaner who became general secretary of a militant union] to join the Defend the Constitution Women's League, which eventually became the Black Sash, at their two-day protest in Pretoria. They were protesting the fact that the Coloured people's right to vote had been taken away by an unconstitutional maneuver by the Nationalist Party. Several of us from the federation went to join that protest and slept at the foot of the Union Buildings [the government's administrative headquarters]. There were about two or three hundred women camped out in the middle of winter. It was bitterly cold except that we had mattresses and lots of blankets. I shared a bed with Johanna Cornelius and nearly died of suffocation, not cold. Every time I pushed the blankets back, Johanna pulled them up again. But she was bigger than I was!

I was very impressed with this protest: women coming together to defend the constitution and to protest against the rape of the Coloured voter. So I reported on it to the next federation meeting, and when I had finished, Margaret Gazo, the chairwoman of one of the ANC Women's League branches, stood up and said from the floor, "The white women went to Pretoria to protest against their grievances, but they did not invite us. Now we will go to Pretoria to protest against our grievances, but we will invite the white women." It was a very historic statement.

And within no time it had turned into a resolution, and the whole conference was talking about going to Pretoria and staying at the foot of the Union Buildings. I sat on the platform with my knees literally knocking together. All I could think about was babies and loos [bathrooms] and things like that, but all these women were determined to go to Pretoria and stay there. Finally, it got whittled down to one afternoon. Thursday afternoon was chosen because that is nanny's day off, so domestic servants would be able to attend.

The Women's March of 1955

We called for all women to come to Pretoria on 27 October 1955 to protest four different laws: the pass laws, Bantu Education, Group Areas, and Population Registration. These were very general issues chosen to include as many different racial groups as possible. Our letters to the various ministers saying we were coming were, of course, ignored. A person who must be mentioned here—though, alas, she is dead—is Lillian Ngoyi, because she was the great leader of all time. She dwarfs all other women leaders. For me she always will. She was the Transvaal president and I was Transvaal secretary, and we worked together to organize the march. How we worked!

I was one of the few people who had a car, so we went night after night to townships, sneaking in at the back door. We didn't aim at anything really grand. We thought if we got a thousand women, we would be doing very, very well. We applied to the Pretoria city council for permission to hold a public meeting, but the government got alarmed. Only three days before our protest was due to start, the city council turned down our request. We didn't know what to do. All these women would be going to Pretoria to hold a meeting, and now the meeting was forbidden.

I consulted with sympathetic lawyers in Pretoria, and we hit upon a scheme. I said to them, "Look, if I want to deliver a letter to the minister in Pretoria, not send it by post, and if Mrs. Van der Merwe down the road also wants to take a letter to the minister, and also doesn't trust the post, and if Mrs. Sibeko in Orlando also wants to do it, and if we all go on the same day, is that a gathering?" And they scratched their heads and said, "No, you are all going there on your individual purposes. But see that every woman has a letter in her hand, signed by herself." We only had about forty-eight hours to organize this. Two days before the protest, the transportation board rescinded all the licenses for the buses that the women were hiring to take them to Pretoria. So a comrade, Robert Resha, and I leaped into different cars, and we rushed madly to all the townships up and down the east and west Rand saying to the women, "No buses. Go by train. Put the word out. No buses. Go by train." But I thought it was the end of our protest. However, I was wrong, as I so often was.

On that Tuesday night, the ANC called a meeting in Brakpan. They filled the local hall, and they explained that the government had taken away the buses and the women would have to go by train, and that it was going to cost twice as much. The traditional way for political meetings to raise money is that, in the middle of the meeting, you have a session of freedom songs and, while we are singing the freedom songs, practically everybody leaves their seat, walks up, and throws money on the platform. It is so impressive. They raised four hundred pounds* at that meeting, and they went to the station and bought a composite ticket for four hundred or so women to go to Pretoria. So when people ask me, "What support did you get from the ANC?" I answer that the support was unlimited. Some researchers say that the men wanted to hold the women back. It's not true. That is how they supported us.

Two of us drove out to Orlando at six thirty in the morning on the day of the protest to pick up Lillian Ngoyi. On the way there, we came to the great railway embankment, and what do you think we saw? A train with all these arms stretched out of the windows and women singing freedom songs! The women were on their way to Pretoria! You know what I did? I burst into tears. I knew then that it couldn't fail.

Afterwards we heard what happened to these women. They went down to the stations in Soweto, and the booking clerks refused to issue them tickets. They had been forbidden to issue tickets for women to go to Pretoria. So the women walked along the tracks to the next station, got on the next train without tickets, and paid when they got to Pretoria. Then they all massed together at the foot of the Union Buildings. We still didn't know exactly what we were going to do, since we weren't permitted to have a meeting. We had the letters and pencils ready for every woman to sign. Someone would be at the top of the amphitheater steps to receive the women's protest letters, and then we would come down again. I could see a beautiful never-ceasing flow of women up the steps, then down, which I thought would be wonderful.

Next we got a report that the taxi drivers were overcharging. So I

---

* Pounds, shillings, and pennies were the units of currency in South Africa before rands and cents were introduced.

went tearing out to the railway station with a couple of ANC assistants. We got the taxi drivers to agree never to charge more than sixpence. When I came back, the women were gone. I learned that when they got to the top of the steps, they said they were tired, so all two thousand of them marched into the amphitheater and sat down. They took their babies off their backs and said they would stay there for a bit. I've never been up any steps so fast in my life. I got to the top and saw the women sitting there hand in hand. We then collected all the protest letters that had been handed in, and went off to the offices of the ministers. The ministers weren't there, so we left the letters outside their door, then came back, and told this to the women. With that, they stood up and sang the African national anthem—*"Nkosi Sikelel' iAfrika"* ["God Bless Africa"]. Then down the stairs they went.

When the four hundred women from Brakpan got back home, the men were waiting for them at the railway station and escorted them through the location with a band. Such a tribute to women from African men is very rare. I believe some of the husbands actually embraced their women in public, so overcome were they by what the women had done. The whole demonstration made a tremendous impression.

The 1956 March of Twenty Thousand Women

Passes started to be issued to African women in 1955. There were great protests against it and resistance from the women, and by March of the following year, 1956, we held a meeting in the city hall. I think it coincided with International Women's Day. Our feelings were running very high about passes at that meeting. Representatives were there of the Winburg women* who had burned their passes when they discovered how they had been tricked into carrying them. Somebody from the floor at that meeting said, "Last year the women went to see the ministers to protest. Now we must go to the prime minister and say that women do not want to carry passes." And before we left the meeting, everybody was talking about our organizing a protest of twenty thousand women from all over South Africa. And me? I was nearly paralyzed with shock.

I want people to understand that neither of these protests were planned. They were proposed absolutely spontaneously from the heart,

---

* It was the African women of Winburg who had successfully resisted the issuing of passes in 1913.

which is very unique. Having been proposed to us, we now had to organize it. So we wrote to the national committees and did a tour around the country and organized people as we went. We knew what to say this time: "No buses. Travel by train. Get to Pretoria the day before." And it happened. Twenty thousand women of all races came to the Union Buildings. We collected their protests and took them to the office of the prime minister. He wasn't there, so we dumped them all over the floor and came back. Lillian Ngoyi was our great leader of this protest. She stood on that little rostrum and said, "The prime minister was not there. He has run away from the women." And for almost the only time in my life, I experienced what a groundswell means. I could feel the rage of these women that the prime minister had run away from them when they were so angry. Then Lillian simply put her thumb up as she said, "We shall now stand in silence for thirty minutes in protest." As she said it, the clock struck a quarter to three, and twenty thousand arms went up and stayed up for thirty minutes. I couldn't do it today. I stood with my hand up on the platform, and once again the tears were pouring down my cheeks. I couldn't even blow my nose. There was dead silence for thirty minutes. I heard the clock strike three o'clock, then a quarter past three. Then Lillian began to sing "Nkosi Sikelel' iAfrika." Ah! I've never heard it sung like that before or since. Never ever! And then they sang a new song that one of the women had composed. It is a song that was addressed to [Johannes] Strijdom, the prime minister then. It is well known now. "Strijdom, you have struck a rock. You have tampered with the women," and it went on to say, "You shall die." Sure enough he did, a year later. And the women are convinced that they had something to do with it.

It took them seven years before they dared make passes for African women compulsory. That lapse in time was simply due to the stand of the women, not only in Pretoria, but all over South Africa. But the federation became nonviable in the 1960s because wave after wave of our women leaders were arrested, banned, exiled, jailed, and in the end we really couldn't function. The federation itself was never banned; it never dissolved itself; it just fell apart.

House Arrest and Imprisonment

I was the first person to be house-arrested in South Africa, though I have never understood why. It happened on 13 October 1962 at ten o'clock on a Saturday morning. It was initially for a period of five years, then it was renewed for another five years. I lived in this house which I love, but for nine years I couldn't go out at night or at the weekend, and I wasn't allowed any visitors at all. I had to be here from half-past six in the evening to half-past six in the morning and all weekend. I could go out in the daytime to earn my living because the government wasn't going to support me. I managed to meet my friends at work, but I wasn't allowed to be with more than one person at a time. But you can't do a job and keep to that, so I broke my ban all the time. I had to report to the police every day at midday when I wasn't under twenty-four hour house arrest at the weekend. I forgot to report once, and I had to go to jail for a few days for that.

Certain things happened that made house arrest difficult for me, like telephone threats and obscene calls which were absolutely horrible. But I learned how to recognize the voices and how to deal with them. Occasionally I still hear the same voice, and I just put down the telephone receiver. Then there was the violence that was aimed at me, like when gun shots were fired at my house. I now have plastic sheeting over my bedroom window so I can at least sleep safely. Then a bomb was tied onto the gate, and there were a few other things like that. But it is all in the past now, and I think that it's terribly important that one leaves these things in the past. Also, you must realize that at the time when I was under house arrest, the people who were closest to me were serving life sentences on Robben Island. How could I be sorry for myself?

By the fourth year of the second term, I went to have a mastectomy. Cancer is such a frightening word, it even frightened the government! They thought, "This old girl [she was then over sixty] is going to die in the hospital, and it won't look very nice if she's still under house arrest." So they lifted the banning and the house arrest while I was in the hospital, but I remained listed,* and I still am. I also had another two-year banning order served on me in 1980.

I was in prison in 1978, long after the house arrest. Barbara Waite [a friend of Joseph's], Ilona Kleinschmidt and Jackie Bosman [both old friends of Winnie Mandela's], and I went to Brandfort, the place where Winnie Mandela had been banished to. We all refused to make any statements to the police because they would have been used against Winnie. They subpoenaed me to make a statement, but it was unthink-

---

* Listing is another form of political restriction, less severe than banning but equally arbitrary, that usually involves curtailment of the listed person's freedom of movement, speech, and assembly.

able for all of us. Ilona went to jail for three months as a result. I spent two weeks in Klerksdorp jail. I was alone there for the simple reason that I was the only white female prisoner. They were really very good to me. They were so frightened that this old woman was going to die at the wrong moment and cause an international scandal that they wrapped me up in cotton wool. They even brought me paperbacks to read, and the time really didn't pass too unpleasantly.

Out of my participation in the struggle, I have received so many incredible riches in the way of friendships and sharing. Being designated the "mother of the struggle" is the most wonderful thing. And I have known people like Lillian Ngoyi, Dora Tamana, Annie Silinga, and Mary Moodley as my sisters. These are riches beyond anybody's deserts.

If I didn't believe in what the revolution will bring, I wouldn't have been able to carry on for as long as I have. I have never doubted it for a moment, in part because I know the people in the struggle. I went through the 1950s and through the treason trial with Nelson Mandela, Walter Sisulu, Moses Kotane, and Ahmed Kathrada [ANC leader sentenced to life imprisonment in 1964]. All these people are my personal friends. We became very much a family during the treason trial. It is all these experiences that have made me so convinced that we are walking toward the light at the end of the tunnel.

I also don't doubt for a moment that the revolution will result in a nonracial society. I have just come from being a patient in Groote Schuur Hospital [in Cape Town] where they now have integrated wards. For the first time in my life, I have seen it working. The patients were mixed, the staff were mixed, and the medical officers were mixed; it was totally integrated. It was beautiful. White and black together. And it works. To me that is terribly exciting.

16
The Black Sash: White Women Confront Apartheid

"I struggle terribly with the whole issue of violence. One cannot expect people against whom the government has armed itself not to want to defend themselves. I know that change could come about peacefully if the government laid down its arms. But it's not going to, and therefore it's within that context that I absolutely understand the use of violence on the part of people who are directly exposed to it every single day of their lives."

DI BISHOP

*O*F ALL THE WOMEN interviewed, Diana Bishop—Di, as everyone calls her—has held the highest position in the white power structure in South Africa. She was elected for five years to the Provincial Council—which she described as "the second tier of government"—for the Progressive Federal Party in 1981. She is also a leader in the Black Sash, a largely white women's anti-apartheid organization.

Bishop's husband, Brian, was killed just over a year before the interview, at the end of 1985, in a tragic car accident, in which she herself was seriously injured. In the accident, Molly Blackburn, a well-known white woman activist, political colleague, and friend of Bishop's, was also killed. In her interview, Bishop describes how this tragedy has deepened her relationship with an African woman, Nyami Goniwe, whose husband Mathew had been assassinated just months prior to Brian's death. This relationship illustrates the deep bonds that can develop between black and white women in South Africa, despite all efforts by the government to prevent them.

Bishop was born in Cape Town, where she has always lived, except for three years when she attended Stellenbosch University* about sixty miles away. She obtained a B.A. and an honors degree in social work there, then worked as a social worker for ten years before becoming involved in politics. Bishop struck me as a woman of profound integrity, who combines a sharp intelligence and thoughtfulness with great empathy, feeling, and sensitivity. She was also exceptionally open about questioning some of the policies of the Black Sash. For example; while, on the one hand, she felt that the Black Sash has demonstrated that women have an equal contribution to make to society and political work, on the other, she admitted that "because our concern and activity is focused on political issues, we haven't grappled with women's issues in the way that we might otherwise have done." In elaborating on this point, Bishop mentioned that one member of the Black Sash became actively involved in the rape issue and tried to get the Black Sash to discuss it. But, while Bishop agreed with the way this woman had related the issue to the problems of racism and sexism, "I only have so much time," she said.

* This is an Afrikaans University, attended by very few English-speaking South Africans like Bishop.

214

Bishop went on to say that, "because the Sash leadership has taken a position against abortion personally, they seem reluctant to move into areas where the majority of the organization may decide to support the demand for abortion. But that's undemocratic, and I think it would be healthy for us to be addressing women's issues in a more comprehensive way."

Growing Up White

I first experienced apartheid when I compared the way we and my friends were allowed to speak to the women who worked in our homes as domestic workers. My mum worked full-time when we were children, and Doris looked after us when we came home. She came to work for us when I was about nine or ten. I remember the day she came. She loved it when we went to meet her at the bus stop. I also remember very well Mum saying to us, "You know, Doris is not a slave. She's our friend." We were never allowed to give her any instructions. We had to make our own beds and help with the washing up. She was an integral part of the family, and we had to treat her as such. Because of the training that my Mum gave us, I was very conscious of the wickedness of treating a woman with disdain who is really another mother figure in the home.

My first political statement was at the age of eleven. It was 1961 when South Africa became a republic, and all the school kids were organized into various activities to celebrate this. Amongst other celebrations there was a military display, and I refused to go to it. That wasn't so much a sin in the eyes of my dad as that I influenced my younger brother and sister not to go. We had our pocket money cut for a week. I cannot recall why I felt so strongly about it, except that I hated apartheid.

The Black Sash

In 1975 at the age of twenty-five, I married Brian—who was fourteen years older than me. It was through Brian that I joined the Black Sash. Men don't have full membership in the organization, but Brian had an enormous admiration for it. After we were married, he said to me, "Why don't you think about joining the Black Sash?" My image of the Black Sash was formed by derogatory remarks that were made about an aunt in my family who had been a member in the early years, and who had participated in the demonstrations. She was regarded as rather quirky for having done that. The thing that pushed me to join in 1977 or 1978 was related to my work as a social worker. The majority of people with whom I was working in Cape Town were classified as so-called Coloured. I realized that an enormous gap in my understanding of African people must exist, as I had had virtually no contact with them. In my training at Stellenbosch, I wasn't taught anything at all about the particular problems that African people struggle with. The Black Sash had for me the image of relating very closely to the problems and the struggles of black African people.

In 1979, Brian's business started to be very successful, so it wasn't necessary for me to do salaried work full-time. I started to work in the Black Sash's Advice Office on a voluntary basis, and I took a part-time job at the University of Cape Town doing social work student supervision, which was marvelous. Working in the Black Sash revolutionized my thinking. My social work experience had been mainly focused on pathology as opposed to the inequalities of society and the devastating problems that people have to grapple with because of the laws in South Africa.

One of the things that I plugged into virtually straight away in Black Sash work was going to the Langa Pass Law Court on a regular basis. The Black Sash monitored what happened in these courts so as to create an available presence there to people who may want to consult with one of us. Or if someone felt they would like to be defended legally, they knew that they could consult us about how to approach a lawyer. We were also anxious that there should be a white face in those courts, other than the white faces of the magistrates and the prosecutor, as a demonstration of our concern for and solidarity with people who landed up in this kind of situation. This exposed us to the way in which those courts functioned, which enabled us to put together information which we made more widely available. We used to take many visitors to these courts. I believe that whole process contributed toward the exposure of the terrible, visible injustice of the pass laws, which in turn contributed toward their being changed.

I used to go to the Pass Law Court once a week. I remember the first time I was there, I saw a woman who had been arrested on the street with a babe in arms, another baby tied to her back, and two other little ones. They had been kept in a police cell overnight. They had been transferred to the court cells and brought into the court that morning, totally bewildered by the experience. And that mother stood in that dock with her four children accused of not having a pass! It was such an incredibly powerful, poignant experience. It was unbelievable that this was happening to people, unbelievable unless you had the direct experience of it yourself. I couldn't quite grasp that people who are just being human could be exposed to that kind of treatment. This woman was being charged as a criminal. She was given a warning and a suspended sentence. Generally the sentences at that time were seventy rand [$35] or seventy days in jail. If the magistrate was in a particularly compassionate mood, he might suspend the sentence. We were unable to monitor whether our presence in the courts had an affect on the sentencing, but we believe that it did. Some of our African workers in the Advice Office were involved with our court monitoring. When we were unable to be there, they would see that the whole procedure was more hasty, the remarks that were made in the court were more indiscreet and the sentences were harsher.

I found that if I missed a week in the court, the intensity of my commitment to working for change was not as great. It was that exposure which kept me involved and prepared to speak out and to stand on the streets and address meetings. People often ask me, "Why do you do it to yourself? What motivates you?" Although I am not a mother, I felt very deeply for those women who are mothers, and an immense amount of empathy with them.

Of course many of these people could not pay the seventy rand, which is why the jails were so full. I never came across women who carried around that amount of money in their pockets. But a lot of men who were working illegally in Cape Town regarded the possibility of arrest as a very normal hazard and something to be expected. Rather than getting a lawyer and going through the rigmarole of having a case remanded and taking that much more time, maybe causing them to be dismissed for absenteeism, they would carry seventy rand in their pockets. If they were lucky, they would be processed through the court on the same day as their arrest. Maybe they would lose no more than a half day or a full day of work.

If the person didn't have the money on them, they would either land up in jail or they would organize to get the fine paid. There was a type of prisoners' friend at the court who could contact family members, and the township networks are very effective at getting messages out. The courts were full of family members who'd get to the court on the day that somebody had been arrested. Or if somebody didn't come home at night, the first place they would go and look for that person the next day would be in the Pass Law Court. People knew that they should have seventy rand with them so that they could immediately pay the fine and the person could be released. Seventy rand is a lot of money today. In the 1970s, it was an *enormous* sum. But it still paid people to come to town despite the hazard of repeated arrests. If they could work in-between the arrests, they would still earn more and have a better chance of survival or of supporting their families than if they stayed in the homelands.

By the time I joined the Black Sash, demonstrations with people holding placards no longer occurred because the laws had been changed to stop this. The only legal way we could demonstrate was to stand singly, but we were not allowed to stand at all within quite a large area around Parliament in Cape Town (the government introduced special legislation to try to prevent this). We started to stand individually around 1980. If you can see another person standing, then you may be construed to be a part of a demonstration or gathered for a common purpose, which is illegal. It's quite ridiculous, but a lawyer's advice was that it was legal to stand in relays, so that's generally what we did. We would stand for either half an hour or an hour, depending on how good our legs were, and then somebody else would come and take over. But if one were seen handing the placard to the next person, one would be considered a "crowd" and gathered for a common purpose. So at the end of your time of standing, you had to sit in your car or meet your follow-up person somewhere else, and then she would put on her black sash and you'd give her the placard and beetle off very quickly.

Election to Public Office

I was elected as a member of the Provincial Council for the Progressive Federal Party in 1981. The administrator of the Cape made a direct appeal to me in the Provincial Council to stop standing with the Black Sash. He made a long speech about the fact that it wasn't dignified for people who hold public office to demonstrate on the streets, but I refused to comply.

I haven't enjoyed being in the public eye, although Brian was enormously supportive of my public role. There were vituperative attacks on me and Molly Blackburn, who was elected at the same time as me. We were accused of raising issues that were poisoning the image of South Africa overseas. They said they were trying so hard to improve and reform and that we were undermining all of their efforts by talking about the black people—the struggles of little families and ordinary individuals. Black people hadn't been talked about in the Provincial Council in that way before. Both Molly and I believed in the power of personal stories. For example, Molly stood up one day in the Provincial Council, and held up a bloody T-shirt of a child who had been shot by the police. It was a very dramatic act, and they were very angry about it. They said that we were doing things like this for publicity, which was partly true. We used this platform to reach the public, especially the white people who have no idea what is going on in the black townships.

It's a deliberate not knowing on the part of whites, and for those who *do* know, a deliberate putting it out of their minds. It is a consequence of the effectiveness of the Group Areas Act [forcing the different racial groups to live separately]. I hate saying this, but apartheid has worked by keeping us separate. Requiring whites to have permits to enter black areas had a completely intimidating effect on people wanting to enter those areas. And the government has built up such a fear of black people in whites that even today when the permit system only exists in an amended way, the vast majority of white people have never even been into a black township.

Looking for Missing People

I suppose it was through my social work experience that I felt a need to not only work in the Advice Office, but to actually go out when I heard about a problem and to be present in a situation of conflict. In 1980, there was an enormous crisis at the Crossroads squatter area,* and I used to go out there a lot. The Black Sash was quite actively involved in looking for missing people in the wake of police raids on the squatters. I remember the first time that Molly and I ever did anything together was in May 1981. A marvelous rapport developed between us, and our friendship grew very quickly. On this occasion I asked her at the end of a Provincial Council meeting, "Would you like to come with me? I'm going to try to find a woman." So we went to the police station together, and Molly was amazing. She handled the status that she had through being an elected member of the Provincial Council in a very positive kind of way. When we were messed around by the police at the police station, she just puffed herself up and said, "How dare you speak to an MPC [member of the Provincial Council] like that?"

* Crossroads, situated on the outskirts of Cape Town, is the best-known squatter area in South Africa, famous for the people's resistance to the government's repeated and brutal efforts to forcibly remove them.

We said that we were trying to find a man's wife, and we kept being told, "You're in the way here. Get out of this police station." We said, "We may be in the way, but we have been asked to do this, and we have the right to see the register of people who are being held in your cells." We stood our ground, and of course they didn't like that. Eventually we hatched a typical South African plot. We'd gone out and bought a whole lot of milk and Pronutro [a protein-rich additive] because we'd heard that the children inside were not being fed properly. So we said to the man whose wife we were looking for, "You carry the goodies, and nobody is even going to notice you. Pretend that you are the 'boy' in the background who is carrying things for two white women." Eventually we were granted permission to go into the cells, and the man who was carrying all the goodies saw his wife and baby and took the baby out. They hardly even noticed him; he was just "the chappie carrying the goodies." That man had searched for his wife for three days, and amongst other places, he had been to that very police station a couple of times. He had been told that she wasn't there or he'd been pushed aside, but there she was!

Arrest and Civil Disobedience

I've been arrested a good few times, mainly for being in black areas without permits which I never used to get, on principle. The first time Molly and I were arrested was in December 1981. It was the same year we were elected, and it was in Port Elizabeth. It was for being in New Brighton without a permit. We went to a church service which was addressed by Helen Joseph who had just been unbanned. There were about thirty-one whites there, and we were all arrested, but the charges were subsequently withdrawn. I wasn't really worried about that kind of arrest. Molly and I were arrested together in Cradock for the same offense and we refused to pay the admission of guilt fine. So we stood trial in Cradock and we were convicted, but we weren't actually given a sentence. We were warned that we must get permits in the future. But I still never got a permit.

Things really caught up with us after the state of emergency was declared in 1985 and Molly and I entered the township in Fort Beaufort. It had been included as one of the thirty-six magisterial areas which were declared to be under a state of emergency. This required of nonresidents special permission from the police to enter certain townships. We didn't realize that Fort Beaufort had been included under those regulations just the day before we went there. We were arrested in Fort Beaufort on a Saturday. The police were hopping around filled with glee at the possibility of our getting ten years in prison or a fine of twenty thousand rand [$10,000]—the penalty for contravening any regulation promulgated under the emergency. They were saying to us, "You know what you're in for, don't you?" We were standing in the street trying to meet with the people we'd arranged to see. There had been a very, very effective boycott of the white-owned shops in Fort Beaufort. The emergency regulations gave the police the power to close any business that was deemed to be a threat to any other business. This allowed them to close black-owned businesses which were being supported by the black community. But rather than just closing down a business, what they had done in Fort Beaufort was to detain the shop owner and his wife. When that couple was detained, the wife's parents who had experience in helping to run the business, had moved into the shop and were running it. So the police detained *them*. One of the assistants in the shop then kept the shop open, so they came and detained her. The son of the family, who was working in Port Elizabeth, had approached Molly and asked, "If you are going to the area, wouldn't you see if my granny and grandpa are all right?" The granny and grandpa had been released by then, but were also too afraid, I think, to go back into the shop. So we'd gone to see the granny and grandpa, but they were too afraid to be seen with us because of the possible repercussions for them.

We were standing in the street talking when an army vehicle full of soldiers came past, then another, then a third. Four loads of soldiers drove past us—which was an amazing experience. They were clearly having a look at what we were about. On this particular occasion, we'd been asked to take an American appeal court judge, Nathaniel Jones, to various places in the eastern Cape to give him an experience of what it's like there. He had hired a very flashy Mercedes Benz which wasn't the kind of car we usually travel around in. I suppose the police and the army weren't quite sure how to handle people who drive this kind of car. The soldiers were, of course, white [South Africa's conscripts are all white], and I remember thinking to myself that I could well have known some of those young people who had been posted to the eastern Cape and who were having to patrol those townships for the first time. Some of them had been in correspondence with me and shared the agony of being drawn in whilst politically they were on the other side. I remember these young soldiers going by and some of them obviously feeling embarrassed about us also being white. Their attempt to demonstrate their friendship toward the people was to wave to the children, which was very poignant.

After the army had gone by without interfering with us, the police zoomed in on us, first a police van, then a casspir full of policemen all wielding guns. Two of them actually trained their guns on us while the officer got out and said, "Do you have permission to be here?" When we didn't produce permits, he said, "Follow us. You're under arrest." We were in the Mercedes, and the police van was in front of us, and a casspir was behind, again with all the guns trained on us. And we were conducted like that to the police station. I remember passing some of the children that we'd been playing with and chatting to. As we were driven away, a very brave little child gave us a clenched fist in such a way as to look like a wave instead of a fist. We were told by the security policeman who interviewed us that we were going to be locked up.

The best part of this experience was that Judge Jones is black. Of course, there is no such being as a black judge in South Africa. The furthest thing from the mind of the security police was that he was such a prestigious person. The warrant officer asked for our names, and when he got to the judge, he addressed him in Xhosa. This officer was a real showoff and was using his position of power as much as he possibly could. We tried to contain ourselves from laughing. The judge was dressed in a very American lumber jacket with a camera around his neck, and he just stood and said nothing. You could see that the thought that was going through the policeman's mind was "Why doesn't this cheeky black reply to me?" Then he said in English, "What is your name?" So the judge said, "Jones," with his obvious American accent. You could see that the policeman's reaction was, "Don't mess around with me!" It was an unreal scene. Then the policeman got to asking, "What's your occupation?" So Nathaniel said, "I'm an appeal court judge," to which Molly added, "You can't get any higher than that." Nevertheless, they refused to allow him to make a telephone call from the police station, and he was fingerprinted along with us.

We were all charged, but something changed their minds about locking us up. I think that they must have decided it would be quite difficult to find a suitable place to lock up an American judge. I'm sure that the police cells in Fort Beaufort are awful. Where they'd have locked up two white women, I'm not quite sure either. The other thing that irritated them terribly was that Molly and I were very complacent when this kind of thing happened to us. We were held in police stations so many times while they decided what to do with us, and it was so time consuming, that we used to take our knitting. On this occasion, too, we sat and knitted. My little niece has lots of jailhouse jerseys as a result.

The Black Sash: White Women Confront Apartheid

Of course, a contravention of the emergency regulations was a bit more serious than contravention of some of the apartheid laws. Also, since it was untested we weren't quite sure what they were going to do. But we were together, and that helped us not to be fearful. Another thing that saved me from being afraid is that those men represented visible evil to me. We were simply responding to a call from desperate people, and there's no way that can be wrong. There's no way that the love and the friendship and the acceptance which we experienced everywhere we went in the townships that we visited could be wrong.

I employed a woman for a very long time to help me at home without ever registering her or paying the levy that one is required to pay, because I objected to it. But the acts of civil disobedience in which I have participated have been as an individual. I think one of the reasons why the Black Sash has survived so far is that it has always acted within the law. There's a tremendous debate about whether we ought not to be participating increasingly in acts of civil disobedience as an organization. And many other members besides myself participate in individual acts of civil disobedience. As the options narrow, I think we will inevitably be drawn more into this form of resistance.

In 1985, there was another death in detention. Two of our Sash members who are mothers—one was pregnant with her third child—were outraged by this. They had decided that the next time somebody died in police custody or in detention, they would chain themselves to the railings of Parliament. A thirteen-year-old youngster was the next person to die in police custody, so these girls made their demonstration and were arrested. Brian and I, Molly Blackburn and a couple of other white people from the eastern Cape, went to the funeral of that youngster, Johannes Spogter, and his cousin, Mzwandile Miggels, who had also died. I think the most important aspect of the demonstration of these two women was the effect that it had on the little black community that the victims came from. Although it was publicized in the press in Cape Town, I'm not sure what effect it had on the white community. But people in the black community they came from knew about it and they couldn't believe that two white women, one of them pregnant, had actually done something like that and had been arrested for somebody stuck away in a little rural town called Steytlerville. The young people there kept asking us, "Is it true that they were white?" "Is it true that they were women?" "Is it true that they were arrested?" "Is it true that one of them was pregnant?" "Are they still in custody?" "Are they all right?" And we felt very privileged to be able to say yes to all of those questions—that yes, we knew them, and that yes, it was their very deep concern for the situation that had caused them to do what they did. That was the first time that those people who were fighting for a nonracial future actually had any kind of an experience of nonracialism.

The Consequences of Anti-Apartheid Work

I was absolutely appalled when tear gas was fired at our house in September 1985. Then, in November 1985, I was away addressing a meeting when my car was burned right outside our house. Brian's car also had petrol [gas] poured over it that night, but the perpetrators were alerted somehow by the neighbors' dogs, and they pushed off before they'd managed to ignite it.

The threatening phone calls are pretty awful, though you kind of get used to them. We had a couple of death threats on the phone, and I had death threats through the post as well. I could handle this because we had each other. Brian and I were very, very close and involved in so much together. Having each other helped us to cope with these attacks and the exposure to danger. We took the death threats seriously initially, but we laughed about them later. Some of the letters were so illiterate, and some of the things that were said were so stupid, like "You're a bitch and a lover of black babies."

Whenever I was quoted in the press as having said something, I could be sure one man would ring the next day. He was quite clearly a policeman. I think the middle-of-the-night calls were also probably bored policemen. Last year when I was struggling in the aftermath of Brian's death and living alone at home, I didn't get the calls. But the minute I started to become active again, I got a couple. Now I get calls where the phone rings once, twice, or three times, then stops. If I get to the phone in time to pick it up, I hear somebody putting the phone down. It's a terrible irritation. Recently it's started to happen in the middle of the night, but it's usually in the wake of some kind of publicity.

I also see Brian's death as one of the consequences of my work. I don't believe that our accident was caused by the police, although there are many people who do believe it—particularly our black friends in the eastern Cape who wouldn't put anything past the government. But I cannot help feeling that I would still have Brian and Molly if it wasn't for the fact that we were fighting against apartheid. We were driving back to Port Elizabeth on the Langkloof Road on a Saturday night after visiting a township to gather affidavits about police brutality. Suddenly in front of us there was a pair of very bright headlights. The car was traveling on the wrong side of the road. The driver was found at the inquest to be under the influence of alcohol. He was a man from a little town nearby who gave people lifts, and was apparently on his way to fetch some people. Some people believe that this chap had been killed before being put back into the car, and that it was possible the police had programmed the car in such a way that it drove into us. I suppose it is a possibility, but I have put it out of my mind because it's easier for me to feel that it wasn't planned by them.

Both my legs were broken in the accident, and I had a couple of broken ribs. I had a cracked skull, and I was unconscious for a while. But I think the person who suffered most terribly because she never lost consciousness was Judy Chalmers, Molly's sister, who was sitting behind me in the back. She was alone in that car before help came, with Molly, who died instantly, beside her—with Brian who lived for about twenty minutes, unconscious, and myself unconscious. When I came around, people had stopped and it wasn't long before the ambulance came. Judy was also injured. She had a couple of broken ribs and gashes, but she wasn't hospitalized.

A Black-White Friendship

Although the loss of Brian is obviously devastating, it's amazing how, even out of such situations, new opportunities are born. I feel that something very exceptional has happened to me through Nyami [Goniwe] having lost Mathew and my having lost Brian, with us both struggling with the problems of early young widowhood. We have developed an amazing friendship. Both of us are social workers, and we are now employed by the University of the Western Cape in an action research project. We are working in two new posts which have been created to look at whether the university can relate more closely to the struggles of communities and towns in the rural areas. We've only been at it six months in my case and Nyami for four months, so it's still very new. But it's fantastic to have a whole university supporting us.

My first knowledge of Nyami was through Molly, who had met Mathew in 1983 for the first time. I remember her phoning me and saying, "Di, I met somebody who you have *got* to meet. I know that you are going to love him. And he has a wife who is a social worker, and I know that you are going to want to meet her, too." After Mathew died, Nyami came to stay with Brian and me for two weeks, and that's when we got to know her. Because of Nyami's interest in and commitment to political struggle, unlike many other friends, she has been a very, very special person for me in this period as I have tried to find myself.

Being offered the job at the University of the Western Cape (which occupies such a unique and important place in South Africa today [because it is both black and politically radical]) with Nyami, and the exposure that I have had to the richness of life in South Africa through having been able to cross some of the barriers that divide us—these experiences have contributed toward the fullness of my life. And I don't exclude from that the experiences to which I was exposed when Brian died. There were the most incredible demonstrations of solidarity toward me and my sufferings when I was struggling with loss. I didn't realize before how important friendships—particularly those across the color line—are to me. And the things that people did, and have continued to do, to demonstrate their support for what I'm doing, mean so very much to me. For example, in the middle of the night on Old Year's Night last year, a very ordinary chap that I'd met in the course of my travels, phoned up and said, "I'm just thinking of you at the end of this very difficult year for you." Then he gave me a little pep talk on how to stay strong in the struggle. When I was so incapacitated last year in a wheelchair and with my legs in plaster, one of the women I'd met in my work moved into my house and helped to run my home for me. These demonstrations of solidarity have the long-term effect of keeping me involved. There is no doubt for me that I am committed to living and working and staying in South Africa because of experiences like these.

17

Feminism and the Anti-Rape Movement

"The police take rape very lightly, especially in black areas. They repeatedly let even the most violent men out on bail. Some rapists attempt to rape the same woman again to intimidate her into dropping charges against them. The police don't even withdraw the bail in such circumstances."

ANNE MAYNE

*R*APE CRISIS *is the most significant feminist organization in South Africa. It was started by Anne Mayne, together with four other women, shortly after she took a crash course in feminism at the United Nations International Year of the Woman Conference in Mexico City in 1975 and a subsequent visit to the United States. Indeed, I believe it would be accurate to say that Mayne was the original impetus behind the anti-rape movement in South Africa. In this chapter, as well as describing how Rape Crisis began, she talks about her personal history of gang rape and battery which led to her organizing efforts. Her experience of incestuous abuse in her own family has also played a major role in her life and work, but space considerations preclude inclusion of her account of this ordeal.*

Born in Egypt in 1940, Mayne emigrated to South Africa with her parents when she was seven years old, settling first in Johannesburg and then in the Cape Province. Mayne, who is an English-speaking white woman, left school after completing standard eight (tenth grade). Her academic performance was unimpressive, and her headmistress discouraged her from completing high school. Although clearly an unusually bright woman, Mayne has not yet fully recovered from her headmistress's misassessment of her talents, and has never gone to college. She studied graphic art for a while, then dropped out in her second year to go to England. Of her work history, she said, "I worked in all kinds of odd jobs, never staying in any of them for long because I wasn't interested in them."

Feminism totally changed Mayne's life, unleashing some of her remarkable creativity. "Before the UN Conference," she said, "I was a complete nonentity. I never took responsibility. I never initiated anything. I was very unhappy most of the time. I was very frustrated. I just drifted. But after 1975, I really achieved things. I did a lot of educational work, and I did it well. People listened to me. I became effective. From being a total nothing, I became a very focused person." This kind of radical transformation through feminism is a familiar phenomenon to feminists.

It wasn't only Mayne's experience in Mexico City, but also her travels in the United States afterward that changed her: "I feel I was able to resolve my sense of having been damaged by the rape. It would have taken years of therapy and education to achieve this under-

standing." One year later, Mayne became a lesbian—not an easy identification to have in homophobic South Africa where homosexuality is outlawed. Being a feminist there also takes a lot of courage.

As well as describing the founding of a Rape Crisis center in Cape Town, Mayne explains in her interview how the Battered Women's Shelter began and continues to operate. In addition, she offers a critique of the sexism she experienced in the United Democratic Front, as well as her experience of arrest and detention for merely trying to publicize a UDF celebration. Although the punitiveness of her prison experience is insignificant in comparison with what black South Africans commonly suffer, it nevertheless shows the trivial activities that can cause one to be detained in the South African police state of today.

Growing Up White

I didn't come from a political family, so I was a typical white South African racist who bought all the myths. My father saw himself as quite upper class. A lot of people in his family are listed in the British Directory of National Biography. Many of them were in the military. My mother comes from a more working-class background. Her uncles and aunts were gardeners and shoemakers and small-time farmers in Lincolnshire. Many of them couldn't read or write. But my mother's father became a company director, so she was brought up in quite a comfortable home. But a class war went on in my family the whole time I was growing up. My father was always putting my mother down in terms of her class and implying that he was better bred than she was. He used to talk about women, children, Coloureds, and dogs, as belonging to the same subgroup. I took my mother's side, and I also always felt an affinity with the servants. I didn't enjoy my father's ghastly wealthy friends with their terrible attitudes toward women. And I always gravitated toward people whom I felt were being badly treated.

I was totally unaware politically until I went to Britain when I was twenty-one years old. I got a terrible shock when I met people there who spoke to me about the racism of the regime I lived under. And I met black women who didn't know they were supposed to be inferior! So I came back to South Africa with my eyes wide open.

After returning from Britain, I met a man who ended up beating me very violently. I first worked for him and then lived with him as a lover.

I stayed with him for eight years because he taught me so much about politics and history. He politicized me enormously. But it was a *disastrous* relationship. He beat me up badly and totally terrified me. I was a complete nervous wreck when we split up.

When I was thirty-two or thirty-three, I was gang-raped by gangsters. I was extremely frightened and didn't expect to live. My rapists didn't injure me physically, possibly because I didn't panic, but they injured me psychologically so badly that I was in shock for years. I almost went psychotic. I was completely out of control. I was very scarred emotionally, and there was no one to go to for help. I couldn't speak to my mother because I didn't have a good relationship with her, nor with my father, so I went to see the first psychiatrist listed in the telephone directory. He helped me work through the experience, but he also did the bizarre thing of making me get undressed and examining me. I couldn't understand why he did this because I had no physical injuries.

I was radically changed by my experiences of battering and rape, and I became obsessed with finding out why these things had happened to me. I even asked my rapists, "Why are you doing this?" I also kept asking the man who battered me, "What are you doing this for?" His violence didn't make sense to me.

When I told some of my friends about the rape, they responded in a completely blank or inappropriate way. I didn't feel any support from anyone until I read a book a friend gave me for my birthday, *The Sourcebook on Rape* by the New York Radical Feminists. Reading it was the most incredible experience because it broke my isolation.

I started becoming political at the time that the Liberal Party was banned in 1966 or 1967. I realized it was the party I should join the very week it was banned. I joined the Young Progressives instead, and I worked with total dedication canvassing door to door. But I experienced a lot of abuse by males within the organization. My ideas were stolen. I was confined to being a shit worker. I was sexually harassed. It was the same story that every woman who has worked with the male-dominated left has to tell. Although the Progressive Party was a new and quite exciting nonracial party when I joined, I found that I had terrible problems in getting close to people across the color line in that organization. No real connecting was going on.

The Rape Crisis Center

The first Rape Crisis center in South Africa began after a brief article was published in the *Cape Times* newspaper in late 1976 saying that a group of women were interested in talking to and helping women who'd been raped. We expected only a few calls, but the phone rang nonstop for three days. It was overwhelming. There were only four or five of us to handle them, though I and another woman called Ann Levett took the brunt of the early work. But the other three women—an Indian doctor (the only woman of color in the early stages); a medical receptionist; and an accountant—also stuck with the organization.

Two women who had been raped, one very young woman who was in a terrible state and the other a middle-aged woman, came to talk with us. Some of the other women who phoned just wanted to talk for an hour about their experiences, which they did at all hours including late at night. We became very scared. We felt we weren't strong enough to handle the response, but we managed somehow.

Our first public speaking engagement was at a Rotarian luncheon. The accountant and I went together, but I did all the talking. I spoke very emotionally and very angrily about the situation that women are in when they are raped. It obviously had an effect because they paid for the printing of four thousand information leaflets for us. Then a pharmacist phoned and gave us a medical beeper so we could answer calls. Armed with four thousand leaflets and a little beeper, four or five naïve women took on the system.

We didn't have to work to find rape victims. There was obviously such a need for this kind of service that we were phoned endlessly. We were also constantly invited to give talks. Having spoken at one Rotarian luncheon, all the Rotarians wanted us to "entertain" them. So we went from luncheon to luncheon, from the Rotarians to the Lions, to all the different service organizations, then to the women's book clubs and the women's Christian groups. The invitations to speak never stopped. The director of the National Institute for Crime Prevention contacted us and gave us a lot of clout and credibility by supporting what we were doing and by confirming that our statistics, gleaned from U.S. studies, could be applied to South Africa, although no comprehensive study had been done at that time. The National Council of Women took us under their wing and gave us public platforms, as did the business and professional women. I found myself unable to stop and think because the demands were so constant.

A lot of women came to work with us. We would sit around at meetings in a small women's center and discuss how to deal with cases. We used to tell the rape victims, "Look, we've never done this before. We've never taken anyone through this particular procedure. But we'll be with you and support you all the way." The women were always so grateful for any kind of support that they always welcomed our efforts.

One of the things that excited me about getting Rape Crisis going was the opportunity to work closely with people of every ethnic group. I thought it would help to break down our racism. Most of us had been raped ourselves, and I felt that our sharing and supporting each other and working on a very gut level with women in serious emotional crises would break down all kinds of barriers. And indeed it did.

We helped the women who came to us enormously. We got them proper medical treatment. We sometimes managed to get them an abortion if they needed it. We got them better treatment in court and told them the kinds of things they would have to put up with, so at least they were prepared for what happened. The rapists usually weren't convicted, which always horrified them [the women] despite our warning them about the likely outcome. We also developed really good relationships with them which both we and they very much appreciated.

Very few studies of rape have been done in this country. But a well-documented study on crime shows that there's a very high crime rate in the low socioeconomic areas. The people there have been completely disrupted by being moved without their consent from long-established homes and family networks into dreadful, low socioeconomic housing schemes where they don't know their neighbors, where they're suspicious of everyone, where they are very vulnerable, and where very organized and ruthless gangs attack people. Most of the townships are controlled by very violent gangs who do a lot of the raping that occurs. People say that a large percentage of the Coloured male population in Cape Town is involved in gang activity. The women in these areas are absolutely terrified of these gangs. Neighbors are even terrified to *help* a woman who has been raped, to even let her use their telephone if they have one, because they don't want the gang members to know that they support the rape victim. They're afraid the gang will turn its attention on them.

The incidence of crime *across* ethnic lines is very low. We were responsible for a question being asked in Parliament about this. The answer was that, according to a police report, a significantly higher incidence of rape of black women by white men was reported to the police than vice versa. If a *police* report is saying this, you can imagine how many more cases of black women being raped by white men there really are! Very few black women report their experiences of rape by white men because they're usually laughed out of the police station. I remember in about 1980 the police statistics gathered by the Johannesburg central police station showed that there were eighty reported rapes by white men of black women in that area and only twelve reported rapes by black men of white women.

Both white and black audiences are surprised when we report these statistics because they've really bought the myth that blacks are more inclined to be rapists, and that whites don't do such nasty things as rape and batter their wives. We spend a lot of time trying to undo these myths. We speak to a lot of black groups about them. When we talk about this to domestic workers, tremendous activity immediately starts in the audience, and everybody starts telling stories and agreeing and saying, "Yes, yes, yes. We *know*." *They* know more than any other group how badly white men rape black women.

I had an extraordinary experience when I spoke in Paarl—a completely Afrikaans rural town. I told the audience that more white men rape black women than the other way around, and a woman came up to me afterward and said, "I totally agree with you. We know that it happens here in this very town. Many white men go to the pub for a couple of drinks, then they cruise the routes that domestic workers take home. We've had reports of these men forcing these women into their cars or driving to a place where there are bushes, then jumping out and raping the domestic workers," she said. "We know this happens a lot."

Domestic workers are seen as people whom whites can use for anything and everything. Some sons of white employers force the domestic worker to have sex with them. They see the situation as providing them with an opportunity to practice having sex. They know the domestic worker won't talk because she has no power and no rights whatsoever. This happens often at all levels of white society. We have had many domestic workers come to us with these kinds of stories, and pregnancies as a result of these rapes.

A substantial number of black and Coloured women come to every training course we offer. They are mostly women in professions like social work and nursing who are concerned about the problem and want to learn to deal with it more effectively. Some black women and Coloured women have been working in the organization for five or six years. But they seldom come to meetings, and as a result, they're not very influential in terms of forming policy. They don't come to meetings because of residential segregation, the long distances they have to travel, and the long hours they have to work. They can't come to an evening meeting that ends at midnight and then drive back alone to the dangerous areas they live in. Even though most of them have their own cars, it's not safe. But they are on the counseling roster, and we meet with them on various occasions. If they generate a talk in their area, they usually come to it. And we work on cases together if a case needs two people.

At one stage we had our meetings in Mitchells Plain [a Coloured area], which is a good half-hour drive away from most of our homes. But the problem was that we sometimes have forty people to a meeting and the women's houses were too small for such large groups. This was the case even for the middle-class women. For example, we quite often went to the home of one of the senior social workers at the child welfare agency, who did her master's degree on battered women in Mitchells Plain. Although she had one of the more comfortable houses in Mitchells Plain, there wasn't room for all of us to sit down. Her children were in one room, her mother in another, while her husband was trying to work in the bedroom. So it was too difficult to meet there. It was also *very* dangerous to travel at night in those areas because of the gangs. So we normally meet in the child guidance clinic in a white area—not in private homes. It has a nice big conference room where we have access to video machines and any other equipment that we might need. And it's accessible to people who don't have cars.

A lot of the women who came to Rape Crisis for help were Coloured women. Still today about sixty percent of them are Coloured and the rest are white. Very few black [African] women seek our help because they don't hear about us. Many of them don't have time to read the papers, and they don't have telephones. The black women who do come to us usually come as a result of their employers who phone us and say, "My domestic has been raped and I'd like you to come and see her." I don't think black women expect to be helped by anyone for free, and they rarely have money to pay, so that is another factor that keeps them away.

We have spoken about our work to various nurses' associations and teachers' associations in the black townships, but they haven't called on us very much. We've tried for years to encourage black women to set up Rape Crisis services in their own communities. We share our information and discuss the whole process and hope that they will adapt what we do to their situation. Because many of them don't have phones or cars, they need to work out a different system from ours. But because they work very long hours and are forced to live very far from their work, they don't have time for volunteer work, so almost nothing has happened so far.

Feminism and the Anti-Rape Movement

Aside from Cape Town, there are rape crisis groups in Pietermaritzburg, Durban, Grahamstown, and Bloemfontein. Every year we have a national conference in a different city. We [in Cape Town] trained the group in Grahamstown, but the other groups developed on their own. We gave them literature and all kinds of information. The Johannesburg group, People Opposed to Woman Abuse, focuses more on battering than on rape.

We in Cape Town are the biggest organization. We've had an office for three years now. There are usually only about seven women at a major policy-making meeting in Johannesburg or Durban. Pietermaritzburg and Grahamstown are even smaller, while we always have over twenty-five and quite often as many as forty women at our meetings, and we have approximately sixty active members. We have a very good comprehensive training course with two sessions a week for six or seven weeks. This includes a political section that covers how to act in a democratic way. By the end, people are very knowledgeable about legal and medical issues pertaining to rape.

Feminism and Rape Crisis

In the old days a lot of the women in Rape Crisis didn't identify as feminists. I was constantly told by some of the other women that it was very important that we *don't* identify as feminists because otherwise we'd be seen as a bunch of loonies. After about three years of this painful debate, those of us who disagreed said, "To hell with this! We *are* a feminist organization and we *do* have a feminist analysis." A lot of the nonfeminist women dropped out after that. Nevertheless these women were empowered by their experience of working in Rape Crisis. They all moved up notches in their work or improved their lives. They became more assertive and rose to more challenges. More recently a couple of liberal feminists dropped out because they didn't think we should align ourselves with the democratic struggle [the anti-apartheid movement]. They felt that our doing so would stop many women, like policemen's wives, from coming to us. They thought we should remain a service organization. They left Rape Crisis after we decided at a national conference that we couldn't use the state media any more because they are a propaganda machine for the government.

In the early days of Rape Crisis, I went on national television with the director of the National Institute of Crime Prevention, a member of Parliament's wife, and a professor of law. Our debate made quite an impact. I was stopped in the streets by people saying, "We saw you on TV and we thought what you said was wonderful." But the second time we were on TV was a disaster. They distorted our information and reinforced the myths. So we didn't ever use them again.

The women in Rape Crisis today are all feminist activists, and they're usually involved in some kind of anti-apartheid work as well. Feminists gravitate toward Rape Crisis in order to work with women. And a lot of left-wing women came into Rape Crisis because they were very unhappy about the male domination in the left. They are able to express their feminist ideology more comfortably here.

I became radicalized through my work with Rape Crisis. The more I worked with the system in this country, the more appalled and politicized I became.

In 1985, Rape Crisis made a public statement at a national conference about our decision to align ourselves with the democratic struggle. We started an organization called Campaign Against Sexual Abuse and made links with the Repression Monitoring Group. From then on, we were on call if a woman was raped in detention and needed to be counseled. And we linked up with UDF-staffed advice offices located throughout the community that give legal advice as well as advice about rent and other daily life concerns. They call us if they have rape cases that they can't deal with. We also run training courses on rape for the people working in these offices so they can be more effective in counseling people. And we always send somebody to make solidarity statements at major political meetings. So we're making ourselves more visible than we used to.

The Battered Women's Shelter

Two years ago [1985] we developed a section of our Rape Crisis training on battered women. This was followed by a twenty-four-hour phone-in. Again, we got an alarming number of calls, but this time we had many shifts of women fielding them. There were seven phone lines coming in for twenty-four hours. Listening to the stories of so many women who have been battered is a shattering experience. We were shell-shocked. We really felt ill. Another three hundred calls came into the office over the next week because we'd leafletted at railway stations and bus terminals. Quite a lot of black and Coloured women came into our office or called us from the townships.

Our next step was to launch a big public campaign to get a shelter started. The community responded amazingly supportively, and we were given a house for which we only have to pay twenty-five rand [$12.50] a year. The place was totally furnished within days by donations of fridges and stoves and carpets and curtains, and it was full of battered women within a week. It can take up to twenty-five women and their children.

Our shelter is only a year old. Except for having different bank accounts, it is totally integrated with Rape Crisis. There are three paid workers, and every battered woman who comes into the shelter gets a support worker. When people answer the Rape Crisis line, they may get a call from a battered woman or a rape victim. With battered women calls, counselors have been trained to assess whether she needs a shelter and if so, the counselor becomes the support worker for that woman. She visits her in the shelter and works with her throughout her stay there. Unfortunately there's a waiting list, but women can stay for three months once they're admitted. We work very hard to get their divorces through or whatever it is they need to get their lives reorganized. There are weekly house meetings to iron out any problems that come up in the shelter.

The shelter has been a very empowering place for women. Men aren't allowed there, so women do whatever work is needed. Rape Crisis volunteers have made bunk beds for the children and done all the house repair work and painting. The women who live there get a tremendous kick out of learning to knock in nails and glue wood. It's great fun when we have a work party there from time to time.

There are some basic rules, like no men, no violence if possible, no beating of children, and no alcohol or other drugs. And we don't take any psychiatric cases because we can't deal with them. Most of the women who come there are Coloured, though we've had quite a few black women and some white women there, too. The atmosphere there is often wonderful. Many talented women have stayed there; for example, we had an upholsterer who did a superb job upholstering all the second-hand furniture that we were given. The lounge looks beautiful now. And there are some wonderful cooks. The smell of cooking makes you *weak* when you go there at supper time. There have been pastry makers and dressmakers, a psychologist, nurses, and other professional women. The wives of two leading activists in UDF are in the shelter at the moment.

Of course, tensions do arise. There's only one bathroom for all those women, and sometimes the plumbing doesn't work very well. But often there's an amazing atmosphere and an extraordinary bonding occurs between the women. They say, "I was so isolated. I've never had friends before." And they keep up with these friends after they leave.

Participation in the United Democratic Front

I joined the UDF within the first month or so of its being launched in 1983. Their first public meeting was the most exhilarating experience that I have ever had. It was so wonderful to be able to participate in the mass excitement and to shout slogans that I normally only whisper. Most of us are so frightened in this country. It was wonderful to hear statements like "The people shall rule" said loudly. It was exciting to see how high people's confidence was. It was always so orderly. There were never unpleasant experiences or incidents. I'd never before been with mobs of people of all colors in this country. It was so peaceful, and there was so much goodwill. It was wonderful to let off steam and to dance and to sing and to learn protest songs.

Once a month or once every two months, there'd be a massive meeting at a big stadium addressed by some prominent leaders. Then there'd be lots of small meetings every weekend at public halls or church halls or cinemas where not-so-prominent people would speak. But after the initial excitement of hearing so many articulate black people speaking, I became increasingly bothered by the sexism in the organization. The men were usually the organizers and the speakers at the meetings. I became sick and tired of the fact that I never saw women on the platform, except for Cheryl Carolus [a former member of the National Executive of UDF]. I realize that I can't work in organizations with men because they can't *hear* women. And I couldn't bear the sexism that I was experiencing in my area meetings. The guys seemed to be posturing most of the time. Some of the UDF women in my area had husbands or lovers who were talking about women's rights and feminism, but they didn't really *understand* it. So I began to fade out of UDF after about six months.

In 1985, in the early days of the United Democratic Front, a "People's Weekend" of activities was planned all over the western Cape. I had joined the UDF group in my area, and twenty-six of us went in a motorcade, two people in each car, to advertise the People's Weekend. We planned to drive through business areas with UDF banners on our cars so people could see us. We looked quite spectacular, but the police stopped us after we had driven only a very short distance. They impounded our cars and took us to jail. We were fingerprinted and photographed and warned that we had been part of an illegal gathering, though no motorcade had been seen as an illegal gathering before. They set our bail at two hundred rand [$100] each on a Saturday afternoon when very few people had access to that amount of money. But people lent us money so we all got out at about 2 A.M.—sixteen hours after our arrest. They were thinking of holding us the whole weekend because they wanted to spoil the People's Weekend, but they didn't succeed.

It was a *very* interesting experience but very frightening. I was locked up in a women's prison with the other women in our group. It's terrifying to be so powerless: not being able to use a phone; having to ask permission to go to the toilet. There were big iron bars that slammed behind us, then a steel door slammed on top of the iron bars. We couldn't see anything. There was heavy mesh over everything. I felt that the place could hold a herd of rhinoceros or elephants. "What on earth are they doing having bars this size, a door this thick, for *us*?" I wondered. I felt like a squashed insect. It was the most *dreadful* feeling. I felt as if I'd been raped again.

Maybe if I'd known that I was going to be put in jail, I wouldn't have been so shocked. One mother looked ten years older as a result of the experience. Her child had expected her back home at midday so she was desperate for someone to look after him. She finally managed to get a message out, but the experience wrecked her.

We were made to stand in a filthy, smelly area where people had vomited. We were stripped of everything—earrings, glasses, shoelaces, belts, and any kind of jewelry. It made me feel so stupid. We were told not to speak, so we stood there watching the police eat sandwiches. When they'd finished eating, they threw their garbage at us. We begged them for food at about 10 P.M. because we had had nothing to eat all day. The police finally brought us some food from a nearby hotel.

Our cars were confiscated for two weeks and held as evidence, so we had no transport during that period. But the people in our area were wonderful, and a car pool was set up so we knew who to phone if we needed a car for a certain number of hours. Those of us who had been detained got to know each other and were very supportive and enjoyed each other's company. And then we went to trial. Our case was even taken up by the Supreme Court because it was a test case of what constitutes an illegal gathering.

There was quite a bit of publicity around the trial. A wonderful gray-haired old black man who had been on Robben Island for years came to support us. I was so touched when I thought of the nonsense that we were being tried for compared to what he had suffered. He'd had nervous breakdowns because of all the torture he'd been subjected to. But he wanted to give us his support. We all stood around him and asked him about his life, which he was very happy to tell us. In the end, we were fined only fifty rand [$25] each.

Three of us who had been detained, and who were born outside South Africa, were phoned by the Special Branch and instructed to bring in our passports. They told us that we would be deported. I was absolutely terrified. Luckily, our lawyer told us we didn't have to follow their instructions. It was all a bluff. But had I done what I was told, the police might have held my passport for six months. The truth is that I'm a naturalized South African, and I *have* no other country.

18

The United Women's Congress

"[The revolution is] going to be hard, it's going to be long, but we are all committed to it. We know that we're going to suffer. We know that we *are* suffering. Lots of us are in detention. Lots of us are not sure whether we can actually give our address on the telephone. So our lives have been changed. We aren't naïve about the struggle. We *know* it's going to be hard, but we're prepared for it."

GERTRUDE FESTER

*A*FTER SPENDING *two hours with thirty-five-year-old Gertrude Fester and other friends, and explaining my project to her, I asked her whether I could interview her. Fester, who is Coloured, said she would have to tell the United Women's Congress, of which she was a dedicated member, about my project, and, if they wished to cooperate, they would let me know whom I could interview. Since she was in hiding from the security police at the time, she instructed me to wait for her to call me. Weeks went by. Finally, a cryptic message took me to the house where Fester was hiding out.*

I found her there with sixty-five-year-old Mama Zihlangu and fifty-two-year-old Mildred Lesia, two of the founders of the United Women's Organization which had preceded UWCO. Both Zihlangu and Lesia were then in deep hiding, staying at different addresses for a few nights at a time; "on the run" would well describe their situation. I had the impossible task of trying to interview all three women at one sitting—an interview situation that I had told Fester wouldn't work, but the requirements of a totally democratic process took precedence over this reality. At the end of it all, I asked her whether I could come back to interview her further, since she hadn't gotten to say much out of deference, I believe, to her two colleagues; and this time she agreed.

Fester received a B.A. from the University of the Western Cape, after which she studied at the Third World Institute in Holland from 1980 to 1982. She teaches at a training college for teachers in Cape Town. Ever since her first political involvement with UWO in 1982, she has been extremely active in the anti-apartheid movement. She was on the executive of UWCO in 1986 and has been part of the Area Committee of UDF and a member of the Western Cape Teachers' Union. Although she has been asked to be on WECTU's executive committee, she decided to give all her attention to UWCO "because women are my first priority." Fester, who believes that "women are much more militant than their male comrades," commented that "If you divide your attention, the women's issues often get lost."

Fester divorced her husband a few years ago after he became violent. She speaks eloquently in this interview of the pain of being a black child in a white world, of her student days, her participation in the Black Consciousness movement, and her gradual awareness of sexism, especially owing to having had a violent husband. She de-

scribed how frightened she was when she was detained for the first time in 1983 for going house to house with six others to gather signatures against the tricameral parliamentary system being proposed by the government. "The most frightening thing," Fester explained, "was the feeling that no matter what we said, no matter what our rights were, no matter who we were, we had to do what these people [the police] wanted us to do." When Fester tried to insist on her right to make a telephone call, she was smacked and told to "shut up."

Fester was arrested a second time the same year when she and two other women put up posters at night, an illegal activity in South Africa. "What is frightening in South Africa," Fester explained, "is that if people don't know where you are, there's nothing that can be done about it. No one saw us being arrested. We could just disappear. We'd heard of people who had disappeared." However, on both occasions she was released after a few hours.

When I interviewed her, Fester was staying in a house with other women friends. She believed that the police were not aware of her whereabouts, and was trying to keep it that way. For example, she mentioned that she usually plays music to prevent conversations from being recorded through the telephone. Despite such precautions, she wasn't sure how much longer it would continue to be safe for her to remain there.

In July 1988, I learned that Fester had been in detention for a month, and that she was likely to be accused of terrorism. No one has been allowed to see her—not even her closest friends. In April 1989, I was told that her trial was about to begin.

Growing Up Coloured

I come from quite a comfortably off Coloured family. There are five of us. I have two sisters and two stepsisters, and I'm the second youngest. My family is not politically involved, although they're very sympathetic. My parents are very conservative and very religious, but my mother now understands why people are involved and she gives the necessary support. My sisters, however, are not politically involved at all. One of them is studying for a master's degree in clinical psychiatry and has a family, and my youngest sister is a born-again Christian who emigrated to Australia last year because she felt she'd never get a chance in this country.

I remember going to the park to play as a child. Although there were no "Europeans only" signs up, we knew we weren't supposed to enter, so we went in when no one was around and played quickly, feeling very scared. When the white children came, we'd sometimes be defiant and stay there and fight them.

My mother comes from a rural area, and I remember going there every holiday. It was really terrible because we couldn't go into shops. We had to use a little window at the side. We couldn't go into cafés to get a cold drink. We couldn't even go to a public toilet. These restrictions became part of my consciousness. I will always be scared to go into a restaurant. It's not easy to unlearn these things. Experiences like this give you a permanent inferiority complex. For example, I was studying in Holland in 1981. I'd been living there for a year when I walked down the street one evening looking for a pub with a whole group of mostly black students. But every time we came to one, I'd say, "No, we mustn't go in there." I rejected about ten or twelve pubs in this way, so people asked, "What's wrong with you?" I realized that I was scared to go in! I've had these kind of scared feelings my whole life. Most of the cinemas in South Africa are open to black people now, but I don't have the courage to go to many of them. It's the same with a new restaurant.

My sister, a radiographer, was living in England for sixteen years. She came back here with her husband on holiday two years ago. We traveled up the coast stopping at a lovely restaurant. My mother was hovering outside until I brought her in. She is normally a very confident woman, but she became completely subservient. Before we left, my sister said she wanted to go to the toilet. She asked us, "Are you sure it's safe to go in?" In the end, she didn't go because she was scared despite having lived out of this country for sixteen years.

Becoming Politicized

I started to realize that something was wrong about all this when I was thirteen or fourteen. But there were no anti-apartheid organizations around then for me to join.

I went to the University of the Western Cape [a black university] at a time when male students had to wear ties and we had to wear dresses. All our lecturers were white Afrikaners with a paternalistic attitude of helping poor black people.* First, there was a tie boycott, and then one

* This university has since become such a progressive, anti-apartheid institution that the ANC does not include it in its academic boycott because they consider it to be "part of the struggle."

day in 1971, I decided to wear jeans to class. I was the first woman on that campus to wear trousers. I remember walking into class and hearing people say, "She's wearing her trousers!" Four other women wore trousers the next day, and today we all wear trousers or anything we want to wear. There are many more black professors now, though they're still less than fifty percent.

Feeling inferior because you are black is something that takes a very long time to get rid of. Perhaps being out of South Africa and mixing with other people in another country helped me to value myself for what I am. And participating in the Black Consciousness movement helped a lot too. That was the beginning of my political involvement. Through it I came to understand that there's nothing wrong with me because I'm black. It's important to be proud of what you are. All of us were involved in it in 1975 and 1976, the time when black students broke away from NUSAS [the largely white National Union of South African Students] and started SASO [South African Students Organization]. Steve Biko was a very charismatic person. I remember the saying we had that "Black Consciousness is not a color, it's a state of mind." We sought mental emancipation. We were very militant and anti-white at that time. I remember being part of a black theater festival. We were so angry when some whites came in, we threw them out saying, "We need to get together as black people to decide our futures. We have been the slaves of whites for too long."

Then in October 1977, SASO was banned along with nineteen other black organizations. But there are still little pockets of Black Consciousness all over the country. The leadership can be banned but you can't ban ideas. On the other hand, Black Consciousness only has a very small following today. They are very élitist, and their largest following is on the university campuses. I consider Black Consciousness an important phase of the struggle, but I also think it's shortsighted because there cannot be a meaningful struggle in South Africa without whites. Because some whites have created a fiasco in this country it doesn't mean that we should hate all whites.

My awakening to sexism was a gradual one. It took me going through marriage to realize that I was being oppressed as a woman. I saw that the brunt of the work in marriage has to be done by women. My husband and I both worked, but it wasn't equal. He was supportive of my political work as long as it didn't take up too much of my time, and as long as the washing was done and everything was nice and clean. The reason I didn't want to have children was that I knew I would be the one to have to stay home. And I often said to my husband, "Look, there are so many problems in this country. Do we really want to bring a child into it?" But everyone thought that there was something wrong with me for not having a child. Whether to have children or not is quite a debate among us activists. Some feel that by having children you bring in more cadres for the struggle. I feel that it would curtail my activities.

I took a course in Holland on women and development at the Institute of Social Studies with about thirty other women from different countries. I realized that no matter which society, which culture, women are *always* oppressed whether it's through female infanticide, female circumcision, or whatever.

My husband was violent in the last two years of my five-year marriage. I still get upset when I speak about the violence. I didn't get support from people, even my own sisters. I remember my one sister saying, "Perhaps you deserve it." It has created quite a lot of tension between me and my family, and I'm still not completely open with them. I was very involved in the United Women's Organization then. I got the understanding and support there that my family didn't give me. That was a very hard time in my life. I didn't have a place to stay. There was no battered women's shelter then. And because of the socio-economic conditions of black families, there isn't space for additional people to stay. Also, we don't speak about violence, especially not people from middle-class backgrounds like mine. So I felt I had to stay in my marriage.

His violence was definitely connected with my involvement in UWO. He was very threatened by it. Everyone in UWO was a lesbian as far as he was concerned. A woman who is very strong and who doesn't wear makeup is not a true woman in his eyes. Articulate women were threatening to him. And if women prefer other women to men, that was even worse. That was also probably the reason my family supported him. They agreed that it was a bit unsavory for women to be getting together. The time came when the violence was unbearable. He fractured my ribs, et cetera, et cetera. Fortunately, there was a woman I had taught with years ago who had a place for me to stay.

Police Harassment

I've had numerous run-ins with the police. My most frightening experience was when five security police came to the previous house that I lived in with my friend Lynn. Although the state of emergency had not yet been declared, we didn't stay in the house most of the time because our neighbors had told us that the police had been coming there quite often, and we didn't want them to find us. On this particular day I was alone at home and there was a knock on the door. It was a very loud ferocious knock, and I was a bit frightened. I peeped out and saw these five big policemen. I sometimes think they must handpick these people because their mere stature absolutely frightens you. They shouted at me, "Why are you taking so long? Open the door!" I answered, "Who are you? I'm not opening the door." They said they were security police, so I told them I needed to see their identifications. After they showed them to me, I realized I had to open the door because otherwise they'd kick it down. They've done that with lots of other people. So I opened the door, and they searched the house.

The absolute power these men had over everything in my house was frightening, in addition to the way they pushed me around personally. I was frightened on two levels: as a woman I was scared of them because they were men, and I was also scared that I would be detained. At one stage I was standing alone in a room and all five of them *barged* onto me throwing questions at me, ready to push me around if I didn't answer soon enough. "Who are you? Where are you going? What is this? Who are these people?" I had never been so scared in my life! I was afraid of being sexually assaulted. I had been doing interviews with some UWCO members who had been in detention, so I had a very vivid understanding of what type of things they can get up to. And I realized that if I shouted no one would come.

After that, the police came to our house about three or four times a day. Fortunately we were out most of the time. We had quite a good relationship with the neighbors who told us about their visits. In black areas there is much more community spirit than in white areas. A black neighborhood is often a tightly knit group, and people will ask you what's going on. Sometimes people haven't been arrested because of the sheer numbers of people asking the police, "Where are you taking her?" or "Why are you taking her away?"

Living in Hiding

On 25 October 1985, we were babysitting for someone when Hettie [see chapter 21] phoned to tell us that the state of emergency would be declared in Cape Town at twelve o'clock that night [so the police could detain people without having to make a charge]. It was then 11 P.M. or 11:30 P.M., and we *ran* to our house and fetched our clothes and whatever we could grab, and we never went back. Apparently the police were parked outside the house at the time. Later we sent people to fetch our clothes, and on one or two occasions I summoned up courage to go back to the house. It's terrible not having a book or whatever you need with you, but it was so frightening to go back. I didn't put any lights on even though it was dark, and I kept very quiet in case someone came to the door.

We came to this house which was safe at that time. Now I'm not sure how safe it is, because sometimes we forget and use the telephone. And three months after we moved into this house, the police ransacked my cousin's house further up the road though she's completely uninvolved in politics. She heard two policemen saying, "Now which old white house can it be?" She told my mother she thought they must be looking for this house. But thus far they haven't found it. We are still in hiding, but not as seriously as many others. I don't ever divulge any information on the telephone. I won't give my telephone number to many people. As far as possible I don't tell people where I am.

We are trying to avoid detention if possible because there's a lot of work to be done outside prison. Most people who are politically active have to move a lot, particularly around certain dates like before and after 16 June [the anniversary of the Soweto uprising], and before the white elections. The government is scared of activity, so these are the times they really clamp down.

Fear of Rape

The worst thing about living in hiding is being frightened, especially as a woman. I know women who have been stripped while they were detained. They were threatened with rape, and their children were similarly threatened with rape. They are trying to pin a treason charge onto our chairperson, Noma-India, who is detained now. She probably won't be out for ten to twelve years. One day a black policeman walked in and brought her a bowl of porridge with cigarette ash on it. She said to him, "Do you expect me to eat this?" He replied, "Of course, why not?" She said, "I refuse to eat it." Then he started walking around her and looking at her in a very lecherous way, while touching himself and masturbating. Noma-India was very frightened because his whole demeanor was "I'm going to get you now."

The police want to break down strong women [in detention] because they don't give them the information they're seeking. Sexual violence epitomizes that whole dynamic of cutting women down to size, which is why it is such a powerful element in torture. Noma-India realized she had to do something, so she took the bowl of porridge and threw it into his face. He left, leaving her cell door open. But she decided that she wouldn't try to escape because she felt that it may be a ploy to kill her in the process. What is strange is that he didn't even report her misconduct to anyone. Knowing about such experiences I must admit that I am frightened.

The United Women's Organization

It is important to organize as women now because we don't want to have a new society where we are still second-class citizens. We mustn't wait for a revolution to organize women. We've got to learn to share housework now. UWO's constitution says that we will learn to share housework, to share childcare, and to work equally.

Although UWO actually started in 1979, it was only formally launched in 1981. I came back from my two years in Holland in 1982, joined the branch of UWO in the area where I live, and immediately became very involved in it. This was the first political organization to emerge after years of repression. I remember being astounded by the way people talked about their oppression at the first mass meeting I attended.

UWO is based in the western Cape, although we have been instrumental in forming other women's organizations in other areas. There were about one thousand members at the time I returned to South Africa. Perhaps ninety percent of the membership today are African women.

My branch is mixed [racially] because different people live in this area, but many of the branches are racially segregated because of the residential segregation that exists in this country. There used to be large white branches of UWO, but after UDF was launched many of the whites became more active in that organization. The branches do projects that are important to people in their area. For example, the KTC branch [a squatter camp] concentrated on getting more taps and doing something about the lack of garbage collection. KTC is still in existence because of the work of UWO. Reaching women through organizing crèches [child care] is a very big project in most township branches.

Everything I did in UWO was a learning experience. For example, in my branch we started a children's play group in a very poor, deprived area where the women often have lots of children. It was a very exciting project, but it was very demanding, too. There'd sometimes be four or five of us to look after 150 children who were *yearning* for attention and love. We would become *exhausted*. Initially, we thought that a children's group would lighten women's burden, thereby drawing them in gradually to our organization, but we came to realize that the children were just as important as their mothers. We need to give them attention because they are our future society.

We also pursued self-education. For example, a group of us went away for a weekend to consider the importance of feminism and how it relates to women's role in the national democratic struggle in South Africa. Then we held an open forum to which the entire organization came, and we discussed the struggles in different countries like Algeria, Nicaragua, Cuba, the Philippines, and the peace movement. We tried to get hold of resources written by Third World women like *Feminism in the Third World* and *National Struggles in the Third World*, which was compiled by a number of Third World women writers. We studied the history of the struggle, the ANC, the history of South Africa. We had workshops on media skills, how to compile pamphlets, writing, etc. We studied the Freedom Charter and discussed its relevance fifty years later. And about two years ago, we formally adopted the Freedom Charter.

A Comparison of UWO and UDF

UWO was largely instrumental in the formation of the United Democratic Front in the western Cape. With the advent of UDF, many of us are active in both UWO and UDF, so we have an action-packed program. There were times we only slept three hours a night. We did door-to-door distribution of pamphlets every night for two years. It was work, work, work! If it wasn't writing up a pamphlet, it was printing five thousand posters for our meeting. UDF is very action-oriented, and UDF was where it was at, with the result that all of the other organizations suffered, the youth and civic organizations as well as UWO.

The pace of UWO meetings was much slower than UDF: for example, we had to have translations in English and Xhosa and sometimes in Sotho as well. We dealt with squatter women from rural areas who didn't understand urban politics. We had to explain some things over and over again. But this is part of being in a women's movement. It was a political training ground for women. It *has* to be slower if you want to bring all your members along with you.

The United Women's Congress

Two years ago women were coming late for meetings or forgetting them, so I said, "Look. We've got to have diaries, and we must write down our meeting dates." We gave each woman a booklet, but they still didn't write *because they couldn't write.* So we had to teach them literacy. When we send out letters in English because we don't have time to translate them, there are people who won't understand them. We always try to rotate chairpeople in our meetings so that many women can acquire the skill, but this also slows things down.

In contrast, a UDF area committee can call an important general meeting tomorrow night at eleven, and people will be there. Most of them have cars, and they're not mothers with children. They're not living in the township where there's no transport. So there's a material difference in UDF student-type activists as opposed to a mass-based women's organization where the majority are black. But if you truly believe in trying to actively change the role of women, it's slow work and you've got to be patient. And sometimes I forget that I'm speaking to someone in what may be their third language.

UWO Becomes the United Women's Congress

Women's Front was a small group of township-based women that formed much later than UWO. I don't know if it had even a hundred members. But UDF said that there can't be two separate women's organizations in the same area with the same constitution both affiliated to UDF, so they told us to merge. It took us about two and a half years of discussions to actually do this.

There were personality clashes between two of the founding members who were very strong women. And some people said that UWO was dominated by whites, which was definitely unfounded. Most of our executive members were black people—mostly domestic workers; and all our chairpeople have always been black women. It's important to us that the people who represent our organization are representative of the majority of women in South Africa. We finally merged on the twenty-second of March 1986. We really haven't had any major problems during this first year. When we elected our eight executive members, we made sure that there was a Women's Front and a UWO chairperson and two secretaries from each of these groups. There are about two thousand five hundred members of UWCO now.

UWCO is the biggest nonracial organization in Cape Town and always has been. Because the UDF area committees are area-based, these committees are mostly one "race"—though, of course, we reject that concept. UWCO is an organization with branches from Guguletu [an African township] to the Gardens [a white suburb], so automatically we are more representative and nonracial. In contrast, the youth and civic groups are only organized in black areas. But the UDF has done *wonders* nationally to break down barriers. Apart from the UWO meetings in the western Cape, there were never mass meetings with people from all [racial] groups before UDF.

I was on the executive committee of UWCO a year ago [1986], but we're not allowed to be on it for more than two years. Being on the executive committee gives you an opportunity to think things out politically, to speak to people, to gain confidence, so we want all our women to have these experiences. If we believe in a truly equal society, we must avoid developing specialists. I've mentioned to the education and training group that we must have a public speaking course this year because we need more speakers. Apart from the language problem, we have complexes as black women about speaking out publicly.

Sexism and the UDF

At the annual general meeting of the Cape Town region, we looked at questions like: Do we promote nonracialism? Do we promote working-class leadership? Are we democratic? Are we sexist? We were all in small groups, and one comrade said about sexism, "I think that sometimes it's women's own fault because they don't assert themselves enough." I was so angry I couldn't speak. Fortunately a male comrade said, "I don't think that's fair." And after further discussion, we concluded that we are sexist. We reported this to the plenary session when everyone came together. The comrade who reported this said that male comrades need to think carefully through their actions, and that "our female comrades will also tell us when we are sexist." And I said, "That's really nonsense. No one will ever make a racist joke because they know it's too sensitive a matter. So why do male comrades have to be *told*? Why don't you develop the same kind of sensitivity that you have about being racist?" The chairperson responded, "Look. We don't have much time. We have to go on to the next point."

The next point was working-class leadership, and the discussion of this went on and on. Sometimes I'm very confrontationalist, but this time I told myself, "Gertrude, shut up!" Then a male comrade got up and said, "Look what's happening now. We didn't have enough time to discuss sexism, but we can go on and on about working-class leadership." So there is an awareness on the part of some male comrades, but the theory and the practice don't always coincide. And when one looks at the personal lives of some of the comrades, they also leave much to be desired.

The Federation of South African Women

At the moment we are involved in trying to relaunch a new Federation of South African Women. The women working on it are encouraging all women's groups to be part of it, including the women's sections of mixed groups like the trade unions. All these groups may not share the same ideology: for example, the Black Sash has agreed to be part of the federation although we don't always agree politically. The goals of the federation are to bring women together and for women to give political input and political guidance to the UDF. Like UDF, it will be an umbrella organization for different women's organizations to affiliate to.

Unity is one of the things we need most urgently in this country. When people are separated as they are in this country, they learn to accept the stereotypes about each other. For example, a woman in a new group I spoke to yesterday said, "I always thought that African people stink because that's what I was taught. I realize it's not true now that I'm mixing with Africans." Many black people think that all white people are arrogant and oppressive because in our daily lives we only have contact with white people within a very hierarchical structure. For example, when my friend Lynn [who is Coloured] and I lived in a house in Observatory with Louise who is white, Lynn's mother came to visit one day. Louise brought her a cup of coffee, and Lynn's mother went home and told people, "This white woman actually brought us a cup of coffee!" She'd never had that experience of actually being together in an organization and working together with people from other groups.

We are trying to get groups of women like homemakers, et cetera, into the federation. When we approach people we explain that it's important for women to come together, to speak with one voice, and to develop a common understanding in this country with so many barriers and so many groups of people separated from each other. We must develop relationships with each other. There is a draft constitution that needs to be approved at a later date. This will mean discussion of issues like maternity leave and equal salaries. I agree with the woman who said, "Women's liberation is not an act of charity, and it can never be achieved by men."

19
Feminist Pavement Politics

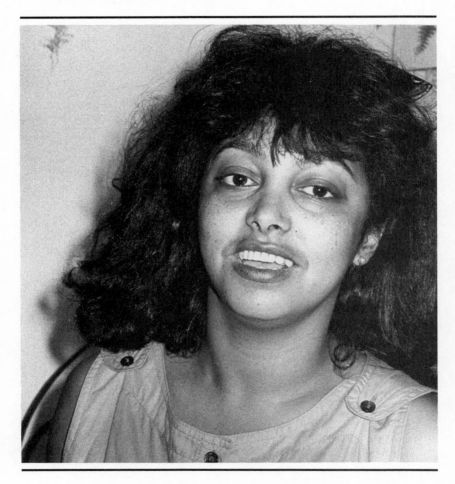

"My reason for highlighting rape and sexual abuse is that I feel people ignore them. They are not interested in these problems because they think they are personal and domestic issues. But if so many women experience them, then surely it can't just be personal and domestic."

ROZENA MAART

*R*OZENA MAART was, at twenty-four, the second youngest of the women I interviewed. She was living with a racially mixed group of friends in a so-called gray area of Cape Town where the Group Areas Act, legislating residential separation by race, has not been strictly implemented for a while. Here I interviewed Maart and also subsequently visited her a few times.

Maart, who has a B.A. honors degree in social work from the University of the Western Cape, had been working as a social worker at Groote Schuur Hospital for the past two and a half years in gynecology and the emergency unit. She mainly sees survivors of rape, incest, and extrafamilial child sexual abuse, counseling them within a feminist framework that she says she developed when working in Rape Crisis.

Maart is a bright, flamboyant, and gutsy woman with tremendous energy and independence of mind. For example, her response to the common left accusation that feminism is divisive, is: "It's patriarchy that is divisive, not feminism." She is a committed feminist whose risky "pavement politics," as she calls them, are as original as they are daring. In the past, the government has often dismissed feminist politics as not threatening to the apartheid system, but Maart's group, Women Against Repression, engages in unusually risky actions. In this interview she describes the formation of WAR and some of its novel activities such as picketing against child sexual abuse and graffiti spraying, showing in the process how male dominated the society is. Maart has also worked out a political theory of her own to justify her protesting sexism rather than apartheid. She critiques the common defense by people in the anti-apartheid movement of certain customs like lobola—that they are just cultural phenomena—by pointing out that "ten years ago it was culturally acceptable to call a black man 'kaffir' [the equivalent of nigger] and 'boy.' What is seen as culturally acceptable depends on men's definitions, which change when it suits them," Maart declared.

When I saw her, Maart was expecting soon to interrupt her political activities to go to England on scholarship to do an M.A. in women's studies at the University of York—an opportunity that she felt justified her leaving her work in WAR.

Growing Up Coloured

I am the oldest of nine children. My father had five women. Three of them were wise enough not to marry him, including my mother, so Maart is my mother's surname. I come from District Six,* but we were forced to move from there to Lavender Hill [another black area, but one lacking a sense of community] when I was twelve years old. I lived with my mother, granny, sisters, and uncles. There were about twenty-four of us in a three-bedroomed house.

I felt very, very unhappy about being uprooted from District Six and having to leave all my friends. At the time I thought going to live in Lavender Hill was the worst experience in my life. District Six is less than four minutes drive from where I now live. Whenever I drive past there, I am still upset by seeing the flattened space where my home used to be.

There were no shops for miles in Lavender Hill. There were no schools. We saw ourselves as absolutely oppressed when we went there because it was like a dump, and that's what we called it. We went to school in Cape Town for a year after that, rather than going somewhere nearer by, because we wouldn't accept the fact that we lived in Lavender Hill. When I started going to high school in Lavender Hill, I began to realize what it means to be Coloured. I only learned what it means to be *black* later on when I made connections between myself and other black people.

The women in my family are very strong. My great-grandmother, my grandmother, and my mother had a feminist consciousness long before I even realized what this meant. Their standing up for themselves made a strong impression on me. I was brought up to believe that I can do anything I want to do. But I wasn't interested in school. There were boycotts and marches and placard demonstrations that were ten times more interesting than studying. I only passed by the skin of my teeth with D's and E's.

I wanted to study drama at university. My mother said I couldn't do it, and my friends said I shouldn't because it would have required me to go to the University of Cape Town [a largely white university; the university designed for Coloured people, the University of the Western Cape, has no drama department]. UCT has a permit system for all its

---

* District Six was a black community in Cape Town that was totally destroyed because of its proximity to white residents.

black students, now called a quota system, which means it has a permit to have black and Coloured students there. Had I gone there, it would have meant that I accepted this system, so I went to the University of the Western Cape instead.

I participated in the protests at UWC because I felt they were important despite the fact that they never addressed the oppression of women. The fact that all sixteen of the students on the Student Representative Council were men for two years in a row says a lot about this lack of awareness. It took me about two years to decide that I wasn't going to have anything more to do with campus politics. Instead, I got involved outside of campus. But this was also frustrating because there was no place for women there either. At meetings I'd only see the women at the interval because they'd have been in the kitchen all the time preparing for the food break.

Rape Crisis Work and Feminism

I joined Cape Town Rape Crisis in 1982 and was very active in it for a time. It was incredibly influential in my thinking. By acknowledging that "sexual abuse is personal abuse is political abuse," rape crisis centers have played a very important role in this country. Usually sexual abuse is regarded as something you go to a hospital for and then don't talk about with other people. The community organizations don't do anything about it. Rape Crisis has made people aware that sexual abuse exists and that there are ways and means of handling it.

It was only when I joined Rape Crisis that I regarded myself as a feminist, although I hated that word. I didn't want to be known as a feminist. But now I do because I know what it represents to me. It no longer has an American, academic, white connotation. I do whatever is comfortable for me. I wear makeup because I enjoy it. I wear pants a lot because I like them. Feminism has very little to do with the kind of clothes you wear, whether you wash dishes or not. It's got to do with how you see yourself in relation to other people, whether you are oppressive or exploitative, and how you relate to people.

As a feminist/activist I consider my most important work to be picketing against sexual abuse and drawing analogies between state violence and violence against women. I'm not saying that all the other protests I have participated in haven't meant a lot. But, in the history of South African politics, organizing a feminist demonstration is much more groundbreaking.

ROZENA MAART

Women Against Repression

Five of us got together in April last year [1986] to look at what we felt the shortcomings were of South African women's organizations. We are all black women, and four of us are or were Rape Crisis members. I'm fairly middle class in terms of having a job and earning a professional salary. The other four women were university students, so we all had a university education. We have always been friends who rail about the same things, and we felt that there was a need for another women's organization. So we founded a group we call WAR—Women Against Repression.

There are now thirty people in our organization, so it's grown a lot in seven months. A lot of them are working-class women. There are also a lot of people like Kevin [a housemate and friend] who don't come to meetings regularly, but who take part in actions. Men aren't full-time members. They understand that we want the organization to be comfortable for women. They [men] get involved in the actions but not the other activities like public speaking, workshops, and education. White women are also involved. We feel that white people have a role to play. We are not sectarian in any way. The fight is not against whites, it's against white domination. We want to encourage everybody to take up that fight, and not to exclude anybody because they are white or male.

Rape Crisis looks at sexual abuse and tries to politicize people about the analogy between the state oppressing people and beating them and men oppressing and raping women. The United Women's Congress, a largely black women's organization, believes that black women are oppressed because they are black and tries to encourage women to join mainstream politics. We have a more in-depth approach than either of these organizations in terms of looking at social, cultural, legal, and economic aspects of women's oppression.

If you make a logical argument as to why feminism is valid, why it is relevant, why it should be part of mainstream politics, people will often agree with you. But they'll say that it's not so important and can wait 'til after the revolution. I think it's going to be a long fight, and part of WAR's program of engaging in that kind of struggle is to be very action-oriented. We've only been going officially since August of last year [1986], and we've done a helluva lot of stuff. We've had three pickets [demonstrations] already, and we've spoken to people at schools.

Feminist Pavement Politics

At one school a teacher tried to rape a student he'd given a lift to. There were graffitied slogans on the wall opposite this school like "FIGHT APARTHEID" and "WE STAND BY OUR TEACHERS" because the principal and one of the teachers had been in detention. We said to the teachers at this school, "On the one hand, you're trying to politicize and conscientize the students. On the other hand, you are sexually abusing them. How the hell can you do this? It's denying them the right to control their own bodies." And they answered, "That's a different issue." So we organized a demonstration there. Instead of a sign saying, "HANDS OFF OUR TEACHERS," we made one that said, "TEACHERS, HANDS OFF OUR STUDENTS!" and "HANDS OF THE TEACHERS OFF THE STUDENTS."

When we went to talk to the principal of this highly politicized school about the fact that sexual abuse of students by teachers is also a political issue, he responded, "But it's not the same thing." Then he said, "I'm dealing with it in my own way. Do you people want to see blood?" We said, "No, we want dismissals of these teachers, and not just from this school, but from being allowed to teach at any school." We argued, "If one of your teachers was heard calling one of your children 'kaffir' or some other racist term, what would you do?" He said, "I'd kick him out of the school." We said, "But why aren't you doing the same now?" He said, "It's different." We said, "No, it's the same thing." But the principal saw the rape as the student's fault. He said, "Oh, these girls look for these things. This girl wears long nails and a short skirt. She wanted it."

The principal wouldn't let the teachers tell the students about the rape. We thought that if the female students knew about it, they at least wouldn't take lifts from these teachers. So at about three o'clock one morning, we graffitied the slogans on the school sports stadium. When five hundred students arrived at school the next morning they all knew about the sexual abuse.

The Western Cape Teachers' Union is an organization that looks at how teachers can work with oppression in schools and in the community. In their constitution, it states that they should fight discrimination on all levels. WAR was told about some cases of teachers sexually abusing students at schools, but when we took this issue to WECTU they didn't want to deal with it. So we told them, "If you don't do something about this, we will have a picket about it." So they said "O.K., we'll think about it." WECTU now has a subcommittee on sexual harassment, but they have done nothing else about this problem. It's bad enough if children are sexually abused, but if so-called progressive activist teachers are actually doing the sexual abuse, it's ten times worse.

We have had calls from several schools and teachers from quite a few of them came to our meetings. They asked us to take up the issue of sexual abuse rather than going to Rape Crisis because they wanted to go beyond offering counseling to victims. They wanted the problem to be made public and for people to do something about it. But the teachers involved in protesting the sexual abuse were the ones to be dismissed. The reason for their dismissal wasn't stated, but it was very clear it was because of the stand they had taken before they even got involved with WAR. They didn't participate in our picket, but they had insisted in a school meeting that something be done about the problem. They were told that there would be no position for them the next year. But the teachers who sexually harassed students are all still teaching despite the fact that we spray-painted "GET RID OF EDGAR WILLIAMS AND BRIAN ADONIS" [the perpetrators] on the school wall. Another slogan was "SEXUAL ABUSE EQUALS PERSONAL ABUSE EQUALS POLITICAL ABUSE."

There have been a lot of child rape-murders of little girls and boys in Mitchells Plain [a Coloured area near Cape Town]. WAR organized a petition against the sexist rape laws with slogans like "SEXUAL HARASSMENT, A COMMUNITY ISSUE." It's usually assumed that it's women's job to take up such issues. We wanted to challenge why when somebody is called a "kaffir," it is regarded as a political issue, but rape is not. Our goals were to encourage so-called political community organizations to deal with rape and sexual harassment and to create an awareness about these problems which have been kept very much under cover.

Picketing is scary to do because it's illegal. You have to get permission to picket. But there's no point in our asking because it would never be granted, especially in view of the fact that we make it quite clear that we aren't only picketing against somebody who sexually abused a child, but we draw analogies between this and state violence. Our pickets are designed to get publicity and to put pressure on the schools. I phone people who I know and trust at the *Cape Times*, the *Argus*, and all the newspapers the night before a picket and say, "There's going to be a picket. Be there!" They appreciate it and half the time they get there before us. We only actually stand there for about fifteen minutes to half an hour. One time I asked for the photo of me to be cut out of a larger picture because of my job. (The other picketers were all students.) The journalists cooperate with requests like this because they're people that I know. One time we were picketing in the middle of Cape Town and only left a few minutes before the police came. It was a very close call. But the risk involved in picketing isn't as great as it is for doing graffiti.

Feminist Pavement Politics

When we want to mobilize people for an action like a graffiti spree, we phone people and say, "There's a joll [party] tonight. Meet at so-and-so's house," and they know what it means. They all pitch up with a spray can or two, and we decide on the slogans before we go out so that we don't have any that are not in line with WAR's philosophy. For example, our slogans for International Women's Day were "WE FIGHT MALE DOMINATION" and "WOMEN FIGHT FOR THEIR RIGHTS." We *don't* say things like "AS MOTHERS AND CHILDREN WE STAND BY OUR MEN." We call these actions pavement politics.

We also respond to newspaper articles. For example, there was an article about a woman who was raped by a policeman. He was only fined eighty bloody rand [$40] for the rape. We responded by writing a letter to the newspaper and by doing graffiti.

Spraying graffiti is considered a serious offense, particularly because of the state of emergency. We all know the risk involved. We are always very scared when we do this. We try to be as careful as possible. But we are not going to be dormant because there is a state of emergency. We don't have money to pay for ads in the paper so we have to make people aware by using other methods, because the state of emergency is going to continue until the revolution.

There are only about six of us in WAR who are willing to participate in the graffiti actions. But it's okay that other people don't want to. It's their choice. For me, if I have to think, "I can't do this or that because I may be detained," I might as well not live. Whether there's a state of emergency or not, I'm still going to do something to bring about change. If I have to go underground at three o'clock in the morning, then that's what I am prepared to do. We've done graffiti actions about six times now. There is always somebody waiting in a car in case we need to escape in a hurry.

Maart's Ideology

I don't regard what I do now as less political than demonstrating against apartheid. I think it is the same thing. I think that women's oppression is political, that the personal is political. But fighting sexism is more significant to me because it is an analysis I have made for myself. I didn't go on our pickets because I felt it was part of being in the mainstream, but because it was my choice and because I believe in it. I am not saying I didn't believe in the student protests, but participating in them was a case of being part of the flow and feeling that if I didn't, I'd be making a statement that was *a*political.

I'm not so thrilled about the whole idea of sisterhood. A lot of politically active women that I know are completely antifeminist, and they commit suicide to their feminist potential because their whole orientation in life has been geared to pleasing men. And then there are a lot of men whose comradeship I share because they have a feminist analysis even while they have problems with the word *feminist*. Just as the African National Congress is not exclusively African, so our women's organization is not exclusively for women. We believe that the fight is against male domination and the system of patriarchy, not against men and not against whites.

I subscribe to an analysis that challenges race, class, and gender. I think that the fight against male domination must not become a woman's issue in the sense that it must not only be fought by women. When people talk about "the people shall govern, the people shall this, the people shall that," I wonder if they mean women. Which is why we came up with the slogan "WOMEN'S DEMANDS ARE PEOPLE'S DEMANDS."

Although I see gender as only one of the three priority issues along with race and class, it is never acknowledged. That's why all the activist work that I do is centered around feminism. I would prefer for my work to have more balance, but it can't because so few others work on sexism.

The Consequences of Political Activism

I'm not afraid of people finding out what I'm doing. Most people know that the organization exists. When we do pickets, people know that it's us because it's in the newspaper. So far nothing has happened as a result of our actions. But we don't see ourselves as an organization that can't be brought in for questioning. The newspapers don't report what we say against the state, because of the press curbs, and they also choose pictures that don't challenge the state. They'll cut out the part of the picture in which the picket says "SEXUAL ABUSE EQUALS PERSONAL ABUSE EQUALS POLITICAL ABUSE" for publication purposes. This is probably why we haven't been hassled more so far.

One of the terrible things about being involved in mainstream politics is that one sometimes finds that male-activist men become the enemy, because gender politics requires one to see how people deal with their personal lives. Of course people don't like this because it's threatening. Men worry: "Somebody's watching how I talk to my wife or somebody's looking at what my wife does." One of the personal consequences for me of my political activities is that I'm ignored in some circles. For example, when I went to a union gathering, a lot of people didn't look at me or talk to me because they know what I do and they think it's terrible that I'm not fighting in mainstream politics. I go through different phases in my life where I feel I need to get recognition for what I am doing, but I don't feel I need it now. I've got my own circle of friends, and I feel that what I am doing is valid, important, and uplifting. Women's oppression is one facet of the oppression in South Africa, and I don't see my focusing on it as any different than somebody else focusing on trade-union work. But none of the mainstream political organizations address the issue of gender, which makes me feel more and more that there is never going to be a rightful, equal place for women, including after the revolution.

When the ANC is the new government, it will definitely still be a male-dominated government. Maybe the male domination won't be as severe as it would be without the influence of feminists. Quite honestly, I don't think it's all that important which political organization comes into power after the revolution.

PART V

THE MANY FACES
OF ANTI-APARTHEID
ACTIVISM

"I always draw a parallel between oppression by the regime and oppression by men. To me it is just the same. I always challenge men on why they react to oppression by the regime, but then they do exactly the same things to women that they criticize the regime for."

—SETHEMBILE N.

THE SPEAKERS IN this section focus more on some of the issues some political activists are tackling than on organizations. Sethembile N.* [pseudonym], for example, shows why Chief Gatsha Buthelezi's Inkatha movement is seen by both the government's security branch as well as anti-apartheid groups as a major obstacle to the South African liberation struggle. Since Buthelezi—who has a significant international reputation, particularly in the United States—opposes divestment and indeed encourages foreign investment in South Africa, claiming it is good for black people, the international business community has enthusiastically embraced him. Business leaders ignore the fact that all the black leaders of the anti-apartheid movement are in favor of sanctions and divestment. I realized how important it is for the international community to hear about this other side of Chief Buthelezi. It was impossible, however, to find a Zulu woman who was willing to talk

---

* This way of naming the woman is intended to remind the reader that her real identity is not being revealed.

about him without using a pseudonym, so fearful are critics of retaliation by him or Inkatha—the movement that he heads.

While Sethembile N. chose to use a pseudonym to protect her life, Hettie V., a rebel against her Afrikaner heritage, decided not to use her real name in an effort to keep a low profile so as to continue with her political work as long as possible. Although not the only Afrikaner I interviewed, Hettie V. is the only one represented in this volume. She has a fascinating tale to tell, starting with her learning to shoot at the age of ten with other Afrikaner children who were members of an organization called the Young Voortrekkers.

Rhoda Bertelsmann-Kadalie, a Coloured woman, describes the consequences of her marriage to a white Afrikaner both before and after intermarriage became legal. One of the much-heralded reforms of the current government was to repeal the Mixed Marriages Act, which outlawed marriages between members of different races, along with the so-called Immorality Act, which had made interracial sexual relations illegal. Bertelsmann-Kadalie shows how these reforms have not stopped the harassment of racially mixed couples.

Leila Issel, the thirteen-year-old daughter of Shahieda Issel [see chapter 4], describes her political activity from the age of seven, and the police response. Since children are playing such a crucial role in the South African liberation movement, I felt it important to include the voice of at least one child.

Finally, Sheena Duncan, a prominent leader in the Black Sash with an extraordinary fund of information about the racist legal system in South Africa, describes the appalling scope and destruction that has resulted from forcing millions of people, mainly Africans, to move from their homes to uninhabitable dumping grounds. This massive dislocation is part of the government's insane dream and malevolent belief that apartheid can and must be implemented.

20
A Refugee from Inkatha

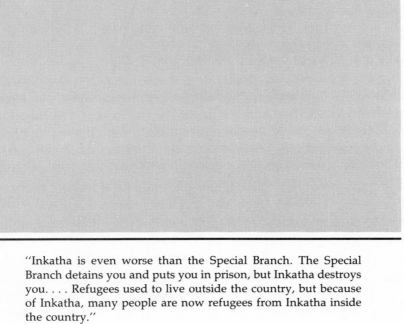

"Inkatha is even worse than the Special Branch. The Special Branch detains you and puts you in prison, but Inkatha destroys you. . . . Refugees used to live outside the country, but because of Inkatha, many people are now refugees from Inkatha inside the country."

SETHEMBILE N.

*S*ETHEMBILE N. is, as a Zulu, particularly vulnerable to Inkatha's efforts to punish Zulus who belong to UDF-affiliated groups
instead of showing loyalty to their Zulu chief, Gatsha Buthelezi.
Thus, she finds it necessary not only to use a pseudonym here* but to
hide out illegally in the so-called white neighborhoods of Durban. In
this interview, Sethembile N. describes the events—including the
murder of a friend's father—that led to her decision to become a
refugee from Inkatha and go into hiding.

*Thirty-four years old in 1987, Sethembile N. is the mother of three
daughters, the eldest of whom is fourteen and the youngest, seven. A
teacher for many years before her political activities made it impossible to continue, she was also a battered wife who left her husband and
has become an able and dedicated leader in the National Education
Union of South Africa. Sethembile N. describes both of these experiences in some detail. Although I didn't ask her whether she considers
herself a feminist, her active and outspoken commitment to gender
equality earn her this label in my mind. The stories of Sethembile N.,
Gertrude Fester, and Anne Mayne lead me to wonder whether women
who are battered or raped are more likely to become feminists, or
whether feminists are simply more willing to reveal these experiences. (I did not specifically ask about experiences of male violence.)*

*I interviewed Sethembile N. in the Durban house I was staying in
one day after the election on 6 May 1987. The UDF had called a
national stayaway to protest the all-white elections and to highlight
their demands for the unbanning of the ANC, the release of the
leaders in prison, the return of those in exile, the lifting of the state of
emergency, and the withdrawal of troops from the townships. Sethembile N. described herself as "really inspired" by the effectiveness of
the stayaway. "Although the South African Broadcasting Corporation
would underplay what is happening," she said, "they reported that
sixty percent of the workers in Natal participated in the stayaway
yesterday. This degree of support was unexpected because of Inkatha's repression in this province. The participation was highest in
the Transvaal, and in Port Elizabeth and East London it was eighty*

---

* Other major figures in Sethembile N.'s story have also been given pseudonyms for
security reasons, at her request.

percent to one hundred percent. This morning Capitol Radio said that the participation today is even higher. So it has been very successful."

Sethembile N. has a strong personality—direct, assertive, energetic, exuberant, and very present—and is definitely a leader. May she have the opportunity fully to realize this ability.

Growing Up African

My father is illiterate, and my mother was a domestic worker until her health got bad. When I was only eleven or twelve years of age, I had to work during my holidays for the white holiday makers. I washed dishes and looked after their children to help pay my school fees. My parents had to save all their money to be able to send me to boarding school for standards nine and ten. I started nursing after I matriculated. But I quit after three months because I couldn't take the regimentation. When I was seventeen or eighteen, I went to work in a factory for five rand [$2.50] a week. Then I decided I wanted to be a teacher. Because I had no money, I had to work as a private teacher for five years before I could get my training. I was also never able to study full-time at the University of Zululand for financial reasons. I found it very tough to study for my B.A. courses after work.

I got married in 1972. I was interested in politics during my married years but remained passive because my husband wanted me to confine myself to going to work and household chores. He and I were both teachers, but he would go and drink after work, while I was expected to go home and look after the kids, do housework, then be scolded for having ironed a blue shirt rather than a pink one. He felt threatened if I wanted to go to a political meeting, so I was prevented from involving myself as fully as I wished.

When I tried to further my education, my husband tore up my notes and said, "You want to make yourself better than I am." He was violent and drank a lot. I have a scar on my head where he stabbed me with a knife. I was staying with my in-laws and sitting in the lounge peeling a peach with a knife. My husband came into the room and said, "Why are you looking at me?" Then he picked up the knife. Usually I ran away from him in these situations, but that time I wanted to see if he intended only to threaten me, but he stabbed me for no reason.

If he discovered that I was talking happily with his mother, he would say, "Are you gossiping about me? You are against me." When he drank alcohol, he felt threatened and inferior. Sometimes he was violent toward me seven days a week. Most of the time I wanted to end the marriage, but society always expects a woman to persevere. I had to wait until everyone realized that things were very tough for me, otherwise I would have become an outcast.

In 1981, I said "To hell with everyone!" and I divorced him. But getting away from him was very difficult. I had to sneak out of the house and leave the kids with him. I knew he was a drunkard and that anything could happen to them, but I had to save my life. I went to the magistrate who was fortunately very sympathetic about my reasons for leaving. He said, "Do you want your kids?" I said, "Yes." After about a week, a court order was issued requiring my husband to bring the kids to the magistrate's court and hand them over to me. Then I legally handed them over to my mother. I didn't even need a lawyer to fight the divorce, because I had such a strong case against him. He was very overwhelmed by this and has never been brave enough to approach me himself since then—though he has sent people to tell me he wanted to reconcile.

Political Activity

I taught Zulu [one of the major African languages in South Africa] and became very involved in education politics after my divorce. As a literature teacher I was able to bring up relevant issues in class and to use methods that conscientized the students by encouraging their creativity and critical thinking. Since 1984, I have been the chairperson in Durban of a nonracial teachers' organization called NEUSA—the National Education Union of South Africa. Teachers who belong to NEUSA have to be quiet about their membership because we challenge the government's system of education. NEUSA is the only nonracial teachers' union in Natal. Most of its membership is black because we are the most oppressed. We have a lot of support from students and a great deal of credibility amongst the communities.

In the northern Transvaal and in the eastern Cape, there was a time when the students would ask a teacher, "Are you a member of NEUSA? If not, get out!" We don't separate politics from education but see education as part of politics. Right now we are discussing the question of "people's education." We are concerned about education *for* liberation and education *after* liberation. But since we are not in a position to take control of the education system, the first step is for our people's education programs to run parallel to the official system of education that exists now. We are critical of the biased history syllabus that only begins after the arrival of Western people in South Africa and that sees black people as troublemakers who stole the sheep of the white people. People's education tries to rectify these kinds of biases.

The government has now banned the very term *people's education* because they consider it to be teaching communism and revolution, so the materials we compile cannot be used yet. But before the state of emergency was declared, people's education was being taught in some schools in Soweto. After it, the South African Defense Forces have been present in the schools, which has made it very difficult to implement our programs. So we have to plan weekend workshops for students on topics like democracy within the schools, the history of the educational struggle in South Africa, and so on.

The recent state of emergency has hit us very hard. Most NEUSA teachers have been kicked out of school. Last year we could not even afford a national conference. One of our NEUSA members was called into the security offices simply for addressing the teachers about NEUSA. I was forced to resign from teaching in January [1987], which is what so often happens to NEUSA teachers. My school was closed down last year in September because the majority of the teachers there were NEUSA members and the rest were supporters. Many of us were transferred to schools in distant places. My friend Tozi Dlamini was sent to Zululand to teach at a school whose principal was a member of Inkatha from KwaMashu, where her father had been killed by Inkatha. I was transferred to Ermelo primary school, which is near Swaziland. If I refused to go there, I was out of a job.

Some teachers went where they were sent only to find no accommodation had been prepared for them. Others were told by the principal, "I don't know anything about you." This is what happened to Tozi. The school chairperson said to her, "I don't want you. If the department is interested in giving us an additional post, they should tell us, and we will look for a teacher we want." So they sent her up to Ermelo instead. Our lawyers fought this case, so she was then transferred to Pietermaritzburg, where she teaches in a primary school, although she is a secondary schoolteacher with higher qualifications than anyone else in the school. They have her teaching sewing.

I have a job now that provides academic support, financial support, and assistance in finding accommodation for disadvantaged, mainly black students. I will have to keep this job, but my main interest is in education, and I miss teaching because I enjoy the interaction with the kids, and they enjoy it, too.

Gatsha Buthelezi and Inkatha

A significant problem in Natal is that most African schools in this province are in the KwaZulu area [the Zulu "homeland" run by Buthelezi], and Chief Gatsha Buthelezi has said that teachers' jobs will be threatened if they join our union. A bill was passed in the KwaZulu parliament saying that teachers who get involved in politics will be sacked. In 1986 the teachers in KwaZulu were forced to sign pledges saying that they would not denigrate or villify Buthelezi's name, the KwaZulu parliament, or Inkatha. As well as the pledge, teachers had to make an oath in front of a commissioner of oaths.

Inkatha is not popular because it is tribalistic, and the chief minister, Gatsha Buthelezi, is not democratic. Most of the people who are involved in Inkatha don't understand politics and what Inkatha is all about. They join to get jobs or for business reasons. A lot of information about Inkatha attacks are leaked by Inkatha people because so many of them aren't very committed to it. Only about two percent of the Zulu people are voluntarily Inkatha members. Pensioners won't get their pensions in KwaZulu unless they are card-carrying members. And at the beginning of each year, when students have to pay school fees, there is a fifty-cent fee for Inkatha. The lists of students and pensioners are then used by Inkatha to make the membership appear very large. But it's not a voluntary membership.

The Amabuthos, the Inkatha vigilante group who physically attack people, are not even members of the organization. They are migrant workers and unemployed people. Inkatha is able to get their cooperation because they need permission to stay in town. They are also rewarded with money and beer. The press interviewed the Amabuthos who attacked those of us attending the National Education Crisis Committee conference, and many of them said, "We didn't know what it was about. We were just told that we must get into the bus."

In January 1985, the examination results of our standard ten students were withheld by the Department of Education. An Education Crisis Committee consisting of parents, students, and teachers was formed to deal with this, and I was one of the two teachers elected. We demanded that the Department of Education release the results of the students' examinations, but they refused. One day a woman phoned us to say that the police had told her that Inkatha would fix us for being the instigators of the boycotts by the Durban school kids who were protesting the withholding of their exam results. She asked them, "But why do you say Inkatha? Isn't Inkatha involved in the liberation struggle?" The chief of the Special Branch, Drane Meyer, said, "No, Inkatha is working with us. Just give us three months." We were very frightened by this threat because we feel that Inkatha is even worse than the Special Branch. The Special Branch detains you and puts you in prison, but Inkatha destroys you.

I lived in a place called Hambanati when I was still married. It is about forty kilometers from Durban. In 1984, Inkatha attacked all the people they considered UDF elements in Hambanati and burned down their houses. The whole UDF community in Hambanati was uprooted and their houses destroyed. I was one of those who lost my house there. I was not staying there at the time because I had to be near Durban for study purposes, but I had intended settling there with my kids after I had completed my degree. I didn't go back there, but most of the people wanted to return, so there were negotiations between Inkatha and the UDF about this. But the people who returned to Hambanati were attacked by Inkatha again, so they had to move out permanently.

In May 1985, I was living with two other women in a cottage in the Umlazi township. We were living under great tension. If there was a movement outside, we thought, "Oh! Inkatha has come." Then we thought, "No, these people are just trying to intimidate us and discourage us from carrying on with our activities." I was a part-time B.A. student at the university at that time, and one night in May—fortunately for me—I stayed the night in Lamontville where I was teaching. One of my colleagues told me, "Inkatha has attacked your house." They had thrown petrol bombs at it and burned it down. The other two women had been in the house but managed to escape with their children—a baby and a five-year-old. I left the township after that because it was too dangerous for me to live there any longer.

We reported the destruction of our house to the police, but when they came, they only asked, "This has never happened in Umlazi before, so why did they come and attack you? Are you involved in politics?" There were some petrol bombs at our house that hadn't exploded and some bottles which we gave to the police for fingerprints. When we asked them later, "Where are the bottles for fingerprints?" they said, "We didn't need them so we've thrown them away." This shows the attitude of the police when we report to them about Inkatha. I started to stay in a white suburb after that because I didn't know what would happen next in Umlazi. My kids are now staying with my mother, where they are safe.

Somebody phoned to tell us that there were rumors that Inkatha buses from KwaZulu were on their way to attack people in KwaMashu where Tozi's family, the Dlaminis, lived. Tozi is a close friend of mine as well as a teaching colleague and a member of NEUSA, so I phoned to tell her of these rumors. Tozi said, "But why would Inkatha attack us?" Since the Dlaminis didn't see any reason for an attack, they didn't run away. Very late that night the phone rang, and it was one of Tozi's sisters saying that Mr. Dlamini had been killed. Robert and another friend of ours in the house drove to KwaMashu to try to rescue them, not knowing whether the Amabuthos were still there. When we arrived, they had left and the casspirs were there. The Dlamini family was sitting outside with a neighbor waiting for the dawn. Next to them was some of their furniture and a bundle of things that hadn't been destroyed. Smoke was still coming from their house.

The Dlaminis had heard shots from the front door of their four-room house. There are still gunshot holes along the window sills and around the door. The Amabuthos are not very well trained, so they were just firing at random. There is a small bedroom at the back of the house, where the children stayed. Tozi was recovering from a caesarian delivery, and her two-week-old baby was with her. While some Amabuthos were shooting in the front of the house, others were trying to get in through a back window. Tozi doesn't know how she gained strength, but she took an umbrella and beat the men who were trying to enter through the window. She had pushed the wardrobe against the window and was beating them fiercely from behind it. Then a spear stabbed through her coming out just under her chin. It was very fortunate it didn't kill her.

One of the Amabuthos who had entered the bedroom said, "All the women must move out! Out!" He told the other Amabuthos that they must only fight with men. So the women managed to escape from the house, while Tozi's father and Thabo [Tozi's brother] remained inside. Thabo managed to escape because he is a fast thinker. The Amabuthos started to loot before they killed anyone, so Thabo joined them in looting as if he were one of them. Then he escaped. His father was an old man whom they shot and stabbed to death when he tried to run away. Then the Amabuthos attacked and burned the house. After hiding in people's toilets, the other members of the family returned to find Mr. Dlamini lying outside dead.

A Refugee from Inkatha

Inkatha attacks people suspected of being active in UDF. Tozi was in NEUSA, which is affiliated to UDF; Thabo was in the Youth Congress in KwaMashu; and their mother had resigned from Inkatha. Some time back in the mid-1970s, Mrs. Dlamini had been very active in Inkatha. At some stage she discovered that Gatsha was a liar. Her kids had also kept discouraging her from being involved in Inkatha activities. Inkatha might have had a grudge against her for resigning. They might have assumed that meant she had joined a UDF group. But Mr. Dlamini wasn't involved in any political group at all. He had never been arrested or anything. Most people who have been victims of Inkatha are not even activists in UDF, but if you are against Inkatha, they assume you must be UDF. If a boy is in the SRC [Student Representative Council] at school, they think he is UDF. This is why most people have been killed and most houses have been burnt by Inkatha.

During my friend Robert's interrogation when he was in detention, the Special Branch drew a diagram with the state on one side and the opposition on the other. Groups like ECC [End Conscription Campaign], NEUSA, and UDF were written in as members of the opposition. Robert deliberately mentioned Inkatha as opposing the state, and the Special Branch said, "No, no, no! Inkatha is on the *government's* side." He was shocked that the Special Branch would actually say that. The Special Branch has also said to some people, "You must be happy to be in detention, because if we let you out, Inkatha would kill you." Clearly, Inkatha and the government work hand in glove with each other. Each time the people take a stand against the government, Inkatha attacks them. For example, when NECC [National Education Crisis Committee] encouraged people not to buy books or pay school fees in 1985 because they pay taxes and there is a high rate of unemployment and the government should provide for education, Inkatha attacked people.

In March last year, the NECC had a national conference here in Durban. NECC announced that the government should respond to their demands within three months; otherwise, there would be another conference where people would decide what to do next. This conference had nothing to do with Inkatha, but Gatsha made a statement that it was being held in Durban to provoke him. Although it was in a white area, Inkatha attacked us. I ran for my life into a shop and asked the owner to close the shop, then peeped into the street through the glass door. The shop owner wanted to phone the police, but I told him, "The police aren't going to do anything against Inkatha." Many people have been killed by Inkatha, but no arrests have been made. On this occasion the police came when Inkatha buses were arriving. After the war was over, they escorted them back into their buses.

Inkatha has killed hundreds of people. Last month nine school kids were killed in KwaMashu, and in Claremont, I can't say how many. In December, thirteen were killed in one family on one day. I am only talking about the very prominent incidents. In contrast, the UDF always *avoids* confronting Inkatha.

I am staying with Robert, who was detained last year. The police now realize that people use the white suburbs for hiding, so during the last state of emergency they concentrated their searches here. Each night we had to move to another house. When Robert was released from detention after about four weeks, he was shocked to find that I was still here to welcome him. He had been told in prison that I was a terrorist involved in the bombings that were exploding around Durban at that time. He had become convinced that I was using his house as an ANC base. The Special Branch had worked on his mind when he was in solitary confinement, and he had come to believe what they told him.

Being in hiding is very, very taxing. I become paranoid. I am suspicious of every car that stops and every telephone call. I can't even go to the shop. I actually detain myself. I can only move at night in disguise. I had to disguise myself yesterday to get my driver's license. I wore a domestic worker's uniform and a head scarf to the driving school. But it is still safer in a white area as far as Inkatha is concerned, and I prefer detention to being killed. Quite a few black people live in white areas or non-KwaZulu areas. Refugees used to live outside the country, but because of Inkatha, many people are now refugees from Inkatha inside the country.

The Consequences of Political Work

I'm not able to live with my kids because there is no place for us to stay together. They stay with me here at Robert's house over the holidays, but we receive telephone calls asking, "What are those black children doing here? Go back to the township." When I returned from meetings, my kids would say, "Ma, this telephone caller phoned again." It was very tough for them, but even so, they want to stay with me. But if I kept them here, who would look after them? I have to go to work and attend meetings, so it is much better that they stay with their granny, who is always at home.

A Refugee from Inkatha

There used to be phone calls even when the kids were not here. Anonymous callers would say things like, "Kaffirs should get out of that house." Last December my kids were in the house when the Special Branch came through the window and raided us. That night there was a telephone caller who threatened, "Remember the necklaces and the hand grenades," and then banged down the telephone. The three children were sleeping on mattresses on the floor when there was a bang, bang, bang on the window. I jumped up thinking, "Today is our last day." I went to the other room where Thabo, Tozi's brother, sleeps and said, "The AWB* have come!" The police opened the window and entered the house. They looked around and wanted our identity papers. They didn't want to identify themselves, but we saw they were police because they had guns with them. They said they were going to take Thabo, but they left the house without him.

I think they raided us because Robert's house had become notorious by that time. I am not staying there right now because we were expecting raids there before the elections. I had planned to go back to the house today until I got the message that Robert was arrested at a demonstration this morning, so they might have a follow-up raid on the house while Robert is in prison.

I am now staying at another white man's house with a NEUSA friend, Vusi, whose life has also been threatened by Inkatha. He is also out of teaching now. An Australian guy who is staying there said that there was a street meeting of white people who were complaining about their black neighbors. Although this is defined as a white area by the Group Areas Act, there is a legal loophole according to which a black person can be here for ninety days. So the police have to prove that we have been here for more than ninety days, which is difficult.

Robert's big three-bedroom house has now become a home to me. One room is Robert's, another is mine, and there is a very big room that is used by other people who pop in and out. Tozi's brother started staying there continuously after his father was murdered by Inkatha last May [1986]. There is a difference between a home where I live and a place where I need to go when I am seriously hiding. I still use Robert's house as a hideout as far as Inkatha is concerned, but it is no longer a hideout as far as the state is concerned. I moved out during the state of emergency last year, but Robert stayed because he felt that he was not involved in anything serious. Then he was detained.

* The Afrikaner Weerstandsbeweging, meaning Afrikaner Resistance Movement in English, a white supremacist group founded in 1972 whose members wear swastika-like emblems, are sometimes armed, and have been known to have tarred and feathered a professor whose views they disliked (Omond 1985).

The Costs of Sexism

Women are doubly oppressed; we are oppressed by the regime and by our fellowmen. Even within the movement itself we have to fight against male domination. But it is different with NEUSA. I am the chairperson in Durban and the Soweto chairperson is also a woman who has been in that position since it started.

I became aware of sexism because of what I had to do as a wife. One time the classroom I was teaching in wasn't swept. The kids have to sweep the classroom themselves. I said, "Why is the classroom so dirty?" And the boys said, "It is these girls." I used the whole period to deal with the issue of sexism, and the following day the boys jumped up to pick up papers to impress me. By the end of the year, their attitudes had changed. My experience of marriage was very useful to me in looking at men and relationships critically, and it strengthened me as well. I always draw a parallel between oppression by the regime and oppression by men. To me it is just the same. I always challenge men on why they react to oppression by the regime, but then they do exactly the same things to women that they criticize the regime for. I tell them that they are doing the job for the regime. The regime wants few people to be involved in the struggle so it will be ineffective, so the men are supporting the regime when they say, "You stay at home while I go out to meetings." After the meetings they go back home and tell their wives about it. Often the man actually says at meetings what the wife was saying to him behind the scenes.

21
An Afrikaner Rebels

"I don't see myself as having any career in this country other than working for the struggle. . . . That's all I want to do, and that's all that makes me happy. I couldn't lead a life that is separate from it."

HETTIE V.

*H*ETTIE V. *grew up in a typical Afrikaner home, joining the Voortrekker Youth Movement when she was a young child. This is an Afrikaner nationalist, Christian organization which tries to involve young people in cultural activities, including politics and religion, to try to keep Afrikaners on the right path and close to the Afrikaner nation. Most of the small minority of whites who oppose apartheid with any degree of conviction are English-speaking South Africans. Afrikaners who reject the government's conservative, racist policies usually become alienated and cut off from their own people, and thus have more to lose than English-speaking South Africans. Hettie V. has had the courage and motivation to risk such loss.*

Thirty-one years old in 1987, and single, Hettie V. is a feminist who lives with a woman friend in one of the "gray" areas of Cape Town. She dropped out of university after only a few months to involve herself in political work more or less full-time, working in overcrowded, impoverished, and ruthlessly persecuted squatter communities. Often supporting herself by working at odd jobs, she finally landed a position as a journalist in 1983. She describes the dramatic political events she covered in this capacity—the 1985 march on Pollsmoor Prison to demand the release of Nelson Mandela, the police harassment of the black squatter camps on the outskirts of Cape Town—as well as the earlier upheavals and stayaway of 1976. Active in the women's movement since 1977, she is an acute observer of black and white women's differing attitudes toward feminism. Fearless and committed, Hettie V. lives on the edge, politically and financially. Security is not what she wants, but excitement and meaningful action, and she forgoes white privilege whenever possible to contribute to the struggle.

Growing Up Afrikaner

I grew up in a small Afrikaans community within a larger English community where everyone knew everyone else. I come from quite a middle-class family, but my parents sent all of us children to a very working-class high school to develop a social conscience. The school had been set up for poor Afrikaners, so we were among the wealthiest people in the school, though we weren't that wealthy. It was a pretty conservative Nationalist Party–type of environment, though my family is relatively liberal on both my mother's and father's sides. But even as liberal Afrikaners they were Nats [members of the conservative Nationalist Party] and belonged to the Dutch Reformed Church because there wasn't anything else to be. Although they didn't step very far out of line, they had a more humanistic approach to people and weren't out-and-out racists.

I was one of four children and the only girl. I was always a very rebellious child and questioned things around me, even though it was often interpreted as "cheeky." I would often stand up for other kids.

I was a member of the Voortrekker Youth Movement until I was about seventeen. We all learned to shoot guns at about ten years of age, and we used to go to camps where we'd participate in staged battles. Some of us would stand guard against the "terrorists" who would attack the camp in the middle of the night. I wasn't a willing or good Voortrekker. In fact, I was quite a rebel within the movement.

We were being prepared to deal with the "black onslaught" [the expectation of being attacked by black people], and we used .22 guns which were loaded with real bullets. We learned about politics, basic survival, how to operate a two-way radio, how to do first aid. It was designed to fit us all into the civil defense system. In general, children learn to shoot in Afrikaans schools from the age of about twelve. It is part of the school cadet system for men, and the Youth Preparedness Program teaches both girls and boys to shoot. In 1976 [the year of the Soweto uprising], the school cadets patroled our school with guns from the school armory. People stood guard at night and over weekends in anticipation that the school would be attacked, though this never happened.

I didn't mind being a Young Voortrekker because I thought it was useful to learn to shoot. Afrikaners are not like English people, who don't like to argue and to get emotional. We talk and argue about religion and politics all the time. Those are our favorite subjects. All my uncles are in the Broederbond [a secret society of Afrikaners dedicated to furthering the interests of their people], and we often went on holidays where a couple of dozen people in my extended family would sit and argue all night. They still liked me because I'm one of them, even though I didn't agree with them. Afrikaners are very political people. You'll never find an Afrikaner who is undecided about anything.

I also had endless arguments with people in the Young Voortrekkers, and I eventually resigned on a point of principle. We'd get these badges like the Boy Scouts do, and one of the tests for the last badge remaining for me to get was to prove that I had a sound understanding of the political situation in South Africa. The person who tested us was the Nationalist Party's secretary for the town I grew up in. I had a blazing argument with him, and he failed me, which finally gave me a good enough reason to resign.

I became politically conscious in primary school at about ten or eleven years of age. But a lot of it was just rebelliousness. I remember during the Six Day War between Israel and Egypt, I was the only person in primary school who supported Egypt. I did so because everyone else supported Israel. I always identified with the rebels. My parents were very freaked out about me because I had pictures of Yasir Arafat and Fidel Castro on my wall when I was a child. A lot of this was just to be provocative. But it became more than that when I was about twelve. Because the school was not an academically prestigious place, the teachers were people who cared, and they encouraged us to have debates about politics. I was anti-apartheid then, which wasn't a popular position in the school at all, and my brothers followed suit. We were known as the commies, the reds. When people didn't want to write a math test, they would start an argument with the teacher about communism, and they knew that we'd take up the whole period arguing with him, so they would get out of their test.

Two of my brothers and another friend were also very politically active at school. When I was in standard eight, one of us was in each of the high school classes. We took over certain organizations like the debating society and the school magazine, and we went to things like the Nationalist Party Leadership Training Conferences for high school students and tried to subvert them. We also organized a strike at our school. The girls still had to wear hats at that time, and we decided that this was nonsense, so we got everyone to throw their hats in the dustbins. We didn't have to wear hats any more after that.

I really don't understand why I grew up as I did. The only explanation I can think of is that my parents were more left than their parents, and we were more left than them, and that it may have been a kind of generational progression. Also, the kind of attitudes that they taught us toward people forced us to look at things in a more critical way and to question things. Basically, my parents are very kind, even though they're probably racists. They would never consciously undermine another human being's dignity. If a beggar or a drunk came to the door to ask for money, they treated that person with respect.

An Afrikaner Rebels

I had a very unsexist upbringing. We always did the same chores at home and had the same rights. I got the same toys. My parents encouraged me to stand on my own feet. They told me that they realized that I was going to be an independent type, so I should know how to look after myself. I was confronted with a sexist world when I went to school, so I naturally rebelled against that, too. I was also very involved in sports like rugby and cricket. I was called a tomboy, but there wasn't a stigma against this in the community I grew up in. It was only when I hit puberty that I was supposed to change.

Working in Squatter Communities

I always wanted to be part of an anti-apartheid group, so that's why I went to an English-speaking university. There were no anti-apartheid groups at Stellenbosch [an Afrikaans university]. My parents really wanted me and my brothers to attend an Afrikaans university. They feared if we went to UCT [University of Cape Town], we would become involved in politics. However, we eventually did go to English-speaking universities and did become involved in student politics. But I left university after six months because I quickly became very disillusioned with it.

While I was still at UCT, I started working in squatter camps around Cape Town, and I worked there full-time after I quit university. A lot of my friends supported me financially while I did this work, but I also started a scrap recycling project with a few other people. There was a big rubbish dump just outside Cape Town where we collected glass, bottles, cardboard, and metal, to sell. And we cut firewood, which we also sold. I didn't really worry much about money.

These squatter communities had absolutely no access to resources like sewage systems or water. The people there wanted projects that would strengthen the organizations and politicize people, so together with others I did literacy teaching in a consciousness-raising way using the methods of Paulo Friere [a Brazilian theorist and radical activist who devoted his life to trying to advance the fortunes of impoverished peoples]. We also tried to train barefoot lawyers and barefoot doctors in the community and helped to get vegetable gardens going.

A lot of the squatters where I was working were Coloured people who had been moved out of white areas. Insufficient housing had been provided for them in the areas where they were supposed to go, or they were too far from their places of work, so they had no choice but to squat. At that stage there was a three hundred thousand housing shortage in Cape Town for Coloured people. In those days most squatters had corrugated-iron shacks, whereas today far more of them have plastic and cardboard shacks, which are much worse. A lot of them were quite settled communities that had sometimes been there for years. They were relatively secure on the land because most of the squatting laws hadn't been passed yet. But they were still very poor, very unorganized, and very crime-ridden. Especially in the Coloured areas, there are lots of gangs, and they are also very vulnerable to gangs from other areas.

I remember speaking to one woman in a very small squatter camp who had been raped fourteen times by gangs who came in a truck on weekends. These gangs would go through the community, bash down all the doors, take everything, rape a few women, then leave in their truck. A committee tried to organize a system where someone would blow a whistle as soon as the gangs came, to rally other people for help. But people ran away into the bush when they heard the whistle. Because this woman's house was the first one, she got hit every time. She reported what happened to the Divisional Council which was in charge of the land, and she and others asked to move their shacks closer to a big community to get some protection. But the Divisional Council said, "No. Once you've built a shack, you're lucky if you're allowed to stay. You can move to a proper housing area, but you can't move around here and make it easier for yourself."

People wouldn't try to lay charges against the gangs for the rape for fear of being killed in retaliation. Gangs are one of the reasons why the Coloured areas aren't as politically organized as the African areas. Someone said that about eighty percent of Coloured boys belong to gangs. Some of the gang members make their living by being drug dealers, but most just engage in petty crime or violence in their own communities. And the police have never tried very hard to get rid of them or to control them because they keep people scared and inside their houses rather than going to meetings and getting involved in the community. The gangs have got a hell of a lot of power and quite a lot of wealth in some areas. Some community organizations are trying to work with them to change their attitudes.

The community leaders and committees in the Coloured areas were almost all female. Women are exceedingly strong in the Coloured community because traditionally they work. The major industries in Cape Town are garment and textile production and food and canning, both of which employ many Coloured women. So Coloured women are often quite stable wage earners, whereas Coloured men often work in more unstable and seasonal jobs like fishing, farm labor, and construction. Coloured women have traditionally worked, brought up the children, kept the house; in squatter camps, they have often also built the house, worked in the community, sat on the committees, been active in churches, and slaved their guts out to get their children educated. A lot of them are fierce, strong women.

Police Brutality and Political Resistance in 1976

Nineteen seventy-six was a very dramatic time. The unrest in Soweto spread to Cape Town, and there was a hell of a lot of action here. The squatter camp I worked at most of the time was close to a lot of it. The repression got much worse around that time. Our tires were slashed outside our homes or outside the squatter camps all the time. We were always being stopped by the police and searched and had to find back ways to go into the camps. A lot of the roads were closed because the cops set up roadblocks. Sometimes I got through by telling lies to the police if they didn't know me. I'd tell them that I was from Stellenbosch University and that I was teaching Bible classes to squatters. I told them I wasn't scared to go in because God was on my side and this kind of work had to continue, especially at this time. Sometimes they'd even give me an escort.

After June 1976, the police told everyone who attended our literacy groups that they would lose their houses if they continued to come. Most of the people didn't come back so we had to change our strategy, which was actually very good. We trained the people who were already a bit educated, and who were in leadership positions, to teach the classes themselves. So the work became less visible, and it didn't create dependency relationships. White people going into communities was always a very suspicious thing to the cops. They knew that we discussed politics because there were police informers in our groups.

In 1976, there were school boycotts, fighting in the streets, barricades. A lot of people were shot. For three days there were riots in Adderley Street [the main road in Cape Town]. A stayaway had been called, and black people decided to go to [largely white] Cape Town because white people had been so isolated from the unrest that they didn't have a clue what was going on.

The stayaway started with a march by a group of Coloured school kids who had taken a train into Cape Town. People from all over joined them, and within half an hour there must have been ten thousand people walking up and down Adderley Street. After a while all the shopkeepers closed their doors and put down their burglar bars. The cops were armed with guns and teargas and truncheons—wooden batons with lead in the middle. They formed two lines on either side of Adderley Street, then marched toward each other so that all the people were squashed up the side roads. Then they shot teargas and clobbered people with their truncheons.

I got clobbered over the head by a cop who had probably been watching me. I wasn't doing anything, but I was with black people so I obviously wasn't a shopper. I thought I had been shot because the cops had started shooting over the heads of the crowd. I was unconscious for about ten minutes. I woke up with everyone running over me, and feeling a pain in my head. I thought, "I have a bullet in my head. I'd better not move because then I'll die." I was paralyzed for a few minutes. People carried me into a shop, and a guy said, "No, you weren't shot. You were just clobbered. I saw the policeman do it." Then somebody else looked at my head and said, "No, there's a bullet in your head," and I promptly became paralyzed again. The blow had cracked my head a bit, and I still have a dent in my skull from it. But I'm never scared in these situations. When there's shooting, I just hit the ground. I'm always a bit terrified *afterward*, when I realize what has happened.

The next day I went back to Cape Town—but with a crash helmet! As soon as a group gathered, the cops would disperse them with tear gas and baton charges. Eventually there were about a hundred people in front of the city hall on one side and the cops on the other side in two vans. Two black guys were walking between the two groups when the cops ran across, grabbed them, and started dragging them to their vans for no apparent reason. About a hundred of us surged forward to go to rescue these two people when the cops pulled out their handguns and shot at us. Two people were killed. Then thirty police vehicles arrived, and the police started charging us. A group of us ran into the city hall followed by about a hundred policemen. Eventually they arrested and beat so many people that the demonstrations stopped. This kind of crisis went on until the end of 1976. They didn't call a state of emergency, but they killed and injured many people. All the people killed were black.

The police did all kinds of other ugly things during that period. For example, they announced that they had found pamphlets that called for a "Kill-a-White Day." Every black person was meant to kill a white on a particular day. We knew the pamphlets were coming from the cops to increase white paranoia so as to detract from the real issues and turn the unrest into a racial war. On the "Kill-a-White Day" a lot of white people didn't move out of their houses. They had their overnight bags packed and their guns ready. But not a single white person was injured in the whole country in spite of the wide distribution of these pamphlets. This shows how much maturity there is in the black community despite months of harassment. People knew that the call wasn't coming from their people, or even if it was, that it was something that should be ignored.

Feminism, the Left, and Anti-Apartheid Politics

I joined the women's movement at the end of 1977. It was very small at that stage and not very active. It had started in 1975 when Juliet Mitchell [British feminist author] came out from England to give a lecture here. We confronted white left-wing organizations a lot with their sexism. We organized a walkout of a National Union of South African Students' conference in 1978 by about sixty percent of the women on the grounds that they didn't take women's issues seriously, that they saw us as peripheral to the struggle, that the leadership positions in NUSAS were very male-dominated, and that we didn't agree with the hierarchical nature of the leadership positions. It caused an incredible trauma and took about two years before the women got properly integrated into the left again. We were accused of dividing the left. Despite this, feminism was at the height of its popularity on campuses in 1978–79. The women's movement was much noisier then than it is now, but there are probably more feminists around today. Feminism is now more accepted by the left because of the kind of noise we made then.

But in those days the women's movement was a very white, middle-class thing. Feminism didn't take off at black universities. In fact, there were no active black women's organizations, other than church ones, and there were no nonracial political organizations like UDF. So whites basically worked on campus, and feminists worked in organizations like Rape Crisis. A lot of the criticisms of us—like that we were too Western —were valid because we took feminism straight from America and Europe and fought for the same things here. Nevertheless, we felt that the issues we focused on had to be taken up, and that we weren't just being divisive.

When black women formed women's organizations, they chose to get involved in more grassroots community issues like rent, housing, and food. With the birth of nonracial organizations, most feminists chose to get involved in anti-apartheid organizations rather than to remain an outside pressure group and be branded as lunatics. They worked within these organizations to push for equality of women within the struggle and for other women's issues like child care. Issues like contraception or women's right to determine their own reproduction are more problematic. Although thousands of women have back-street abortions, there's no way that abortion will be taken up as an issue. [Abortion is still illegal in South Africa.] In the black community, people are relatively conservative about things like this and quite religious. This makes it a difficult issue for white women to take up because if we do, it becomes a case of cultural domination. And contraception is a very dicey issue in South Africa because family planning is used by the state against black people in such a racist way.

I don't think the struggle will ever stop for feminists. The conclusion I came to last year, which is quite a drastic one because I see myself as a revolutionary, is that feminism will always be a reformist struggle in this country. Whoever is in power, we will still have to chip away at things. There will never be a mass-based feminist movement that will threaten or challenge the system, whoever is running it. So we have to adapt our strategies accordingly.

Feminists in this country have to commit ourselves very firmly to the struggle in general if we want to have any effect afterwards; otherwise, we're just going to be seen as fence sitters. It's not a question of being manipulative and saying, "O.K., we'll adopt these strategies because that way we'll achieve our hidden agendas." It's recognizing that housing and schooling and torture may not be "feminist" issues, but that they are important issues. And as feminists, we cannot ignore the important human issues. Our position is very difficult, because a lot of people who are very strong feminists are also white and middle-class. That means that we have to triply earn our credibility, and we're viewed with triple suspicion.

Working as a Journalist: 1983–86

About four years ago, I became a freelance journalist. I covered politics, labor, education, housing, and a little bit of central government stuff. And I did a lot of features on community issues like removals and demolitions in squatter camps that were very horrifying.

An Afrikaner Rebels

Whites weren't allowed into the black townships in those days, so I often had to be smuggled in. I would put on a balaclava and a blanket, and then the taller people would walk in a group around me so that I wasn't obviously a white person going in there. Had the cops caught me, they would have taken my tapes and thrown me out and they also might have arrested me.

For example, in 1983 a new squatter camp called KTC was started with twenty houses made of sticks covered with black plastic rubbish bags. Because of demolitions in other squatter camps, KTC kept growing. But every day the cops and the administration board would demolish and burn people's shelters. It became a big issue in the community, and some people who had houses elsewhere put up shelters there out of defiance. Within two or three weeks there were ten thousand people living there, most of them women. And it was the women who organized the resistance. A lot of them had come to Cape Town to join their husbands, who had been living in the [so-called] single men's hostels as migrant workers. Other women from Cape Town joined them.

Although it was winter, the cops' raids got bigger and bigger. Sometimes it would be raining, but the cops would still come and bash down the houses, and whole families with kids would have to sit there in the rain all day until it was dark enough to build their shelters again. Eventually people started breaking down their shelters early in the morning and burying their materials so that they wouldn't lose everything when the raids came, because it was impossible to get any sticks or rubbish bags anywhere any more. A lot of people dug holes in the ground and put plastic over the top because they said the police couldn't demolish holes. It was a nauseating business. People would have prayer meetings and sing and watch the cops demolishing their shelters and the cops would then shoot tear gas to get them to move away from the scene. This went on for about four months. One day hundreds of cops came in and demolished the shacks, then put barbed wire around the place, parked a few casspirs there, put search lights up, and stayed there for weeks and weeks so people couldn't rebuild at night. So most of the people moved to Crossroads [the most famous squatter township in South Africa] and the demolitions then started there.

I also covered all the school and university unrest in 1985 until the state of emergency was called in October 1985.* It was a very dramatic period for journalists because people were being shot every day or two.

---

* When the state of emergency was imposed on 20 July 1985, it excluded certain areas like Cape Town. Presumably, this is why Hettie V. mentions October rather than July as the month it began.

The unrest [in the western Cape] started in August 1985 with the march on Pollsmoor to deliver a message of support to Nelson Mandela who was imprisoned there. The march was meant to start at Athlone Stadium, so I went there at five o'clock in the morning, but the whole of Athlone had been cordoned off with armored vehicles making it impossible to get through to the stadium. There were alternative plans, but no one knew what they were. Some people went to Athlone, but the cops whipped them and forced them away. One segment of the march started with about four thousand people from Hewat, a Coloured teachers' training college. The cops whipped them and trapped a lot of them in a hall, then threw tear gas into the hall causing a big commotion. About a thousand more people marched from UCT. Eventually the planning committee for the march started marching from just outside Pollsmoor, and they were all arrested. After that, all hell broke loose everywhere.

The police became very paranoid about the kind of press coverage they were getting, especially from the journalists with foreign connections. They started shooting at journalists with tear gas cannisters or rubber bullets. Rubber bullets are four inches long and about one inch wide and made of very hard rubber. The police call them rubber batons. They are cylindrical in shape so they've got sharp edges. If they are shot in the air and then drop down on someone, they're not lethal. But if they are shot at someone at close range, they're as lethal as anything. People have been killed by them, especially when they get hit in the throat or in the eye. And I've seen people with furrows cut through their skulls from being hit at too close range with them. Instead of shooting them in the air, the cops shot them right at us.

I was hit by a rubber bullet once on my hip, but it wasn't serious. I had a huge bruise and a mark from it which took months and months to go away. The cops were shooting tear gas at the students at the University of the Western Cape because they were stoning a bus, and I got caught in the middle. Suddenly there were stones raining down on me, so I jumped into a ditch. I was hit by a rubber bullet just as I was jumping. I thought, "Oh, shit, I've been hit!" but I had to get out of there in a hurry because the cops stormed onto the campus and started arresting people and shooting real bullets at them. So I ran with some people and hid in a lab. I put on a white coat that I found lying around, then walked out as if I was a member of the university staff. A group of students recognized me and called me because someone had been shot in the head and they wanted a journalist to take pictures of this. Then we organized one of the caretakers to try to get the victim to a hospital in the maintenance van without being arrested. By that time I'd forgotten that I'd been hit.

It felt a bit like being a war correspondent where, although you're on the sidelines, you're actually on one side. And the cops knew it. You can't maintain a position of neutrality in such a situation. The whole concept of journalist-as-observer disappeared when cops started targeting us. I became totally dependent for protection on the people who could hide me or carry my tapes out. If the cops came toward me, I'd pass all my tapes and my film to anyone and say, "Please keep it." And to get my stuff back, I'd give them my phone number and hope for the best.

I've often been tear-gassed, which is the most *awful* feeling. The police don't use a tear gas that makes you cry, like in the States. It's something that attacks your nerve endings wherever you're wet on your body, like in your mouth, your eyes and throat, your lungs, under your armpits. It gives you a sharp unbearable pain, so you stop breathing. If you put water on your skin, which a lot of people do because that used to help with the old kind of tear gas, your whole face feels as if it's on fire. There's another kind of tear gas they use less often that makes you vomit.

We've discovered all kinds of remedies for tear gas. I always used to walk around with a lemon, because it helps if you put lemon on a piece of cloth and breathe through it. Without lemon, it becomes so painful that you don't want to breathe, and you can't see where you are going because your eyes are aching so much. It's a very effective crowd disperser. As long as it's around, you're almost totally immobilized, and you feel sore for hours afterward. If somebody comes close to you and smells it on your clothes, they'll feel sore as well. People have died of suffocation from it, especially when they're in confined spaces. I'm far more scared of tear gas than of anything else, because with rubber bullets you still have a chance to see if someone is pointing a gun at you, or you can hit the ground, or they may miss. I understand why tear gas causes people to panic completely.

I've seen people who've had six-month-old scars from being hit with sjamboks. They cut the skin and leave huge weals. One of the cops' favorite things is to hit women across their breasts with them. When they disperse gatherings, they're meant to only use as much violent force as is necessary, but they'll often hit people until they fall to the ground, then carry on beating them which, of course, *prevents* them from dispersing. They like doing that to journalists because they hate us.

I've covered a lot of white student protests and seen people getting completely freaked out from being sjamboked. This is a very normal reaction in one sense—in that it's a very invasive, abusive, and violent experience, and some students complain of nightmares afterward. But people in the townships [black people] experience it all the time and don't make such a big deal of it.

People didn't understand the concept of a progressive journalist in those days, so the press was seen as part of the system during the first few weeks of unrest. We were in the crossfire a lot, and it became very dangerous. Journalists had their cars stoned and petrol bombs thrown into them, and they were always being stopped at roadblocks—*people's* roadblocks, not police roadblocks. It took about a month before people realized that some journalists served a useful purpose, and then they started being more protective toward us. Usually what happens is that the people are on one side, in a school yard or at a university or in the street, and the cops are on the other side, and the journalists stand in the middle somewhere, but slightly to the side. We'd go and interview the people, and if we had the guts, we'd go and interview the cops, but we didn't want to be seen talking to the cops. Then somebody would throw a stone or somebody would shoot, and it was like watching a war being played out in front of you.

There had been school boycotts since June of 1985 which all the Coloured and African schools participated in. Every day something awful happened at some school, like the school kids would be having a meeting or a demonstration in the school yard, and the cops would come and shoot lots of people, and some would be killed. The cops were trying to force people to stay in classrooms, so they'd be posted outside the classroom doors or in the classrooms to see that the teachers were teaching. Eventually the government closed down all the African and Coloured schools in Cape Town. They said, "If you want to boycott the schools, we'll close them down." People then decided to reopen the schools because they wanted them to be *changed*, not shut down. So on 17 October 1985, parents, teachers, and children planned to reopen the schools everywhere.

One of my most terrible experiences occurred at a school called Alexander Sinten in Athlone. I went to the Athlone area [a Coloured suburb of Cape Town], because I thought there would be the most trouble there. There were a couple of kids standing around singing in the quad when I walked in, and parents and children were arriving to open the school [Alexander Sinten]. I went to interview the headmaster, who was standing at the gate when two vans and about six cops arrived and arrested us. They arrested me for trespassing on government property. Then they put guards at the entrances to the quad and said that all the children were under arrest. Next they called for reinforcements to come and take about one hundred seventy of us away. Meanwhile, more and more people kept arriving to reopen the school. There are three other schools in the area and a teacher's training college, and lots of people came to see what was going on. Although the cops had closed the gates almost immediately, about four thousand people gathered outside. By this time I was under arrest in the back of a police van with a lot of other people.

The people outside the gates took all the cars that were parked on the pavements, picked them up, and stuck them in the middle of the road so that the casspirs couldn't come in to take the rest of us away, and they got the local butcher to park all his refrigeration trucks in the road. After about forty minutes the place had been cordoned off by the people and was absolutely impassable to traffic. I was still sitting, as hot as hell, in the back of a van with the teachers and headmaster and some of the students. By this time the cops were absolutely panicking because it was only three days after a cop had been killed by a Muslim crowd at a funeral in Salt River [a neighborhood nearby]. Cops don't often get killed in South Africa, and there were a lot of Muslims outside the school shouting for holy war. The cops were standing right next to our van, not knowing what to do.

An imam [Muslim priest] came to try to negotiate for our release. He said that the people would stop the blockade if those of us inside the gates were let out, but the cops said, "No, we're never going to get out of here alive unless we have these people in the back of our vans." And it was true. By this time the stones were raining down on that place, and we were kept there for four hours. They wouldn't even let us go and wee or get water or anything. Then a huge army truck that's used for towing broken-down casspirs and other large vehicles drove over the back fence of the school, flattened it, and brought in a lot of troops and riot weapons, because up to that point the cops only had guns.

We shouted from the vans to try to warn people that these guys were coming in from the back. Then they started firing tear gas at the crowd to try to clear them away. I stopped counting after about fifty-six canisters, but the people just picked them up and threw them back. All the cops had on gas masks, but we had to sit in an open police van in an absolute cloud of tear gas. We thought we were going to die. Cops then charged from all sides, and the people moved a few blocks back. The breakdown trucks came and towed all the cars off the road, enabling the cops to drive off with us in the backs of the vans. They also brought in more vans, loaded about half the people into them, and charged out of there. Somebody threw a stone at the guy who was driving our van, while everyone shouted, "*Amandla!*," and he pulled out his gun and started shooting.

We spent the rest of the day in jail, until the lawyers came and got us out because they'd arrested us for nothing. I was the only white person there, but it took them a while to figure out that I was white because a lot of Muslim people are lighter than I am. They put all the women, girls, boys, and men in separate cells. In the women's cell there were twenty-three of us, two teachers, myself, and the rest were mothers who had come to support their children. They were people who hadn't been in prison before, and they became more and more defiant as the time passed. A cop came in to find out if anyone had any medical problems, and one woman said she wanted pads. He said, "O.K., I'll see what I can do." Then another woman said, "I want maternity pads," and somebody else said, "I want Liletts [a kind of tampon]." They went through all the brand names for sanitary napkins, which made him very embarrassed. He was blushing when he said, "I'll bring toilet paper and that will handle it all." That sort of incident cheered everyone up.

One woman said, "I don't know what's going to happen to my house because my children are also here today." Another said, "Well, my husband is here, too, so I don't know what's going to happen when my primary-school children get home." They'd compare notes as to how many of them were united in this thing. It was very sweet. But eventually the cops put me in a separate cell because they realized I was white.

I have been in police cells a number of times for being in the wrong township at the wrong time, but I've never been in serious trouble. The longest time I've been in is overnight. The cops would tell a crowd to disperse but I'd want to be where the action was to record it. I'd often end up being the last one to get away, and that's how I got hit a few times.

After the 1985 state of emergency was declared, journalists were suddenly much more restricted. We couldn't report on police action. We weren't allowed to take sound recordings or film recordings any more. Restrictions became even worse after the state of emergency was renewed on 12 June 1986. We weren't allowed to be at the scene of unrest.

There were very heavy penalties for breaking this and other rules—like ten years in prison or a fine of twenty thousand rand [$10,000] or both. After that, the restrictions kept getting worse and worse. Basically we could only cover the police's side of things. Then they centralized it all, so that we couldn't even interview local police any more, and we had to get the information from Pretoria. So I quit being a journalist.

On Being White in the Anti-Apartheid Movement

Before 1976, whites were involved peripherally in the labor movement and in work like I was doing in the squatter camps. After 1976, there was a huge Black Consciousness movement, and whites were not part of the mainstream anti-apartheid movement. After 1980, the nonracial democratic organizations were being born all over the place, and the nonracial organizations like the UDF became the strongest. I've never experienced animosity from anyone in any of these organizations on a racial basis, which surprises me.

It also surprises me that I could go into a riot in a squatter camp without anybody threatening me or being hostile toward me. I don't understand it. I think that there is something very, very special about black people in this country. People are prepared to listen to me and to judge me as a human being and not merely as someone with a white skin. It amazes me every time I experience it because I don't think that I would have that tolerance if I were in that position. And I don't think white people in general would put up with so much and then still be open to people as human beings.

I don't have any doubts that there will be a place for progressive white people in this country in the future. I think the paranoia common among white people is very unfounded. I have always organized my life so that I could focus on my political work. That's all I want to do, and that's all that makes me happy.

22

Marriage Across the Color Bar

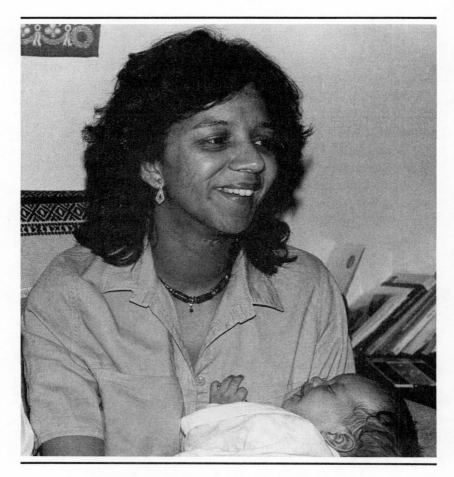

"I don't just believe that the personal is political, as most radical feminists do, but that the political is also often very personal, as my story of 'love across the color bar' shows."

RHODA BERTELSMANN-KADALIE

R HODA BERTELSMANN-KADALIE was born in 1953 in District Six, the low-income black community that was completely destroyed by the government's efforts to separate black and white residential areas described by Rozena Maart in chapter 19. "Because of the Group Areas Act, we had to move around Cape Town quite a lot," explained Bertelsmann-Kadalie, a Coloured woman, thirty-four years old in 1987 when I interviewed her.

After graduating in 1975 from the University of the Western Cape,* a black university, Bertelsmann-Kadalie completed an honors degree in social anthropology there, then went to the University of Cape Town to study for an M.A., also in anthropology. She didn't complete this degree, but in 1986 obtained an M.A. in women and development studies at the Institute for Social Studies in the Hague, the Netherlands. Bertelsmann-Kadalie was on maternity leave from teaching at UWC at the time I interviewed her, nursing and caring for her few-months-old baby, Julia.

Although Bertelsmann-Kadalie didn't tell me that her grandfather, Clements Kadalie, had been a famous organizer of workers in the 1920s, other people did. Perhaps pride in her family name, as well as her feminism, accounts for her desire to maintain her father's name. But she also wanted to take the last name of her white husband, Richie Bertelsmann, to emphasize to the South African authorities that she was married to him, despite the illegality of this union in their eyes. There are many different ways to rebel against apartheid, including ignoring the racist laws against interracial marriage, as Rhoda Bertelsmann-Kadalie did. Most of her story is taken up with the police harassment she and her husband experienced owing both to their marriage and to their political activities.

Growing Up Coloured

I come from a big family with nine children. I was aware of apartheid from a very young age. When I was six years old, we moved to a white area in Cape Town because my father was transferred there. He was in

* The university attended also by Gertrude Fester and Rozena Maart, and where Di Bishop now works.

charge of the municipal laundries where white people used to come and bring their washing. We were the only so-called Coloured family living in the area. So from my second year of school onward, I was living in a white area while always being made aware that I was Coloured. For example, I used to play with a white minister's daughter in the neighborhood. Her mother used to say to her, "You can only play with Rhoda for five minutes because she's black." After school I used to meet a white girl called Paddy to play with her before we went home. One day I walked her home and at the door said, "Bye-bye, Paddy." Her mother said sternly, "*Miss* Paddy to you." I said, "But she doesn't call me Miss Rhoda." "She's saying that to you because you're black," my mother explained. And one day I was suddenly told, "You can't play here any longer because it's a park for white people." I registered these experiences as a little girl, though I couldn't make sense of them.

My father became a minister, and when he complained about the apartheid in the churches, another minister—whom he thought was a friend—said, "You sound like a communist." I had a lot of white Christian friends who would be friendly with me in the church but wouldn't look at me in the local supermarket. I used to run interracial camps. Many of my white friends used to invite me to their parties, and they would say, "Oh, meet my nice friend who's not at all bitter." I would be asked to address white schools on my experiences as a Coloured student, and when I began to show my indignation and anger about the way I was treated, I wasn't asked as much any more. My younger sister and I have been thrown out of restaurants because they were for whites only or because we went in the whites-only entrance.

Marriage and Police Harassment

I met Richie at the University of the Western Cape when he joined the staff as a new lecturer there in 1980.* A colleague of mine was already acquainted with him, and the three of us went to see a very poignant play on migrant labor and the difficulties it creates for family life. I was very impressed by what he thought about the play, though I also felt that he was trying to impress me politically. He kept saying to me, "Well, don't you think I also feel disgusted about the situation in this country?" We dated each other every week from then on.

---

* Just as women's colleges in the United States have male faculty members, so black South African universities employ faculty who are white.

Marriage Across the Color Bar

At that time I was the youth leader of our church in a Coloured township where the crime rate was very high. Richie isn't particularly religious, but he went to our church with me, and he was very impressed by our efforts to provide recreation and political outlets for the people. He loved doing that kind of thing with me. It was the first time in his life that he was involved in a Coloured township activity, because he had grown up in Pretoria and had attended very middle-class white schools. After courting for two years, we realized our relationship was becoming serious. I had wanted to break it off several times because my father was opposed to it because Richie isn't a Christian, and I felt I couldn't cope with my father's pressure. While Richie's father opposed our relationship on racial grounds, his parents were also apprehensive about the problems which we as a "mixed couple" could encounter in a society like ours. When we decided we wanted to marry, they realized there was nothing they could do about it so they might as well accept it.

It was still illegal for people of different races to marry then. We decided to stay because we felt that too many people in our situation had left the country and not opposed that law. We thought the best strategy would be to buy a house, so we looked for one before we even told anybody we were getting married. As university employees we qualified for a subsidy, so it was quite easy to get a house. We bought one in Observatory—a white working-class area [in Cape Town]—because it is more tolerant than most. Communes in which white students live with their black student friends are flourishing here. We bought the house under Richie's name because only he qualifies for a house in this legally-defined white area.

Marriage was the next step. We decided to fly to Namibia* over a weekend, marry, then come back, and move into our house. So in December 1982 that's what we did. The Mixed Marriages Act had been repealed in Namibia in 1978, but that didn't mean that the people there liked marrying us. The white magistrate didn't even look at us, and during the marriage ceremony he asked: "Do you, Richard Bertelsmann, white man, marry Rhoda Kadalie, Coloured girl?" He tried to rub it under our noses that we were breaking the law in South Africa and that he hated having to marry us. I wanted to keep my maiden surname for feminist reasons. But for political reasons I decided to adopt Richie's name to rub it under their noses that, "I am married, and you will have to accept it whether you like it or not."

* A neighboring country, illegally ruled by South Africa. In 1989, South Africa's withdrawal is still in the early stages.

After our return, the police drove up and down the street about five times a day to intimidate us. They would stop at the gate and look at us but not say anything. I remember one night we went to a party and came home very late. We were sitting in the car kissing when a cop car parked next to us. The cops looked at us, and we looked at them, and then we rolled the window down to say, "Hey, what's this all about?" but they left before we could question them. They never physically intimidated us as they've done to many other mixed couples. For example, we know of the police having entered the home of a mixed couple and having tried to get a video of them in the act [of having sex]. Maybe they are reluctant to prosecute us because we teach at a volatile and politically explosive university. The students might protest and cause disruption if they do anything to us. We also have a lot of influential friends who would come to our aid if anything happened. People who don't have the connections and the student support we have get screwed by the police for living together.

Once we looked after the children of a well-known anti-apartheid leader while he was away for a fortnight, and the police phoned us the first day we were home. A police officer said, "We would like you to come and report at the Wynberg Magistrate's Court tomorrow at 8 A.M." I asked why. "Because," he said, "I have a copy of your marriage certificate, and we would like to question you about contravening the Group Areas Act, the Mixed Marriages Act, and the Immorality Act." I replied, "If you have our marriage certificate, you know everything about us already, so why should I come?" He got a bit cross and said, "Look, we want to know all the details about your marriage." I told him I'd consult my lawyer, which made him more annoyed. "You don't need a lawyer," he said. "You just have to sign a paper." I said, "You'll hear from us." I immediately linked this call with our having stayed with this well-known family. Their phone was tapped, and this political leader was hot property at that time. The government tried to get him in all kinds of ways.

The same police officer phoned us again to say that we should fill out a form and come in for questioning. This time we went, and they asked Richie all about his background, his education, his family, where he grew up, and so on. Richie speaks perfect Afrikaans, and their attitude was "How could a sweet, innocent Afrikaner like you go wrong?" The police officer was shocked to learn that he had studied at the Rand Afrikaans University. Throughout the interview the officer ignored me. He didn't even look at me or address me, as if I didn't exist to him. He didn't recognize me as the wife of this man. But when they were finished with Richie, the sergeant looked at me and asked, "Do your friends recognize you as white or as Coloured?" I said, "I have the kind of friends to whom that doesn't matter." When I wouldn't answer any more of his questions, he said, "You have to sign this form to the effect that you are breaking the Mixed Marriages Act, the Group Areas Act, and the Immorality Act." We refused to do this and said we'd consult our lawyer and then bring the form back. But we just kept the form and never went back.

University Protests and Further Harassment

The University of the Western Cape was established by the government in 1960, specifically for Coloured people. Many of us rejected the racist grounds on which the university was founded, but nevertheless enrolled as students since the mainline, predominantly white universities were closed to the growing number of black matriculants. At the time, many of us registered under protest, determined to fight for the deracialization of the university. It is for this reason that the university became an active site of struggle against the intervention of the apartheid state in our daily lives, particularly in our education. In the course of time, the university developed a strong tradition of protest, where demonstrations, boycotts, and marches against repressive laws and undemocratic practices meted out by the government on a regular basis became the order of the day.

I often joined these protests, alongside fellow progressive staff members, by refusing to teach during boycotts. A case in point was when a small group of staff together with students decided to protest against the newly created tricameral parliament and the new constitution in 1984. We campaigned vigorously against the Coloured and Indian elections, and joined students in making posters, picketing and marching, much to the chagrin of the rector. Many of us did not care whether we would be fired or not, and we felt very strongly that our rejection of this new parliament should be recorded for history's sake, no matter what the consequences.

The United Democratic Front asked the lecturers at our university to monitor the polls for the Coloured elections of this new tricameral parliament because we suspected that the polls would be rigged. Richie monitored the polls at Woodstock Town Hall, and I at the Cape Town Civic Center. That morning there were more policemen than voters! The police were angry with us because of our monitoring, so they intimidated us every five minutes. They wrote down our names and phoned the security police to check on our files. When they found out that Richie and I were both monitoring the polls, they said, "So you're not only breaking laws. You're also involved in subversive activity." I was nearly arrested that day. The police were getting agitated with a friend and me for monitoring for too long, so at noon they came to us and said, "You're under arrest." For some reason they took her but not me. To me they said, "See that you get out of here as soon as possible." I was horrified and frightened, and they followed me until I was out of Cape Town.

The next day the police officer who had been responsible for dealing with our marriage phoned. The police had checked up on us on election day and discovered that we hadn't been prosecuted. Apparently, the sergeant had got into trouble for this. We were then compelled to return the form, but decided to indicate in writing that we were married on 3 December 1982, in Namibia. The government was talking about reforms at the time, and everybody knew that the first item on the agenda was the scrapping of the Mixed Marriages Act. So we were angry with the police and said to them, "If you prosecute us, we will make a big stink about it. Why do you want to do this when the government is trying to get support for reform?" They said, "This is going to the attorney general, and we'll inform you about what he says." We never heard anything more, and they never did prosecute us. This happened just prior to our recent trip abroad. Ironically, we left on the day that they scrapped the Mixed Marriages Act—17 April 1985. I went to the Netherlands to study, and Richie went to Germany. Incidentally, there was an article about our marriage in a German newspaper on our arrival in Germany.

Soon after our return from study leave overseas, the Department of Internal Affairs sent us a letter saying, "You must apply for validation of marriage. Here is an affidavit to fill out in front of a commissioner of oaths, and, if approved, we might send you a marriage certificate." They are keeping our original marriage certificate, which Richie sent them when he applied for a new identity document on his return here from Germany. If I didn't have a copy, we'd have no marriage certificate. Because our marriage isn't recognized, our daughter Julia will probably be illegitimate. Although they treated us as a normal couple when we registered her at the Wynberg Magistrate's Court, we're now waiting to see if she's going to get her birth certificate. Normally these get issued about two weeks after the registration of birth, but we've been waiting about a month now, which I think is deliberate.

Richie also wrote a letter saying, "We are not applying for validation of our marriage. We left the country to marry because we feel that you have no right to decide who should marry whom." I phoned "mixed couple" friends of mine who had also married in Namibia and who then divorced. I told them about this letter telling us that our marriage wasn't recognized. They found this very strange because they had divorced like any normal couple. This means that *their* marriage *was* recognized.* This is how they [the government] force one to submit to their laws; the rule is scrapped, but under the new law, you have to apply for validation. If our marriage is invalid because it has been contracted outside South Africa, then it follows logically that all marriages contracted outside South Africa are illegal. My German friends who got married in Germany should then also be required to apply for validation of their marriages in South Africa. But this doesn't happen, which means that it's purely a racial issue. So I don't care if they register Julia as illegitimate; I'm not prepared to apply for validation of our marriage.

I feel that we should take this up with the newspapers now. It would embarrass them and make the public aware of the cosmetic nature of the changes our country is making. They are now allowing couples of different "races" to marry, but then prosecuting them for breaking the Group Areas Act. They have prosecuted many mixed couples because the black partner was living in a white area. The Mixed Marriages Act, the Group Areas Act, and the Population Registration Act are the pillars of apartheid, but if they get rid of the one, they have to get rid of the others. I think they know this, but they can't cope with it. And they are angry that marriages have occurred across the color line. Implementing the Group Areas Act is their way of punishing those of us who have done this.

Other Problems for Mixed Marriages

Because Richie is white, and I am Coloured, I don't automatically inherit from Richie when he dies. Because of the Group Areas Act, I can't get this house, for example. I'm not allowed a house in a white area, so Richie has to make out a will in order that I at least benefit from the sale of the house.

Another disgusting thing is that they tax us jointly as a married

---

* This is also an indication of how arbitrarily the government goes about prosecuting people.

couple. I'm going to challenge them on this. I plan to say, "You don't recognize my marriage, so pay me back all the taxes you've taken from me." I want to take this to the newspapers as well. Also, men as husbands have property rights, not women. As a married woman, they won't allow me to own a house, so I'm also going to oppose this from a feminist's point of view. I shall *not* leave this house. They will have to take me out of here physically.

Schools are also a problem for children of mixed couples. Racial classification itself is a problem. I plan to find out more about how this situation affects children—for example, how they're classified racially —because this has a lot of implications for their schooling. I don't care how the government classifies me, but children suffer because of it. Other children might say to my child, "Your mother is black," or, "Your father is white," or, "You're a half-caste," which is unpleasant for a child.

A mixed couple is never anonymous in this country. Many people stare at us when we go to a restaurant or to the beach. In fact, I was kicked off a beach once. Two years ago Richie and I went to Muizenberg Beach. I knocked my toe when I was walking on the beach, so I went to sit in the car because it really hurt. Two policemen came by and circled my car. Then the white policeman told the Coloured policeman to tell me to leave. (Whites are always getting Coloured people to do their dirty work.) So the Coloured cop told me to leave. I said, "Why?" He said, "You don't belong here." I said, "Why?" He said, "You shouldn't be here." But he wouldn't tell me *why* I shouldn't be there. I kept asking, "Why?" and saying I wouldn't leave. So he went back to report to the white policeman, then came back and said, "My colleague says you must leave." I repeated that I wasn't leaving. Then he said, "Are you white?" I said, "No, I'm not. And you're not either. What are *you* doing on the beach?" He said, "Don't backchat me. Just leave." I said, "I can't leave because my husband is on the beach, and he's swimming." This made them even more annoyed because now they thought that there were *two* Coloured people on the beach! So they waited and waited. When Richie came, they were confused. I told him what was happening, and he went to take a shower. They circled and waited at the exit until we left. But they didn't come up to him and say, "Why are *you* here?" But I'm not intimidated by the police. Being at the university strengthens me. I think I would probably be chicken if I didn't have that political base.

With the scrapping of the Mixed Marriages Act, it's amazing all the people who are emerging from the closet. In contrast, Richie and I decided we were going to treat our marriage like any normal marriage. We hold hands on the streets and on the beach. And if our marriage doesn't work, we'll end it, like any other marriage. People often imply that we get on well because we want to show the world that this marriage works. People ask me, "Don't you find that there's a big cultural difference between you." But Richie has more in common with me than with an Afrikaner woman, for example. Of course, they wouldn't ask that question if he had married an Afrikaner.

The fact that they decided to call us into the police station for questions shows that they felt that we were being too brazen in openly flaunting our marriage, and they just wanted to remind us "to know our place." If we become more active politically, it's also possible that we could face a Group Areas charge. That is why we have kept a low profile politically since our marriage. We wanted to get our marriage off the ground before having to cope with all these other kinds of political pressures. I would have liked to have been more actively involved with the UDF, but decided it was safer to be involved at the university.

If the government really intended to reform, why do they hassle harmless people like us about the Group Areas Act and the Mixed Marriages Act?

Feminism

I was the only girl for sixteen years with seven brothers, so I've always felt very oppressed by men. I didn't particularly like men, and I decided never to marry. After I graduated, I worked and had a car and dated a lot of student guys who often felt inferior to me. They always measured me by the fact that I earned a salary, and they felt intimidated by that. For example, since I had a car but my boyfriends didn't, they would insist on driving if we were to go somewhere together. I would say, "No, it's my car. Why should you drive?" I think I was a feminist long before I knew it. And then working in a white, male-dominated department at the university made me terribly aggressive about my rights as a woman.

If we women are sure of ourselves and our identity, then we don't need to compete with men. The slogan "women who want to be equal to men lack ambition" is very true for feminists here in this country. We don't just want to be equal to men, but more than that, we want to live a full, self-determined life and have the power to control our own bodies within and outside the home. Feminists are fighting for a more just social and economic order, where all forms of inequality, domination and oppression will have been removed.

What we need in this country is a healthy combination of liberal, radical, marxist, and socialist feminism—so that one realizes that to fight for the right to control one's own sexuality, to fight for better education, to fight against rent increases, or to fight as women for the right to live with one's migrant husband, are all feminist struggles. Women fight not as neutral subjects but as gendered beings. To make a dichotomy between political issues per se and issues of sexuality is to lose sight of the fact that the struggle for national liberation itself has a gender content.

In one of her books, Jackie Cock [feminist sociologist and author of *Maids and Madams*, 1980] writes that white women have tended to mobilize around issues of rape and violence, whereas black women are concerned about fighting for the vote, democratic rights, boycotts, and things like that. But even though the distinction is there organizationally, black women actually talk about both kinds of issues. Of course, white women don't have to fight for the vote, but they should fight for black people's right to vote.

The Future

When the level of struggle escalated in 1985, I was still overseas and I thought the time for a revolution was at hand. Then when my friends or family came to visit, they'd still be the same. One friend said, "Rhoda, you're going to be a grandmother before you see change." Now that I'm back, I really feel like that is true. I saw a documentary on the military might of South Africa, and I am convinced that the government will fight to the death before it changes. So I think I'll be one of the many who will not remain to tell the story.

23
A Child of the Struggle

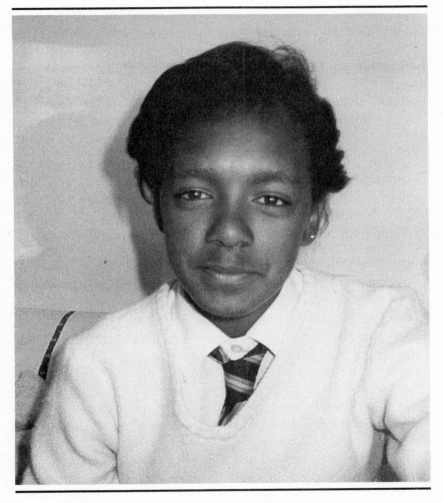

"The police began harassing us more and more. My mother had
to take us to see a psychiatrist last year because we couldn't cope
with our work or with other people any more."

LEILA ISSEL

*L*EILA *is the eldest of Shahieda (see chapter 4) and Johnny Issel's three children. Her two brothers, Yasser and Fidel, were eleven and nine years old in 1987, and she was thirteen.*

I picked Leila up from Alexander Sinten Senior School in Athlone* *—a so-called Coloured area in Cape Town—to take her to her home for the interview. The walls by the school were covered with political graffiti. The government appears to have given up trying to clean it up in the black areas of town, but I noticed that in the white areas it would often be gone in a day or two. Leila directed me to her mother's home in Mitchells Plain, normally an hour's bus journey for her each way. She said that she used to go to Moslem school after arriving home, but now it's over by the time she gets back and instead she usually plays the piano.*

In her interview, Leila describes how it has been to grow up from the cradle being harassed by the police, owing to her mother and father's political activity. She speaks of her own "first arrest," of how she rescued her father, of how she and her brothers lived during her mother's imprisonment, and of political activity at her school. In South Africa schoolchildren typically wear school uniforms, as Leila did on this occasion. When I asked her what Mitchells Plain and South Africa would be like if she had her druthers, she answered, "They would be like in America, where the children have their free will and can wear what clothes they like to school."

My father has been gone or arrested most of my life. He was in hiding when I was a few months old. Apparently, the police barged into the house, grabbed me, and asked my mother where he was. They said that if she didn't tell them, something would happen to me. So my father came out of hiding because he has a soft spot about his children being harassed.

There was a mass rally here at the Rockland's Civic Centre [in Mitchells Plain] when I was seven years old. I was asked to speak there on behalf of my father, who was banned at the time. Afterward, the police threatened my mother, saying, "We're going to fetch your daughter at

---

* The school where Hettie V. had one of her "most terrible experiences" (see pp. 293–294).

school, and you're never going to see her again." I had to go to my teacher's home each afternoon after school, then she took me to my home at about six o'clock. Someone always had to be with me wherever I went to stop the police from getting me.

At the meeting to launch UDF [1983] I spoke about my father being banned, and I read from the papers that the police had given to him when they banned him about how he'd be arrested if he went past a particular place. I said how my father could only visit us or take us to the beach one day every three months. Some of the people there got angry and excited and marched out of the hall. They wanted to go to the nearest police station and knock it down.

My father helped me with my talks the first few times, and he'd tell me to be brave. I've spoken more than seven or eight times, and find it much easier now.

I was arrested once when I was seven years old, but it was only for a few hours. Two ladies asked me if I would stand with them with a placard saying "RELEASE MY FATHER AND ALL DETAINEES," if my mother would allow it. I don't remember what organization they belonged to, but they were white. The police arrested us and took us to the police station, where we were put in a cell for about four hours. It was my first arrest, and I was very scared but the other people in the cell seemed to feel very at home. They were washing their hair and stuff like that. The two ladies were asking how the police could arrest a seven-year-old child. They didn't used to arrest such young children at that time, although now they're arresting children of six or seven years old.

My father visited here [her mother's house] sometimes when I was ten years old. The police sometimes broke down the door at night to look for pamphlets and other things. Once they found an ANC flag, and they put it on the bed with the pamphlets and all the other stuff they wanted to take away. My father told me that he could be arrested if they took away the flag, and asked me to try to take it outside and hide it under a blanket. I used to take drama classes, and I was very good at acting, and I managed to get the flag and hide it under a blanket in my room. There were about seven men standing by the bathroom with rifles, so my father decided not to try to escape. They took him away for almost a year because of what they found in the house and also because he speaks at mass rallies.

Once we were all standing on the steps here, and the police barged in and took my father to their car. I threw a stone at them, and one of them got out, and I almost smacked him because he was saying a lot of nonsense about my parents, like that they are very bad people. The police just drove off.

Last year [1986] my father was on the run. My mother and two of her friends and myself and my two younger brothers were at home after supper on a Thursday night when the police barged in to ask my mother questions. I asked them, "About what?" I told them, "If you don't answer me, then you can't take my mother away." I got upset and started to cry. We went next door to the friends we go to when my mother or father are detained; then the police took my mother away. My mother's elder sister came to take us to my granny's, where we slept for a few nights. My mother returned after almost a week.

I was playing outside with my brother one night last year when my granny called us in and told us that our mother had been arrested. She was detained for a month, then released, and then detained again. The police used to tell my mother [when she was in solitary confinement] that her family was turning against her and that her children didn't want to hear anything more about her. If my grandfather hadn't gone to visit her in that week, she would have gone mad because of all the things they told her that weren't true. She was very scared when she came out of prison. She looked thin and very different. When I came home one Friday afternoon, everyone was crying. Then I saw my mommy sitting there, and I was very happy that she was home.

Sometimes it makes me very sad when my mother is being harassed, but I don't speak about it much. When I was very young, I didn't understand what was going on. Later my brothers and I felt sad most of the time, and our schoolwork got worse and worse each year because of all our worries. We were always staying with my granny. The police tried to get at us when they looked for my father. They used to come to ask my grandparents where we were. We had to stay in the house and lock the door so no one could come in. The police began harassing us more and more. My mother had to take us to see a psychiatrist last year because we couldn't cope with our work or with other people any more. My younger brother used to come home and tell my mother he had no friends at school. The children at our school know the situation our father is in, and they used to say untrue things about the ANC, like that ANC people are bad, they're "sellouts." Then they stopped being his friends.

I and my two younger brothers are supposed to stay indoors when there is rioting around here, but we went outside one time because we wanted to see what was going on. People were burning cars, buses, and trains. The police came and threw tear gas, shot rubber bullets, and used their sjamboks. The children ran away, then ran back and shouted "*Amandla!*" and "May the struggle continue!" The police got angry and ran after us shooting rubber bullets. We came home at half-past five because our grandparents come home at six o'clock. We put the food on the stove and said, "We were in the whole day, Mama."

Our vice principal at school, Mr. Swarts, was arrested last year in June or July, then released last week after nine months. He is about sixty. He was involved in the struggle and used to speak openly to us about what is happening in South Africa. He is now at home recovering from detention. His son is still detained. We have quite a few teachers like that. The majority of our school is politically involved. At the beginning of the year, when he was still arrested, we had a walkout [in protest]. We had a walkout rather than a placard demonstration to avoid violence. The police would have come and shot tear gas and then said that we had started throwing stones and provoking them.

There was a mass rally today [8 April] at UCT [University of Cape Town] to tell people what is happening in this country and that they should stand together. Quite a lot of students from my school wanted to go, so one bus wasn't enough to take us. A police van was standing there as the children filled the first bus. I was going to go in the second bus, but it never turned up. A student I know said that some of the children were arrested and that those who got away were just lucky.

24
Forced Removals Mean Genocide

"The women made a plan to dig their own graves and they said, 'We will stand beside our graves because we are not moving from here. You can shoot and we will lie in our land forever.'"

SHEENA DUNCAN

Forced Removals Mean Genocide

I MET *Sheena Duncan at the annual National Black Sash Conference in Cape Town in 1987 and arranged then to interview her many weeks later in Johannesburg, where she was born, grew up, and still resides. I had previously seen her in a documentary on South Africa in which she spoke eloquently about the massive scale of forced removals imposed by the South African government, and wanted to interview her about this subject to help disseminate this information more widely.*

Duncan, a white woman, was born in Johannesburg in 1932. The eldest of five children, she is the only one currently living in South Africa. Her sister married a Scot and lives in Scotland, her two younger brothers became chemical engineers and reside in the United States, and her eldest brother left long ago to make a home in London. Duncan also went abroad, studying at the Edinburgh College of Domestic Science in Scotland and qualifying as a teacher of domestic science in 1953. Two years later, she married a Johannesburg architect and moved with him to Salisbury, in what was then Rhodesia (now Zimbabwe). After living there for eight years, during which time Duncan gave birth to her two daughters, she returned to South Africa with her family in 1963.

Duncan is one of the 8 women out of 112 political people listed in the first edition of Who's Who in South African Politics, *according to which "her political involvement arose entirely from her sudden and adult conversion to active Christianity and her conviction that there could be no justice or peace unless one attacked the political causes of hunger and suffering" (Gastrow 1985, p. 79). The author Shelagh Gastrow also notes that Duncan has published widely "in press articles, reports, booklets, pamphlets, and magazines both in South Africa and abroad." The main topics of her published works include the pass laws, forced removals, the government's "homeland" policy, the legislation that deprives South Africans of their citizenship, and "the consequences of these legislative enactments for political and constitutional development in South Africa" (Gastrow, 1985, p. 79). Someone told me that Duncan probably knows more about racist South African laws than almost anyone else in the country—a knowledge acquired by over two decades of voluntary work at the Johannesburg Black Sash Advice Office.*

Here Duncan describes the founding of the Black Sash by her mother and five other women in 1955; the almost fatal role of the press in ignoring the work of this women's organization; the magnitude and severity of the forced removals still being implemented in South Africa, despite the government's claim that apartheid is dead, and that it is now interested in reforming its policy of racial discrimination; how the reforms that are undertaken are designed to co-opt and divide black people; the effect of the abolition of the pass system; what she thinks about Chief Buthelezi; and the underappreciated role of women in the anti-apartheid movement.

Growing Up as the Daughter of a White Activist

I can't actually remember when I wasn't politically conscious. I was very fortunate because I went to Roedean [a private girls' high school in Johannesburg] which had a very eccentric, but remarkable woman as principal. She had personal friendships with people like Trevor Huddleston and Alan Paton [two well-known anti-apartheid writers and activists], and she brought much more content about the South African political situation into our school lives than normally occurred, or than happens today. Also, my mother [Jean Sinclair] became very politically involved in United Party politics after the war, and she eventually became a city counsellor in Johannesburg. So political discussions were constantly going on around the house. She was also one of the founding members of the Progressive Party when it was formed. And she was one of the six women who started the Black Sash in 1955. She did this about the same time that I married and left the country.

The Black Sash

I joined the Black Sash immediately after I came back from Rhodesia in 1963. My children were only three months and three years old at that time, but the Black Sash did things in those days that allowed me to participate while being at home with the children. When they went to school, I extended my activities to working in the Advice Office one morning a week. It was very new, and we used to sit in the office with our knitting and our letters to write, and if a customer arrived, we all jumped to our feet to see who would be the first to be able to help. It took a long time for the idea of an advice office to catch on, especially in the political climate shortly after Sharpeville [see page 8] and the banning of the ANC. The repression and the state of emergency [in 1960] succeeded in crushing black resistance for a whole decade. People have often asked me why I joined the Black Sash rather than something else. The reason is that there *wasn't* anything else at that time.

In 1955 the government had introduced a senate bill to pack the Senate with its own supporters in order to get the necessary two-thirds majority to change the constitution so they could stop Coloured people from having a vote. It was this act by the Nationalist Party that brought the Black Sash into existence in the first place. Looking back on it now, I think that the mass of women who joined the Black Sash in the early years couldn't have cared two hoots about whether Coloured people lost their vote. They cared about the fact that if the government could maneuver in that very immoral way, it could also stop the English language from enjoying equal rights with Afrikaans.

The Black Sash has had to change quite a bit since those early days in the 1950s, because the situation has changed. In the beginning it was a mass movement of women who really believed that if there was a substantial public outcry, the government would have to desist from whatever it intended to do. After its last major mass protest against the Sabotage Act of 1962,* the women realized that the government paid no attention whatsoever to public opinion. The Black Sash then entered a period in the 1960s when the membership dwindled away to practically nothing. At its peak it was about 10,000, whereas by the beginning of the 1970s it was about 1,100, and I think it's now about 2,700.

Another factor in our dwindling numbers was that the Black Sash had changed its constitution in the early 1960s to open the membership to any interested woman resident in South Africa. Previously membership had been limited to voters—which meant white and Coloured women only. This change in our constitution led to a mass exodus from the movement.

In the very beginning [of the Black Sash], women rallied incredibly. The group of six women who met in 1955 didn't mean to start an organization. They were just chatting over coffee and talking about how

---

* This act permitted ninety days detention without any trial or other evidence of guilt being necessary.

desperate everything was, and decided that women should do something. Then they got on the telephone, and each of them got ten other women to come to a meeting. Within ten days they had the three thousand or so signatures needed to petition the mayor to call a public meeting. And there was a huge march of thousands of women to the public meeting, where they were received by the mayor on the city hall steps. When I look back at the old photographs, it is very exciting to see this sea of women who turned up.

They called themselves the Women's Defense of the Constitution League in those days. But when they started wearing a black sash across their right shoulders and tied at their waists on the left as a sign of mourning for the constitution, the press started calling them the Black Sash. Because it was obviously a much snappier name than the one they had chosen, they adopted it.

My mother was the Black Sash president for fourteen years, and I was elected president when she retired in 1975. I told the organization that I would not do it for more than three years because I think it is very important that leadership is spread across a wide range of people. So at the end of three years I refused to stand again, though I did another term later. We now have a whole range of leaders in the Black Sash, so they would have to pick off a lot of people before they could cripple the organization.

During the 1960s, when there was so little opposition to the government outside Parliament, our focus was twofold: one was to protest when particular legislation was introduced. We frequently did silent stands [demonstrations in which women stood still while holding placards] before they were prevented by law. In about 1962 the government banned all gatherings within one mile of the city hall and within a certain radius of Parliament in Cape Town, so we had to find other places to protest. We also protested in all sorts of other ways like writing letters to the newspapers. But we had to struggle with the newspapers at that time because they didn't like the Black Sash. My mother told me that the editor of the *Rand Daily Mail* once told her that it was very foolish to keep this organization going and that she should rather be working in the United Party. Subsequently the newspapers changed their minds, but it was a real struggle to get any coverage in those years. If you wanted an article in the newspaper, you really had to bleed for it. If it hadn't been for my mother the Black Sash wouldn't have survived the 1960s. It was her determination and drive at a time when people said, "What is the use?" and "What can you do?" that kept it alive at all.

The other activity that developed during those years was the advice offices. The first one in Cape Town began as a bail fund to get black women who had refused to carry passes out of prison while they awaited trial so that they could be with their children. Involvement with those women led to a better understanding of the persecution which the pass laws involved. So advice offices were gradually opened in different cities, and it was this work that really established the Black Sash's credibility. We became the only experts in that field of law in the whole country. There was only one lawyer in Johannesburg—who was banned and left the country—and then her successor who would help with these sorts of cases. Other lawyers didn't know anything about the pass laws; this information wasn't included in their training in law schools. So when the press wanted to know something about the pass laws, the Black Sash was the only place they could come to. We didn't just understand the law. We knew what it meant to black people because we were dealing with the problems caused by these laws. By the end of the 1960s, we were in a much better position because the press was prepared to publish our material and people were prepared to hear us.

The Policy of Forced Removals

In 1962, our East London group discovered a resettlement camp in the Ciskei known as SADA, where black people had been dumped. From that time on, the removal of people to the homelands became one of our major focuses. The dispossession of black people from their land had been going on ever since Jan van Riebeeck arrived [in 1652], but it was only in 1962 that it became public knowledge that the government had begun this process of deliberately moving people as part of a larger program.

On discovering SADA, we started trying to expose it, though our efforts were unsuccessful for a very long time. We found out where the people had come from and why, but it was some time before we realized that this was part of a much larger picture. The real impetus came when the people at Maria Ratschitz were moved to Lime Hill [a resettlement camp] in 1968, and Cosmos Desmond, the Catholic priest at Maria Ratschitz, journeyed around South Africa identifying all the resettlement camps. He published a book about it all called *The Discarded People* [1971] and was banned for his pains. That book was very valuable because it gave a much clearer idea of the overall picture, but the real breakthrough didn't come until the 1970s when the churches suddenly started taking the issue seriously.

317

In the early 1970s, I was on the Anglican church's Challenge Group which tried to combat racism within the church, and it was extraordinary to hear ministers in rural areas say, "Oh, yes, those people did suddenly appear." But they had never asked any questions about *why* they had suddenly been brought there and where they had come from and what it was all about. When the churches finally did address the problem, the work became much easier because that brought international interest and made removals and resettlement household words.

Since then, forced removals have become very politically costly for the government. Mogopa [in western Transvaal] was the last one—I think it was in 1984—where the army and police surrounded the community and just picked people up and forcibly took them away. At Mogopa they also dismantled all but one of the water pumps. They tried everything, but the Mogopa people still refused to move so they were moved by force. The government has now devised all sorts of new strategies to avoid using that kind of physical force again. For example, they knock down the schools in July when the children are in the middle of their school year so the people will say, "I must go for the sake of my children." That is their [the government's] way of "persuading" people to move "voluntarily." But there have been some major successes on the part of the people in communities like Driefontein, Daggakraal, and KwaNgema, all in the eastern Transvaal.

Driefontein, for example, is a farm that was owned by the members of the community who had bought the land before the 1913 Land Act prevented any more such transfer of land to black people. The government wanted to remove them to Oshoek [an African settlement], but the people said they didn't want to be moved and they weren't going to go. I was reading some of the minutes of one of their meetings with Dr. [Piet] Koornhof [a government minister] who turned to them and said, "But you must go because you are all squatters." And they said, "But we *own* this land." He then made the incredible statement that, "All black people in South Africa are squatters if you are outside your traditional lands."

The negotiations and meetings went on and on, but the people never faltered. They continued to say that they weren't moving. Then the police arrived at a meeting of the community in the schoolyard, and a policeman called Nienaber shot and killed their leader, Saul Mkhize. That was the turning point in their struggle. Saul had been in the schoolyard, and the policeman was outside a high wire fence, but he claimed he was in danger of his life and that's why he shot Saul dead. The people remained firm and said, "On no account are we going." The women made a plan to dig their own graves, and they said, "We will stand beside our graves because we are not moving from here. You can shoot and we will lie in our land forever." This statement had quite an effect on the local police.

The people of Driefontein had come to the Black Sash long before Saul's death because of the kind of resources we can offer, like organizing press conferences and getting press and diplomatic people to go there and meet them and getting foreign governments interested. The government was saying that the community had to move because of a new dam that had been built there. The people said, "But the dam is only going to cover a few of our fields and our houses. Why don't you give us more land on the other side?" A legal action was prepared for their neighbors and at least one lawyer thought it might be possible to force the government to empty the dam. Before that case proceeded the matter had been concluded, but I think the threat of legal action was a factor in the outcome because the government didn't want to lose the enormous amount of water if they had had to empty the dam.

The people of Driefontein succeeded in staying on their land due to a combination of international pressure, public interest inside South Africa, and their own determination. This is one of the few success stories, but it gave a lot of people hope.

Sometimes when people are resettled, they are given tents, sometimes nothing, and usually there's no water or sewerage facilities. The early removals were a particular scandal. The people who were moved to Klipgat were dumped there without water, sanitation, or shelter. They are still living there with no water and no sanitation, but they have built their own houses. Some of these people said that they had been moved there from the farms in the Transvaal as early as 1957, but I think the mass removal to Klipgat happened in the early 1960s. The terrible conditions into which these communities were moved was the first thing that one was able to get public pressure about.

To focus public attention on the issue, David Russell [the author's brother] lived for six months on the very meager rations these people had to live on. This was very important because it raised public interest in this scandal. The government responded by preparing the resettlement areas better, so the first indication now of a new resettlement camp is a sea of tin latrines. And every row of latrines now has its tap. The people are then moved onto a site and told they can build their homes there.

But the terrible conditions are not as important as the fact that *people are removed from where they were.* Some of them were doing a lot more than surviving: they were producing a surplus of crops, or the people in urban areas were living there because that was where they could work. When you move people, it means total impoverishment for them. They lose their means of survival. The only way of getting work then is to get locked into the migrant labor system.

Because black people didn't voluntarily go to work in the mines in the early days, English-speaking South Africans introduced policies to deprive them of land and thereby force them to work. A whole series of laws were passed—for example, limiting black people to owning land in the reserves. Within the reserves the laws of inheritance were changed so that only the eldest son could inherit the land, leaving the rest of the brothers landless. Hut taxes and polltaxes were also introduced to force black people to need a cash wage. So the motivation for the creation of black homelands was to create reservoirs of labor to force people to work.

But then mechanization on the farms and in the cities and the needs of industry changed, so instead of a mass of cheap, unskilled labor, more settled, more stable, more skilled, better educated, and fewer workers were needed. So the purpose of the homelands then switched to their becoming places to dump the surplus people. In fact, that was the very phrase used by one government minister. And another minister referred to wives, children, and old people whose labor was not required in South Africa as "superfluous appendages." This has led to the even greater impoverishment of the people who live in those homeland areas, because even migrant labor gets cut down as employers use more workers who are settled in urban areas.

The estimates are that over three million people have been forced to move. About seven hundred thousand of them are white, Coloured, and Indian people who have been moved into residential areas set aside for their own racial groups. The rest are African removals, some of whom have been removed from urban areas. Particularly in Natal and the western Transvaal, whole [African] townships were disestablished and the families moved into Bophuthatswana [an African "homeland"]. The men so moved had to come back to their old jobs as migrants. The government never thought they could actually remove Soweto, but they had a rule that any black township that was within twenty-five kilometers of a homeland border must be eliminated. Some of the townships they removed were actually much further away than that. But I think partly because of political pressure, that process was first suspended and then stopped. It was also stopped because the thinking was, "O.K., if you've got to have black workers, they'll be quieter and more pacific if they are living with their families." But hundreds of thousands of people had already been forced to move.

Then there was the whole group of [African] people living on white-owned farms who were affected by removals. These were people who may well have been on that land long before the whites ever appeared in the interior. After that they worked as sharecroppers for white farmers until it was outlawed. Then they became labor tenants or registered squatters. Labor tenants were allowed to stay on the farm and had their own fields and cattle in return for doing three months' work for the farmer for no pay. Then both the labor tenant system and the squatter system were made illegal, and all sorts of controls were put on farmers so they could only have a small number of families living on their farms. So there were massive removals from the white-owned farms.

A third group affected by removals are the black [African] people who owned their own land and who were moved into the homelands and lost their land in the process. Even when they were given compensatory agricultural land in the homelands, nine times out of ten it is not as good as the land they left. Secondly, they never get ownership again because, if the homeland is independent, tenure of land in the homelands is invested in the president.

In terms of human suffering and impoverishment and destruction of people and communities, these forced removals must be the greatest evil in South Africa. I once used the term *genocide* to describe them, and I don't use that term lightly. But if genocide is the destruction of a people, that really is what forced removals does, not just in terms of deaths but in terms of destroying people's spirit. If you go to these resettlement areas now, you see a totally disorganized, apathetic group of people, even in places that have been there for a long time. The establishment of any kind of community and life as it is meant to be lived is totally destroyed, and hopelessness and poverty prevail. I consider that genocide. It has been a terrible, terrible sin, and the consequences for the future are enormous.

Any new government in the future will have to act very fast to respond to the needs of these impoverished people. It is going to mean state intervention in the distribution of land in particular. We are not going to be like Zimbabwe where Mr. [Robert] Mugabe has been able to carry out his land resettlement without expropriating land. Part of the reason this was possible in Zimbabwe is that fifty-four percent of the land was set aside for black people, so he has been able to manage by having the owners of the land offer it for sale. In South Africa less than fourteen percent of the land belongs to Africans, so we have a much bigger problem. I think there is going to have to be massive expropriation here, which, of course, means trouble, because there will be resistance from the landowners. I suppose one would start by expropriating the land of people who own more than one farm, and then the whole world will say, "You see, we knew we'd get a communist government in South Africa." But how they are going to cope otherwise, I don't know. The solution to this problem cannot be left to the free market. All that the free market would do is transfer the land to other people who are rich.

Nor will being given land deal with the psychological destruction of these people, coupled with the fact that severe malnourishment in the first five years of life destroys people's brains. It means they very often become unteachable and certainly not people who are going to be able to absorb the education required to participate in a free society. Forced removals are causing generations of damage. At the moment Operation Hunger, a private charitable group here, is feeding over one million people every day with about seventy thousand other people waiting for food. And they don't believe they are close to feeding all the people who need to be fed. This is really obscene in a country as wealthy as this.

The Abolition of Passes

Now with the abolition of the pass laws, we have so-called freedom of movement. But what has happened is that the control of people's movements by the government is now entirely, and much more effectively, administered through housing policies. Although a man from a homeland, provided it's not independent, is free to move anywhere he wants to look for work and can take a job without any permission, he can't bring his family with him because there is no affordable accommodation. And the reason for the lack of affordable accommodation is that the government controls the land and is not setting aside new land in the metropolitan areas for massive building of affordable housing. So although it's not written in his pass any more, this man who now is free to move from a homeland and come to Johannesburg to seek work, has to remain a migrant laborer. So he still only sees his wife and children once a year.

Forced Removals Mean Genocide

The whole reform structure is there with one purpose only, and that is to preserve apartheid. One has to understand that the policy of apartheid is designed to maintain power in white hands, and in order to do this and to entrench it, certain things have been relaxed at the level of social race discrimination. The reform process has been one of co-optation as far as possible—co-optation through improving the quality of people's lives. That is why the Sullivan Codes and the European Community's Code [employment codes for American and European businesses in South Africa] fit in very well with government policy. The government actually hasn't minded those codes because what they want is a stable group of better-paid, better-educated workers in the urban areas. They are doing things like electrifying townships to improve the quality of life so as to create a black middle class which they hope will keep the lid on the revolution. What black people can do, and which black people are in urban areas, becomes much more a matter of what they can *afford* to do. A black person who can afford it certainly has a much better quality of life now. The humiliations of being excluded from theaters and cinemas and restaurants and so on have disappeared almost entirely in Johannesburg. In another town you might find that it is a bit further back in the process, but that is what reform has been about. The freedom of movement fits in with this because employers have wanted it.

I am not saying that we are not thankful that the pass laws, as they were, have gone, but it has exposed how much worse off the people from the independent homelands are. Although they have been considered aliens in South Africa since the day their particular homeland obtained "independence," they are now dealt with in terms of the Aliens Act.* This means that people asking for permission to work outside their homeland are given the same huge complicated four-page form to complete as an immigrant from Britain wanting to come here on a temporary work permit. An employer is also supposed to get permission from the Department of Manpower to employ a foreigner, and the department only gives that certificate if it is satisfied that there is no South African available to do the job. The employer then has to approach an immigration officer for a temporary work permit, which has to be renewed every year or two. So black people in the independent homelands are in a much worse position than they were before the pass laws were abolished. It is a great boon that other people can work or

---

* This was the case at the time of this interview. Although the law has not been changed, citizens of the independent homelands are no longer being victimized in this way (Duncan, personal communication, September 1988).

look for work without being constrained by passes, but their abolition has not resolved the problems that follow in the wake of the migrant labor system—a breakdown of families and community.

Also, we have had reports of old-style pass raids where black people are stopped in the street and told to identify themselves. The police say that they are looking for illegal aliens. We haven't yet been able to verify these reports because what happens is that some white person phones to say that she has seen the police doing this in the street, but she never knows the names of anyone who is arrested, and without that we can't trace them.

Comparing South Africa and Nazi Germany

I've been reading William Shirer's book on Nazi Germany [1959] during the period 1934 to 1938. The Reichstad fire occurred one week before Hitler's election, and I see parallels with the kind of things that happened during the week to ten days before our election [in May 1987]. We saw on our television screens allegations that union members had murdered railway workers, though there is absolutely no evidence that this is the case. And I'm jolly sure the murders weren't anything to do with the union because they don't operate like that. Shirer talks about how even though he was a foreign correspondent with access to the international press, which he read regularly plus listening to the BBC every day, he found that his judgment was affected by reading German newspapers and listening to German radio day after day. He began to believe things merely because of the skillfulness of the propaganda onslaught. In this country it is exactly the same now.

Early this year I was sensing a real fluidity in white opinion. By April that fluidity had disappeared. White people were bombarded by television, radio, and the government press, which is where they get their information. Its effect was incredible. White people stopped thinking. They were fed this steady diet about the threat of the ANC–SACP [South African Communist Party] alliance. The ANC was never talked about as a separate organization. Whites just absorbed and repeated what was told to them. The parallel with Nazi Germany at that time is very striking.

The other thing Shirer pointed out was that the early concentration camps in Germany were used for political dissidents; and at that time, he said, they weren't the huge deal that they became. There were only about twenty thousand people in detention. And I thought, "Well, we're at that stage now." Twenty-four thousand people* have been detained since June last year, more than four thousand of whom are still in, as far as we know. But there is nothing to stop the process of more elaborate concentration camps being developed and more and more people being locked away for years and years. Shirer doesn't mention children being detained in large numbers at that early stage in Germany, as we have here. Our system of repression is much more sophisticated than some of the other brutal regimes that have existed around the world.

On Chief Buthelezi

Throughout the history of the Black Sash, we have never experienced antagonism from black organizations or black groups, with the exception of Chief Buthelezi. He doesn't like us at all at the moment because we have been critical of him. We have accused him and his government and Inkatha of using and provoking violence. When there is proof that the UDF has attacked somebody, we have spoken out against that, too. The difference is that the UDF leadership does not like people claiming to be their members using violence against others, and they try to stop it, whereas Chief Buthelezi takes it as a personal affront when one says Inkatha encourages vigilante groups. Also, we oppose his participation in the homeland structures. I think the argument of the early days is no longer valid: that in order to build a power base, in order to be able to operate in opposition, it is necessary to make use of the government's structures. And Chief Buthelezi has never drawn the line anywhere. He goes on taking all the paths that are offered to him, short of independence. Therefore he is very much part of the process of the breaking up of South African society.

One always has a feeling of fear when criticizing Chief Buthelezi. His and P. W. Botha's personalities seem to be terribly similar. Both of them are ruthless. Both of them desire power in a very personal sort of sense. They're very arrogant, and they don't like criticism. But Chief Buthelezi does have another side; he can be the most charming and charismatic person. Some people see one side, and others see the other.

---

* Thirty thousand is the figure given by Audrey Coleman and the *Weekly Mail* for the number of detainees between 1986 and 1987 (see p. 15).

The Black Sash and the Struggle Today

We are a resource for the much bigger black movements that are now carrying the load of opposition and resistance in this country. I have described our role as a resource for people who do not wish to be moved. We also serve as a resource for other issues. Judging by the way we are so widely used, we have information that many people want and need for their work.

Secondly, we try to inform the white community inside South Africa as well as people in the Western democracies. I was in America twice in 1985; and at one meeting with white American church people, a white woman asked me, "Why are you coming here to tell us about what happens to black people in South Africa?" I said, "Because I was invited, but more importantly because you hear it when I tell you. If a black woman comes from South Africa to tell you, you might say 'Oh, shame!' but you don't hear what she says." And a black American woman said, "Sheena is absolutely right. People don't absorb what I tell them as a black American, but if one of my white friends tells them the same thing, they hear it." We always try to be as accurate as possible with our information, and people come to rely on it because they know we don't exaggerate. If we are not sure of something or it is unconfirmed, we say so. And they know it is based on our daily work, not culled from the newspapers or other sources.

And the third thing of value that we do is to uphold ideals—the freedom of the press, no detention without a trial, the importance of the rule of law. We have to keep on talking about these principles for the sake of the future. I was up in Lusaka last week, and I saw Mr. Tambo. He was very warm and said many nice things about how people admire the Black Sash. It is very nice to know that people don't think we are irrelevant.

Police Harassment

I take phone tapping for granted like anybody who is in any way actively engaged. In fact, this entire conversation is probably being tapped. I took the receiver off the hook because I thought we'd be sitting outside. I think when I lift the receiver, it activates the tapping device and it stays active for four minutes after I've put it back, so they can pick up what we're saying in this room.

I and my family have received quite a few telephone threats, from heavy breathing to threats to my children when they answered the phone. Somebody said to my daughter, "Aren't you sorry that the newspapers published your mother's address?" It must have been election time when the newspapers have to publish the names and addresses of all those who write letters they publish. My daughter was still young, and she got jolly scared. And we went through a period when they kept chopping up my hosepipes [garden hoses]. I would find the hosepipe with a piece cut out of the middle and another piece somewhere else, which was very irritating.

But I've never been subjected to the worst things, like having a whole load of coal deposited on my driveway, which has happened to other people. The other day, somebody ordered sandwiches for two hundred and fifty people from a little shop near Khotso House [the headquarters for many anti-apartheid groups]. The shop closed down for the day because they couldn't have prepared that enormous order and handled their customers. So these vast amounts of sandwiches were delivered to Khotso House, and the South African Council of Churches paid the shopkeeper because otherwise he would have made a major loss, then took them out to some children's home. Those sorts of things can be frightening.

The Black Sash hasn't been harassed in the way that black organizations have been and continue to be. The security police float in and out of the office from time to time in a very arrogant manner without introducing themselves. Several of our members were detained and then released with restriction orders.* I think everybody now is expecting a major clampdown of the kind that occurred on 19 October 1977† when they banned all the Black Consciousness groups, two newspapers, the Christian Institute [an ecumenical organization whose goal —before it was banned—was to unite Christians of all ethnic groups], Beyers Naudé [a previous member of the conservative Afrikaner Broederbond who became a leader of the anti-apartheid movement], and other individuals. But banning across the board as they did then is not possible now because the UDF consists of 840 or so grassroots organizations all over the country. So another way to achieve a clampdown is to cut off all overseas funding for anti-apartheid groups. We are expecting such legislation very soon.‡

Who they ban and detain is quite arbitrary. Avoiding any logical

---

* Banning orders are being replaced by restriction orders so that the government can claim, as one of its reforms, that it no longer bans people.

† Duncan states that such a clampdown happened in February 1988 (personal communication, September 1988).

‡ This legislation was withdrawn due to intense international pressure, but a modified version is expected to be introduced in the near future.

pattern to what they do is part of creating an atmosphere of fear and terror. Astonishing people are detained, and people say, "Why him? He's never done anything," and other people are not detained who have been very high-profile. This leads to an air of uncertainty and fear. One has to not allow oneself to be overcome by these feelings. I'm not afraid of being banned myself, though it would be exceedingly frustrating to be prevented from working. Imagine not being able to prepare anything for publication and not being able to talk to two people at once. But then you look at somebody like Beyers Naudé who performed very important work through his years of banning by counseling the people who went to see him one by one. He was never out of the mainstream of the struggle all those years. I guess I'd find new ways of contributing. If I let those sorts of fears weigh on my mind, I would be immobilized.

The Role of Women in the Struggle

Outside South Africa I think the role of women is a bit like Israel and Zimbabwe, with women being part of the army [*Umkhonto we Sizwe*] just like men. They have exactly the same training and tasks as the men. Nonsexism is much better understood by the ANC-in-exile than inside South Africa. Because Black Sash trains people to work in advice offices inside the country, community groups come to discuss with us whether to open one. Frequently, only men will be on their committees. I am forever saying, "Haven't you got any women where you live?" But South Africa is terribly backward in this regard. Although South Africa has produced some incredible women like Albertina Sisulu, Helen Joseph, and Lillian Ngoyi, there are very few high-profile, high-level women leaders, and women at lower regional and local levels are not given the same leadership opportunities as men.

I think the Black Sash is much stronger because it is a women's organization. We have a much more immediate way of responding to things than men do, and there is a great strength in that. I like working with women compared to my work in the church, which is very male-dominated. My church work is very much more frustrating than it would be if women were accorded their rightful place.

I think women are playing a terribly important role in South Africa, but the potential of women is simply not recognized by most organizations.

25

Conclusion: The ANC, International Pressure, and the Role of Women

"We are asking the caring world to strangle Pretoria [the administrative capital of South Africa] so that the money that is used to finance our oppression dries up. It is only the caring international community that can help us realize the dream of a peaceful transition from a government by the minority to a government by the majority."

—WINNIE MANDELA

As well as asking women about their lives, their anti-apartheid work, and the consequences they have had to pay for their political activities, I asked them how important they considered international pressure to be for the fate of South Africa, and for their opinions on the African National Congress, and the role of women in the liberation movement.

After reading these twenty-four stories of pain, of hope, and of courage in the face of a brutally repressive regime, many readers will want to know what they—as individuals and as part of the international community—can do to alleviate this ugly situation, or, better, how they can contribute to real change there. And, since the African National Congress is clearly the most popular and significant of the different strands of the South African liberation movement, it is important to know what a broad spectrum of political activists in that country think about this organization. Finally, since this book focuses on women in the anti-apartheid movement, and since women are often not given the credit they deserve for their contributions to social movements, their differing assessments of their role in this vitally important movement complete the picture.

The Significance of International Pressure

International pressure can take many different forms: economic sanctions, divestment and disinvestment,* sports, cultural and academic boycotts, verbal denunciations and resolutions, withdrawal of ambassadorial and other foreign representatives, educating the international community about what is happening in South Africa so as to encourage progressive intervention, and so on. Economic sanctions and divestment are the forms of international pressure addressed most frequently by the women I interviewed, most of whom believe that such pressure has been, can be, or will be crucial to their struggle.

"With international pressure on the South African regime, we would be liberated tomorrow," insisted the ANC member Connie Mofokeng, now living in exile in Zambia. Those opposed to international efforts to pressure the South African government into dismantling apartheid—on the grounds that other countries have no right to interfere—often ignore the long history of international efforts *in support of* the apartheid system. As another ANC spokesperson, Mavivi Manzini, put it: "The South African regime has been, and still *is* being, sustained by the military, economic, and cultural supports that it gets from other countries. It is being propped up by multinationals, without whose assistance we would have been able to deal with the regime a long time ago."

Similarly, the trade-union leader Lydia Kompe maintained that "South Africa cannot survive without outside help. Countries like the United States and Britain don't put more pressure on South Africa because they make a lot of money from all their investments here. These countries could make it change if they really wanted to." According to these women, then, the goal of the divestment movement is therefore to *withdraw* the international support that has bolstered white supremacy in that country for decades.

Almost every woman I interviewed stressed the importance of international pressure in the struggle for democracy in South Africa. "Winning the support of the international world hasn't been easy," said the ANC leader Ruth Mompati, "because South Africa is a highly developed country, a friend of the Western world, a friend of NATO, and a

* "*Divestment* occurs when a church or university or city authority, for example, sells shares in a foreign company because that company does business in South Africa, or does it in an unacceptable fashion. By contrast, *disinvestment* occurs when the foreign company closes or sells its South African operation and withdraws, repatriating what assets it can" (Orkin 1986, p. 17; emphasis mine).

country in which the majority of the Western nations are heavily invested."

Albert Luthuli, the 1961 Nobel Peace Prize winner and former president of the ANC, started calling for sanctions in the 1950s. "But the call fell on thin air," declared the veteran political activist Helen Joseph, who concluded, "If they'd applied economic sanctions thirty years ago, we wouldn't be in the mess we are in now."

Despite these criticisms of the role that the international community has played with regard to South Africa, Mompati also pointed out, "Through the years, we've enjoyed the support of progressive movements the world over, anti-apartheid movements, women's organizations, churches, as well as the Organization of African Unity. The pressure from these groups has definitely made an impression on South Africa."

Some of the women I interviewed expressed considerable gratitude for international pressure. For example, the co-president of UDF, Albertina Sisulu, said, "It is very important that some of the countries that South Africa has depended on are now pulling out economically. We must congratulate the outside world, especially the anti-apartheid movements. They have done a tremendous amount." And Winnie Mandela expressed even more enthusiasm: "International pressure is extremely important. The international community must realize how much it means to us that they have mounted pressure against the South African government, that they have applied sanctions. I hardly think we would have had the energy to go on without it, particularly when the going was tough, had it not been for the aid of our allies, the caring international community.

"The global protest against apartheid has given us tremendous inspiration by focusing attention on our country and highlighting the black man's problems. It has done a great deal to get the Afrikaner to shift away from his brutality, even if to an infinitesimal degree. For example, although the pass laws haven't really come to an end, at least one no longer sees the humiliation of the ordinary black man and woman in the street being stopped by squads of police to ask to see their passes."

Although supporting sanctions against South Africa meets the legal definition of terrorism in that country, and can result in incarceration, the trade-union leader Emma Mashinini's response to the risk involved in speaking out in favor of them was typical: "I'm not afraid to support sanctions publicly because I've been detained before without knowing why. People get into trouble for nothing. What have the ten-year-olds in detention done? Anything and everything can be an offense in South

Africa. If you give in to that, you will become afraid of your own shadow."

Most of the women argued forcefully in support of sanctions, although a few also expressed reservations about this strategy. Mandela articulated the view of many women when she said, "We see sanctions as the only peaceful way to force the government to abandon its abhorred apartheid system of government. To us the only alternative to sanctions is a call on each and every one of our people to take up arms against Pretoria. If international pressure is not concerted enough, the only solution that is left for us is the armed struggle. But we will do anything to stop this if we are provided with an alternative. Anything! We know we are going to suffer. But we also know that we are the victims of apartheid. And we would prefer mandatory sanctions to the armed struggle."

Ruth Mompati also argued that "we in the ANC believe that sanctions are the *only* international strategy left that can minimize the bloodshed that is going to take place in our country." The Domestic Worker Union's leader Florence de Villiers explained her support of sanctions even more succinctly: "I prefer sanctions to war."

Many of the women addressed the common objection to sanctions: that they will hurt rather than help black South Africans. For example, Ruth Mompati said: "We have been told that sanctions will harm us. But how can we be more hungry than we already are? Our children are dying from malnutrition, from *kwashiorkor* [a form of extreme malnutrition]. If your child is dying from malnutrition, can it be more hungry than that? We are told that people are going to be laid off. We say, 'Yes, we know this. And we know that we are going to suffer. But if we suffer so we can win our freedom in the shortest possible time, then we are prepared to go through that hardship.' "

Mompati cited the widely used strategy of consumer boycotts as evidence of black people's willingness to endure hardship in pursuit of political goals: "Our people themselves have decided to boycott certain shops in South Africa, not because they don't need the goods in those shops, but because they've been very successful. They show that people are not only asking others to boycott, but they are also prepared to suffer."

On the other hand, the former Natal Indian Congress leader Ela Ramgobin objected to this argument on different grounds: "I don't agree with the argument that sanctions affect the Africans most of all. From the early 1980s, there has been a steady increase in unemployment, and divestment has only started recently, so they can't blame it on divestment."

The ANC, International Pressure, and the Role of Women

Two of the members of the Black Sash whom I interviewed expressed some reservations about sanctions. Di Bishop believes "that individual families are being very seriously affected by the reduction in the number of jobs available and the withdrawal of companies from participation in South Africa." She also argued that "sanctions could be effective if they were very tough and the struggle was for a very short time. They could have a kind of shock effect on our society and bring about change in record time. But I don't believe that it's going to happen like that."

Nevertheless, Bishop concluded, "I also hear what black people are saying, and I agree to the extent that I am able with their saying, 'For many of us, it couldn't be worse.' When I hear of what happens in rural towns where there has been vast unemployment for a very long time so the people there are only marginally affected by the imposition of sanctions, and when I hear what the quality of life is like for people who are discarded by the government, then I listen when they say, 'Sanctions are a way in which the international community can, in a nonviolent way, demonstrate its rejection of participation in the system in this country.'"

While not arguing against sanctions, the Black Sash leader Sheena Duncan mentioned that "the unions inside the country are reviewing the divestment/sanctions issue. They are trying to decide whether its results so far have been positive or not. This doesn't mean they are turning away from sanctions in general, but they are saying that *conditional* divestment might be better than the kind that merely sells the company to South African interests and makes our monopoly capitalists more and more wealthy."

The Afrikaner rebel Hettie V. was the most skeptical about the efficacy of sanctions: "The way that sanctions have been imposed hasn't really affected things because they've been implemented in such a wishy-washy way. The government is laughing about it because Afrikaner capital is buying up the stock of a lot of the companies that are pulling out, and it's strengthening the whole economy. All the American companies that have pulled out make sure that they have very good relationships with the people who take over the companies. They still sell them all their spare parts and import everything from them. We aren't suffering any shortages, which was the big threat in 1985 that made the government consider releasing Nelson Mandela." Here Hettie V. is arguing not against sanctions or divestment in principle, but against the way they have been and are currently being applied.

The detention expert Audrey Coleman also believes that the efficacy of sanctions depends on the manner of their implementation: "If the outside world gets to the stage where it says, 'It's obvious that the government isn't going to reform in a meaningful way, so we will totally isolate them,' it could have a tremendous impact on this country, because South Africa cannot go it alone. We are a capital-importing country, so when the outside world refused to renew the loans here, this country was in a terrible state. But to be really effective, all countries must *unify* in their efforts."

Aside from the isolation of South Africa that rigorously applied sanctions would effect, other women argued more specifically that such isolation would facilitate revolution. According to the United Women's Congress member Gertrude Fester, for example: "International pressure is a very important arm of our struggle. The role of sanctions is important because this government knows that economic crisis is the sure way to revolution. Suddenly businessmen are flitting to Lusaka when they were among those to support the state of emergency. And all these years these very same businessmen were exploiting—and still *are* exploiting —the black workers of this country. There's already an economic crisis, but the capitalists and the government are afraid of a worse one. And I'm sure that sanctions could bring this about."

Addressing the issue of *why* other countries should apply sanctions and other international assistance to the anti-apartheid movement, the ex-detainee Elaine Mohamed argued, "We need people to be conscious of what is happening here so they can't pretend that it's just a domestic problem. Because other countries have dealings with South Africa, their economies work alongside ours. Whatever happens in any country to human beings should be of concern to everybody in the world. People have a duty to other people to help them, to try and make things right."

Di Bishop also believes, "There's an obligation on the part of the world community to focus attention, as it has done, on the evils of apartheid. But it distresses me that the capitalist countries of the West are unrealistic about how we are going to achieve a radical change in our society, which is obviously necessary. There seems to be a naïve belief in the idea that by pushing for the emergence of a black élite of better educated black people, by pumping large amounts of money into certain projects in this country, that that is going to achieve a redistribution of the wealth. But there's no way that it is. I think that is one of the reasons why there's a rather angry reaction against America, which has overtly stated the aims of its U.S. aid scheme in this country as being to sustain and bolster the capitalist future. It's a shame that there isn't a more realistic acceptance of the fact that redistribution of wealth is not going to come about in that kind of way. It's a revolution at that level that we so badly need."

Albertina Sisulu stressed the watchdog function a concerned international community serves: "When our government does wild things now, they know that there is an eye that is watching them. In past years they used to do all these atrocities knowing that nobody would know about them. They are very shaken by the fact that they are losing friends in the outside world, and we are very happy about this." Ruth Mompati similarly argued that the South African government has definitely been affected by the international pressure, but emphasized another of its important functions: "Support from international groups gives our people courage. It makes them feel they're not alone in the world, that they've got friends outside there somewhere."

According to Sheena Duncan, "The more support our government gets from Western governments—even if it is only tolerance—the stronger they feel. I think international pressure could be much more effective than it now is because basically white South Africans want to be loved like everybody else. They want to be part of the Western world." Duncan advocates, however, the use of other kinds of pressure that "don't have as difficult consequences as sanctions." For example, "the United States' stopping the South African Airways from landing there so that it is no longer possible to fly direct from Johannesburg to New York is very irritating to powerful businessmen who have been used to coming and going more easily. This sort of action has a greater impact on whites than blacks, and doesn't cause a loss of jobs. Things like visas should be denied to us. Why should we be allowed to travel? Although this would affect me because my eldest daughter is going to live in Britain, it is something I would be prepared to put up with for the sake of trying to find nonviolent means by which we can resolve this terrible situation."

Elaine Mohamed also mentioned another way to assist the South African liberation movement aside from divestment and sanctions: "It's important that people in the movement can go to other countries if they need to." Several other women mentioned the need for funds. For example, the ANC representative Mavivi Manzini said, "The liberation movement needs material support. Presently there is an education crisis inside South Africa. We have seen the Reagan administration taking advantage of this need by dishing out scholarships to the wrong people with the aim of building up a middle class in South Africa to dilute the struggle, to create false needs in people, and to introduce the American way of life. But giving scholarships to enable the *correct* people to further their education is the best way to help us so that when we take over, we're not faced with a nation of illiterates.

"We also have many projects that need financial support. For example, we are trying to build a new kind of person at our school, a person who is different from the one developed under apartheid. We hope this school will be a model for schools in a free South Africa. We need support to buy educational equipment, toys for the children, clothing, food, medicines, etc. And the women's projects inside the country need money."*

And the UWCO member Gertrude Fester also talked about the need for financial assistance within South Africa: "Even though we don't want to be dependent on financial aid, we do need money. For example, people in hiding often have to give up their jobs so they need money to survive. Money is needed to get people out of the country. Bail money and legal fees are needed. The Dependents Conference [an organization that assists the dependents of political prisoners] is refusing to pay for the court cases of people involved in public violence. They say it's criminal to throw stones. But the people who are arrested for throwing stones often haven't done so. Also, if *I* was confronted by a casspir and a couple of guns and I could find a stone, I promise you, I would throw it!

"I don't want to reduce our struggle to a financial one, and I also want to get away from the idea that the only help other countries can give us is financial support. But we mustn't deny that we are working with people who are either unemployed or receiving a pittance. Sometimes if we don't supply women with bus fare, they can't come to meetings. Paying for telephone calls is often a problem. Getting pamphlets printed and translated into Xhosa costs money."†

While all the women argued that international support of the anti-apartheid movement is important, several emphasized that it is only important as an adjunct to the internal struggle. "It's important that international pressure be put on the government to make it see that what it is doing is not acceptable," said Elaine Mohamed, "but there's no use pretending that sanctions or any other international pressure will, on its own, make the government change." Ela Ramgobin put it this way: "International pressure plays a large part in the struggle, but

---

* Readers who specifically want to help the Women's Section of the ANC can donate money to it at the following address: P.O. Box 31791, Lusaka, Zambia, and earmark it for that section.

† Readers who would like to donate money to the United Women's Congress should send checks to it c/o P. O. Box 120, Athlone, 7760, Western Cape, South Africa.

not a decisive part." And the ANC representative Mavivi Manzini said, "We think that international isolation, by applying sanctions, will go a long way in assisting our struggle—but, of course, there have to be internal forms of struggle to complement this."

Finally some women—Gertrude Fester, for example—emphasized that despite the importance of international pressure: "We in South Africa must remember that this is our struggle, and that we can't *depend* on sanctions and international pressure." Similarly, Elaine Mohamed declared, "It's *our* struggle, irrespective of what Britain or the United States does or what they're hoping will happen here."

The Role of the African National Congress

"The ANC is the organization that has the most legitimacy in this country. If tomorrow the ANC were to be unbanned and there were a general election, the leadership of the ANC would definitely be voted into office. Without the ANC there can't be freedom in this country because it is the legitimate organization of the people."

—ELA RAMGOBIN

In addition to the subject of international pressure, I asked all the women I interviewed about the role of the African National Congress in the struggle. Some women, like the Black Sasher Sheena Duncan, found it difficult to answer because "inside South Africa it's hard to know where the ANC begins and ends because it is banned and can't operate openly, and I have no way of knowing whether there are contacts between the exiled ANC and people inside the country." She went on to say, however, "I have the feeling that were the ANC to be unbanned, the UDF would disappear, because the people in UDF also support the Freedom Charter [the basic document that sets out the political philosophy of the ANC and other like-minded groups]. The COSATU unions, which are part of the UDF structure, certainly would never disappear, but they too would be allies if the ANC was allowed to operate." Many others expressed a similar view.

Almost all women who were willing to risk expressing an opinion on this subject said that the ANC is the most significant of the liberation organizations and is certain to play a key role in the creation of a new South Africa. "I think the ANC will be the ones to lead us there," said Florence de Villiers. "The ANC is supreme in the struggle. Supreme! It is the organization which leads the people, and rightly so," declared Helen Joseph, with great intensity. "The ANC is enjoying maximum support from the South African people," maintained Sethembile N.

Gertrude Fester concurred with Sethembile N.'s assessment: "The average person in this country definitely supports the ANC. And I must say, I'm very impressed with it. It is very well organized. It is addressing the needs of our future society—for example, post-apartheid education. In some countries the ANC even enjoys diplomatic relations and diplomatic privileges. And for many people it is their government-in-exile."

Ela Ramgobin defended the ANC against the criticism to which it is most frequently subjected: "I feel strongly when people try to dismiss the ANC as communist or communist-linked. The people have the right to decide what they want, whatever the philosophy. They can take bits of capitalism and bits of communism and adapt it to suit the circumstances here. One thing is very definite. The state has created a situation where there is such a big gap between the 'haves' and the 'have-nots' that, no matter which government comes in, if there is going to be peace and justice in this country, there has to be some sharing. How this is effected is another matter that has to be discussed. I would like to see it coming peacefully. But for that sharing to occur, some people will have to make sacrifices."

Emma Mashinini also protests the view of the ANC as an organization of violent, bloodthirsty terrorists: "The ANC is not hungry for blood. They want to come back home. But who has got the key to them coming home? If people want to avoid blood being shed, apartheid has got to be dismantled. The ANC's constitution doesn't have a clause that says that they have to be violent. They were forced to take up the armed struggle by this government. But who is more violent? The government's own statistics show that they and their soldiers and their police have killed more people than the ANC has killed. The government has said they don't want to negotiate with people who are violent, but *they* are the violent ones."

Similarly, Duncan commented, "I don't believe that the ANC wants a violent revolution. Hearing them speak at a conference last week [May 1987], it came across very clearly that theirs is a very reluctant commitment to armed struggle. I also got the very strong impression that armed struggle is quite different in their view from necklacing or petrol bombing people's homes so that children are killed. Someone asked Oliver Tambo [the ANC president] about this, and it was quite clear from his answer that he wouldn't condone these kinds of violent attacks. But he also emphasized that we have to persuade people who think otherwise of the political reasons why we believe they are wrong.

"Whites don't get anywhere in talking to black people about violence if they start off by saying, 'I totally condemn violence.' Because even if black people don't believe in violence themselves, they are naturally very sensitive about criticism from whites on this subject, having been subjected to so much violence from whites. And they want to know what have whites ever done to show that there are better ways."

Of course, a small percentage of South African whites don't disagree with the ANC's methods. Indeed, for several years the head of *Umkhonto we Sizwe* was a white man, Joe Slovo. As Hettie V. pointed out, "The ANC has always had active white members who have gone to prison for working for them. They also have white people in leadership positions." Hettie V. shares a common view in appreciating the ANC's strong stand for nonracialism, which, in the South African context, includes their willingness to work with whites as well as members of all other ethnic groups.

Despite the overwhelmingly positive statements about the ANC from most of the women I interviewed, some criticized the organization on the issue of gender. For example, Gertrude Fester commented, "A lot of the people in leadership positions are from the 1950s, and with all due respect to them—they've sacrificed and they've suffered a lot and set a very good tradition—I think they are slightly out of touch with what's going on with women now. I think the traditions and experience of the older comrades need to be blended with the demands of the younger ones. That is why the [soon-to-be-relaunched] Federation of South African Women is so important. It will show that we have more and new demands in the 1980s." Sethembile N. also criticized the ANC: "We always hear the names of ANC men leaders being popularized. Not a single ANC woman is mentioned. This means that even after liberation women will still have to go on struggling for recognition." (Other criticisms of the ANC on the issue of gender are presented in the next section.)

According to the ANC Women's Section officer Mavivi Manzini, the ANC is currently engaged in important new policy making about gender issues, including the controversial topic of *lobola*. It will be interesting to see the results of these discussions about what should go into a bill of rights for women. Despite concern on the part of some women about how the ANC is addressing sexism, there was virtual consensus among those I interviewed that the African National Congress is of supreme importance in the current and future struggle for a new South Africa.

The Role of Women in the Liberation Movement

"The UDF and the ANC will never be able to ensure women's
equal role in the new society. Women have to be organized to try
to ensure that."

—GERTRUDE FESTER

Many of the twenty-four women whose voices have filled the pages of
this book commented on the extraordinary strength and tenacity of
black South African women. Some believe that women have more
courage than men, even when tortured. This conclusion will be devoted
to the views of the women whose comments on women's contribution
to the struggle to transform South Africa were not included earlier.

All the women I interviewed believe that women play an important
role in the anti-apartheid movement. For example, Hettie V. said,
"Women have always been pretty active in that they've done a lot of the
invisible work and the organizing work in the movement." Some
women even maintained that women play a more important role than
men. Thus, Sethembile N. stated, "I think women are the people who
are most involved and active in the struggle, but that the men are in
control because of the social structure and because women are made to
feel inferior. The struggle is retarded," she pointed out, "when fifty
percent of the population is not fully involved in it. How will the
movement even *get* liberation if women are waiting *until* liberation to be
involved?" Ela Ramgobin agreed with Sethembile N.'s conclusion, adding that "It is always the case with any oppressed group that unless you
assert yourself, you will remain there. Other people are quite content to
leave you where you are. But we must actively participate in the struggle
and not just stand back and say, 'You must give us freedom.' We must
go and get it and show that we are capable of getting it."

Elaborating on Sethembile N.'s point, Elaine Mohamed observed,
"Many men find it difficult to accept and to work with women on an
equal level. Women get put down and often are not taken seriously
when they talk, even by political people. But even though women often
don't say a lot," Mohamed continued, "I think they're more radicalized
than a lot of the men because they're far more emotionally involved in
the pain and the trauma of what's going on in this country. It's there in
their daily lives when they pay the rent. They are the supportive base in
holding their families together. Like Ma Sisulu [Albertina Sisulu, see
chapter 10], for example. She doesn't just have to cope with political
life, but with bringing up children and having a husband in prison for

life. If men had to cope with the responsibilities that women shoulder, their role would be much more difficult."

Audrey Coleman further addressed Mohamed's opinion that women contribute to the movement in many other ways aside from direct participation in it. For example, Coleman pointed out that it is women who are most involved with assisting political detainees, particularly those who are children. In addition, while most people understandably focus on the plight of the detainees, that is no reason to forget that "it is the women who are left stranded when their husbands are detained. They have to carry on keeping the household together monetarily, caring for the children, doing the chores. They have to bear the costs of transport to and from lawyers, police stations and service centers to seek aid, as well as maybe losing their jobs because of the enormous amount of time that is spent on these activities." Coleman went so far as to conclude, "One of the most significant factors in the repression in South Africa is the enormous burden that it places on women."

Other women disagreed with the view that women are as involved as men—or *more* involved—including in the nonleadership positions of the anti-apartheid movement. Helen Joseph, for example, said that, "although women have as much to contribute as men, certain age-old traditions and family pressures hold them back, so there aren't enough women in the movement. They have a double job, going out to earn money in the daytime and looking after the family at night." Nevertheless, Joseph believes that there are many women who are ready to take up leadership positions, and capable of doing so.

When it comes to African women, Winnie Mandela expressed a very different view from Joseph and many of the other women I interviewed. Mandela argues that "the black [African] woman has had to forego the old cultural cobwebs of a woman belonging in the kitchen. This has been imposed by the domineering Afrikaner race themselves since the days of colonialism. When they removed our husbands and our fathers from the rural areas to work in the mines, when they imposed their migratory labor system, they changed the pattern of life of black society. Suddenly the black woman found herself acting as head of her family. As well as raising her family, she had to look after the cattle and till the land. So it has not required any special transformation for women in the urban areas to be in the forefront of the struggle. We transcend sexism because we are not given the opportunity to feel that we are women." Albertina Sisulu made a similar argument in chapter 10.

Nevertheless, Mandela did concede that "women do need to meet as women," but only "to meet as mothers concerned about our children." Women in the ANC and the UDF have tended to talk about women as though the term were synonymous with *mother*. "Motherhood is very important," said Gertrude Fester, "but not all of us are going to be mothers. The mother image must be toned down a bit. I'm not a mother, and I have no intention of becoming one, and people like me have got to be catered to." Mandela went on to elaborate why she believes that "the role of a black mother is ten times more difficult under apartheid." "We are expected to bring up our children to be the decent citizens of tomorrow," she said. "We are expected to teach them the difference between right and wrong, that if they break the law they will be jailed. But in our country, the situation is reversed. If you haven't been to prison, if you have never had an encounter with the law, then there must be something wrong with you. You must be on the other side, a part of this immoral system." It is noticeable that in her discussion of the role of women in South Africa, Mandela sees the entire problem for women as being the responsibility of white society. She is silent about sexism in her own community, perhaps out of a sense of loyalty.

With regard to the ANC in particular, Rhoda Bertelsmann-Kadalie had no compunction about being critical. "The ANC is known to be very patriarchal and very conservative with regard to women's issues," she declared. "They are certainly very sexist and male-dominated. Sexism will continue to be a big problem in a post-revolutionary society. This is what has happened in socialist countries throughout the world. But women in the ANC [in Lusaka, Zambia] are fighting now to be recognized as equal partners, which will filter through to organizations inside the country."

Bertelsmann-Kadalie went on to talk about tensions between the older ex-ANC women and the younger ones. "The old women still believe that the men run the show together with a few important females. They don't think that what the younger women are fighting for is as important as the national struggle. I feel that the message often comes from the top that we should subdue our feminist or gender struggle for the broader national struggle, and that there will be time for the gender struggle later."

Bertelsmann-Kadalie is also willing to criticize the Women's Charter, the women's version of the Freedom Charter: "I wish it would spell out the gender struggle much more clearly than those nebulous statements like, 'As women, we're going to fight for our rights.' Implicit in its constitution is the view that 'it's a plot of the government to make us believe that our men oppress us. It's the *government* that oppresses us, and together with our men, we must fight against it and not against our men.' If one even raises questions about these issues, the men in the hierarchy tend to get very cross.''

Florence de Villiers agreed that the ANC should involve more women in its organization, and added "It is still a man's world in the ANC, the UDF, and COSATU as well." Nevertheless, when it comes to the anti-apartheid women's organizations like the United Women's Congress, the members didn't even debate about whether or not men should be allowed to join. "Even when UWCO was one of the only political organizations that existed in the Cape," stated Hettie V., "nobody asked, 'Why is it women only?' There was no *way* they would have men in it. It wasn't even an issue. In that way these organizations are strongly feminist." Nonetheless, Hettie V. went on to emphasize that, for the most part, both women and men in the struggle "consider it very important that women organize around all issues, and equally important that men are involved in women's issues, like organizing for child care in a community. The line here is that *women's issues are people's issues and people's issues are women's issues.* Anybody who says anything different is seen as divisive." The view that feminism is a divisive force is common in the anti-apartheid movement—a criticism to which Rozena Maart responded, "It's *patriarchy* that is divisive, not feminism!"

The role of sexism in the lives of white South African women is different in significant ways, as in any upper class or caste system. As Paula Hathorn said, "I think white South Africa is a *very* sexist society. White women have pretty much been relegated to the role of looking after men and providing a home for them." Many employ twenty-four-hour-a-day domestic workers to cook, clean, iron, and garden for them, as well as to raise their children. The function of white women is to demonstrate that white men can afford to own and financially support decorative appendages, many of whom spend their time discussing their problems with their domestics over tea, arranging flowers, hosting dinner parties, and pursuing other such nonproductive pastimes.*

Di Bishop expresses a prevalent view in characterizing the situation of white women as "very privileged." Unfortunately it is frequently a crippling privilege which undermines their creativity and autonomy, resulting in a remarkably passive and timid group of people. Bishop correctly points out that "they have the time and the means to be using their time constructively, not only in welfare-type activities, important

---

* The role of white women, particularly as employers of domestic workers, is brilliantly captured in Mirra Hammermesch's documentary rendering of the South African feminist sociologist Jacklyn Cock's *Maids and Madams* (1980).

as they are, but also in more political-type work. [White] women should be working much harder to make the contribution that they are so very well placed to make." While granting that white women "are sat upon in many ways, and men aren't going to change that," Bishop stressed that they "must prove themselves as equals and take up issues and actively campaign." She is, of course, an example of a white woman who has done just that, as are all the other white women in this book and in the anti-apartheid movement in general.

Typical of the strength and courage demonstrated by the women whose stories appear in this book, Feziwe Bookholane stated that she has never regretted her political work nor the six years she spent in prison: "I learned a lot from it." Bookholane went on to say that she believes that women have a special role to play in bridging the divisions between the different anti-apartheid groups: "I feel this is something women are capable of doing. Women need to unite and stand up together, then maybe we can earn some recognition." Emma Mashinini agreed with this view: "Are we South African women still going to be led by men when we get our liberation, although we were oppressed together with them, and fought against this oppression together?" Bookholane's answer to this question is: "People must recognize that women can also be the liberators of this country."

Epilogue:
The Kick of a Dying Horse

"There has to be a revolution some time because repression like this can't last forever. You can't kill the human spirit or the ideas. But the longer it is delayed, the more likely that it will be a very violent and bloody revolution because people get angrier and angrier. And they say, 'Where has nonviolence got us?' "
—SHEENA DUNCAN

Assuming that there is no longer any doubt in the minds of readers that radical change is long overdue in South Africa, the question is what will bring about this change? Only one of the women interviewed believed that reform was still a possibility (Feziwe Bookholane). Most of the other women agreed with Rozena Maart that "there will have to be a revolution here because all other methods have proven to be insignificant." A common explanation for white resistance to change was—in the words of Florence de Villiers—that: "This government has too much at stake to reform. They will do anything in their power to keep what they have." Unfortunately this is true—not only of the government but of the whites it represents.

Several women pointed to the insignificance of the reforms undertaken by the government in recent years. Gertrude Fester, for example, pointed out that those that have been made "only affect the most privileged class. All the five-star hotels are now open to blacks, so if I can afford to pay twenty-seven rand [$13.50] for a meal, I can go there. But how come there's no reform in terms of salaries, education, and group areas [residential segregation]? What about the millions of people who don't have work, who cannot come to the urban areas, who don't have houses? Never before have we had children of nine years old in prison. Never before have we had thirty thousand people in detention."

Sheena Duncan explained how some of the reforms *are* effective, not in bringing about the radical change needed, but in co-opting people: "The army and the police surround an area and remove the leadership, doing a house-to-house search to make sure they get all of them." Then they use the vigilantes [reactionary blacks] against them. Having created

345

a leadership vacuum, they then move in with upgrading programs—better housing, electrification, and those sorts of things. So the sterilization and pacification of a community is followed by co-optation."

Rhoda Bertelsmann-Kadalie and Fester pointed out how the members of the tricameral parliament are also being co-opted onto the side of the whites. "I see them as black Nats [Conservatives]," said Bertelsmann-Kadalie disparagingly; and Fester observed, "They are just there for the money. In fact, I think they inform on their own people to the government. People are being bought all the time."

Similarly, although Di Bishop and others consider the eradication of passes to be one of the few significant reforms undertaken by the government, she also believes that "apartheid is just being given a new more acceptable front. The whole homelands system is still in place, and the government continues to divide the insiders from the outsiders. The new struggle is around citizenship, and the burden for thousands of black South Africans is now to prove that they are South African and not citizens of the bantustans."

Women's views varied greatly on how soon they believe the revolution will occur. At one extreme was Ruth Mompati who argued, "In a way, we are free already because we have freed ourselves from the fear of brutality. Our people are no longer afraid of the guns of the whites. Even our children are not afraid. So what remains is the day when we take over. And we don't think that day is far away. I can't say it's tomorrow. I can't say it's next week. But as Mandela or Helen Joseph has said, 'We are as certain that freedom will be won as we are that the sun will rise.' "

Similarly, Mashinini predicted that "Revolution can be tomorrow. Revolution can be next year. Revolution can come about any time. As long as black people are being pushed into their corners, people will be angry. They would rather die. All I know for sure is that it's going to happen some time." Helen Joseph was equally confident: "I haven't any doubt that it *is* coming. But nothing can convince me that it can come peacefully." A majority of the women I interviewed shared these women's optimism that sooner or later the revolution will succeed. "There is no turning back now," said Fester emphatically. "I don't envision myself, nor anyone I know, ever not being part of the anti-apartheid movement. In fact, our commitment will only increase."

At the other extreme (in terms of the timing of revolution) are women like Duncan, who thinks it will take two or three decades before one occurs. Maart figured it may take twenty years. More common was the view that it may take five or ten years. Regarding the quality of these years, Fester predicted, "It's going to be hard, it's going to be long, . . . but we're prepared for it."

As the only Afrikaner to be included in this book, Hettie V. provides insight into why Afrikaners have such a do-or-die attitude, making revolution the only possible means to real change: "Revolution is going to be a hell of a hard and bloody process. The Afrikaners don't have anywhere else to go so they will stay here, and a lot of them are going to fight it out. Many English South Africans have more options. They and Jewish people are the ones who are emigrating. But where can Afrikaners go? I couldn't go anywhere in Europe, Australia, New Zealand, Canada, or America because I've got no blood ties there and I've got no qualifications that would make them want me. Myself aside," Hettie V. continued, "no country is going to want a few million Afrikaners. People like my family say, 'No one will want us. We'll just have to work it out here.' "

With regard to the participants in the anti-apartheid movement, there seemed to be virtual consensus that, despite the ongoing third state of emergency and the violent government repression, particularly since the upsurge in anti-apartheid activism in 1985, "the spirit of resistance has not been broken, and it never will be" (Di Bishop).

As I write this in the safety and comfort of my house in California, where words like *detention, banning,* and *house arrest* have to be explained to most people, I see the faces of the South African women I met for whom these methods of persecution are an all too familiar reality. And I wonder, How much longer will their struggle continue? Will Winnie Mandela and Albertina Sisulu ever get to live with their husbands again? Will Leila Issel be able to spend more than a fleeting visit with her father? When will Ruth Mompati, Connie Mofokeng, and Mavivi Manzini be free to go back to their homeland? When will Gertrude Fester and Shahieda Issel be able to relax at home without fearing a knock on the door? Will Helen Joseph live to see the new South Africa to which she has dedicated the last thirty years of her life?

In 1974, I concluded my *Rebellion, Revolution, and Armed Force* by applying to South Africa the lessons I had learned from my comparative study of seven successful and seven unsuccessful twentieth-century revolutions. Arguing that progressive international intervention against white minority rule in South Africa is a *necessary* condition for radical change to occur there, I pointed out, "The nations of the world must choose whether to allow such a regime to continue its oppression for the foreseeable future, or not" (1974, p.89).

Like Mavivi Manzini, I maintained that, by investing in South Africa and by carrying on normal diplomatic and trade relations, most Western countries have been intervening on the side of the white supremacists. Recently progressive, as opposed to regressive, interventions have increased significantly. Important as these efforts are, they are not enough.

The question then is, How long will it take for the international community, particularly Britain (as the biggest investor) and the United States (as a big investor and world leader), to decide that white minority rule in South Africa must end? When will they decide that there have already been too many deaths from starvation, too many people destroyed by forced removals, too many people detained without trial, too many tortured and incarcerated children, too many years of unnecessary suffering? Unnecessary because South Africa is a wealthy country, not one in which a more equitable distribution of income would mean misery for all.

I agree with Connie Mofokeng that, if the world cared enough about the suffering and injustice in South Africa to apply sanctions and other forms of pressure in a rigorous and determined way, there could be change in the very near future. The longer they take, the more frightening are the prospects. And I wonder, with Audrey Coleman and many others, what the next generation of ever more desperate and angry opponents of apartheid will be like. The world must not wait to find out.

It is not enough to be anti-apartheid. We have to recognize that because of the recalcitrance of the white government and its white supporters, because they *will* not change until they are forced to, we must support revolution in South Africa. Just as it required an anticolonial revolution for the United States to liberate itself from Britain, so a revolution is required in South Africa in order to obtain majority rule by an enfranchised population. The whites know that if they grant all South Africans the right to vote for freely chosen representatives, their own monopoly on power would end. That's why they will never voluntarily permit it.

White South Africans will change when they are forced to, as most whites did when black majority rule was finally won in 1980 in neighboring Zimbabwe. Those who cannot adapt can leave. If the nonracial politics of the ANC remain the dominant force in the anti-apartheid movement, there will be a place in South Africa for whites who are willing to change, as well as for those who changed long ago—not only because of the magnanimity of black South Africans, but also because the skills and know-how of the white population will be needed in the new South Africa.

Being pro-revolution in South Africa also means supporting the African National Congress, since that is the organization most black people support. Its popularity is well deserved. It is fighting for democracy, justice, and nonracialism. What nobler goals can there be? Even though the ANC has been forced to take up arms—an absolutely essential step given the intransigence and violence of the white regime—its leaders are "not hungry for blood," as Emma Mashinini put it. It is a strategy that they must employ, along with their other strategies for educating the world and planning how they will turn South Africa into an equitable and just society when they finally have that opportunity.

Apartheid and sexism are, in some instances, so intertwined that fighting one entails fighting the other. They are inextricably linked, for example, in a Nationalist Party leader's declaration that "this African labor force must not be burdened with superfluous appendages such as wives, children and dependents who could not provide service" (Bernstein 1975, p.12). In other cases, sexism and racism *can* be separated. When husbands expect their wives to be subservient to them, and think they have the right to beat them and force sex on them, we are seeing the horrors not of apartheid but of patriarchy. And when being beaten by a policeman is considered more reprehensible than being beaten by one's husband, we are hearing sexist, not racist, values.

It is clear that inequality in the family, domestic violence, and sexual harassment and assault can obstruct women's political participation in the struggle, and that the overall oppression women suffer outside prison follows them inside.* I agree with those women in this book who believe that giving priority to the struggle for national liberation in South Africa does not mean ignoring experiences like these. Acquiring a fuller understanding of women's oppression in the overall picture of black oppression is not divisive—unless men make it so. It would provide an even richer and more devastating picture of the horrors of apartheid.

Although a revolution is in progress in South Africa, its end is not in sight. The timing depends on the role the different players play, and the energy and commitment they bring to their parts. As is clear from the interviews in this book, some members of the anti-apartheid movement

---

* The terms *rape, sexual assault, sexual abuse,* and *sexual harassment* do not even appear in the index of the researcher Don Foster's otherwise excellent *Detention and Torture in South Africa* (1987)—omissions that indicate the extent to which women's experiences in prison are still being erased in South Africa.

are bringing enormous dedication and bravery to the struggle. Since the international community is a major player, I hope my readers will be moved—as I was, by the goals, the caliber, and the courage of the women involved in this revolution—to work in whatever way they can to bring about a new and just South Africa. Let us try to ensure that Ruth Mompati is correct in believing that the current behavior of the white regime in South Africa is just "the kick of a dying horse."

Chronology of Major Events in South African History*

Circa A.D. 300	Ancestors of Bantu-speaking Africans settle in South Africa.
1652	Dutch East India Company establishes a trading station on the site of present-day Cape Town.
1658	Slaves imported from West Africa.
1659	First battles by the indigenous Khoi against dispossession of their land.
1806	Occupation of the Cape by the British.
1816–28	Rise of the Zulu kingdom; warfare and upheaval among Africans in southeastern Africa.
1834	End of slavery in the Cape.
1836	Beginning of the Great Trek, the withdrawal by the Afrikaners into the South African interior to escape English rule.
1860	Indian indentured labor introduced in Natal.
1878	Xhosas' final battlefield defeat.
1894	Founding of Natal Indian Congress.
1899–1902	Anglo-Boer War.
1906	Suppression of Bombata rebellion ends the first phase of armed resistance.
1910	Union of South Africa established.
1912	Founding of the African National Congress (ANC).
1913	Natives Land Act prevents Africans from acquiring land outside of "reserves," then only seven percent of South Africa; women successfully resist having to carry passes.
1932	African women organize passive resistance against curfew regulations in the Transvaal.
1936	Native Trust and Land Act increases "reserves" to thirteen percent of South Africa; elimination of African parliamentary voting rights.
1939	Prime Minister Jan Smuts leads South Africa into war on the side of Britain, against opposition of the Nationalist Party, which was sympathetic to Nazi Germany.

* This is a severely edited version of chronologies in David Mermelstein's book (1987), Kenneth Carsten's article (1987) and personal suggestions (15 March 1989).

1948	Nationalist Party comes to power on apartheid platform.
1950	Suppression of Communism Act; Group Areas Act.
1952	Defiance Campaign launched by ANC and South African Indian Congress; eight thousand five hundred arrested for civil disobedience.
1953	Bantu Education Act; outlawing of strikes by African workers.
1954	Formation of the Federation of South African Women, whose goals are articulated in the Women's Charter.
1955	Adoption of Freedom Charter to establish an equitable nonracial democracy in South Africa; founding of the Black Sash; two thousand women demonstrate at the Union Buildings in Pretoria.
1956	Twenty thousand women protest the extension of passes to women on 9 August, which becomes South African Women's Day; Coloureds in Cape Province removed from Parliamentary Voter Roll.
1956–61	Treason Trial: 156 leaders charged but ultimately acquitted of high treason.
1959	Formation of Pan-Africanist Congress.
1960	Sharpeville massacre; first state of emergency declared; ANC and PAC banned; Chief Albert Luthuli, president of ANC, awarded Nobel Peace Prize.
1961	South Africa becomes a republic, leaves the Commonwealth; formation of *Umkhonto we Sizwe*; U.N. General Assembly votes for sanctions against South Africa.
1962	Sabotage Act becomes law.
1963	Arrest of *Umkhonto we Sizwe* leaders at Rivonia.
1964	Mandela, Sisulu, and other members of the ANC sentenced to life imprisonment.
1967	Terrorism Act permits indefinite detention without trial.
1969	South African Students Organization (SASO) formed by Steve Biko and other opponents of white domination.
1975	Formation of Black Women's Federation.
1976	Soweto revolt begins (16 June); Transkei, first of the government's homelands designated independent.
1976–77	Uprising spreads: over seven hundred deaths, detentions, stayaways, school boycotts.
1977	Steve Biko, Black Consciousness movement leader, killed while in detention; U.N. Security Council imposes mandatory arms embargo on South Africa; eighteen organizations and two newspapers banned.
1979	Qualified legalization of some African trade unions.
1981	Launching of United Women's Organization in the Cape.
1982	South Africa Defense Force raid on Maseru, Lesotho, kills forty-one; Neil Aggett, first white to die in detention.
1983	Whites give sixty-six percent approval to a new constitution with limited power sharing for Coloureds and Indians in the form of a Tricameral parliament; formation

	of United Democratic Front; founding of Natal Organization of Women.
1984	Nkomati Accords, restricting ANC activities inside Mozambique borders; current phase of revolutionary resistance begins; Bishop Desmond Tutu awarded Nobel Peace Prize.
1985	Mixed Marriages Act repealed; Immorality Act amended to allow interracial sexual relations; 20 July—state of emergency imposed; mass detentions; Pollsmoor march in Cape Town; Reagan administration imposes mild economic sanctions on South Africa by executive order (heading off stronger congressional actions); international banks refuse to renegotiate South African loans.
1986	State of emergency lifted in March 1986; government imposes a more severe nationwide state of emergency on 12 June; virtually unlimited power given to security forces; even more severe restrictions placed on media coverage; one thousand said to be detained the first day; U.S. Senate voted 84 to 14 to impose new sanctions on South Africa; pass laws repealed; founding of the United Women's Congress in the Cape.
1987	General elections held 5 May for whites, Coloureds, and Indians; national stayaway, organized to protest the exclusion of Africans from election.
1988	Women's Congress established, uniting UDF-affiliated women's organizations; relaunching of National Federation of Women; UDF, ECC, DPSC, and twenty-eight other anti-apartheid organizations banned; widespread strikes, school boycotts, and other protests.
1989	Many detainees participate in a fast to protest their incarceration without trial, resulting in the release of many; Winnie Mandela accused of beating four anti-apartheid activists, and some of her bodyguards charged with the murder of one of them; plan to replace President Pieter Botha with Frederick de Klerk.

Glossary and Abbreviations*

African	Refers to the indigenous peoples of South Africa (Zulu, Xhosa, Tswana, et cetera).
Afrikaans	Language, evolved mainly from Dutch, spoken by Afrikaners and majority of Coloureds.
Afrikaner	South African white descended from early Dutch, German, or Huguenot settlers.
Amandla	"Power to the People" exhortation.
ANC	African National Congress, the most important liberation organization; founded in 1912 and banned in 1960.
apartheid	Government's policy of compulsory and systematic racial segregation, including the creation of independent "homelands."
Azania	Name for South Africa used by PAC and Black Consciousness supporters.
AZAPO	Azanian People's Organization, a Black Consciousness group; banned in 1988.
banning	The imposition of many severe restrictions on freedom of movement, speech, work, social and political activities without charge, trial, or recourse to a court of law, to punish and immobilize political radicals.
Bantu Education	The legally imposed inferiorization of education for Africans implemented in 1953.
bantustans	Official term for reservations designated by the South African government as homes for the various African ethnic groups (also referred to as "homelands" and "reserves").
Black Consciousness movement	Movement originating in the 1970s espousing need for black pride and autonomy.
blacks	Term used by opponents of apartheid and others to include Africans, Coloureds, Indians, and other people of color.
Black Sash	A political women's organization started in 1955 that has radicalized over the years. Largely white membership.
Boer	Afrikaner; sometimes any white with a reactionary, racist mentality; also farmer, police, or prison official; *boer* is the Afrikaans word for farmer.

* I have borrowed several of these definitions from David Mermelstein (1987).

Glossary and Abbreviations

Broederbond	A secret society of Afrikaners dedicated to furthering the interests of their people.
casspir	A large army vehicle.
Coloured	Racial classification for South Africans of African-European descent.
COSATU	Congress of South African Trade Unions.
disinvestment	Foreign companies selling off their South African assets.
divestment	The selling off of shares in a foreign company outside South Africa because it does business in South Africa.
DPSC	Detainees Parents' Support Committee.
ECC	The End Conscription Campaign.
European	White person.
FEDTRAW	Federation of Transvaal Women.
forced removals	The involuntary resettlement of people (mostly black) in areas not of their choosing.
Fort Hare	Formerly a prestigious African university, undermined by the imposition of Bantu Education.
FOSATU	Federation of South African Trade Unions.
Frontline States	South Africa's neighboring countries that support the liberation movement: Angola, Botswana, Mozambique, Tanzania, Zambia, and Zimbabwe.
gray area	Residential area where racial segregation has not been strictly enforced.
Group Areas Act	Legislation that set up segregated zones in towns and cities to enforce residential separation of the races.
homelands	An alternative name for "bantustans" or "reserves."
house arrest	The most severe form of banning; includes being forbidden to leave one's house for twelve or twenty-four hours a day usually for five years.
Inkatha	A movement of the Zulu people headed by Chief Gatsha Buthelezi.
kaffir	Derogatory word for African; the equivalent of *nigger*.
lobola	Payment by a man to his prospective bride's family for their permission for the marriage.
listed person	A person subject to certain restrictions without charge, trial, or judicial review, because of his or her political opposition to the government; less serious than banning or house arrest.
matric	Short for matriculation; final examinations taken at the end of high school.
Namibia	Territory on the northwest border of South Africa, formerly known as South West Africa; still illegally controlled by South Africa.
Nationalist Party	The party supported largely by Afrikaners, in power since 1948; members are sometimes nicknamed "Nats."
NEUSA	National Education Union of South Africa.

NOW	Natal Organization of Women.
NUSAS	National Union of South African Students.
PAC	Pan-Africanist Congress; broke away from the ANC in 1959; banned in 1960.
pass/passbook	Identity document required for Africans over sixteen (officially called a "reference book") to restrict their movement; abolished 1986 and replaced by other means of control.
PFP	Progressive Federal Party (formerly Progressive Party); moderately liberal white parliamentary opposition party, supported largely by English-speaking South Africans.
rand	Unit of South African currency worth approximately $0.50.
reference book	The official name for a pass, or passbook.
reserve	An alternative name for "homeland" or "bantustan."
resettlement camps	Dumping grounds for Africans removed by the government for political reasons.
restricted person	New term for a person who is banned.
Robben Island	Maximum-security prison near Cape Town for black political prisoners.
SACP	South African Communist Party, banned in 1950.
SASO	South African Students Organization, a black organization started by Steve Biko; banned in 1977.
sjambok	Animal-hide whip used by police.
Soweto	Largest African township; population over one million (acronym from *So*uth *We*st *To*wnships); near Johannesburg.
squatters	People who reside, without the government's permission, in makeshift homes in so-called white areas.
standard	Grade in school: standard six is the equivalent of the eighth grade; standard eight, of the tenth grade; et cetera.
townships	Black residential ghettoes located near "white" cities.
Transkei	The first reservation designated "independent" by the government in 1976.
Tricameral Parliament	Parliamentary system implemented in September 1984 with one chamber each for whites, Coloureds, and Indians, but with the power still in white hands and no representation for Africans.
UCT	University of Cape Town, a largely white institution.
UDF	United Democratic Front, an umbrella organization of more than eight hundred anti-apartheid groups and over two million members.
Umkhonto we Sizwe	"The Spear of the Nation"; the military arm of the ANC; sometimes abbreviated to "MK."
UNISA	University of South Africa, a correspondence school.
UWC	University of the Western Cape, a largely Coloured institution.

Glossary and Abbreviations

UWCO	United Women's Congress; formed by a merging of UWO and WF; affiliated with UDF; started in 1986.
UWO	United Women's Organization; started in the Cape Province in 1979.
WECTU	Western Cape Teachers' Union, a UDF-affiliated organization.
WF	Women's Front, a township-based UDF-affiliated group in Cape Town.

References and Selected Bibliography on South African Women

Akhalwaya, Aneen. 1988. "The Mother of the Struggle." *Africa Report,* May-June: 60–62.

Baard, Frances. 1986. *My Spirit Is Not Banned: Interview with Barbie Schreiner.* Harare, Zimbabwe: Zimbabwe Publishing House.

Barrett, Jane; Dawber, Aneene; Klugman, Barbara; Obery, Ingrid; Shindler, Jennifer; and Yawitch, Joanne. 1985. *Vukani Makhosikazi: South African Women Speak.* London, England: Catholic Institute for International Relations.

Beall, Jo; Hassim, Shireen; and Todes, Alison. 1987. " 'A Bit on the Side'? Gender Struggles in the Politics of Transformation in South Africa." Paper presented to the Eighteenth Annual Congress of the Association for Sociology in Southern Africa, University of the Western Cape, South Africa. June 29–July 2.

Beall, Jo; Friedman, M.; Hassim, Shireen; Posel, R.; Stiebel, L.; and Todes, Alison. 1988. "African Women in the Durban Struggle, 1985–86: Towards a Transformation of Roles?" *South African Review* 4.

Beard, Linda Susan. 1986. "Bessie Head in Gaborone, Botswana: An Interview." *Sage: A Scholarly Journal on Black Women* 3 (2):44–47.

Benjamin, Anne. 1985. *Winnie Mandela: Part of My Soul Went with Him.* New York: W. W. Norton.

Benson, Mary. 1986. *Nelson Mandela.* Harmondsworth, Middlesex, England: Penguin Books.

Bernstein, Hilda. 1975; 1985 (rev.). *For Their Triumphs and for Their Tears: Women in Apartheid South Africa.* London, England: International Defence and Aid Fund for Southern Africa.

Bertelsmann, Rhoda. 1987. "International Feminism and the Women's Movement." *South African Outlook* 117 (139):62–66.

Burman, Sandra. 1984. *Woman and Property.* New York: St. Martin's Press.

———. 1988. "When Family Support Fails: The Problems of Maintenance Payment in Apartheid South Africa." Parts 1 and 2. *South African Journal for Human Rights* 4.

Carstens, Kenneth. 1987. "A South African Timeline." *Social Education,* February:110–12.

Cock, Jacklyn. 1980. *Maids and Madams.* Johannesburg, South Africa: Ravan Press.

References and Selected Bibliography

————. 1988. "Keeping the Fires Burning: Militarisation and the Policy of Gender in South Africa." *South African Sociological Review* 1 (1):1–22.

Cole, Josette. 1987. *Crossroads: The Politics of Reform and Repression 1976–1989*. Johannesburg, South Africa: Ravan Press.

Coleman, Audrey. 1986. "Children under Apartheid." Unpublished speech to the Conference on Children in Stockholm, Sweden (25 November).

Davis, Stephen. 1987. *Apartheid's Rebels: Inside South Africa's Hidden War*. New Haven, Connecticut: Yale University Press.

Desmond, Cosmos. 1971. *The Discarded People*. Harmondsworth, Middlesex, England: Penguin Books.

Foster, Don. 1987. *Detention and Torture in South Africa: Psychological, Legal, and Historical Studies*. Cape Town, South Africa: David Philip.

Friere, Paulo. 1986. *Pedagogy of the Oppressed*. Trans. by Myra Bergman Ramos. New York: Continuum.

Gaitskell, Deborah. 1983. "Introduction" to Special Issue on Women in Southern Africa. *Journal of Southern African Studies* 10 (1):1–16.

Gastrow, Shelagh. 1985. *Who's Who in South African Politics*. Johannesburg, South Africa: Ravan Press.

————. 1987. *Who's Who in South African Politics*. Number 2. Johannesburg, South Africa: Ravan Press.

Giddings, Paula. 1986. "The Struggle from Without: An Interview with South African Exile, Tandi Gcabashe." *Sage: A Scholarly Journal on Black Women* 3 (2):48–51.

Ginwala, Frene. 1986. "ANC Women: Their Strength in the Struggle." *Works in Progress* 45:10–11.

Goodwin, June. 1984. *Cry Amandla! South African Women and the Question of Power*. New York: Africana Publishing.

Gordon, Suzanne. 1985. *A Talent for Tomorrow: Life Stories of South African Servants*. Johannesburg, South Africa: Ravan Press.

Harrison, Nancy. 1985. *Winnie Mandela: Mother of a Nation*. London, England: Victor Gollancz.

Hermer, Carol. 1980. *The Diary of Maria Tholo*. Johannesburg, South Africa: Ravan Press.

International Defence and Aid Fund for Southern Africa. 1981. *To Honour Women's Day: Profiles of Leading Women in the South African and Namibian Liberation Struggles*. London, England: IDAF.

————. 1981. *Women Under Apartheid*. London, England: IDAF.

————. 1989. "Women Political Prisoners in South Africa." Unpublished pamphlet. London, England (February).

Joseph, Gloria; and Lorde, Audre. 1986. "In Memory of Our Children's Blood: Sisterhood and South African Women." *Sage: A Scholarly Journal on Black Women* 3 (2):40–43.

Joseph, Helen. 1987. *Side by Side*. New York: William Morrow.

Joubert, Elsa. 1981. *Poppie*. Sevenoaks, Kent, England: Coronet Books.

Kimble, J.; and Unterhalter, E. 1982. " 'We Opened the Road for You, You Must now go Forward': ANC Women's Struggles, 1912–1982." *Feminist Review* 12:11–35.

Kuzwayo, Ellen. 1985. *Call Me Woman*. San Francisco: Spinsters Ink.

Landis, Elizabeth. 1976. "Apartheid and the Disabilities of African Women in Southern Africa," in *Women in Apartheid South Africa*. Michigan: Sun Press. (Excerpts from a paper prepared for the Unit on Apartheid of the United Nations.)

Lapchick, Richard E.; and Urdang, Stephanie. 1982. *Oppression and Resistance: The Struggle of Women in Southern Africa*. Westport, Connecticut: Greenwood Press.

Lawrence, Merlyn. 1984. "The Problem of Marital Violence in Mitchells Plain and its Implications for the Future of Society." Master's Thesis, University of Cape Town, South Africa.

Lawson, Lesley. 1985. *Working Women: A Portrait of South Africa's Black Women Workers*. Johannesburg, South Africa: Ravan Press.

Lelyveld, Joseph. 1985. *Move Your Shadow: South Africa, Black and White*. New York: Times Books.

Levine, Janet. 1988. *Inside Apartheid: One Woman's Struggle in South Africa*. Chicago: Contemporary Books.

Lipman, Beata. 1984. *We Make Freedom: Women in South Africa*. London, England: Pandora Press.

Maart, Rozena. 1988. "A Feminist Agenda for Anti-Apartheid and Anti-Capitalist Politics in South Africa." Master's Dissertation, University of York, England.

"Mamphela Ramphele Speaks." 1987. *Stir: A Journal from Southern African Women* 1 (4). (*Stir's* address: P.O. Box 11214, Vlaeberg 8018, Cape Town.)

Mandela, Nelson. 1987. "I Am Prepared to Die," in David Mermelstein, ed., *The Anti-Apartheid Reader*, pp. 220–28. New York: Grove Press.

Meer, Fatima. 1984. *Factory and Family: The Divided Lives of South African Women Workers*. Durban, South Africa: Institute for Black Research.

———. 1987. "Women in Apartheid Society," in David Mermelstein, ed., *The Anti-Apartheid Reader*, pp. 236–40. New York: Grove Press.

Mermelstein, David, ed. 1987. *The Anti-Apartheid Reader*. New York: Grove Press.

"A New Generation of South African Women." 1987. *Leadership* 6 (5).

New York Radical Feminists. 1974. *Rape: The First Sourcebook for Women*. New York: New American Library.

Omond, Roger. 1985. *The Apartheid Handbook*. Harmondsworth, Middlesex, England: Penguin Books.

Oosthuizen, Ann, ed. 1987. *Sometimes When it Rains: Writings by South African Women*. New York: Pandora.

Orkin, Mark. 1986. *Divestment, the Struggle and the Future: What Black South Africans Really Think*. Johannesburg, South Africa: Ravan Press.

Parks, Michael. 1987. "Miners' Strike Results in Shift of Power," *San Francisco Chronicle*, 23 September, pp. Z–6, 1, 4.

Pillay, Pendy. 1985. "Women and Employment in Southern Africa: Some Important Trends and Issues." *Social Dynamics* 11 (2):20–36.

Qunta, Christine, ed. 1987. *Women in Southern Africa*. Braamfontein, South Africa: Skotaville Publishers.

Ramphele, Mamphela; and Zille, Helen. 1987. "Life in Transition." *Leadership* 6 (5):67–71.

References and Selected Bibliography

Ramphele, Mamphela. 1988. "The Dynamics of Gender Politics in the Hostels of Cape Town: Another Legacy of the South African Labor Migrant System." Unpublished Paper, Cape Town, South Africa.

Ringelheim, Joan. 1985. "Women and the Holocaust: A Reconsideration of Research." *Signs: Journal of Women in Culture and Society* 10 (4):741–61.

Russell, Diana E. H. 1974. *Rebellion, Revolution, and Armed Force.* New York: Academic Press.

———. 1980. "Banned and House-arrested in South Africa: A Personal Account." *Worldview* 23 (5):6–9.

———. 1988. "Detention in South Africa: A Woman's Experience." *Feminist Issues* 8 (2):3–24.

———. 1989. "Life in a Police State: A Black South African Woman Speaks Out." *Women's Studies International Forum* 12 (2):157–66.

———. In press. "Fatima Meer: South African Community Leader and Fighter against Apartheid." *Sage: A Scholarly Journal on Black Women.*

Shirer, William. 1959. *The Rise and Fall of the Third Reich: A History of Nazi Germany.* New York: Simon & Schuster.

Simon, H. J. 1968. *African Women: Their Legal Status in South Africa.* London, England: C. Hurst & Co.

"South African Women Fight Apartheid." 1986. *Third World Women's News* 1 (1).

Speak Collective. 1987. "No to Rape Say Port Alfred Women." *Speak* 13 (January-March). (*Speak's* address is Office 14, The Ecumenical Centre, 20 St. Andrew's Street, Durban 4001, South Africa.)

Van der Vliet, Virginia. 1984. "Staying Single: A Strategy Against Poverty?" Unpublished University of Cape Town Carnegie Conference Paper, No. 116. Cape Town, South Africa.

Van-Helten, Jean; and Williams, Keith. 1983. "The Crying Need of South Africa: The Emigration of Single British Women to the Transvaal, 1901–10." *Journal of Southern African Studies* 10 (1):17–38.

Walker, Cherryl. 1982. *Women and Resistance in South Africa.* London, England: Onyx.

———. 1987. "Women's Studies on the Move." *Journal of Southern African Studies* 13 (3):433–43.

Weekly Mail. 1988. 4 (13 [8–14 April]).

Wren, Christopher. 1988. "White South African Women Step Off Their Pedestals to Fight Apartheid." *The New York Times International,* 25 December:3.

Index

Index

Child bashing, 130–31
Child labor, 67–68
Children: brutalization of, 87–88; detention/imprisonment of, 15, 81–82, 87–90, 345; of mixed marriages, 304; murder of, 151, 260; police harassment of, 307–11; politicization of, 78, 87–88; protests by, 272–73; sexual abuse of, 199, 255, 260; torture of, 88–89; See also Issel, Leila; Soweto uprising (1976)
Christian Institute, 173
Circumcision, female, 191
Cock, Jacklyn, 306, 343
Coleman, Audrey, 80–90; on black-on-black violence, 16; Black Sash Advice Office work, 83; on brutalization and politicization of children, 87–88; Detainees Parents' Support Committee (DPSC) and, 84–87; detention of children and, 15, 81–82, 88–90; detention of son, 84; growing up white, 83; on guilt of detainees, 14; on international pressure, 333–34; on length of detention, 29; on police harassment, 87; politicization of, 83; radicalization of, 81; threat of restriction order on, 81; on women's role in liberation movement, 341
Coleman, Keith, 83–84
Coleman, Max, 81
Coloured, defined, 355
Coloured activists. See Bertelsmann-Kadalie, Rhoda; de Villiers, Florence; Fester, Gertrude; Maart, Rozena; Mohamed, Elaine
Coloured areas, 284–85
Commercial Catering and Allied Workers' Union, 179, 183, 187–88
Communism: ANC and, 117–18, 324; charges of, as government ploy, 7; government's paranoia about, 30, 117–18
Communist Party. See South African Communist Party (SACP)
Comrades, defined, 47
Congress Alliance, 204–5
Congress of Democrats (COD), 83, 204–5
Congress of South African Trade Unions (COSATU), 166, 188–89, 337, 343, 355
Congress of the People, 141
Conscientious objection to military service, 156; See also End Conscription Campaign (ECC); Hathorn, Paula
Conscientizing, defined, 101
Conscription, 157–58; See also End Conscription Campaign (ECC); Hathorn, Paula
Constitution, new (1984), 301–2, 352
Consumer boycotts, 55, 332
Contraception, 288
Cornelius, Johanna, 206

Crime, 232–33
Criminal Procedure Act, 14, 89
Crossroads (squatter camp), 174, 219, 289

Dad's Army, 157
Debt, foreign, international banks' refusal to renegotiate, 10, 353
Defend the Constitution Women's League, 206; See also Black Sash
Defense and Aid Fund, 112
Defiance Campaign (1952), 93, 100, 134, 136, 147–48, 204, 352
Demonstrations, illegality of, 159, 218
Dependents Conference, 336
Desmond, Cosmos, 317
Detainees Parents' Support Committee (DPSC), 84–86, 180, 353, 355; actions of, 85; Coleman in, 81, 84–86; repression of, 82
Detention(s), 71; arbitrariness of, 327–28; for being student leader, 89; of Bookholane, 58–64; of children, 15, 81–82, 88–90; conscientizing effect of, 180; deaths during, 223; deaths during, suicide as explanation of, 48, 70; detainee fasting to protest, 353; DPSC publicity about, 85; extent of, 15, 24, 29, 85; of Fester, 242–43; gender differences in, 31, 37–43; goals of, 29; goals of, to instill fear, 89–90; of Hathorn, 159–60, 162–63; international pressure against, 15–16; as internment camps, 14–16; of Issel, S., 71, 74–77, 310; of Mandela, W., 96, 102–4; of Manzini, 125–26; of Mashinini, 179, 183–87; of Mayne, 238–87; for membership in street committee, 89; menstruation during, 37–38; of Mofokeng, 47–48, 52–53; in Nazi Germany, 324–25; under 1986 state of emergency, 353; for noncriminal reasons, 84; pregnant women in, 15; racial differences in treatment of detainees, 162, 212; rapes during, 38, 51–52, 76, 230, 248–49; sexual harassment during, 71, 74–75; of Sisulu, 148–49; traumatic effects of, 37–38, 186–87; without trial, legality of, 14–15; of women, 15, 29–30; See also Arrest(s); Physical assaults during detention; Solitary confinement; Torture
de Villiers, Florence, 168–77; on ANC's role, 337; Black Women's Federation and, 173; as domestic worker, 171–72; Domestic Workers' Union and, 175–76; educational aspirations of, 170–71; growing up Coloured, 170–72; harassment by security police, 177; on interna-

Index

Index

Index